Labour Regime Change in the Twenty-First Century

Studies in Critical Social Sciences

Labour Regime Change in the Twenty-First Century

Unfreedom, Capitalism and Primitive Accumulation

Tom Brass

LABOUR REGIME CHANGE IN THE TWENTY-FIRST CENTURY
Tom Brass

First Published in India 2016

ISBN 978-93-5002-438-6

Published in agreement with Koninklijke Brill NV, Leiden, The Neatherlands for publication and sale only in the Indian Subcontinent (India, Pakistan, Bangladesh, Nepal, Maldives, Bhutan and Sri Lanka)

Published by
AAKAR BOOKS
28 E Pocket IV, Mayur Vihar Phase I, Delhi 110 091
Phones : 011 2279 5505, 2279 5641
aakarbooks@gmail.com; www.aakarbooks.com

Printed at
Sapra Brothers, Delhi 110 092

For Amanda,
Anna, Ned and Miles;
for my mother, Gloria Brass,
and in memory of my father
Denis Brass (1913–2006)

CONTENTS

ACKNOWLEDGEMENTS

This book is an attempt to provide an answer to one of the central theoretical questions posed historically by the social sciences. That is, about the way a capitalist labour regime develops and changes, why and with what implications for the workers caught up in this process. In doing so, it draws on articles by me published since the year 2000 in a number of different journals, including *Critical Sociology*, *Capital and Class*, *The Journal of Contemporary Asia*, and *The Journal of Peasant Studies*.

The argument made here was formulated initially after fieldwork conducted in Peru during the mid-1970s, which revealed the acceptability to capitalist producers of bonded labour. Both the fact and the significance of this link were confirmed subsequently in the course of research undertaken in India during the 1980s. At the time, however, the prevailing orthodoxy informing social science discourse in general and the development studies agenda in particular was much rather the opposite: that the spread of capitalism would lead to the eradication of unfree labour. Evidence to the contrary notwithstanding, this orthodox view remains entrenched, even today.

For this reason, the main focus of the analysis which follows is theoretical: to trace – and to assess the validity in the light of current economic development – the epistemology structuring different historical interpretations of the link between capitalism, unfreedom and primitive accumulation. Conventional wisdom is that – on the issue of the incompatibility between a 'fully functioning' capitalism and unfree labour – there is an unbroken continuity between Marxism, and the ideas of Adam Smith, Malthus, Mill and Max Weber.

Such a view is challenged in this book, which argues that Marxism does indeed accept that, where class struggle becomes acute and spans the globe, capitalist producers can and will employ workers who are unfree. The theoretical reasons for this are traced to the conceptualization by Adam Smith of labour as value and by Hegel of labour as property, and the subsequent interpretation by Marx of labour-power as commodity that in a capitalist economy can be bought/sold. From this stems the initial and continuing importance of the distinction between workers who are free and those who are unfree, a difference that informs the process of becoming, being, remaining, and – crucially – acting as a proletariat.

Although the continued existence of unfree labour within capitalism is now being recognized, its relation to capital is still a source of difficulty. Adherents of an ethical/moral discourse opposed to debt bondage perceive the state as a disinterested enforcer of human rights. By contrast, the semi-feudal thesis and disguised wage-labour framework attempt to redefine such relations as free. Other analyses – currently fashionable in the social sciences – redefine capitalism itself: as a form of primitive accumulation (= 'accumulation by dispossession') giving rise to an 'empire' composed not of classes but of 'multitudes'. In each of these interpretations, agency is no longer that of class struggle designed to achieve a socialist transition, but rather to achieve citizenship by means of redemocratization, or the realization of a civil society within capitalism. All such approaches, it is argued here, correspond in the end to a political avoidance/postponement of socialism.

For nearly two decades I edited *The Journal of Peasant Studies* (1990–2008) – making me its second longest serving editor – and much of the research for this book was undertaken during the last eight years of editing the journal on my own. In the course of the latter period I received the unstinting support of the two reviews editors and members of the editorial advisory board. They made a notable contribution to the success of the journal under my editorship, and I extend my thanks to them for resigning on a matter of principle in 2008.

Special thanks are also due to five other people. To Professor David Fasenfest, the Series Editor, for encouragement; to Rosanna Woensdregt, Mirjam Elbers and Debbie de Wit, of Brill publishers, who guided the book through production; and to my daughter Anna Luisa Brass, who designed and drew the cover illustration. Now studying art at university, she drew the cover for the book *New Farmers' Movement in India.*

This book is dedicated to two sets of kin. As always, to my family: to Amanda, and to Anna, Ned and Miles. Also to my mother, Gloria Brass; and to the memory of my father, Denis Brass, who – as Music Officer of the British Council – gave the first concert performance in Spain in June 1947 of Piano Concerto No. 1 by Alan Rawsthorne, and translated into English the poetry and short stories of the Portuguese writer Miguel Torga.

Richmond-upon-Thames
September 2010

INTRODUCTION

TWENTY-FIRST CENTURY LABOUR REGIME CHANGE

> "How, then?", I persisted. "You will not apply my precept," he said, shaking his head. "How often have I said to you that when you have eliminated the impossible, whatever remains, *however improbable*, must be the truth?"
> – The investigative procedure of Sherlock Holmes, as explained by him to Doctor Watson in *The Sign of Four* (Conan Doyle, 1929: 185, original emphasis).

Among the dystopian visions of the future that circulate historically in the domain of popular culture, one of the most common is that such societies will be places where chattel slavery once again reigns supreme. Such visions are deemed exaggerations, not least because they present us with what might be called a 'whips and chains' image of unfreedom, a picture that conjures up a labour regime associated not with the capitalist system in the present century but rather with depictions of ancient Rome as these appear in Hollywood films.[1] Once we move away from an image-based concept of unfreedom, and particularly that derived from cinema epics, however, it becomes less easy to dismiss dystopian visions of the future as wholly exaggerated.[2]

The reason for this are the many instances of restructuring by 'fully-functioning' capitalist enterprises the world over involving the

[1] The 'whips and chains' image of unfreedom is projected in many film epics about ancient society, such as *Ten Commandments* (1956), directed by Cecil B. DeMille, *Spartacus* (1960), directed by Stanley Kubrick, and *Gladiator* (2000), directed by Ridley Scott. A similar picture of enslaved humanity permeates science fiction dystopias in films ranging from *Metropolis* (1927), directed by Fritz Lang, to *Planet of the Apes* (1968), directed by Franklin Schaffner. An exception to this 'whips and chains' image of unfreedom is the excellent film *Ghosts* (2006), directed by Nick Broomfield, which deals with the way unfree immigrant workers employed in British agriculture are currently exploited by the gangmaster system.

[2] This is *not* to say that all forms of twenty-first century production relations automatically become unfree. Instead of the unilinear unfree → free progression, there is much rather a dialectic between these two relational forms. What is being argued here, therefore, is that in specific circumstances – linked to the acuteness of competition and class struggle – capitalists will indeed employ unfree forms of labour-power. In short, and contrary to received wisdom, capital does – and will continue to – avail itself of such working arrangements.

introduction, reintroduction or the reproduction of labour that is unfree. Many examples in what are not just undeniably areas of capitalist agriculture but also some industrial urban contexts include the following: debt bondage in India and Latin America; the continuing use of peonage, sweatshops and convict labour in the United States; the offshore programme in Ontario, Canada; contract migrant labour in white South African mining and industry and the sunbelt states in the United States; the resurgence of the gangmaster system in British agribusiness; unfree plantation workers in West Africa; and the existence of unfree industrial labour both in the brick kilns of Pakistan and in the export processing zones of China.[3]

Although it is now being accepted, finally, that capitalist development is compatible with labour-power that is not free, the reasons why this is so is still the subject of dispute.[4] As is evident from most current analyses of the capitalism/unfreedom link, there still exists a gulf between what are said to be the conditions that give rise to an unfree labour regime, and those in which such relational forms currently occur. Since it derives from epistemological confusion, and also generates further misunderstanding, this gulf, together with the reasons for its current prevalence, is the subject of the analysis in this book.

To talk about a labour regime in the twenty-first century as entailing an increase in the incidence of worker unfreedom remains controversial, given the degree to which this kind of development is opposed by

[3] These are well documented case studies, referred to both by me – in Brass (1999) as well as in previous and subsequent texts – and by many others (e.g., Lichtenstein, 1996; Krissman, 1997; Martins, 1997; Ross, 1997; Bonnet, 2000; Assies, 2003; Ercelawn and Nauman, 2004; Lawrence, 2004; Bedoya Garland and Bedoya Silva-Santisteban, 2005a, 2005b; Manzo, 2005; Bauder, 2008).

[4] See Brass (2003; 2007; 2008) for analyses of arguments that until very recently continued to question the acceptability to capitalist producers of unfree labour.

[5] There are, of course, other ways in which claims about an increase in worker unfreedom are controversial. One such is the view that there is nothing wrong with such a production relation, since its subject obtains benefits from this kind of working arrangement, the element of unfreedom notwithstanding. This view, which has been applied to all historical forms of unfree labour, corresponds to what has been termed by me the 'subsistence guarantee' argument. Its claim that even unfree production relations are empowering for the worker concerned is disputed, and has been addressed elsewhere (Brass, 1999). That such a view still circulates is evident from a recent text which recycles precisely this claim with regard to the current employment of female labourers in sweatshops. Hence the following argument made by Kristof and WuDunn (2010: 232): 'Sweatshops have given women a boost. Americans mostly hear about the iniquities of garment factories, and they are real – the forced overtime, the sexual harassment, the dangerous conditions… The factories prefer young women, perhaps because they're more docile and perhaps because their small fingers are more nimble

non-Marxist and Marxist political economy.[5] Both the latter, so the argument goes, adamantly dispute the acceptability to capitalist producers of unfree labour, maintaining much rather that a 'fully functioning' accumulation process cannot operate efficiently – let alone profitably – without workers who are free. Whilst this may be true of the way non-Marxist theory perceives the link between capitalism and unfreedom, that it applies similarly to the most important – let alone all – Marxist political economy is disputed here.

Theories in Conflict

Much political economy maintains that unfree labour is incompatible with a fully-functioning capitalism, and that employers always seek to replace unfree workers with free equivalents. In keeping with this, cases of unfree labour encountered currently are categorized as instances of primitive accumulation. Against this view, it is argued here that the centrality of class struggle to the shaping of the accumulation process leads to the opposite conclusion. Labour-power is unfree not because capitalism is in its early or 'primitive' stage – but much rather because it is mature. The importance of this distinction is that the characterization of unfree labour as acceptable or unacceptable to capitalism affects in turn what kind of systemic transition is on the political agenda.

Generally speaking, both non-Marxist and (some) Marxist theory subscribe to three positions about the link between unfree labour and capitalism. First, that capitalist development is in a fundamental sense incompatible with production relations that are unfree.[6] Second, that

for assembly or sewing. So the rise of manufacturing has generally raised the opportunities and status of women.' This positive interpretation of unfree labour is one that has been advanced by defenders of slavery at all historical conjunctures, and amounts to the assertion that simply to have a job – even an oppressive one that pays little – is for the worker a sufficient goal. Such an argument is not only demeaning to the worker concerned and wrong about the supposed benefits, but also no different from the justification used in the past of chattel slavery. As a politically conservative ideology, it ignores both the economic role of unfreedom and also its effect: the 'from above' struggle by commercial employers to drive down pay and conditions, and the corresponding 'from below' struggle – not always successful – by workers against this kind of labour relation.

[6] Unfree labour belongs to the category of what might be termed *a priori* exclusions from the capitalist transition paradigm. This category is composed of socio-economic forms which, it is confidently asserted (mostly by exponents of the semi-feudal thesis), have no place in the capitalist system because they belong unambiguously to the past. Among the other forms consigned to this category are banditry, gangsterism

current approaches which do connect unfree labour and capitalism may indeed be right empirically, but in theoretical terms cannot be said to be Marxist. And third, faced with the dissonance between what is said to be Marxist theory and the acceptability of unfree labour to capitalist enterprises, purportedly Marxist approaches take refuge in the concept of primitive accumulation.

Against these three positions, I shall deploy the following arguments. Although it is important to distinguish theoretical approaches on the part of non-Marxist and certain kinds of Marxist analysis to the link between capitalism and unfree labour, therefore, they nevertheless share a number of assumptions about the capitalism/unfreedom link. Following on from this, there are two distinct and occasionally contradictory Marxist approaches to the capitalism/unfreedom link. For this reason, a distinction exists between the Marxist analysis of unfree labour employed here and a number of other analyses by Marxists of the same relation.

The position adhered to here makes a number of interrelated claims. To begin with, that unfree relations are not merely compatible with a 'fully-functioning' capitalism, but – given their role in the twenty-first century labour regime – perhaps even in certain circumstances its preferred form. That the reason for this lies in the current form taken by class struggle, a view that is indeed compatible with Marxist theory. Accordingly, to interpret the employment by capital of labour-power that is unfree as an instance of primitive accumulation is similarly fraught with difficulties, not least since it boils down to a variation of the first position: namely, that a 'fully-functioning' capitalism and unfree labour are incompatible.

Market, Class and Labour Regime Change

Prognosticating about the elements composing a twenty-first century labour regime nevertheless begs rather two obvious questions. Does the distinction between free and unfree labour-power matter any

and the mafia, frequently dismissed – by, for example, Hobsbawm (1969) – as innately pre-capitalist institutions destined to be swept away as a 'fully functioning' capitalism emerges. Without wishing to dwell on the point, such prognoses have been dramatically wrong footed by developments in Italy, in post-1976 China, and in post-1989 Russia, all contexts where the phenomenon of 'gangster capitalism' has become well established (Blok, 1974; Arlacchi, 1986; Volkov, 2002; Walker, 2006).

longer, and if so why? The answer to the first question is simple: in the form of the class struggle argument, which informs the concept of deproletarianization, yes it does. And in answer to the second, this is because without such a distinction we cease to be able to understand past, present and – most importantly – future developments in the way capitalist labour regimes change, and the implications of this for conflicts which do or do not lead to systemic transcendence.

Broadly defined, the class struggle argument presented here operates at two interrelated levels, ones that are familiar in Marxist theory.[7] Combining politics and ideology, the first concerns the way in which the deployment of unfree workers reproduces debilitating forms of 'otherness' (replacing class identity with that based on ethnicity, gender and nationality) within their own ranks and also the ranks of workers who are free. At the politico-ideological level, therefore, one of the main reasons why capitalist producers employ workers who are not free is the effectiveness of such restructuring in curbing the emergence or – where this has already emerged – the reproduction of a consciousness of class.

The second involves economic considerations of two kinds. On the one hand, unfree labour-power is generally easier to control than its free counterpart, and for this reason also cheaper to employ. Ironically, therefore, free markets that are global in scope mean that unfree labour becomes for capitalists not just an option but in some instances a necessity, as competition cuts profit margins which in turn force down labour costs. If nothing else, this underlines the problematic nature of the oft-heard claim about the insignificance of unfree labour for modern capitalism.[8]

On the other, class struggle waged 'from above' that entails workforce restructuring using labour-power that is unfree also generates a

---

[7] Insofar as it refers to struggle, the semi-feudal thesis uses the term in a very different way. Accordingly, it locates struggle between on the one hand a 'semi-feudal' landlordism and its external allies (imperialism), and on the other a 'progressive' bourgeoisie, plus peasants and workers. Such division licenses struggle along national or multi-class lines, and conflict is thus not primarily about class, in the shape of capital versus labour.

[8] As outlined below in Chapter 4, in his analysis of class struggle in the ancient world de Ste Croix (1981) pointed out that, although chattel slavery in Rome was small numerically speaking, the surplus extracted from this kind of worker was large. Economically as important is the fact that the presence of unfree workers in the labour market exercised a downward pressure on wage levels of those who were free. My argument is that this applies equally to modern capitalism.

crisis of underconsumption, but not in the form usually invoked. Economic crisis results not from the presence in a particular national context of workers who are unfree, the reason why exponents of the semi-feudal thesis maintain incorrectly that bonded labour is incompatible with accumulation. Rather, the presence of unfree workers in one national context triggers difficulties for free labour in other countries; that is to say, in those national contexts – particularly where accumulation has a long history (Europe, the United States) – where the consumption patterns of workers are affected as a result of loss of employment due to capitalist restructuring.

Accordingly, unfree labour is one contributory factor in a specifically capitalist economic crisis. Ironically, although many contemporary observers have until recently had difficulty in recognizing this link, this was not the case historically.[9] During the nineteenth century many commentators who held widely differing political views nevertheless understood the expansionist dynamic informing slavery in the antebellum southern states.[10] Namely, that if not eradicated the 'peculiar institution' as it existed on the plantation system would gather momentum and extend beyond the boundaries of the south, eventually threatening to displace free labour throughout the United States.[11]

---

[9] Those who in the recent past have opposed strongly the view that agrarian capitalists deploy unfree labour have argued either that where coercion is used agriculture cannot be capitalist, or that such workers are free, coercion notwithstanding. Some have now quite simply changed their minds, while others have qualified positions held previously.

[10] This was true also of those nineteenth century commentators such as Sir Arthur Helps who, questioning slavery on moral/ethical grounds, objected to the justification of unfree labour in terms of the innate racial inferiority of non-whites. The inference of the conclusion reached – that as slavery was not an effect simply of race, it could not be confined merely to the labour of non-whites – was that unfreedom might extend to subordinate any and all workers, regardless of race. This possibility was recognized by him (Anonymous, 1851: Chapter IV) in terms of the fact 'that there are no races is respect to which the preceding propositions against slavery do not apply'.

[11] These politically and theoretically distinct commentators included John Stuart Mill, John Bright, Karl Marx and Abraham Lincoln. For the views of Bright and Marx about the expansion northwards of southern slavery, and its implications for free workers, see Chapters 1 and 2. A similar argument was made by Mill (1875: 193), who noted in 1862 that if 'the purposes of the North may be doubted or misunderstood, there is at least no question as to those of the South. They make no concealment of *their* principles. As long as they were allowed to direct all policy of the Union; to break through compromise after compromise, encroach step after step, until they reached the pitch of claiming a right to carry slave property into the Free States, and, in opposition to the laws of those States, hold it as property there...' (original emphasis) Much the same position was advanced by Lincoln in the course of debates about

Trapped in the Capitalist Maelstrom

That the same expansionist dynamic continues into the present is evident from the dilemma facing enterprises committed to ethical/moral business practices. Until the new millennium, the fashion retailer Marks & Spencer publicly eschewed outsourcing in search of cheap labour.[12] It followed a policy of locally produced clothing for the domestic market in Britain itself, an approach praised by advocates of a benign capitalism. Marks & Spencer was soon undercut by rivals in the same market, such as Primark, a company which not only outsources production but has also been accused of employing workers that are unfree. Faced with a decline in profits, Marks & Spencer has had to follow suit, and adopt the cost-cutting restructuring strategies of its competitors (relocation, outsourcing, cheaper workers).

This episode illustrates three things. First, the way in which capitalism now has a vortex-like dynamic, to the extent that enterprises prepared to employ unfree labour set the low standard of cost-cutting labour practices which in turn determine market advantage and generate higher profitability. To remain competitive, therefore, other enterprises in the same market necessarily have to adopt the same practices, or risk being undercut and going out of business. Second, the case also underlines the problems confronting advocates of ethical/moral

---

slavery during the 1850s, when he referred to its spread as 'the nationalization of slavery'. About this process his views were unambiguous (Roe, 1929: 52, 56, 138): 'This thing of slavery is more powerful than its supporters…[i]t gathers strength, like a rolling snow-ball, by its own infamy […] One great trouble in the matter is, that slavery is an insidious and crafty power…[…] Once let slavery get planted in a locality, by ever so weak or doubtful a title, and in ever so small numbers, and it is like the Canada thistle or Bermuda grass – you can't root it out. […] You need but one or two turns further [and you] will receive and support or submit to the slave trade, revived with all its horrors – a slave code enforced in our Territories…to bring slavery up into the heart of the free North.' In this connection it is important to note that – unlike Bright, Mill and Lincoln – only Marx attributed the expansion of unfree production relations to a process of class struggle (see Chapters 3, 5 and 8).

[12] On this see 'M&S comes apart at seams', *The Observer* (London), 19 September 1999; 'M&S sacks British supplier', *The Guardian* (London), 23 October 1999; 'M&S signals 50% profits fall', *The Guardian* (London), 28 September 1999; 'M&S target of child labour claim', *The Guardian* (London), 27 October 1999; 'Desperation time as M&S as profits fall 43%', and 'M&S digs in to stop the slump', *The Guardian* (London), 3 November 1999; 'Marks and Spencer feels a chill wind on the high street', *Financial Times* (London), 3 November 1999; 'M&S gambles on foreign suppliers', *The Observer* (London), 7 November 1999; 'Primark sales boom arouses anti-poverty anger', *The Guardian* (London), 4 November 2009; and 'Indian staff at factory linked to M&S say they were beaten up', *The Observer* (London), 5 September 2010.

opposition to unfree labour. And third, it emphasizes yet again the importance of analysing the capital/labour relation in terms of competition and struggle that are now global in scope.

About the capitalism/unfreedom link, therefore, deproletarianization entails four basic propositions. First, that economically speaking accumulation is not merely compatible with unfreedom but thrives on this. Second, that historically it has been capitalists themselves who actively sought out labour-power that was unfree. Third, that this kind of worker has on occasion been employed by capitalists in preference to free wage-labour. And fourth, that the presence of unfree labour has been used by capital to intimidate free workers contemplating or undertaking strike action.

Why Labour Regime Change?

Workforce restructuring based on the capacity and willingness of employers to replace free workers with unfree ones has accordingly been used – and is used still – by capital as a weapon in the class struggle. For this reason the appearance in the title of 'regime change' is deliberate. It is a reference to the same term in popular culture discourse indicating an intention on the part of western capitalist powers to remove by force any/every government not to their liking. As is well known, 'regime change' highlights the contradiction between the lip-service paid by western capitalism to the principle of political democracy, and the routine undermining or ousting of an administration – regardless of its grassroots support or popular mandate – that challenges its interests.

A similar contradiction operates with regard to the kind of workforce utilised by capital, since here too there is a dissonance between a discourse about the desirability of labour-power that is free, and the resort by commercial employers to an unfree workforce when it suits their interests. This is a transformation that has become more common with the global spread of capitalism, much to the surprise of many development economists. Indeed, it is a change that brings into question the usual categorization of the capitalism/unfreedom link as a contradiction.

Hence the extension to the reference in the title, to one of 'labour regime change', which challenges three shibboleths. That the capitalism/unfreedom link is contradictory; that it is in some sense 'accidental', a working arrangement undesired – and thus not imposed – by employers; and that a benign state can be relied on ultimately to eliminate such production relations. These are the reasons that those who search for solutions within the existing system, invoking an ethical/moral discourse based on 'human rights', 'citizenship', 'civil society', and 'redemocratization', will search in vain for ever. As long as unfree labour yields profits, its reproduction by capital is guaranteed.

Since an ethical/moral discourse opposed to bonded labour leaves unchallenged either the capitalist system or its state, advocates of such an approach tend to look to the state as a disinterested enforcer of 'human rights'. This overlooks the fact that (lip-service apart) the capitalist state has shifted its position regarding the economic role of unfree labour. From being perceived negatively, as an obstacle to economic growth, and thus institutional forms that had to be eliminated, therefore, unfree production relations are now regarded by the state as making a positive contribution to the accumulation process. This in turn undermines the optimistic view that a mere tinkering with the legal apparatus by the capitalist state is all that is needed to eliminate such production relations.[13]

In addressing the theme of twenty-first labour regimes, with particular reference to the kind of future trajectory followed by capitalist social formations, two paradoxes should also be noted. First, speaking about the future necessarily involves looking mainly at the past (late antiquity, the eighteenth and nineteenth centuries), and specifically how different theoretical frameworks (Marxist, non-Marxist) have interpreted labour regimes created and reproduced historically by capitalism. And second, to speak about how this applies to so-called Third World nations involves looking at examples of advanced capitalist nations (United States, Germany, Britain).

---

[13] Thus, for example, Breman (2010: 347–8, 350ff.) persists in seeing the capitalist state in India as part of the solution to the problem of bonded labour, a potentially benign and disinterested institution ultimately willing to enforce human rights legislation designed to eradicate 'abuses' by emancipating unfree workers. Putting too much faith in a well-meaning 'state apparatus that has committed itself to upholding the rights...of all its citizens', Breman (2010: 336) fails to understand that the perception by the state of the economic role of unfree labour has itself changed. As long as unfree labour was regarded as a non-capitalist social relation, the colonial bureaucracy in India saw it as an obstacle to the development of a capitalist agriculture. When the latter process got underway, however, it became increasingly evident that such a view was misplaced, and that institutional forms hitherto characterized as incompatible with profitability, advanced technology and accumulation were perfectly compatible with agrarian capital accumulation.

An earlier analysis by me of unfree labour examined this relation in so-called Third World nations, where the debate about its presence or absence concerns transition to capitalism.[14] The focus then was largely empirical, on instances of unfree production relations deployed by agrarian capitalists; in what follows, by contrast, the focus is on why many influential theorists throughout history have perceived these working arrangements and capitalist development to be incompatible. Here it is intended to look at the prevalence or resurgence of unfree labour in metropolitan capitalism.

Whereas unfree labour in the context of Third World development has been and continues to be regarded as a characteristic of a backward agrarian structure, this kind of interpretation is obviously not possible in the case of the economically advanced agriculture that is a feature of Europe and North America. How, then, is one to account for the increasing use of unfree labour by agribusiness enterprises in advanced capitalist economies?

Themes and (Political) Variations

The book is divided into eight chapters, of which the first examines the impact of non-Marxist assumptions about the capitalism/unfreedom link, and the objections to them. Adam Smith, Malthus, Mill, Bright and Weber all dismissed the idea that unfree labour might be acceptable to capitalists on the grounds that such workers would necessarily be inefficient, unskilled, costly, and scarce. Because it was an obstacle both to market formation/expansion and to the installation of advanced productive forces, they argued, unfree labour was incompatible with a dynamic system of accumulation within particular national contexts.

In the present global capitalist system, however, none of these objections continue to hold. Analysing a twenty-first century capitalism through the lens of class struggle confirms that today unfree workers are more profitable to employ but no less efficient than their counterparts who are free. Deskilling combined with a reserve army that is global in scope now makes it possible for capitalists to use such production relations.

[14] Ethnographic data and case study materials in the earlier analysis (Brass, 1999) chronicled the contemporary presence of unfree labour in India and Peru.

Historical and current approaches on the part of Marxist theory to the same question are considered in Chapters 2, 3 and 4. The epistemological link connecting on the one hand the conceptualization by Adam Smith of labour as value and by Hegel of labour as property, and on the other the interpretation by Marx of labour-power as commodity that in a capitalist economy can be bought/sold, is traced in Chapter 2. A distinction between workers who are free and those who are unfree informs the historical process of becoming a proletariat, itself a result of class struggle between capital and labour.

In the course of such conflict, agency metamorphoses from that conducted by the (Hegelian) subject-in-general to that by (Marxist) subjects-of-a-particular-class. This in turn gives rise to the bonding by employers of landless workers – regardless of whether these are permanent, seasonal, casual, locals or migrants. The latter corresponds to deproletarianization, a process whereby labour-power is either decommodified or recommodified by someone other than its owner.

Chapter 3 examines the semi-feudal thesis, a variant of Marxism which might be called the stages version, whereby one relational form is inevitably replaced by another, a unilinear and irreversible change that signals in turn the accomplishment of a systemic transition. It insists on the absolute necessity of a link between free wage labour and a 'fully functioning' capitalism, an approach which decouples accumulation and unfree working arrangements. The semi-feudal thesis rests on the premiss that unfree relations exist because capitalism has yet to emerge, or is insufficiently developed. Once it has, so the argument goes, then commercial agrarian producers will rush to eradicate all forms of unfreedom.

Chapter 4 considers the 'disguised' wage labour framework, another variant of Marxism. Since it regards capitalism as an eternal systemic form, it recognizes neither unfree labour nor primitive accumulation. By abolishing the free/unfree distinction, and maintaining instead that all rural workers – in late antiquity no less than in present-day capitalism – are simply hired labourers who are contractually free, this view breaks with Marxism and is indistinguishable from neo-classical economic historiography. Locating capitalism in ancient society also reproduces the claim made by cliometricians that capital and labour are ever-present, historically non-specific and thus 'natural' economic categories that cannot be transcended.

Chapter 5 looks at the difficulties in confining unfree labour to the pre-history of capitalism (= primitive accumulation), and thus delinking it from a 'fully functioning' capitalist system. Unlike Marxist theory, in which primitive accumulation is characterized by production relations that are not free, and primitive accumulation itself chronologically prefigures capitalism proper, adherents of the semi-feudal thesis and the 'disguised' wage labour position decouple unfree labour and capitalism, as do exponents of 'empire' and the 'new' imperialism. These attempts both to disconnect unfree labour and capitalism and to dehistoricize primitive accumulation constitute a postponement/cancellation of a socialist transition.

Chapters 6 and 7 present case study material examining if unfree labour is associated simply with primitive accumulation in Germany, North America and Britain, or if its presence in all these contexts is consistent with a 'fully-functioning' capitalism. The continuation of unfree labour long after the ending of southern slavery in the United States, of Prussian serfdom/servanthood in Germany, and of the gangmaster system in Britain confirms that the presence and role of unfree migrant/local workers in the advanced capitalist labour processes over the nineteenth and twentieth centuries is not explained as – and cannot be confined epistemologically to – the 'pre-history' of capitalism.

Nor can it be dismissed in terms of an analogous claim that such production relations are not – and cannot be considered to be – a central feature of a 'fully functioning' accumulation process. Foreign migrants, the gangmaster system and incarcerated workers – the concentration camp in Germany and the commercial leasing of prison labour in the United States – were (and in some instances are still) centrally a feature of 'fully functioning' capitalism in all these national contexts.

Chapter 8 deals with the political implications arising both from non-Marxist and the different Marxist approaches to the capitalism/unfreedom link, with respect to the specific kinds of opposition to its presence (citizenship, human rights), and whether or not these entail systemic transition (a transcendence of capitalism). The Marxist approach deployed here differs fundamentally from a moral/ethical one in that it locates the analysis of unfree labour within debates about political economy.

In contrast to the moral/ethical approach, therefore, the governing criteria of Marxism are what generates value, who has a claim on this, and why. The latter discourse is all about economic growth, efficiency, profit and how surplus generated is to be allocated (the class struggle argument). Once located within this materialist discourse, the reason for the existence and the continuation of production relations that are unfree, together with their intensification under a 'fully functioning' capitalism (deproletarianization) ceases – or ought to cease – to be a mystery.

CHAPTER ONE

THE SMITHIAN INHERITANCE

As many commentaries on the subject confirm, the incompatibility between unfree labour and capitalist development became almost an article of faith where non-Marxist political economy was concerned, particularly during the nineteenth century.[1] Among the reasons for this were the rise of political liberalism, the dominance of *laissez-faire* economic theory, and the emancipatory claims informing colonial discourse about trusteeship. Imperialism and the spread of capitalism were accompanied by a justifying ideology, that posited not just the desirability but the necessity of two conditions: on the one hand political democracy, and on the other economic growth achieved by employing labour-power that was free. Each of these conditions was underwritten by the view of an empowered subject exercising free choice, either in the market or at the ballot box.

Historically, the most influential non-Marxist analyses of political economy – those of Smith, Malthus, Mill, Bright and Weber – all questioned the compatibility between capitalism and unfree labour, mainly on the grounds that this kind of working arrangement was too costly and/or inefficient. More recently, neo-classical economic historians of unfreedom – such as Fogel and Engerman – espouse the same argument but invert its logic: because the antebellum plantation was in their view economically efficient, its workforce must in some sense have been uncoerced, and remained on the plantation voluntarily, attracted by the good pay and conditions on offer there.[2] In the end, these non-Marxists adhere to the same epistemology: as in their view unfree labour is economically inefficient, workers employed by a

[1] For nineteenth century commentaries on political economy that decouple unfree labour and capitalist development, see – among others – Brassey (1872; 1879), Walker (1888), and Bagehot (1911).

[2] See Brass (1999: Chapter 5) for the epistemology informing the arguments advanced by Fogel and Engerman, aspects of which are also considered below in Chapters 2, 3, 4 and 8.

capitalist enterprise that in economic terms is efficient are – and can only ever be – free.[3]

This chapter is divided into three sections, the first two of which examine recurrent themes in the analyses by Smith, Malthus, Mill, Bright and Weber of the reasons why unfree labour is incompatible with capitalism. These include claims about the inefficiency, the costliness, the lack of skill and the scarcity of such workers. Part three considers the extent to which all these objections still hold true.

I

The importance of Adam Smith's contribution to the debate about unfree labour is simply put: it was the first major theoretical attempt to understand the dynamic of capital accumulation, to link labour to the creation of value, and to characterize labour in terms of a wider political economy. Even those who disagreed with him on fundamental aspects of these questions, such as Mill, nevertheless accepted much of what he had to say about the systemic dissonance of unfreedom and its negative economic role in the accumulation process. Epistemologically, therefore, Smithian assumptions about the capitalism/unfreedom link permeate both non-Marxist and – as will be seen in Chapter 3 – semi-feudal Marxist political economy.[4]

Adam Smith on Unfree Labour

It is clear that Smithian teleology concerning the economic inefficiency of unfree labour, and hence its high cost when compared to free labour, can itself be traced back to two of the central theoretical emplacements

[3] A similar argument was advanced by Bagehot (1911: 72), who maintained that a precondition for capitalist development was 'the existence of transferable labour, and I showed before how rare transferable labour is in the world, and how very peculiar are its prerequisites. You cannot have it unless you have a strong government...and you must not have slavery, for this is an imperfect substitute for free transferable labour, which effectively prevents the existence of it. Complete freedom of capital presupposes complete freedom of labour, and can only be attained when and where this exists.'

[4] When Adam Smith contrasts unfree labour with sharecropping, therefore, the inference is that the latter is a free relation of production, a view which overlooks the fact that in India, sharecropping relations involve poor peasants who are themselves bonded by debt, i.e. unfree labour. In contrast to Smith, therefore, sharecropping is not on a relational continuum at the beginning of which stands unfree labour and at the end of which is freedom. Much rather, sharecroppers who begin as free workers gradually lose this economic identity, as they become increasingly indebted to employers.

informing his analytical framework: his view of labour as the source of value and thus of national wealth, and the distinction between productive and unproductive labour. In contrast to the French physiocrats, for whom land/Nature was the sole repository of economic value, Smith allocated this same role to labour, on the productivity of which rested industrialization and with it the capacity to augment national wealth.[5]

The enhancement of labour productivity, however, depended in turn on the installation of advanced technical inputs and machinery, both of which required capital investment and neither of which were in his opinion compatible with the employment of a workforce that was unfree. The presence of the latter was accordingly a twofold obstacle to accumulation: not only was unfree labour itself incapable of operating advanced productive forces, but capital would not invest in a labour process where workers deemed by Smith to be unproductive – that is, slaves and other forms of unfree labour - were employed.

Although he does not explicitly include slavery within the category of unproductive labour, this linkage (slaves = idle = unproductive) is nevertheless inferred. 'Wherever capital predominates,' Smith observes, 'industry prevails: wherever revenue, idleness.'[6] The presence of the latter characteristic is attributed in turn to the absence where slaves are concerned of an incentive on their part to work hard or well, a situation which he contrasts with that of labour which is free, and which for this reason not only responds positively to economic incentives but also works hard and efficiently. Thus, for example, the economically backward character of large feudal estates in England was attributed by Smith to the employment of a work force that was unfree, in his opinion the most costly form of labour-power because – unlike a free worker – one who is unfree has no incentive to work well.[7]

Extending this argument, Smith also claimed that – again unlike free workers – 'slaves…are very seldom inventive', as a consequence of which 'all the most important improvements, either in machinery, or in the arrangement and distribution of work, which facilitate and abridge

---

[5] For the French physiocrats see Beer (1939).

[6] See Smith (1812, II: 12).

[7] See Smith (1812, II: 87–8), where the following oft-quoted passage is to be found: 'But if great improvements are seldom to be expected from great proprietors, they are least of all to be expected when they employ slaves for their workmen. The experience of all ages and nations, I believe, demonstrates that the work done by slaves, though it appears to cost only their maintenance, is in the end the dearest of any.' For the same argument, see also Smith (1812, III: 37–8).

labour, have been the discoveries of freedmen'.[8] He then insisted, rather oddly, that: 'Should a slave propose any improvement of this kind, his master would be very apt to consider the proposal as the suggestion of laziness, and of a desire to save his own labour at the master's expense. The poor slave, instead of reward, would probably meet with much abuse, perhaps with some punishment'. This bizarre argument verges on the nonsensical: even staying within the confines of the logic adopted by Smith, a completely different outcome is in order. Not only would a master not reject an improvement simply because it was suggested by his slave, therefore, but the former would regard it – like the subject who made the original suggestion – as his own property.

From all this Smith concluded that the employment of slaves was the least productive and thus the most costly form of working arrangement. This argument, variations on which are a constant refrain in most of the texts about political economy which follow his, was elaborated by him in the following manner. Accepting that employers preferred slave labour to that of free workers, he argued that whereas cash crops such as sugar and tobacco 'can afford the expense of slave cultivation, corn cannot, and is therefore grown by free labour'.[9] Since tobacco and sugar were sufficiently profitable to justify cultivation with expensive forms of labour, they – and only they – could be grown using workers that were unfree.[10]

Contrasting the *metayer* system of cultivation using tenant labour with that based on slaves, Smith argued similarly that because sharecropping tenants were free, and thus able both to acquire property and to benefit from the application of their own labour-power, they had an incentive to work harder and were thus more productive than slaves, who were unfree.[11] It was to this difference in productivity that he attributed the decline of servitude in European history, although he

---

[8] On this point, see Smith (1812, III: 37).

[9] See Smith (1812, II: 89–90).

[10] Elsewhere Smith (1812, III: 38) maintains that the high price of luxury items produced in antiquity was due mainly to the fact that these goods were the product of slave labour. A similar theme informed the argument about capitalism and slavery advanced at the beginning of the twentieth century by Sombart (1967: 125–7, 142–5), who maintained that slaves were employed on large colonial plantations mainly in order to produce the luxuries for bourgeois consumption in Europe.

[11] Hence the view (Smith, 1812, II: 90–1) that: 'Such tenants, being freemen, are capable of acquiring property, and having a certain proportion of the produce of land, they have a plain interest that the whole produce should be as great as possible, in order that their own proportion may be so. A slave, on the contrary, who can acquire

accepts that 'slavery continued to take place almost universally for several centuries afterwards', until it was abolished 'from above'. Because Adam Smith and others attribute the eradication of unfreedom simply to 'from above' agency, no mention is made of the role of class struggle waged 'from below' in the demise of unfree labour.

II

Since he located unfree labour within a discourse about the necessity of population checks on the poor, Malthus also attributed its economic unviability to low productivity.[12] Like most other economists, Malthus, Mill and Bright recognized that the presence of slaves in the labour market undercut the demand for workers who were free. Unfree labour was regarded by them as unproductive and inefficient, and – like Adam Smith – more costly than its free equivalent, not least because such workers could not reproduce themselves demographically, and thus their supply was not assured. As employers were unable to hire/fire unfree labour according to business requirements, Max Weber argued, it was costly. For this reason, he regarded the use by capital of such arrangements as economically irrational.

Malthus, Mill and Bright on Unfree Labour

Writing about ancient Rome, Malthus noted that, as land was consolidated into large properties under landlord control, erstwhile smallholding peasants were increasingly compelled to rely for their income on the sale of their labour-power.[13] Unable to do this due to the widespread availability of slaves who, because they were unfree were also

nothing but his maintenance, consults his own ease by making the land produce as little as possible over and above that maintenance.'

[12] Malthus (n.d., I: 314–5) outlined his thesis as follows: 'Must it not then be acknowledged by an attentive examiner of the histories of mankind, that, in every age and in every state in which man has existed or does now exist, the increase of population is necessarily limited by the means of subsistence: population invariably increases when the means of subsistence increases, unless prevented by powerful and obvious checks'.

[13] The situation is described by Malthus (n.d., I: 147) as one in which 'the citizens, who were by this change successively deprived of the means of supporting themselves, would naturally have no resource to prevent them from starving but that of selling their labour to the rich, as in modern states; but from this resource they were completely cut off by the prodigious number of slaves, which, increasing by constant influx with the increasing luxury of Rome, filled up every employment both in agriculture

cheaper to employ, such impoverished workers ('poorer citizens') gave rise to what Malthus terms 'a strange and preposterous custom'; namely, 'that of distributing vast quantities of corn to the poorer citizens gratuitously'. However, he perceived the resulting problem to be an obstacle to demographic growth among free workers, who were simultaneously transformed into unproductive/inefficient members of society.[14]

That unfree workers were also regarded by Malthus as innately unproductive/inefficient is clear from his observations about extant forms of agricultural labour in Norway, Sweden and Russia. Noting that tenants in Norway were required to remain in the employ of farmer as unmarried servants, Malthus stated that such tied labourers are 'not remarkable for diligence, and that to do the same quantity of work more are necessary than in other countries.'[15] The same was true of *corvées* in Sweden, and vassalage in Russia, a relational form he associated with worker 'indolence'.[16] As in ancient society, therefore, the presence of unfree labour-power in European nations during the eighteenth century was for Malthus – as for Adam Smith – not only less productive than its free equivalent, and thus a more costly form of working arrangement, but an intrinsically uneconomic one that exerted a downward pressure on the (physical and economic) reproduction of free labour.

---

and manufactures. Under such circumstances, so far from being astonished that the number of free citizens should decrease, the wonder seems to be that any should exist beside the proprietors.'

14 See Malthus (n.d., I: 150–1).

15 See Malthus (n.d., I: 156–7). That he perceived servanthood in idealized terms, an unfree working arrangement which permitted its 'indolent' subject to consume more than s/he produced, it evident from what he wrote about this relation in the case of England. 'The servants who live in the families of the rich,' wrote Malthus (n.d., I: 237), 'have restraints yet stronger to break through in venturing upon marriage. They possess the necessaries, and even the comforts of life, almost in as great plenty as their masters. Their work is very easy and their food luxurious...' This idealized view about the situation of domestic servants in England was one shared by another, equally influential political economist. Thus McCulloch (1967: 62–3) writes: 'And thus it is that domestics owe to the servitude in which they are placed, and the unjustly low estimation in which they are held, their high wages, and comparatively comfortable condition.'

16 Hence the view (Malthus, n.d., I: 185) that 'Russia has great natural resources. Its produce is, in its present state, above its consumption; and it wants nothing but greater freedom of industrious exertion, and an adequate vent for its commodities in the interior parts of the country... The principal obstacle to this is the vassalage, or rather slavery, of the peasants, and the ignorance and indolence which almost necessarily accompany such a state.'

Also following the line of argument laid down by Adam Smith, John Stuart Mill similarly dismissed the possibility that production carried out with unfree workers was – or could ever be – economically efficient. 'It is a truism to assert,' he maintained, 'that labour extorted by fear of punishment is inefficient and unproductive…[a]ll processes carried on by slave labour are conducted in the rudest and most unimproved manner'.[17] Confusing technical skills which enhance production (and profitability), which he agreed slaves possessed, and an understandable reluctance on their part to work as hard as possible, which slaves will not do unless threatened with physical coercion, Mill concluded that slavery and other forms of unfreedom (serfdom) were an obstacle both to the utilization of modern technique and to profitability generated by the application of the latter.[18] For this reason, output by free workers was perceived as superior, and always exceeds in quantity and quality that of those who are unfree: items produced by the latter are consequently regarded not only as inferior but also as dearer than those made when employing free labour.

As with most other non-Marxists, Mill's views about the disjuncture between unfree labour and capitalism were grounded in the defence of the latter, and had little to do with humanitarian considerations. Like Smith, he regarded ancient slavery as generally benign.[19] And, like Malthus and Bright, Mill also perceived the main economic problem with unfree labour to be its inability to reproduce itself demographically: because of this, it was incapable of providing producers with an assured/continuous supply of workers. When examining the conditions favouring the employment of unfree workers over free ones, therefore, Mill – like Bright – identified the supply of unfree workers as crucial.

---

[17] Mill (1849a: 305, 306). For a different view, see Mill (1849a: 589; 1849b: 226), where he accepts that the employment by planters in the antebellum American south of slaves conferred cost advantages on commodities they produced for and sold in international markets that would be eliminated in the event of their having been produced by a workforce that was free.

[18] See Mill (1849a: 306–7), who regarded the quantitative/qualitative gap in output produced by free and unfree labour as unbridgeable, given even the better control and (by inference) the threats of physical coercion exercised over workers who are not free: 'What is wanting in the quality of labour itself, is not made up by any excellence in the direction and superintendence'.

[19] See Mill (1849a: 304).

His coldly pragmatic argument was that, if these kinds of worker could indeed be procured without hindrance, landholders would no longer have to worry about the biological reproduction of the slave population (i.e., accommodate the economically unproductive members of the slave family). In such circumstances, therefore, they could simply work the unfree labourers in their employ 'to death', in the knowledge that such resources of labour-power were both guaranteed and inexhaustible.[20]

In a similar vein, the abolitionist views expressed by Bright in the mid-1860s were linked to his conviction that the continued existence of plantation slavery in the antebellum South was an obstacle to capitalist economic efficiency.[21] At a time when both the market and the demand for cotton were expanding, an increase in the output of this commodity depended on augmenting the supply of labour-power employed in its cultivation. A capitalist whose investment was all in the Lancashire cotton mills, Bright argued strongly that, since the natural demographic growth of the slave population was low, and as only a quarter of all slaves were anyway engaged in cotton production, an increase in the output of this cash crop depended either on resuming the slave trade or persuading free workers in the North voluntarily to migrate southwards and complement the supply of labour employed in cultivating cotton.

Since the Union government would not permit the resumption of the slave trade, and free workers in the northern states would not migrate to the cotton south for fear that they, too, would become unfree, the problem of low output linked to an inadequate labour supply would persist for as long as slavery continued, and it was for this

---

[20] Hence the view (Mill, 1849a:303) that: 'If full-grown able-bodied slaves can be procured in sufficient numbers, and imported at a moderate expense, enlightened self-interest will recommend working the slaves to death, and replacing them by importation, in preference to the slow and expensive process of breeding them. Nor are the slave-owners generally backward in learning this lesson.'

[21] For this argument, see, for example, the speeches made by Bright (1865: 194 ff., 235–9) in London during 1863. In the United States during the nineteenth century, the view about the inefficiency of unfree labour was a commonplace amongst bourgeois economists. Thus, for example, a widely used economics text book (Walker, 1888: 54) of that era advocating 'full and free competition' also observed that, as 'the production of wealth [depended on] the maximum of effect, and the minimum of waste', the main obstacle to this was 'most conspicuously seen in the wastefulness and inefficiency of slave labour.'

(pragmatic rather than humanitarian) reason that Bright advocated the ending of unfreedom in America.[22]

Max Weber on Unfree Labour

A different set of arguments were advanced by Max Weber in support of the same claim, that unfree labour was organizationally 'irrational', expensive, economically inefficient, and thus incompatible with modern capital accumulation.[23] Not only did the purchase of slaves tie up capital, burden owners with additional costs of maintaining the unproductive labour of the slave family, and involve political risks in the form of potential abolition, therefore, but fluctuations in the availability and cost of such unfree workers also precluded both supply and price stability, as well as the installation of advanced productive technique.[24] The latter was attributed by Weber in turn to the absence under slavery of two conditions that contribute to economic efficiency: first, the fact that the latter required a worker to exercise care/responsibility in the labour process (particularly where costly machines/equipment were concerned); and second, to the fact that the intensity of labour was determined by the element of worker self-interest, neither of which in his view were features of unfree production relations.[25]

According to Weberian sociological theory, however, the most important obstacle posed by the presence of unfreedom to the process

---

[22] That it was an increase in cotton production, which depended on ending slavery, rather than just the latter, which interested Bright most, is evident from what he himself wrote and said during the early and mid-1860s. As Bright (1865: 213–4) himself admitted, 'I am speaking now as a matter of business. I am glad when matters of business go straight with matters of high sentiment and morality... from this platform I declare my solemn conviction that there is no greater enemy to Lancashire, to its capital and to its labour, than the man who wishes the cotton agriculture of the Southern States to be continued under slave labour'.

[23] Unsurprisingly, and like some other commentators on the connection between capitalism and slavery, Weber's arguments are somewhat contradictory. Having accepted that slaves were employed in production that was highly profitable, and further that this 'profitableness of slave labour depended upon strict plantation discipline, ruthless driving of the slave, and perpetual importation...and finally exploitative agriculture', he nevertheless denies it any (let alone an initial) economic role in contributing to the origins of modern capitalism: 'This accumulation of wealth brought about through colonial trade,' he notes (Weber, 1927: 300), 'has been of little significance for the development of modern capitalism'.

[24] For these arguments, see Weber (1947: 253–4). Similar arguments concerning the cost disadvantages of employing workers who are unfree were advanced by Brassey (1972: 262–3).

[25] Weber (1947: 254).

of economic rationalization on which capitalist development depends was the consequent inability of employers to recruit/dismiss workers in keeping with business requirements. For this and the above reasons, Weber maintained that it was possible to employ unfree labour only when the following three conditions were met: where slaves could be maintained cheaply, where a large and continuous supply of such workers was assured, and in large-scale agricultural enterprises (e.g., plantations) or technologically underdeveloped (= 'simple') industrial labour processes.[26]

Because of the accruing 'advantages to industrial profitability and efficiency', he argued, unfree relations invariably disappeared once free workers became available. From the viewpoint of the producer, Weber concluded, these advantages took the form of a decline in capital investment/risk, the capacity to shift the cost of family subsistence/maintenance onto the labourer himself, and – crucially – a capacity to hire/fire; that is, both to select suitable workers and to dismiss unsuitable ones, thereby maximizing a worker's self-interest in efficient capitalist production.[27] The latter is, of course, the same argument as that advanced by Adam Smith (see above).

III

Let us now consider the main reasons given by Smith, Malthus, Mill, Bright, Weber, and others, for the incompatibility between capitalism

[26] On this last point, Weber (1947: 215) observes that, where domestic slaves or serfs are employed, '[t]he appropriation of returns of labour may be used by the owner…as a means of profit. In that case the dependent may be obligated to contribute goods or to work on raw materials provided by the owner. The owner will then sell the product. This is unfree domestic industry. He may, finally, be used as a labourer in an organized shop – a slave or a serf workshop.' Although he does consider the case of the antebellum American south, instances of plantations worked with unfree labour are confined by Weber (1927: 80–1, 125 ff.; 1976) largely to antiquity.

[27] On the importance for economic rationality/efficiency of 'the worker's own interest in maximizing…production', see Weber (1947: 218). In the context of a market economy, he notes (Weber, 1947: 240–1), a wage incentive 'appeals immensely more strongly to the worker's self-interest', and '[i]n this sense it has a higher degree of formal rationality, from the point of view of technical considerations, than any kind of direct compulsion to work.' It should be pointed out, however, that – unlike neoclassical economic historiography – Weber did not equate slave emancipation in the American south with the ending of unfree production relations in that context, much rather the contrary: '[t]he negroes are share tenants bound by debt,' he observed (Weber, 1927:84), 'and their freedom of movement exists only on paper'.

and unfree production relations, and evaluate them in terms of their current applicability. These include the argument that unfree labour is inefficient, cannot undertake skilled tasks and cannot be combined with advanced productive forces, is too costly, hinders market expansion, and the supply of such workers is anyway not assured. All these claims are to a large degree interlinked epistemologically: thus the argument that unfree labour is economically inefficient is itself part of the claim that it is incompatible with an increased level of productive forces that characterize a 'fully functioning' capitalism.

Objections to the Smithian Inheritance

To begin with, it is self-evidently the case that many of the objections raised with regard to the employment by capital of labour-power that is unfree apply with equal (if not more) force to the employment by capital of workers who are free. The latter, for example, are not all skilled, neither do they always respond to incentives to work hard, nor is a regular supply of free labour-power always assured. Weber's argument that, together with the unavailability of unfree workers, fluctuating slave prices undermines accounting stability, overlooks the fact that both these conditions operate in situations where workers are free; hence the availability or unavailability of free labour-power is – as in the case of unfree equivalents – reflected in the widespread price fluctuations of this commodity experienced by prospective buyers who are capitalist producers.[28]

The carelessness and inefficiency which many observers attributed to unfree workers, and invoked as a reason why employers always preferred labour that was not unfree, was a characteristic of free labour as well.[29] As the occurrence of sabotage undertaken by workers

---

[28] Perhaps because he was trapped by the epistemological rigidities of his analyses of economic rationality generally, whereby historical forms of unfree labour were uniformly cast as organizationally 'irrational', financially expensive, and thus economically inefficient, Weber was unable to comprehend the extent to which Polish migrant workers employed in Prussian agriculture at the turn of the nineteenth century were not only unfree, but also how the presence of the latter relation contributed to (and was therefore compatible) with modern capital accumulation in Germany. Details about the latter are set out in Chapter 6.

[29] About migrant agricultural workers employed on commercial farms in England during the 1890s, a spokesperson (Rew, 1913: 76) for agricultural producers commented as follows: 'The carelessness and lack of interest in their work of many farm labourers are a common cause of complaint [by employers], and no doubt also a source of annual waste and loss. If it were possible to devise some practical means by which

employed in factories operating in industrial capitalism attests, deliberate acts of carelessness/inefficiency (= 'the conscious withdrawal of the workers' industrial efficiency') have been and are resorted to by free labour as part of the class struggle.[30] Conversely, there are numerous instances historically of commercial enterprises which employed skilled workers – those manual labourers exhibiting precisely technical accomplishments in relation to tasks done, and thus not categorized as careless/inefficient – who were not free. In the case of the commercially important American whaling industry during the nineteenth century, for example, crews were composed of highly skilled workers; the latter were nevertheless recruited/controlled by means of debt bondage relations initiated/reproduced by means of two familiar mechanisms: cash advances and purchases from the ship's store.[31]

---

the labourer could be financially interested in the success of the year's operations, no one, probably, would dispute its desirability.'

[30] On the incidence and impact of sabotage as a weapon used by free workers in industrial capitalist enterprises, see among many others Kornbluh (1968: 51–3), Beynon (1973: 129 ff.), and Dubois (1976). According to Elizabeth Gurley Flynn (1916), industrial sabotage was a crucial part of the class struggle, whereby members of the industrial proletariat engaged in 'putting the machine on strike'. In the words of one member of the Industrial Workers of the World uttered during 1911, '[h]ere we come to the real point on the question of sabotage: it is a *war measure*, made necessary by the nature of the class struggle' (Kornbluh, 1968: 52, original emphasis).

[31] This emerges clearly from the analysis by Hohman (1928: 14), who states that 'the legal status of whalemen at sea, like that of seamen in general, was strongly reminiscent of medieval serfdom...this unfree status resulted from...political weakness on the part of seamen as a class, which made it difficult to secure protective legislation and to enforce those laws which were on the statute books.' Debts incurred as a result of high prices charged by the ship's store, plus cash advances made to crew members, meant that, after having worked for between two and four years, seamen in debt to agents of the vessel were then 'induced...to embark upon another voyage for the same firm' (Hohman, 1928: 234–5). Whaling companies made 100% profit on items obtained from the ship's store, and most of the crewmen who re-enlisted did so because of debts owed (Hohman, 1928: 219, 228, 245 ff.). According to Hohman (1928: 238), this was because 'a large proportion of a man's earnings was required to pay for outfit and (ship's store) articles, and to meet heavy interest charges upon (cash) advances', with the result that at the end of the voyage crewmen not only had no payment coming but actually owed their employer money. In order to clear this debt, a crewman was required to sign up with the same employer for the next voyage. The central role played in reproducing this form of unfreedom was a combination of on the one hand withholding payment due, and on the other high prices charged for items consumed. About this the same source observes (Hohman, 1928: 258): 'If annual or semi-annual settlements had allowed the whalemen to receive a part of the earnings actually due them, it would have been unnecessary, in many instances for them to ask for cash advances.' The outcome is equally familiar. Due in part to the high prices charged by ship's stores and interest charged on cash advances, notes Hohman (1928: 229, 233, 234–5), average wages

Perhaps because of its epistemological roots in a liberal political economy, the claim that workers who are unfree lack an incentive to work hard, and are for this reason inefficient, misses the point entirely.[32] The dynamic is wholly different: tasks are undertaken and completed by a worker who is unfree not in response to the presence of incentives, in form of reward (cash/kind payment), but rather in order to avoid punishment in the event of non-compliance (violence, coercion).[33] Historically, therefore, slaves, serfs and bonded labourers have indeed worked hard, the absence of positive incentives notwithstanding, for the simple reason that such workers are compelled to do so by the threat (or actualization) of violence/coercion. Indeed, avoidance of the latter can be seen as a 'rational outcome' corresponding to Weber's notion of 'worker self-interest'. Accordingly, a labourer who is unfree works as hard as (or harder than) one who is free for a different reason: namely, because of the fear of the consequences if he/she fails to do this.

This point has long been recognized.[34] In the mid-seventeenth century, for example, Hobbes compared the relationship between slave

---

declined over the nineteenth century and the earnings gap between officers and men widened.

[32] Because exponents of *laissez faire* economic theory either banish or underestimate the impact of coercion, they consequently persist in anchoring the expenditure of work effort to idealized notions of pecuniary rewards. An example of this view is Walker (1888: 55), who asserts that 'always and everywhere [slave] labour has been found to be vastly inferior to the labour of freemen. Even the stimulus of the lash fails to command the facilities which instantly spring into activity under the inspiration of an ample reward.'

[33] A tacit recognition of this fact leads, inevitably, to contradictory statements made by some non-Marxist analyses. For example, Bagehot (1911: 73–4, emphasis added) notes: 'Another condition which precedes the free transfer of labour – the first prerequisite of the free transfer of capital – is slavery, *and within its limits this is free enough: indeed, more free than anything else similar, for you have not to consult the labourer at all, as in all organizations you must*.' However, he then goes on to make the usual contrasting assertion, that '[t]he slave will not work except he is made, and therefore he does little.'

[34] Why slaves on the cotton plantation in the antebellum south worked hard is explained thus by Sutch (1975: 342): 'The frequency with which a punishment is administered is a poor measure of its effectiveness… It is the *fear* of eventual punishment which motivates behaviour… A slave need never have felt the lash to know the consequences of disobedience' (original emphasis). Much the same point was made by Roger Casement in his report about the coercive labour regime the Putumayo region of Peru at the start of the twentieth century. On this he commented as follows (Singleton-Gates and Girodias, 1959: 290): 'Wholesale murder and torture endure… and the wonder is that any Indians were left in the district at all to continue the tale of rubber working on to 1910. This aspect of such continuous criminality is pointed to by

and master to that of sovereign and people. Slaves worked hard, therefore, 'to avoyd the cruelty of their task-masters'.[35] His argument was that, in exchange for maintaining peace, and thereby avoid the disorder/chaos of war, society in general transfers legitimacy to any regime that controls the state, the authority of which is then recognized so long as it prevents conflict.[36] The subordination of a slave was consistent with this paradigm, and perceived as a 'natural' condition. Both the fact of unfree labour, and the power such a relation affords an employer over its subject, was accordingly deemed by Hobbes to be valid.[37] Some three and a half centuries later, it could be argued that his views about why those who are unfree work hard accurately describe the kind of control that in a neoliberal global economy is in effect exercised by capital over labour.

Unfreedom and Deskilling

Characterizing unfree labour as inefficient economically also overlooks the contemporary impact of mechanization and technology in deskilling labour-power.[38] The debate about work organization and 'scientific management' over the latter part of the twentieth century has been

---

those who, not having encountered the demoralisation that attends the methods described, happily infrequent, assert that no man will deliberately kill the goose that lays the golden eggs… [The freebooter on the Putumayo] hunted, killed, and tortured today in order to terrify fresh victims for tomorrow.'

[35] See Hobbes (n.d. [1651]: 107), who notes: 'For Slaves that work in prisons, or fetters, do it not of duty, but to avoyd the cruelty of their task-masters.'

[36] On this, see for example Hobbes (n.d. [1651]: 89 *passim*).

[37] Hence the view (Hobbes, n.d. [1651]: 107) that the 'Master of the Servant, is Master also of all he hath; and may exact the use thereof; that is to say, of his goods, of his labour, of his servants, and of his children, as often as he shall think fit. For he holdeth his life of his Master, by the covenant of obedience; that is, of owning, and authorizing whatsoever the Master shall do. And in the case the Master, if he refuse, kill him, or cast him into bonds, or otherwise punish him for his disobedience, he is himselfe the author of the same; and cannot accuse him of injury.'

[38] The concept 'deskilling' is associated principally with the analytical approach of Braverman (1974). Although an important corrective to those who have predicated capitalist development on the skilled worker, this approach has two particular shortcomings. First, a tendency to idealize non-capitalist work organization, and especially traditional farming practices (= 'the natural mode of life of the family') as conducted by self-sufficient independent proprietors, an interpretation similar to that of Chayanov where the peasant family farm is concerned. Hence the view (Braverman, 1974: 272–3): 'So long as the bulk of the population lived on farms or in small towns, commodity production confronted a barrier that limited its expansion. On the United States farm, for example, much of the construction work (apart from basic framing, as a rule) was accomplished without recourse to the market, as was a good deal of house

concerned mainly with the way technology and machinery undermine traditional craft skills, and the corresponding impact of this on the industrial working class.[39] Whilst important, the focus of discussion has nevertheless tended to be on changes affecting the labour aristocracy in metropolitan contexts, and how such manual workers who are employed in industry on a permanent basis have been replaced by a combination of machines and temporary labour. However, little attention was paid to the fact that the installation of machinery also permits employers to replace skilled labour-power with non-skilled equivalents, and even less attention was paid to the implication of this for the kind of relational shift licensed by such restructuring. It is, in short, a transformation that, in a global work regime, simultaneously enables the insertion (or re-insertion) of unfree production relations into a capitalist labour process.

One of the main planks in the argument of those who maintained that unfree labour-power was incompatible with a 'fully functioning' accumulation process stemmed from the assumption that, as capitalism developed, it would require the employment of an increasingly skilled workforce.[40] It is clear, however, that the opposite is the case: a

furnishing. Food production, including the raising of crops and livestock and the processing of these products for table use was of course the daily activity of the farm family, and in a large measure so also was the home production of clothing. The farmer and his wife and their children divided among them such tasks as making brooms, mattresses, and soap, carpentry and small smith work, tanning, brewing and distilling, harness making, churning and cheese making, pressing and boiling sorghum for molasses, cutting posts and splitting rails for fencing, baking and preserving, and sometimes even spinning and weaving. Many of these farm activities continued as the natural mode of life of the family even after the beginnings of urbanization and the transfer of employment from the farm to the factory or other city job.' And second, deskilling is equated unproblematically with proletarianization (Braverman, 1974: 377ff.), whereas – as is argued here – it can just as easily give rise to social relations of production that are unfree: deproletarianization, in other words.

[39] It is important to note the two different ways in which deskilling is effected: one involves a skilled worker employed in tasks for which these skills are unnecessary; the other entails allocating such tasks to workers who are themselves non-skilled. According to Braverman (1974: 113, original emphasis), the object of deskilling is 'the *dissociation of the labour process from the skills of the workers.* The labour process is to be rendered independent of craft, tradition, and the workers' knowledge. Henceforth it is to depend not at all upon the abilities of workers, but entirely upon the practices of management.' Predictably, the critique of capitalist management techniques by Braverman has itself been challenged by those antagonistic to Marxism, for an example of which see the contributions to the volume edited by Giddens and Mackenzie (1982).

[40] This argument, decoupling unfree labour and economic development on account of a dissonance between an employer's requirement for workers who were skilled and

consequence of increasing the level of the productive forces through the installation of machinery and the application of technology, therefore, results in the *de*skilling of the workforce.[41] This in turn enables capitalists to employ those from rural backgrounds who – in terms of the agribusiness and/or industrial labour process – usually possess the least skills, and it is this particular segment of the workforce that is most vulnerable to relational arrangements (debt, coercion) that are unfree.

Unfreedom and the Reserve Army of Labour

Current forms and pace of deskilling also make possible the activation of hitherto unutilized elements belonging to the industrial reserve army of labour.[42] Although the latter encompasses those thrown out of

---

the absence of such labour-power among the unfree, has been made with regard to the antebellum South. Hence the following assertion (Farnam, 1938: 177): 'Viewed in its broadest economic and social aspects, the slavery question involved a contest between the ideals of a static and those of a dynamic society. Slavery was not incompatible with culture, refinement, kindliness, and religion on the part of individual slave owners, and the Southerners could quote good authority in the writings of the Greek philosophers for thinking that a free commonwealth should be based on slavery. But, disregarding entirely the abuses of slavery, and considering it only at its best, it is clear that it is inconsistent with economic progress, certainly with the kind of economic progress which has characterized the nineteenth century. That progress implies a constant increase in wealth by means of the application of science, [and] of mechanical appliances...to the processes of production. This, however, implies a skilled, intelligent, responsible, and, above all, and adapting labouring class.' For the same kind of argument, this time decoupling economic development and debt peonage in Central America, see Munro (1918: 64).

[41] This antinomy is neatly captured by Braverman (1974: 3–4): 'On the one hand, it is emphasized that modern work, as a result of the scientific-technical revolution and "automation," requires ever higher levels of education, training, the greater exercise of intelligence and mental effort in general. At the same time, a mounting dissatisfaction with the conditions of industrial and office labour appears to contradict this view. For it is also said – sometimes by the same people who at other times support the first view – that work has become increasingly subdivided into petty operations that fail to sustain the interest or engage the capacities of humans with current levels of education; that these petty operations demand ever less skill and training; and that the modern trend of work by its "mindlessness" and "bureaucratization" is "alienating" ever larger sections of the working population. As generalizations, these two views cannot easily be harmonized.'

[42] About the perception by bourgeois economists of the connection between the reserve army of labour and capitalism, Marx (1976a: 786) noted: 'Modern industry's whole form of motion therefore depends on the constant transformation of a part of the working population into unemployed or semi-employed "hands". The superficiality of political economy shows itself in the fact that it views the expansion and contraction of credit as the cause of periodic alternations in the industrial cycle, whereas it is a mere

work as a result of mechanization and technification, members of the reserve army can be incorporated by capital into its labour process for two distinct reasons. The first refers to a reserve to be drawn on when market demand expands, and capitalists need further amounts of labour-power. By contrast, the second refers to those who – as a mass of unemployed also part of the reserve army – are drawn on by capitalists not so much to increase production but rather as a weapon in their struggle against those still in work.[43]

In this second role, members of the reserve army are no longer used simply in addition to an existing workforce but now instead of the latter.[44] Replacing skilled, more costly and/or better organized workers

---

symptom of them...When this periodicity has once become consolidated, even political economy sees that the production of a relative surplus population – i.e. a population surplus in relation to capital's average requirements for valorization – is a necessary condition for modern industry.' Against the tendency of bourgeois economics to interpret declining wages and living standards in a national context as an effect simply of demographic growth, he commented (Marx, 1976a: 788, 790): 'Capitalist production can by no means content itself with the quantity of disposable labour-power which the natural increase of population yields. It requires for its unrestricted activity an industrial reserve army which is independent of these natural limits. [...] Taking them as a whole, the general movements of wages are exclusively regulated by the expansion and contraction of the industrial reserve army, and this in turn corresponds to the periodic alternations of the industrial cycle. They are not therefore determined by the variations of the absolute numbers of the working population, but by the varying proportions in which the working class is divided into an active army and a reserve army, by the increase or diminution in the relative amount of the surplus population, by the extent to which it is alternately absorbed and set free... It would be utterly absurd, in place of this, to lay down a law according to which the movement of capital depended simply on the movement of the population. Yet this is the dogma of economists.'

[43] Sweezy (1946: 99, emphasis added) recognized the importance of this distinction, observing that 'the increasing use of machinery, which in itself means a higher organic composition of capital, sets free workers and thus creates "relative overpopulation" or the reserve army. Marx stresses the point that the existence of unemployed labourers is conducive to the setting up of new industries with a relatively low organic composition of capital and hence a relatively high rate of profit... *It would seem, however, that a more important effect of the reserve army is...through competition on the labour market with the active labour force, to depress the rate of wages and in this way to elevate the rate of surplus value.*'

[44] The assumption that those expelled from the labour force by the application of machinery and technology would – after a brief sojourn in the reserve army – find alternative employment, is both pervasive and misplaced. It is linked to the notion that such workers would be employed as a result of investment in new enterprises by capitalists whose enhanced profits derived from the original labour-displacing strategy. This view is problematic, since it applies only when capital and labour are national in scope, and not international. Where the latter is the case, capital is able to do two things: either to invest elsewhere, in contexts where labour-power is available and even cheaper; or to employ (perhaps even to import) migrants who meet the same requirements. Whichever the instance, the outcome is the same: any new jobs created do not

already established in the capitalist labour process with less skilled, cheaper, and/or unorganized ones, enables producers to exert a downward pressure on the pay, conditions and living standards of the proletariat generally, not just in particular national contexts.[45] As is now very clear, such restructuring, based on an enhanced ability to draw on what is a *de facto* global reserve army in order to decompose/recompose the capitalist labour process worldwide, has followed the implementation in the Third World of the Green Revolution programme during the 1960s and *laissez faire* policies in the 1980s.

It is also in this second role – the reserve army composed of deskilled workers drawn into the labour process so as to undermine the bargaining power of free workers in secure employment, with the object of reducing their pay and conditions, and thus maintaining or augmenting profitability – that capitalism finds a use for workers who are not free.[46] According to Marx, the reserve army comes into its own

---

necessarily go to those expelled from the labour process because of technification/mechanization of production. The obviousness of this outcome notwithstanding, it is unfortunately still possible to hear – even from some on the left – the mantra that workers displaced in this manner will automatically find employment in new industries created by capital.

45 The realization of this particular effect – the deployment of the reserve army in the class struggle between labour and capital – was linked by Marx (1976a: 786, note) in turn to the internationalization of the market. He did not, as some insist, confine the impact of the reserve army to national contexts and economies. It goes without saying that, insofar as the reserve army becomes global in scope, such a development licenses racist ideology among the proletariat in a given country, thereby splitting workers along national/ethnic lines. Equally unsurprising is that capital not only benefits from this but also encourages this kind of consciousness, in the process shifting the latter from the sameness of class to the difference of cultural 'otherness'.

46 Both the existence and the importance of a connection between on the one hand deploying labour-power that is unfree, and the processes of deskilling, trade unionization, reproducing the reserve army, capitalist restructuring and the profitability of accumulation are made clear by Marx (1976a: 788, 793, 795) in the following way: 'We have seen that the capitalist buys with the same capital a greater mass of labour-power, as he progressively replaces skilled workers by less skilled, mature labour-power by immature, male by female, that of adults by that of young persons or children. […] The movement of the law of supply and demand of labour on this basis completes the despotism of capital. Thus as soon as the workers learn the secret of why it happens that the more they work, the more alien wealth they produce, and that the more the productivity of their labour increases, the more their very function as a means for the valorization of capital becomes precarious; as soon as they discover that the degree of intensity of the competition among themselves depends wholly on the pressure of the relative surplus population; as soon as, by setting up trade unions, etc., they try to organize planned co-operation between the employed and the unemployed in order to obviate or weaken the ruinous effects of this natural law of capitalist production on their class, so soon does capital and its sycophant, political economy, cry out at the

once the early stage of capitalism – that generally associated with primitive accumulation – has been left behind.[47] Both it and its relational forms – among them the unfree ones which provide employers with a method of controlling the workforce crucial to the success of the whole accumulation process – are thus not confined merely to the initial development of the capitalist mode of production.[48]

Unfreedom and Advanced Productive Forces

Turning to the issue of a supposed incompatibility between unfree labour and the presence of advanced productive forces, it is necessary first to distinguish between two particular situations. Thus it may indeed be true that the existence of unfree labour inhibits the *development* of the productive forces. However, once established, there is no intrinsic reason why capital should not employ unfree workers in conjunction with advanced productive forces. As has been noted above, this is especially the case where advanced productive forces results in

---

infringement of the "eternal" and so to speak "sacred" law of supply and demand. [...] Capital demands more youthful workers, fewer adults.' The role of unfree labour in age- and gender-related capitalist restructuring is noted subsequently (Marx, 1976a: 850): 'A temporary and local shortage of labour does not bring about a rise in wages, but rather forces the women and children into the fields, and constantly lowers the age at which exploitation begins. As soon as the exploitation of women and children takes place on a large scale, it becomes in turn a new means of making the male agricultural labourer "redundant" and keeping down his wage. The finest fruit of this vicious circle thrives in the east of England – this is the so-called gang-system....' As is evident below, Marx regarded female and child workers as unfree.

[47] Marx (1976a: 784–5) emphasizes thus the central economic role played by the industrial reserve army in the capitalist mode of production: 'But if a surplus population of workers is a necessary product of accumulation or of the development of wealth on a capitalist basis, this surplus population also becomes, conversely, the lever of capitalist accumulation, indeed becomes a condition for the existence of the capitalist mode of production. It forms a disposable industrial reserve army, which belongs to capital just as absolutely as if the latter had bred it at its own cost. Independently of the limits of the actual increase of population, it creates a mass of human material always ready for exploitation by capital in the interests of capital's own changing valorization requirements. With accumulation, and the development of the productivity of labour that accompanies it, capital's power of sudden expansion also grows;... The path characteristically described by modern industry, which takes the form of a decennial cycle (interrupted by smaller oscillations) of periods of average activity, production at high pressure, crisis, and stagnation, depends on the constant formation, the greater or less absorption, and the re-formation of the industrial reserve army or surplus population.' Of particular interest is what he says next (Marx, 1976a: 785): 'This particular cycle of modern industry, which occurs in no earlier period of human history, was also impossible when capitalist production was in its infancy.'

[48] For Marxist views on primitive accumulation, see Chapter 5.

deskilling, which in turn enables capitalists to draw from an expanded industrial reserve army, amongst which is to be found workers who are unfree.

Among those who pointed out that farms where labour was unfree were highly efficient economically, not least because such workers were employed alongside advanced productive forces, was Edward Gibbon Wakefield, whose analysis of colonial agriculture was commended by Marx.[49] Comparing large commercial farms in Tasmania with those in British colonies elsewhere, he contrasted the economic efficiency of the former with the relative backwardness of the latter, noting simultaneously that those in Tasmania were operated using the unfree labour of convicts, while the less efficient farms of a similar size in other colonies employed workers who were free.[50] That the employment of unfree workers could be economically efficient was an argument accepted even by some conservatives: those of them who were ardent Catholics objected on the grounds that the spread of liberalism and capitalism

---

[49] Although critical of Wakefield, Marx nevertheless attributed to him insights regarding the kind of labour regime desired by an agrarian capitalist. The generally positive view held by Marx (1976a: 932, original emphasis) about Wakefield is evident from the following: 'It is the great merit of E.G. Wakefield to have discovered, not something new *about* the colonies, but, *in* the colonies, the truth about capitalist relations in the mother country.'

[50] In Tasmania, notes Wakefield (1849: 176–8) 'there are farms, being single properties, consisting of seven or eight hundred acres each, under cultivation, besides extensive sheep and cattle runs, the farming of which is not inferior to that of Norfolk and the Lothians. A description of one of these farms is before me. The eight hundred acres are divided into fields of from thirty to fifty acres each. The fences are as good as can be. The land is kept thoroughly clear of weeds; a strict course of husbandry is pursued; and the crops, especially of turnips, are very large. The garden and orchards are extensive, kept in apple-pie order, and very productive. The house is of stone, large and commodious. The farm buildings are ample in extent, and built of stone with solid roofs. The implements are all of the best kinds, and kept in perfect order. The live stock, for the most part bred upon the spot, is visited as a show on account of its excellence, and would be admired in the best-farmed parts of England: it consist of 30 cart horses, 50 working bullocks, 100 pigs, 20 brood mares, 1000 head of horned cattle, and 25,000 fine-wooled sheep. On this single establishment, by one master, seventy labourers have been employed at the same time. They were nearly all convicts. By convict labour, and that alone, this fine establishment was founded and maintained. Nothing of the sort could have existed in the island if convicts had not been transmitted thither, and assigned upon their landing to settlers authorized to make slaves of them. In this small island, of which the whole population is under 50,000, there have been at one time fifty establishments much resembling that which I have described.' Comparing this situation with the United States, where capitalist producers employed Irish immigrant workers who were free, the same source concludes: 'In British North America, there is not one [large commercial farming establishment] that bears the slightest resemblance to it, in point of scale, perfection of management, or productiveness in

which undermined religious belief also destroyed what they regarded as an eternal and 'natural' (= 'God-given') hierarchy that bound societies together.[51]

In part, the view about the incompatibility between unfree labour on the one hand, and more advanced productive forces necessitated by capitalist technical rationalization on the other, may have its epistemological roots in long-discredited racist ideology which accompanied and justified nineteenth century colonial and imperial rule.[52] Thus, for example, Weberian claims regarding the supposed inability of unfree workers to operate modern technical inputs are themselves based on the view that '[i]f the labour force was dear' on the antebellum southern plantation, it was because 'the negroes could not be trusted with

---

proportion to the capital or labour employed: for the slavish Irish labour of a colony is less easily combined, and less surely retained, than convict slave-labour. I doubt whether in all Canada, though many a first-rate English and Scotch farmer have emigrated thither, there is even one farm of 500 acres, the management of which would not be deemed very slovenly in Scotland or England, or of which the produce in proportion to capital and labour amounts to half that of a Tasmanian farm.'

[51] Thus, for example, Belloc (1924: 99–100, original emphasis) observed: 'One often hears it said that slave labour is less productive than free labour, that is, labour working at a wage under Capitalism. People sometimes point to modern examples of this contrast, saying that places like the Southern States of America, where slave labour was used a lifetime ago, were less productive than the Northern States, where labour was free. But though this is true of particular moments in history, it is not generally true. Free labour working at a wage under the first institution of capitalism – when, for instance, a body of capitalists are beginning to develop a new country with hired free men to work for them – will be full of energy and highly productive. But when what is called "free labour" – that is, men without property working by contract for a wage – gets into routine and habit, it is doubtful whether it is more productive than slave labour. It is accompanied by a great deal of ill-will. There is perpetual interruption by strikes, and lock-outs, and the process of production cannot be as minutely and absolutely directed by the small and leisured class as can slave labour. *There is no reason why a free man working for another's profit should do his best.* On the contrary, he has every reason to work as little as possible, while the slave can be compelled to work hard.' Unlike Marxists, however, Belloc mounted an attack on capitalism from the political right, so as to defend Catholicism and its socio-economic hierarchy.

[52] Hence the view encountered in a late nineteenth century textbook on political economy (Walker, 1888: 54), when considering the attributes of worker efficiency, that 'the labourer's general intelligence…determines his intellectual qualification for his work, his ability to direct his bodily powers, such as they are, to the production of wealth, with the maximum of effect and the minimum of waste. The cause now adduced is moral, affecting the will.' The same text (Walker, 1888: 52–3) equates slave labour with 'wastefulness and inefficiency', because '[t]he capability of dealing with costly and delicate machines varies greatly between different races and nations of men… Even in highly civilized nations the application of agricultural machinery is limited by the inability of the peasantry to use it.'

modern implements and used only the most primitive tools'.[53] To some degree, the same could also be said of the observation by John Stuart Mill that 'it remains certain that slavery is incompatible with...any real efficiency of labour. For all products which require much skill, slave countries are always dependent on foreigners'.[54]

Significantly, Thomas Nelson Page and Ulrich Bonnell Phillips, both apologists for the slave labour regime on the antebellum Southern plantation, regarded the inefficiency of labour-power that was unfree – its incompatibility with the requirements of skilled tasks and careful use of agricultural implements – as an innate characteristic of racial difference.[55] Equally significantly, it was to combat this view of plantation slaves as innately inferior and unskilled that a subsequent revisionist interpretation emerged: the influential neo-classical economic

---

[53] For this argument, see Weber (1927: 82–3). Elsewhere he appears to suggest ('the specifically occidental form of the organization of labour') that the dichotomy between free and unfree labour was overlaid by an additional polarity between 'Western self' and 'Eastern other' (Weber, 1927: 300).

[54] See Mill (1849a: 306, 309), who extended this view (slaves = primitive subjects = technologically backward, therefore slaves ≠ operators of modern techniques, implements, consequently unfree labour = economically inefficient) to 'the Slavonic nations, who have not yet advanced beyond a state of civilization corresponding to the age of villeinage in western Europe, and can only be expected to emerge from it in the same gradual manner [as "Negro-slaves"], however much accelerated by the salutary influence of the ideas of more advanced countries'.

[55] In the opinion of Thomas Nelson Page (1919: 313, 314, 320, original emphasis), therefore, '[s]cientifically, historically, congenitally, the white race and the negro race differ...What of value to the human race has the negro mind as yet produced? In art, in mechanical development, in literature, in mental and moral science, in all the range of mental action, no notable work has up until this time come from a negro... [T]he negroes *as a race* have never exhibited any capacity to advance;...as a race they are inferior.' He concluded (Page, 1919: 338–9): 'They do not appear to possess the faculties which are essential to conduct any business in which reason has to be applied beyond the immediate act in hand,' adding that a 'great strike occurred last year in one of the large iron-works of the city of Richmond. The president of the company told me afterwards that, although the places at the machines were filled later on by volunteers, and although there were many negroes employed in the works who did not strike, it never occurred to either the management or to the negroes that they could work at the machines, and not one had ever suggested it.' This lack of ability and skill in turn underwrote his argument (Page, 1919: 277ff.) that, following emancipation, blacks who had no 'civilization', and could not be 'civilized,' should not be included in the franchise. Ulrich Bonnell Phillips similarly maintained that slave inefficiency in the antebellum South was an attribute of – and proof for – the 'backwardness'/'primitiveness' of workers who were black In his view, therefore, (Phillips, 1918: 339), 'negroes furnished inertly obeying minds and muscles...But in the work of a plantation squad no delicate implements could be employed, for they would be broken; and no discriminating care in the handling of crops could be had except at a cost of supervision which was generally prohibitive. The whole establishment would work with success only

historiography (= cliometrics) associated with the work of Robert Fogel and Stanley Engerman.[56] Ironically, however, portraying black unfree workers in the antebellum South as empowered led neo-classical historians to depict the plantation regime as essentially an harmonious system containing 'choice-making' subjects, a view not so dissimilar ideologically from the one they had initially set out to challenge.[57]

The Costs of Unfree Labour

Because unfree labour is classified as fixed capital, it is perceived as too costly when compared with free labour. This is because an employer is

---

when management fully recognized and allowed for the crudity of labour. The planters faced this fact with mingled resolution and resignation. The sluggishness of the bulk of their slaves they took as a racial trait to be conquered by discipline, even though their ineptitude was not to be eradicated...'

[56] Cliometric approaches to unfree labour include not just Fogel and Engerman (1974) but also and earlier Conrad and Meyer (1965: 43 ff.), Coats and Robertson (1969), Andreano (1970), Parker (1970) and Temin (1973: 337 ff.). It should be noted that until the cliometric intervention in the debate about American slavery began to exercise influence on other fields, the focus of discussion concerning unfreedom – see, for example, the contributions to collections edited by Herskovits and Harwitz (1964), Tuden and Plotnicov (1970), and Bowker and Carrier (1976) – tended to be not so much on its connection with economic development (let alone capitalism) as on the problem of ethnic stratification and plural society. Even though one may disagree strongly with cliometric epistemology, therefore, it nevertheless reoriented the debate in an important way, bringing it back within the domain of political economy.

[57] In a Preface to one edited volume (Engerman and Genovese, 1975) on slavery, Fogel (1975: vii) observed that '[d]uring the late 1960s there were raging debates as to whether black studies and black history had a legitimate place in the university curriculum,' adding that 'now we have this volume which shows that black history has become the leading arena in the effort to apply quantitative methods to historical research.' That the racism of Phillips was the target of much cliometric analysis is evident from Engerman (1973), who counterposes to the view of the former – equating slavery with inefficient black workers, the 'Sambo' sterotype – the findings from his new economic historiography: namely, that slaves were much rather hard workers who responded rationally and efficiently to 'pecuniary incentives'. In this way, the plantation slave was declared empowered and recuperated for neoclassical economic analysis; the coercive nature of the labour regime was correspondingly denied or downplayed, and the plantation declared to be the epitome of a capitalist firm employing what was in effect no different from the free workers used in manufacturing occupations elsewhere. Although such an approach dispelled a central emplacement of racism – that blacks were economically inefficient workers incapable of undertaking agricultural tasks without the supervision of or direction by white planters – it replaced this with an alternative stereotype. Namely, of an unquestioning black worker colluding with planters in his or her own subjection. This, it scarcely needs pointing out, is very different from the view advanced here: that although the plantation was indeed capitalist, its workforce was coerced, an effect of class struggle, and thus not empowered.

unable to get rid of these kinds of workers when there is nothing for them to do, and consequently there are long periods when they are not employed productively (= efficiently). The assumption is that unfree workers – like machinery – have to be paid for during periods when they are not producing commodities, and thus the whole cost is borne by the capitalist.

Significantly, even those opposed to Malthusian views, such as Thomas Rowe Edmonds during the first half of the nineteenth century and Henry George during the second, framed their critique in terms of the relatively more expensive costs of labour-power that was unfree. As advanced by Edmonds, therefore, this opposition took the form of the 'subsistence guarantee' argument: that had the growth of the slave population exceeded its food provision, slavery as a system of production would necessarily have become extinct, according to Malthus.[58] This was because employers would quickly have sought out free workers, thereby avoiding the expense of having to provide slaves with subsistence during times when these unfree labourers were not engaged in productive activity. In other words, compared with free workers, unfree labour was uneconomical.

Although a critic of Malthus, Henry George also subscribed to the view that unfree labourers were expensive when compared with their free counterparts.[59] The reasons for this were the familiar ones

[58] See Edmonds (1832: 21–2). Taking issue with the Malthusian view that population growth necessarily always exceeds food provision, leading to the operation of 'natural' demographic checks (war, famine, plague, pestilence, delays in the age of marriage, etc.), Edmonds argued that famine was due much rather to the export of food, not its insufficiency. In other words, food production exceeds population growth, not vice versa. The accurate and prescient nature of his analysis is evident from the following (Edmonds, 1832: 26): 'At present, it is notorious that more food is raised in Ireland, and in other parts, where the distress is greatest, than is required for the subsistence of the people. At the time that the famine existed in that country, in the year 1826, when potatoes and articles of the lowest description of sustenance were conveyed to the distressed districts; wheat, and articles of superior description of sustenance, were conveyed down the river Shannon for exportation. In this state of things, the language generally used respecting the inadequacy of subsistence is inconsistent and contradictory. Great distress may indubitably exist; but that distress must be traced to other causes than a tendency of the people to outstrip the means of subsistence. A redundant population, proceeding from the scantiness or incapability of the land to afford sustenance, is one thing; a redundant population proceeding from unequal distribution of wealth, is another.' For the importance of Thomas Rowe Edmonds in the Malthusian debate, see Beer (1948: 230–6), who categorizes him as a 'co-operative socialist', and Smith (1978: 198–202).

[59] For the critique of Malthusian theory, see George (1881: 81 ff.).

advanced by nineteenth century political economy. Slavery was described by George as 'a manifest disadvantage to the masters', on account of the costs of supervision, of maintaining them during periods when they were not engaged in economic activity.[60] The latter covered times when such workers were ill, or when there was little demand for their labour-power during the off-peak seasons in the agricultural cycle, making it impossible for slaves to be hired-out to other employers. 'With social development,' he concludes, unfree labour 'entails more and more care, trouble and expense upon the owner'.[61]

However, the argument about the expense of using workers that are not free is faced with three rather obvious problems. To begin with, the objection advanced by Weber about the high cost to the owner of maintaining slave family is valid only where the members of the slave family do not themselves work in the fields, or cannot be sold, neither of which considerations applied historically to the antebellum plantation regime.[62] More importantly, if unfree labour is so costly in comparison to its free equivalent, why then do commercial producers keep on recruiting and retaining such workers where/when possible? And why, if it was so costly, did European capitalists at the start of the twentieth century insist that their competitors should not employ unfree workers to produce commodities destined for the international market?

In these contexts capitalist opposition to the employment of unfree labour had less to do with upholding humanitarian principle and more to do with countering and negating the cost advantages that such practices conferred on economic rivals.[63] Unfree labour is indeed profitable,

---

[60] On this point George (1884: 143) wrote as follows: 'That each particular slave should be owned by a particular master would in fact become, as social development went on, and industrial organization grew complex, a manifest disadvantage to the masters. They would be at the trouble of whipping, or other-wise compelling the slaves to work; at the cost of watching them, and of keeping them when ill, or unproductive; at the trouble of finding work for them to do, or of hiring them out, as at different seasons or at different times, the number of slaves which different owners or different contractors could advantageously employ would vary.'

[61] See George (1884: 143).

[62] As is well known, the objection about the cost to an employer of maintaining kinfolk of unfree workers does not apply to India, where family members of a bonded labourer frequently toil alongside the latter in the fields or in the household of the employer.

[63] This element of inter-imperial commercial rivalry emerged at the start of the twentieth century in the case of the campaign by British cocoa manufacturers against the labour regime on cocoa plantations in the islands of St. Thomé and Principe, both

not only intrinsically – because workers who are unfree are not able to negotiate over the price of their labour-power or sell it freely on the open market – but also because it drags down the price of free labour, which in cases where the latter is more costly the former either cheapens or displaces.

Markets and Unfreedom

The argument that unfree labour inhibits the expansion of a home market for the commodities produced by capitalism holds only where the market outlet for such output remains domestic, and consumers are themselves unfree. Where products made by unfree labour are exported to other (international) markets, the consumers of which are free, the market expansion argument does not hold. There is accordingly no obstacle to employment by capitalist producers of workers who are unfree in situations where a fundamental break occurs between producer and consumer, a characteristic that obtains where accumulation is global in scope.[64]

---

of which were Portuguese colonial possessions. The latter provided cocoa for capitalist enterprises selling to the American market, and the use of unfree labour (*serviçal*) from Angola gave US companies a competitive edge. It was this as much as anything that informed both the opposition to unfree labour voiced by British cocoa manufacturers (Cadbury, 1909; Anti-Slavery and Aborigines Protection Society, 1913) and the refusal by American firms to join them in denouncing the plantation work regime. As noted by a representative of the British cocoa manufacturers (Cadbury, 1909: 3–4), 'A large American firm approached did not, much to our regret, see their way at that time to interest themselves in the subject'. Much of the debate between rival imperialist powers concerned the incidence and causes of mortality rates among plantation workers, the object of those who employed unfree labour being to decouple mortality from the work regime on commercial enterprises. In keeping with the practice of either denying the high incidence of mortality among unfree workers or else blaming this on 'natural' factors unconnected with their pay and conditions, for example, the last governor of German East Africa (Schnee, 1926: 138–9) at first disavowed a link between forced labour and an indigenous population decline. He then accepted that the death-rate among plantation workers was 'at times regrettably high'; however, this was attributed by him not to working conditions but to 'natural' occurrences, such as climate, epidemics and fevers.

[64] Where no capitalism exists, the presence of cheap unfree workers may indeed act as a break to economic growth, but not for the reason given: namely that unfreedom is inherently incompatible with technology. Where unfreedom exists, therefore, capital will not invest because workers possess little purchasing power, and consequently there is no market for its commodities. By contrast, where markets exist elsewhere, capital is no longer dependent on local workers for consuming commodities, and it can accordingly deploy unfree relations in its labour process.

As long as capital accumulation depends on the continued consuming power of workers producing the commodities, it will be in the interests of capital to ensure that wages paid its labourers either retain or increase their purchasing power, a situation which does not favour the employment of cheap unfree labour. This was the logic behind the agrarian reform programmes in Latin America and elsewhere during the 'development decade' of the 1960s, which envisaged that among other things land redistribution would create or enlarge a market – composed of peasant smallholders – for commodities produced by domestic capital. However, once capital no longer has to rely on the purchasing power of its own workers, it can solve crises of profitability by recourse to recomposition/restructuring that entails the displacement of free with unfree labour-power.

The emphasis of current *laissez faire* policy on a low cost export agriculture contrasts with that of the 1960s 'development decade', when the implementation of Keynesian demand management policies was premissed on providing a nascent capitalist class with a domestic market capable of buying the commodities it produced. In Third World nations at that conjuncture this involved creating a mass market composed of peasants and agricultural workers newly endowed with purchasing power as a result of agrarian reform programmes.[65]

Central to this economic strategy was a process of institutional reform, the necessity of which was apparent to normally conservative multilateral agencies. Thus the ILO had during the early 1950s already connected slow industrial growth throughout the Third World to a restricted home market and the absence of purchasing power by rural populations, a problem it attributed in turn to the persistence of feudal tenure in the agrarian sector.[66] By the mid-1970s, even the World Bank had not only incorporated within its own analytical framework the critique of feudal landownership as an obstacle to economic development, but was also using the concept 'feudalism' itself in its own policy documents.[67]

The assumption was that rising income levels in rural areas would generate the consumer demand that would in turn fuel economic

---

[65] For more on this, see Chapter 2.

[66] See the report by the International Labour Office (1953: 317–8, 344, 470).

[67] See World Bank (1975: 16 ff.) for evidence of the fact that, by the mid-1970s, the concept 'feudalism' had become part of the accepted terminology in its policy framework when analyzing development strategy.

development in what had hitherto been underdeveloped nations. Given the latter objective, it is hardly surprising that one of the main reasons for expropriating large landowners was to eradicate the control they exercised over poor peasants and workers via the debt bondage mechanism designed to keep rural wages low. Clearly, an effect of the continued presence of unfree labour in rural areas would have been incompatible with the desire to create a mass market in such underdeveloped contexts.

Where a mass market already exists, as is the case in metropolitan capitalist nations – the employment of workers who are unfree confers a different kind of economic advantage. In such contexts this relation also enables agribusiness enterprises to keep down the cost of labour-power, particularly when this is provided by immigrant workers, thereby lowering the cost to domestic capital of foodstuffs – and through this the bundle of wage goods – consumed by industrial labour in the context in question.

In the current global market, therefore, capitalists can get round this difficulty by supplying commodities produced by unfree labour to the international market, and not the home market. This avoids the contradiction of employers having to pay their own workers more to consume the items produced by capitalism. Once capital is no longer exclusively national, this particular problem is no longer a central consideration. Much the same cause – the internationalization of the market, but this time for workers – is the reason why there are not difficulties with the supply of labour that is unfree.

The argument that capitalists eschew unfree labour because it is in short supply is also open to a number of objections.[68] As with other claims about the incompatibility between unfreedom and accumulation, this objection could as easily apply to free labour. Most significantly, this objection is informed by a subtext which, in effect, undermines it: hence the argument that it is the uncertainty of supply which prevents the reproduction of slavery and other forms of unfree

[68] That such an argument is mistaken, not least because a commercial enterprise can maintain a hold over a supply of workers who are unfree, something that cannot be done where they retain the capacity personally to commodify or recommodify their own labour-power, is on occasion recognized, albeit belatedly. Hence the following admission by Munro (1918: 95): 'In a previous chapter, the author has stated it to be his opinion that the plantations of Guatemala could be operated successfully without a peonage system. The effect of the repeal of the repeal of the labor laws in Nicaragua would seem to prove the contrary….'

relation admits the premises that, in the event of the supply being assured, there would be no reason why such production relations might not continue, a view found even in the framework of some Marxists.[69]

For both Weber and Mill, the inability to guarantee employers of unfree labour with continued access to plentiful supplies of such workers constituted an important obstacle to production based on their use: were such workers to be available in the amounts and at a (low) cost acceptable to producers, they could be 'worked to death', thereby obviating for any supposed shortcomings in the quantity/quality of commodities produced by them. It is these very conditions that are in fact met by modern forms of unfree labour, linked as they are to the global expansion of the industrial reserve army of labour during the post-1945 era.

Conclusion

In non-Marxist political economy which eschews class struggle, the idea that unfree labour might be acceptable to capitalists was dismissed from the late eighteenth to the early twentieth century on the grounds that such workers would necessarily be inefficient, unskilled, costly and scarce. Because unfree workers were an obstacle both to the formation and expansion of the domestic market, and also to the installation of advanced productive forces, it was argued that they hindered capital accumulation within particular national contexts.

The main epistemological roots of this theory decoupling unfree labour and capitalist production are encountered in the political economy of Adam Smith. It was he who connected labour to the creation of value that structured both industrialization and national wealth. Labourers who were unfree were both inefficient and costly, according to Smith, because unlike their free equivalents they lacked not only incentives to work diligently but also the skill required to operate machinery effectively. Since economic growth depended on the installation of advanced machinery, the operation of which in his view was incompatible with an unfree workforce, the employment of the latter was perceived by him as an obstacle to accumulation.

[69] Thus, for example, in his analysis of the reasons why slavery was replaced by serfdom in ancient India, Dange (1949: 176) observes that '[r]eplenishing the worn-out or the lost slave was becoming difficult'.

All these claims surface in much subsequent non-Marxist political economy. Thomas Malthus regarded all forms of tied labour (slaves, serfs, tenants) as inefficient and thus economically unproductive, as did John Stuart Mill and John Bright. Economic liberals and forerunners of neo-classical economic historians who went on to question that slavery was coercive, they connected higher productivity simply with free labour responding to pecuniary incentives. In keeping with the latter view, Max Weber argued that free workers were less costly because employers were able to hire/fire them according to business requirements. For this reason, he regarded the use by capital of unfree labour as economically irrational.

Most, if not all, of these objections are no longer valid. Analysing a twenty-first century capitalism through the lens of class struggle confirms that today unfree workers are more profitable to employ but no less efficient than their counterparts who are free. Labour that is unfree works hard not because of incentives but in order to avoid punishment, and their lack of skills is a view rooted in racist ideology. Because they cannot bargain over the price at which they sell their own labour-power to capital, workers who are unfree are usually cheaper than free equivalents. Deskilling combined with a reserve army of labour and markets that are global in scope makes it possible for capitalists to use such production relations.

It the following chapter it will be argued that, unlike non-Marxist political economists – such as Smith, Malthus, Mill, Bright and Weber – all of whom disavowed the acceptability to capitalism of unfree production relations, Marxists were able to understand this connection. This they were able to do for two reasons in particular. First, because of the centrality to Marxist theory of class struggle, a dimension missing from non-Marxist political economy. And second, because Marxism built on Hegelian epistemology, and was able to shift conceptually from labour-as-property to labour-power as commodity.

CHAPTER TWO

THE MARXIST INHERITANCE

Turning to the way in which Marxism interprets the capitalism/unfreedom link, the usual procedure is to locate it the same theoretical lineage as the non-Marxist analyses of political economy considered in the previous chapter. As in the case of Smith, Malthus, Mill, Bright and Weber, therefore, Marx is perceived as questioning the compatibility between capitalism and unfree labour, on much the same grounds: like them, he maintains that a 'fully functioning' capitalism needs (and cannot do without) a free worker.[1] From this, it follows that Marxist theory about the capitalism/unfreedom link is seen as open to the same kind of objections as those levelled at non-Marxist political economy.

Although superficially plausible, this conflation is in reality questionable. Thus an examination of the views held by many of the major Marxists – Hilferding, Mandel, Dobb, Kuczynski and Guérin, as well as Marx, Engels, Kautsky, Lenin and Trotsky – reveals not just the opposite to be true, but also the reason for this. Because of their role in the class struggle waged by employers, unfree production relations are indeed compatible with a 'fully functioning' capitalist system, an interpretation consistent with Marxist theory.

To understand both why class struggle determines the reproduction of unfree labour in advanced capitalism, and also why this is in fact central to Marxist theory, it is necessary to begin by tracing the genealogy of two prefiguring and interrelated concepts. These are labour-power as the property of the subject, and (therefore) labour-power as a commodity that can be sold by its owner. Building on the Hegelian concept of freedom epitomized by labour-as-property, Marxism then defined as free a worker who possesses and retains the capacity personally to sell (= commodify, recommodify) his/her own labour-power.

---

[1] This view is examined further in Chapters 3 and 4.

In the course of class struggle generated by accumulation, however, labour-power is increasingly estranged from its owning subject. Where this loss culminates in an inability on the part of a worker personally to commodify/recommodify his/her own labour-power, s/he becomes as a result unfree. It is argued here that such a relational transformation amounts to deproletarianization, or a process whereby capitalist producers depoliticize/cheapen/discipline their workforce.

Accordingly, the conceptualization in Hegelian and Marxist epistemology of labour-power both as property and (thus) as commodity is examined in section one of this chapter. Sections two and three consider the implications of this epistemology for the way in which the capitalism/unfreedom link is interpreted by Marx, Engels, Kautsky, Lenin, Trotsky, Hilferding and others. The loss by workers of ownership over their labour-power as a result of deproletarianization, and the consequent importance of this relational development to Marxist analyses of capitalism, is traced in section four.

I

Marxist theory about labour-power as a commodity owned by its subject has its roots in Hegelian epistemology.[2] Both envisioned history as a dialectical process of 'becoming', a trajectory consistent with the attainment of freedom, albeit with different agents, objectives and means. Where agency was concerned, it was the subject-in-general in the case of Hegel, and by the subjects-of-a-particular-class in the case of Marx. Each accepted that reality was distorted, a situation resulting in consciousness that was false, which constituted an obstacle to the realization of progress.[3] Hegel, however, perceived the end-point of this historical trajectory as purely metaphysical (= the attainment of the Absolute Idea). By contrast, Marx saw it in materialist terms, as progress towards socialism by means of class formation and class struggle.

---

[2] That an overlap exists between Marxist and Hegelian theory is not open to doubt, but its extent and ontological immanence are matters of dispute. At one end of the spectrum is not only Lenin (1963c: 87ff.) but also Marcuse (1955: 273ff.) and Lukács (1975), for whom the overlap is both significant and positive, neither of which claims are conceded by those at the other end (Colletti, 1973; Mepham and Ruben, 1979).

[3] Historically, and in specifically Marxist terms, this involves a process of becoming that entails a shift on the part of the proletariat from a consciousness that is false to one that embodies and projects its class interests (Lukács, 1971).

Hegelian Epistemology, or Labour-Power as Property

For Hegel, the freedom of the subject expresses itself in a capacity to transfer various forms of property to another such, a contractual act of externalization (= alienation) which depends in turn on ownership by the subject of the property transferred.[4] Among the forms of property owned by a subject (and thus transferrable), Hegel argued, was his/her 'productive capacity or…services so far…as these are alienable, the alienation being restricted in time or some other way'.[5] In other words, the ownership of what Marx subsequently termed labour-power.

The significance of this epistemological link between Hegel and Marx cannot be over-emphasized, not least since it involves a position not encountered hitherto in political economy. Perhaps because he was writing in the period of the English civil war, Hobbes restricts his interpretation of unfreedom to situations arising simply from conquest/defeat linked to physical strife. Unlike Hegel, therefore, Hobbes misses the extent to which labour-power can be and is owned by its subject, and thus also is something which in an economic sense can be sold/alienated. Although a distinction between freedom and its absence is recognized, Hobbes nevertheless fails to locate this difference in the idea of labour-power as property.[6] In contrast to Hegel, for whom labour-power as property meant that its use could be transferred on a period-specific basis, Hobbes argued that 'every Subject has

---

[4] About this Hegel (1942: 38, original emphasis) observes: 'Right is in the first place the immediate embodiment which freedom gives itself in an immediate way, i.e. (a) possession, which is *property*-ownership:.. (b) A person by distinguishing himself from himself relates himself to another person, and it is only as owners that these two persons really exist for each other.'

[5] See Hegel (1942: 62), where in words that could almost have been written by Marx himself about the role in the capitalist system of labour-power as a commodity, Hegel points out that '[i]n the contracts whereby I part with the *use* of a thing, I am no longer in possession of the thing though I am still its owner' (original emphasis). The same is true when Hegel (1942: 51) comments that '[a]s full owner of the thing, I am *eo ipso* owner of its value as well as of its use.'

[6] Hence the view (Hobbes, n.d. [1651]: 354–5): 'For whereas there be two sorts of Servants: that sort, which is of those that are absolutely in the power of their Masters, as Slaves taken in war, and their Issue, whose bodies are not in their own power, (their lives depending on the Will of their Masters, in such manner as to forfeit them upon the least disobedience,) and that are bought and sold as Beasts, were called Δουλοι, that is properly, Slaves, and their Service δουλεία: The other, which is of those that serve (for hire, or in the hope of benefit from their Masters) voluntarily…are Domestique Servants; to whose service the Masters have no further right, than is contained in the Covenants made betwixt them. These two kinds of Servants have thus much common to them both, that their labour is appointed them by another…'

Liberty in all those things, the right whereof by Covenant cannot be transferred.'[7]

It is clear, moreover, that the retention by the subject of ownership of this form of property was for Hegel (as for Marx) a defining aspect of freedom.[8] The latter necessarily entails that a subject to whom the property belongs engages in a transaction that corresponds to a relative (= 'an event in time'), not an absolute, transfer.[9] Like Marx, therefore, Hegel distinguished between a slave, who is unfree by virtue of him/herself being property (as a result of an absolute transfer, by self or other), and a worker whose freedom resides in retaining personal ownership of his/her capacity to labour (a relative transfer, by self).[10]

This difference emerges in the contrast drawn by Hegel between the position of a lord and his bondsman. In keeping with his idealist epistemology, and unlike Marx, Hegel interprets the lord/bondsman relationship in non-material terms, as antithetical forms of consciousness. Whereas a lord is capable of realizing his selfhood (= being-for-self), the bondsman represents the antithesis of this: that is, a negation of selfhood, and agency based on this.[11] Unlike a free labourer, therefore,

---

[7] See Hobbes (n.d. [1651]: 68ff., 114).

[8] 'Contract is the process,' states Hegel (1942: 57–8), 'in which there is revealed and mediated the contradiction that I am and remain the owner of something from which I exclude the will of another only in so far as in identifying my will with the will of another I cease to be an owner...' Also clear is that for Hegel surrender of the totality of his/her working time to another on a permanent basis is a loss of freedom that identifies its subject as a slave. Hence the view (Hegel, 1942: 54, emphasis added): 'By alienating the *whole of my time*, as crystallized in my work, and everything I produced, I would be making into another's property the substance of my being, my universal activity and actuality, my personality.'

[9] Hence the following view (Hegel, 1942: 52): 'The form given to a possession and its mark are themselves externalities but for the subjective presence of the will which alone constitutes the meaning and value of externalities. This presence, however, which is use, employment, or some other mode in which the will expresses itself, is an event in time, and what is objective in time is the continuance of this expression of the will. Without this the thing becomes a *res nullius*, because it has been deprived of the actuality of the will and possession.'

[10] 'Objectively considered,' Hegel noted (1942: 39–40, 42), 'a right arising from a contract is never a right over a person, but only a right over something external to a person, or something which he can alienate, always a thing... Since my will, as the will of a person, and so as a single will, becomes objective to me in property, property acquires the character of private property; and common property of such a nature that it may be owned by separate persons acquires the character of an inherently dissoluble partnership in which the retention of my share is explicitly a matter of my arbitrary preference.'

[11] Hence the view (Hegel, 1978: 115–6) that there are 'two opposed shapes of consciousness; one is the independent consciousness whose essential nature is to be for

a bondsman owns an ability to conduct neither his own work nor his own existence. This is because in the relationship with his lord, a bondsman has lost what Hegel refers to as his essential selfhood (= personal autonomy), and therefore has no selfhood to realize.[12]

Marxist Epistemology, or Labour-Power as Commodity

On this absolute/relative distinction (bondsman, free worker) Marx based his view of labour-power as a specific kind of property, one that in a capitalist system is owned and personally commodified by a worker, who can and does sell it to an employer, but only – like Hegel – on a time-restricted basis.[13] Despite his critical approach generally to Hegelian theory, Marx nevertheless regarded its conceptualization of labour-as-property and the subsequent ability of the subject to externalize (= alienate/estrange) this aspect of his/her selfhood as an 'outstanding achievement'.[14]

Unlike Hegel, however, Marxist theory unifies two opposites: in the course of class struggle, the individual subject as owner of his/her estranged labour-power is formed into a collective subject. This in turn signals a dual transformation: from the labourer-as-individual to a component part of a class-in-itself, and from the concreteness of

---

itself, the other is the dependent consciousness whose essential nature is simply to live or to be for another. The former is lord, the other is bondsman.' For this reason, the consciousness of bondsman 'sets aside its own being-for-self, and in doing so itself does what the [consciousness of the lord] does to it…for what the bondsman does is really the action of the lord. The latter's essential nature is to exist only for himself…he is the pure, essential action in this relationship, while the action of the bondsman is impure and unessential.' That is, in terms of consciousness, it is not necessary for the bondsman to possess selfhood, since his agency is set in motion – and does not exist independently of – that of his lord.

[12] Even here, however, Hegel (1978: 117, 121) identifies the presence of a contradiction, in that a lord is confronted by a dependent consciousness that – as such – cannot independently recognize and confer validity on his (the lord's) own selfhood.

[13] Not only did Marx (1975a: 181; 1975b: 327) defend Hegel against others, such as Ludwig Feuerbach and Bruno Bauer ('The criticism of the German philosophy of state and law, which attained its most consistent, richest and final formulation through Hegel…'), but he also made clear his own intellectual debt to the Hegelian argument about labour-as-property (see next note).

[14] On this Marx (1975b: 332–3, original emphasis) writes: 'The outstanding achievement of Hegel's *Phänomenologie* and of its final outcome, the dialectic of negativity as the moving and generating principle, is thus first that Hegel conceives the self-creation of man as a process, conceives objectification as loss of the object, as alienation and as transcendence of this alienation: that he thus grasps the essence of *labour* and comprehends objective man – true, because real man – as the outcome of man's *own labour*… Hegel's standpoint is that of modern political economy. He grasps labour as the *essence* of man – as man's essence which stands the test…'

self-hood to the abstract/universal otherness of a proletariat. Because of this, an interpretation based on labour-as-property, and – under capitalism – labour-as-property which is increasingly estranged from its subject, underwrites Marxist epistemology, both about the formation of and struggle over class, and thus about systemic transformation.

In Marx's analysis of accumulation, therefore, ownership of labour-power by its subject remains epistemologically crucial, since it is a form of property which, when retained by a worker, defines him/her as free. What it confers on the owner is an ability to recommodify labour-power subsequently, either to the same or a different employer, or indeed not to sell it at all. It is precisely this aspect of a worker/employer arrangement that for Marx and Marxist theory generally defines a production relation as either free, where the capacity of a worker personally to commodify/recommodify his labour-power is reproduced, or, where this same capacity is for whatever reason absent, as unfree.

Accordingly, Marx perceives free labour as a relation that for a variety of non-free workers (slaves, bondsmen, serfs, etc.) is an achievement historically, but an achievement which nevertheless does not signal the end of struggle, merely a new phase: within capitalism, and this time for socialism. In this materialist teleology, a crucial aspect of which is consciousness not merely as a process-of-becoming but as a misrepresentation of reality, Marx and Marxism generally diverges from a variety of non- and anti-Marxist theory. The latter encompasses not just Hegelian idealism but also marginalist economics, and – where the free/unfree distinction is concerned – the neo-classical economic historiography of cliometricians.

These two distinct and contrasting aspects of freedom are free labour as the apogee and thus the legitimation of capitalism, and free labour as both the outcome of class struggle under capitalism and simultaneously a precursor and necessary condition of a transition to socialism. Whereas the first meaning corresponds to 'consent' as understood by bourgeois economics, the second by contrast informs Marxist theory about continuation of class struggle in order to transcend capitalism. Whereas Marxism and liberalism both privilege free labour, therefore, each draws a very different conclusion from its presence.[15]

[15] As will be seen in Chapter 4, rather than connecting my arguments about deproletarianization to the second of these two meanings – where they belong – Banaji (2003a) wrongly links them to the first.

Labour-Power and 'the Free Exercise of Industry'

The political dangers for capitalism of conceding that labour-power is the property of the worker was an issue not lost on nineteenth century advocates of *laissez faire*. Writing just after the 1848 revolutions in Europe, Samuel Laing recognized that to do so conferred an element of ideological legitimacy on struggles waged by labour against capital.[16] For this reason he departed from not just Marxist but also Hegelian epistemology, and opposed the view of labour-as-property then gaining ground in political economy, arguing that it is so only under the medieval guild system still encountered on Continental Europe, the object of which was to defend specific trades by restricting both entry into and practice of them.[17]

As such, Laing argued, the concept labour-as-property was a protectionist obstacle to economic development. Significantly, what concerned him in particular was that conceptualizing labour-as-property invited its protection in law, a situation that would enable workers thus defended legislatively to resist competition from other workers, competition 'obliging them to work more cheaply'.[18] Accordingly, for Laing an undesirable effect of the interpretation by political economy of labour-power as a form of property owned by its subject was to prevent capital from driving down wages and conditions through recourse to the industrial reserve army of labour.

Unsurprisingly, therefore, Laing dismissed the labour-as-property view on the grounds that it emanated from European socialist theory,

---

[16] See, for example, Laing (1850: 163ff.), who asked 'Is labour property?', and answered that the 'proprietary right…derived from labour [is] a man's own [only] in a state of nature.'

[17] What he described as the 'ancient restrictive system' should, Laing (1850: 167) insisted, continue on Continental Europe, since '[t]here is not room in the world for two Great Britains.' This gives the game away, since what Laing wants is freedom for capital *vis-à-vis* labour, but only in Britain. His fear is that foreign capitalists may exercise the same kind of freedom in relation to their own workers, since this would enable them successfully to compete in the same markets as British industry. In other words, he is that most familiar of apologists for capitalism: a monopolist in the disguise of a free trader.

[18] See Laing (1850: 166), who concedes that labour might be considered to be property, but only where 'it is possible to protect it by law.' He then negates this by claiming that public opinion overrides the law, and that public opinion in Britain 'is opposed to the restrictive system [= guilds] of the Continent', because this amounts to a monopoly over 'the supply of the most necessary products of industry, while the operative members of these corporate bodies are subject to no competition obliging them to work cheaply, expeditiously and well'. He continues in a similar vein: 'The perfect freedom of trade, industry, and labour, is the principle of all our political economy and social arrangements. Restriction is but the exception with us, and freedom is but the exception on the Continent.'

and as such was not in the interests of capitalist development taking place in Britain. Lumping together the guild system and socialism, he maintained that both were anti-modern obstacles to economic growth by attempting – unjustifiably in his opinion – to afford some protection to the worker, and thus imposing an unacceptable restriction on the employment practices required by industrial capitalism.[19]

This insistence by nineteenth century advocates of *laissez faire* on an absolute right of capital to command labour-power, regarding any concession to the latter as an unwarranted 'restriction', recognizes the need of employers to resist even the limited economic autonomy embodied in the ownership by a worker of his/her own labour-power. Within such an ideological framework, deproletarianization as the desired outcome for capitalist producers of a twenty-first century class struggle no longer seems anomalous.

II

If the notion of free labour-power being crucial to a 'fully-functioning' capitalism is so central to Marxist theory, as is claimed, why then do so many Marxists maintain the opposite? Why do not just Marx, Engels, Kautsky, Lenin, Trotsky and Hilferding but also Mandel, Dobb, Kuczynski and Guérin all accept that accumulation does not necessarily require free labour-power, and can indeed do without this? And why currently do 'fully-functioning' capitalists in so many different global contexts accumulate quite adequately using workers that are unfree?

Marx and Engels on Unfree Labour

Contrary to received wisdom, the resort by capital to production relations that are unfree does find support in the views of Marx, both about the specific historical instances – child labour in Britain and plantation slavery in the antebellum American South – and more generally about

[19] Hence the view (Laing, 1850: 168): 'The common principle, common to the old restrictive system of incorporation and to the new communist or socialist theories of 1848, is that labour is property entitled to such protection from law, and that the operative labourer is secured in a subsistence from his property in his craft or trade, in sickness, or when out of work, as well as in health and in full employment. This was the end and object of the incorporations of trades, and the restrictions on the free exercise of industry in the middle ages; and it is the end and object of all the modern schemes of communism, socialism, cooperative labour for a common subsistence, and all the other visions of the working-classes on the Continent in 1848.'

the centrality to the accumulation process of class struggle.[20] Indeed, in describing the impact of the reserve army of labour, and the importance of its role in the reproduction of capitalism, Marx observes that '[a]ccumulation of wealth at one pole is, therefore, at the same time accumulation of misery, the torment of labour, slavery, ignorance, brutalization and moral degradation at the opposite pole, i.e., on the side of the class that produces its own product as capital.'[21]

That child workers employed in the factories of mid-nineteenth century Britain were for Marx a form of unfree labour is clear from two things: not just from the fact that their personal labour-power was sold by others, but also from the comparison he makes between such workers and plantation slaves.[22] Furthermore, he noted that wages paid to such workers were held down by the operation of the truck system,

---

[20] Not the least of the many ironies is that the approach of Marx to the role of child labour in the capitalist economy of Britain during the nineteenth century is very similar to that used by organizations such as the UN and the ILO in their critiques of child labour in India and other developing countries. Acknowledging that many child workers are unfree, a report by the UN Special Rapporteur (Bouhdiba, 1982: 23) noted: 'As has often been stressed, child labour brings down wages and therefore keeps adults in a highly insecure employment position... It is only in appearance that it helps families to survive. Far from improving the household income, child labour helps to reduce it.' This is also the view in a report about child labour published in India itself (Government of India, 1979: 8) some three decades ago: 'Child labour is as much the cause as the consequence of adult unemployment and under-employment. It at once supplements and depresses the family income. Child labour is not only a subsidy to industry but a direct inducement to the payment of low wages to adult workers. The entrance of children into the labour market reduces the volume of employment for the adult and lowers the bargaining power of adult workers.' Such critiques, indicting as they do the economic structures of the capitalist system, are very different from the kind of approach noted above, that seeks merely to verify whether or not such relational forms are prohibited in law.

[21] See Marx (1976a: 799). Anticipating the account by Lenin of Russia (see below), Marx (1976a: 821, 830, 849) refers to miners in nineteenth century England as 'bound' workers – bonded to their capitalist employers for a twelve month period, like attached labourers in India – and endorses the description of agricultural workers as the 'white slaves' of farmers.

[22] About this Marx (1976a: 519) wrote as follows: 'But now the capitalist buys children and young persons. Previously the worker sold his own labour-power, which he disposed of as a free agent...Now he sells wife and child. He has become a slave-dealer. Notices of demand for children's labour often resemble in form the inquiries for Negro slaves that were formerly to be read among the advertisements in American journals.' Elsewhere (Institute of Marxism-Leninism, 1964a: 344) Marx observed similarly that 'the accumulation of capital...transforms parents by their necessities into slaveholders, sellers of their own children.' He went on to observe (Marx, 1976a: 922) that 'the transformation of manufacturing production into factory production and the establishment of the true relation between capital and labour-power' entails among other things 'child-slavery'.

a classic debt bondage mechanism.[23] Most significantly, Marx emphasized that the employment of child labour was made possible by the introduction of machinery, where children worked alongside older female and male labourers.[24] As is well known, the current prevalence of bonded child labour in agribusiness enterprises throughout India is a matter of record.[25]

---

[23] 'Wages', argues Marx (1976a: 599), 'miserable as they are (the maximum wages of a child in the straw-plait schools rising in rare cases to 3 shillings), are reduced far below their nominal amount by the prevalence of the truck system everywhere, but especially in the lace districts.'

[24] 'The labour of women and children was therefore the first result of the capitalist application of machinery... If machinery is the most powerful means of raising the productivity of labour, i.e., of shortening the working time needed to produce a commodity, it is also, as a repository of capital, the most powerful means of lengthening the working day beyond all natural limits in those industries first directly seized on by it', noted Marx (1976a: 517, 526–7). He continued (*Marx*, 1976a: 590): 'In contrast with the period of manufacture, the division of labour is now based, wherever possible, on the employment of women, of children of all ages and of unskilled workers, in short of "cheap labour", as the English typically describe it.' In the *Communist Manifesto*, Marx and Engels (1976: 491) made much the same point: 'The less the skill and exertion of strength implied in manual labour....the more modern industry becomes developed, the more is the labour of men superseded by that of women [and children].'

[25] See the valuable studies by da Corta and Venkateshwarlu (1999) and Venkateshwarlu and da Corta (2001). There are, unfortunately, still those – for example, Lieten (2003: 227 ff.) – who take an idealized and largely uncritical view of child labour in India. The link between on the one hand capitalist competition and maintaining/enhancing profitability, and securing higher output by employing the unfree labour of child workers emerged clearly from evidence presented to the 1931 Royal Commission on Labour in India. The exchanges contained in the latter about the kind of production relations used, and the reasons for this, are remarkable in terms of their frankness (Government of India, 1931: 104–6, B-1367, B-1370, B-1171, B-1172, B-1374, B-1375, B-1376). Because rival producers were undercutting them ('Persia is producing carpets considerably cheaper than we can produce here'), capitalist enterprises in India operating an outwork system to make carpets for the international market extracted greater quantities of surplus labour from their debt bonded child workers ('Until the money is paid back the boy has to work for me'). Master weavers who operated this outwork system made no secret either of the coercive methods used, or that this was the way in which higher output was obtained ('we see to it that the boy is made to work a little more than he ought to work; if it is one rupee's amount of work we see that we get 17 annas out of the boy'). In response to the question 'if the children are playful, and not quick in learning [to work] or do not diligently do their work, how does the weaver get work from them?', a master weaver answered: 'By punishing them.' To the next question, 'What sort of punishment?', the reply was: 'A slight beating'. When asked 'if a boy does not turn out efficient work how do you get him to do it?', the master weaver replied with remarkable candour: 'Beat him, hit him on the face, hit him with the fist and whatever we have handy at the time such as a stick.' Unsurprisingly, the subsequent query concerned the reaction to such maltreatment, the answer revealing the extent to which such debt bondage relations were enforced by kin: 'Does the boy sometimes run away? – Yes. When he runs away how is he brought back to work? – Very few run away; when they do run away we go after them or send the parents after them.'

When accurately translated, it is clear that Marx himself subscribed to the view that owners of American slave plantations were capitalists, thereby confirming that in his view accumulation could occur on the basis of unfree labour.[26] Writing about the conflict in America between the Northern and Southern states at the outbreak of the Civil War, he characterized this not just as a struggle between slavery and free labour, nor as a defensive war to ensure that the South could continue to employ labour that was unfree, but rather as a conflict to extend the latter to the North and throughout the whole of North American society.[27]

In short, were the South to be victorious in this struggle, Northern capitalism in the United States would – in the words of Marx – be the subject of 'a reorganization on the basis of slavery'.[28] That is, a process of restructuring whereby workers who were free would be replaced

[26] For this point, see Mintz (1977: 268–9, note 32), Bowman (1993: 99–100), and Assies (2003: 99). An observation about the way in which this argument by Marx has been misinterpreted deserves citing in full (Assies, 2003: 124, note 21, original emphasis): 'Note that I do not follow the translation by Jack Cohen of Eric Hobsbawm's edition of the *Formen*... The translation states: "If we now talk of plantation-owners in America as capitalists, if they *are* capitalists..." The German text, however, is quite clearly affirmative: "sondern daß sie es *sind*..." A more accurate translation might have saved a lot of ink and paper.' The updated translation that appears in the English version of the collected works (*Marx*, 1986: 436, original emphasis) is unambiguous on this point: 'That we now not only describe the plantation-owners as capitalists, but that they *are* capitalists...'.

[27] On this, Marx (1984: 44, original emphasis) writes as follows: 'A large part of the territory thus claimed is still in the possession of the Union and would first have to be conquered from it. None of the so-called border states, however, not even those in the possession of the Confederacy, were ever *actual slave states*. Rather, they constitute an area of the United States in which the system of slavery and the system of free labour exist side by side and contend for mastery, the actual field of battle between South and North, between slavery and freedom. The war of the Southern Confederacy is, therefore, not a war of defence, but a war of conquest, a war of conquest for the spread and perpetuation of slavery.' Lest there be any doubt about it, this is repeated subsequently (Marx, 1984: 49): 'One sees, therefore, that the war of the Southern Confederacy is in the true sense of the word a war of conquest for the spread and perpetuation of slavery.'

[28] Hence the view (Marx, 1984: 50, original emphasis): 'What would have taken place would be not a dissolution of the Union, but a *reorganization* of it, a *reorganization on the basis of slavery*, under the recognized control of the slaveholding oligarchy.... The slave system would infect the whole Union. In the Northern states, where Negro slavery is in practice impossible, the white working class would gradually be forced down to the level of helotry...The present struggle between the South and the North is, therefore, nothing but a struggle between two social systems, the system of slavery and the system of free labour. The struggle has broken out because the two systems can no longer live peacefully side by side on the North American continent. It can only be ended by the victory of one system or the other.'

by labour that was unfree ('a war of conquest for the spread and perpetuation of slavery').[29] A more succinct definition of struggle involving workforce restructuring – a conflict over decomposition/recomposition of the labour process in terms of free/unfree workers, or what is conceptualized here as deproletarianization – is difficult to imagine.[30]

Capitalist Unfree Labour – A Contradiction?

Since other Marxists have made much the same point about the antebellum plantation economy, it is hard to see quite in what way this

[29] During 1866 Marx issued a warning against attempts by 'big capitalists' to restructure, replacing existing workers with cheaper unfree ones recruited from elsewhere. He delineated its object succinctly, noting (Institute of Marxism-Leninism, 1964a: 367–8, original emphasis) that 'the purpose of this import [of workers] is the same as the import of Indian coolies to Jamaica, namely, *perpetuation of slavery*.' In a review of *Capital*, Engels drew attention to the fact that capitalist production on the basis of slavery was accompanied by the intensification of labour. Hence the following (Engels, 1985b: 252): 'But wherever a nation whose production is carried on in the more rudimentary forms of slavery or serfage, lives in the midst of a universal market dominated by capitalist production, and where therefore the sale of its products for exports forms its chief purpose – there to the barbarous infamies of slavery or serfdom are superadded the civilized infamies of over-working. Thus in the Southern States of America slave-labour preserved a moderate and patriarchal character while production was directed to immediate domestic consumption chiefly. But in the same measure as the export of cotton became a vital interest to those states, the over-working of the negro, in some instances even the wearing-out of his life in seven working years, became an element in a calculated and calculating system....' The same point was made subsequently by Guérin (see below).

[30] That Marx himself saw the dangers of and was opposed to workforce restructuring is evident from the following (Marx, 1985a: 186): 'To counteract the intrigues of capitalists always ready, in cases of strikes and lockouts, to misuse the foreign workman as a tool against the native workman, is one of the particular functions which our Society has hitherto performed with success. It is one of the great purposes of the [International Working Men's] Association to make the workmen of different countries not only feel but act as brethren and comrades in the army of emancipation.'

[31] According to Daniel Guérin (1956) in his Marxist analysis of the race question in the United States, unfree labour was compatible not just with capitalist production but also with advanced productive forces. Hence the view (Guérin, 1956: 29–30, emphasis added) that '...a technological revolution resuscitated the slave system and gave it a new lease on life: that is, the invention of the mechanical cotton gin by Eli Whitney in 1794...[in] the mid-19th century, slavery was not, as one might think, a rather shameful residue, an anachronistic vestige of the past, on the verge of disappearing. On the contrary, it reached its height in the years 1820 to 1860, the period when Cotton was King. *It was not a feudal but a capitalist institution*... Moreover, the steadily declining price which the planters received for their cotton in the markets of New England and Europe narrowed their margin of profit and induced them to redouble their exploitation of the slaves. *The institution of slavery, far from being mitigated, became ever more vile, ferocious and inhuman when modern capitalism revived it and worked it to the*

view can still be considered 'non-Marxist'.[31] Thus the situation is the opposite of what it is usually presented as being: rather than regarding the slave plantation in nineteenth century southern US as pre- or non-capitalist, therefore, what Marx actually said – when not mistranslated – was that the slave plantation was a capitalist unit.[32] Hence the argument that unfree labour was perfectly acceptable to producers who were capitalist is not inconsistent with the theoretical framework of Marx himself.[33]

This is especially so when the dynamic role of conflict is considered, and how the relative economic importance of free and unfree labour is structured by the dialectic. Not only did Marx himself point out that no social form vanishes until all its uses have been exhausted, but Engels (as well as Marx: see above) saw the role of class struggle as central to in the reproduction of capitalism, determining the way in which its production relations are constituted.[34] In a similar vein, both Marx and Engels chronicled historical reversals, whereby in the course of class struggle production relations that were initially free can indeed give way to those that are unfree.[35]

---

fullest.' According to Ingram (1895: 285), following the invention of the cotton gin, exports from the United States of cotton rose from 138,328 pounds to 38,118,041 pounds in 1804 and to 127,860,152 pounds in 1820.

[32] Noting the fact that Marx classified planters as capitalists and/or plantation agriculture as capitalist, some exponents of the semi-feudal thesis then simply deny this as being the case. Thus, for example, having asserted that for Marx slavery was incompatible with capitalism, Byres (1996: 253, 279 note 40, original emphasis) then accepts that '[t]here is a problem here....[t]his is Marx's apparent categorization...of plantation owners (slaveholders) as *capitalists*... slavery clearly cannot be viewed as capitalism and must be seen as quite distinct from it.'

[33] Observing that '[s]lavery is an economic category like any other', Marx (1976b: 167) continued: 'Direct slavery is just as much the pivot of bourgeois industry as machinery, credits, etc. Without slavery you have no cotton; without cotton you have no modern industry. It is slavery that gave the colonies their value; it is the colonies that created world trade, and it is world trade that is the precondition of large-scale industry. Thus slavery is an economic category of the greatest importance. Without slavery North America, the most progressive of countries, would be transformed into a patriarchal country. Wipe North America off the map of the world, and you will have anarchy – the complete decay of modern commerce and civilization.'

[34] Hence the observation in the 1859 Preface by Marx (1913: 12), and the following observation by Engels (Marx and Engels, 1957: 257): 'In modern history at least it is, therefore, proved that all political struggles are class struggles, and all class struggles for emancipation, despite their necessarily political form – for every class struggle is a political struggle – turn ultimately on the question of *economic* emancipation.'

[35] The historical reversal of emancipation – from free to unfree relations of production – as the outcome of class struggle is noted by Engels in his introduction to the English edition of *Socialism: Utopian and Scientific* (1892). There he (Marx and Engels, 1957: 298) wrote as follows: 'The Lutheran Reformation produced a new creed,

Marx hinted at the same possibility when observing that in historical instances where conquest occurs, and plunder entails the enslavement of the defeated population, 'a mode of production appropriate to slave labour must be established'.[36] This could apply just as easily to flows of migrant labour from present-day contexts either that neoliberalism has penetrated economically, or which imperialism has literally conquered. In both cases, the incorporation of such workers into the labour process of the victorious social formation entails changes to – but is not incompatible with – the existing mode of production (capitalism).

Kautsky on Unfree Labour

Although Kautsky appears to belong to the ranks of those who classify unfree labour as economically inefficient, he nevertheless accepted that, where and when large enterprises had access to such production relations, they were able to maintain or enhance their profitability.[37] He also recognized, as did Lenin (see below), that the real economic significance of the small-scale rural 'enterprise' lay in its role as a source of outworkers – composed for the most part of female and child

---

indeed a religion adapted to absolute monarchy. No sooner were the peasants of North East Germany converted to Lutheranism than they were from freemen reduced to serfs.' Observing that 'the honest English farmers...depressed the wages of the agricultural labourers even beneath that mere physical minimum, but made up by Poor Laws the remainder necessary for the physical perpetuation of the race,' Marx (1985b: 145) concluded that '[t]his was the glorious way to convert the wages labourer into a slave.'

[36] See Marx (1986: 35), who was referring to the plantation agriculture in the antebellum South. This was a view echoed by Plekhanov in the 1890s. 'Slavery in the European colonies is also, at first glance,' he wrote (Plekhanov, 1976: 175, original emphasis), 'a paradoxical example of capitalist development. This phenomenon...cannot be explained by the logic of economic life in the countries it was to be met in. The explanation is to be sought in *international economic relations*.'

[37] Despite associating 'the exercise of care' (= economic efficiency in the sense he understood the term) in the labour process with workers only when employed on large farms, Kautsky noted that the conditions licensing such a situation – good pay, good food and good treatment – were not only absent from the majority of capitalist agribusiness enterprises but would also not be introduced voluntarily by these employers. About this he wrote (Kautsky, 1988: 118, emphasis added): 'If the position of most small farmers is inimicable to the exercise of care, conversely the large farm is eminently capable of getting careful work out of its wage-labourers. Good pay, good food, and good treatment have a considerable effect... Well-paid and well-fed, and hence intelligent, workers are an indispensable prerequisite for rational large-scale farming. *This precondition is still undoubtedly lacking in the majority of instances, and it would be naïve to expect any improvement from the "enlightened despotism" of large-scale farmers.*'

labour – on which large-scale agribusiness and industrial capitalists depended in order to boost profitability.

That he did not believe a capitalist agriculture would automatically replace unfree workers with free equivalents was clear from what Kautsky wrote during the 1890s: both in the Erfurt programme, and in *The Agrarian Question*.[38] Not only did he maintain that, with the introduction into the accumulation process of machinery, capital would increasingly replace the labour-power of men with that of women and children, but he also saw depriving workers of their freedom as being the logical outcome of capitalist development.[39] Central to all these processes, Kautsky argued, was the element of class struggle linked to the formation, expansion and reproduction of an industrial reserve army of labour.[40]

The latter took a form that is familiar to all those who study the pattern of agrarian capitalist development in the so-called Third World. Kautsky effects a contrast between on the one hand the big peasant, who works alongside and supervises his labourers, and on the other the small peasant, who is required to overwork his kinfolk/family, making

[38] For translations into English of the 1891 Erfurt Programme and the 1899 Agrarian Question, see Kautsky (1910; 1988).

[39] Like other Marxists, Kautsky (1910: 24–5) argued that, as capitalism developed, the labour-power of males would be replaced by that of women and children: 'There was a time when skill and strength were requisites for the working-man...Now, however, the progress made in the division of labour and the introduction of machinery render skill and strength superfluous; they make it possible to substitute unskilled and cheap workmen for skilled ones; and, consequently, to put...women and even children in the place of men. In the early stages of manufacturing this tendency is already perceptible; but not until machinery is introduced into production do we find the wholesale exploitation of women and children – the most helpless among the helpless.... The labour of women and children, moreover, affords the additional advantage that these are less capable of resistance than men.' On the erosion by capital of freedom, his comments are as follows (Kautsky, 1910: 86–7): 'Private ownership in the implements of labour has long ceased to secure to each producer the product of his labour and to guarantee him freedom. Today, on the contrary, society is rapidly drifting to the point where the whole population of capitalist nations will be deprived of both property and freedom.'

[40] 'We have seen that the introduction of female and child-labour in industry is one of the most powerful means whereby capitalists reduce the wages of working-men,' notes Kautsky (1910: 29, 32, 34), adding that: 'To the capitalist this reserve army is invaluable. It places in his hands a powerful weapon with which to curb the army of the employed. After excessive work on the part of some has produced lack of work for others, then the idleness of these is used as a means to keep up, and even increase, the excessive work of the former...unemployment becomes greater the harder and the longer the workman toils; he brings enforced idleness upon himself through his own labour.'

them 'slaves without a will of their own'.[41] A peasant smallholding is able to reproduce itself not because it is inherently efficient economically, let alone able to compete successfully with capitalist units, as populists maintained, but rather because it constituted a labour reserve on which large commercial farms drew for the purpose of accumulation.[42]

This meant, Kautsky pointed out, that the large commercial unit had 'at its disposal very cheap forced labour. If the source of this *cheap forced labour* dried up the large-scale enterprise became unprofitable and was replaced by the small one.'[43] This was the central thesis of his argument concerning the seemingly irrational survival of peasant cultivators in an agriculture that is capitalist: namely, that because smallholdings are a source of labour-power, they are never wholly displaced by large farms.[44] This, and not their economic efficiency, is the reason why peasant economy survives.

This labour-power was provided, Kautsky pointed out, on a casual, seasonal or permanent basis by members of the peasant family farm, and controlled by large capitalist producers through the debt mechanism.[45] By itself, however, the creation or reproduction of peasant

---

41 For this description, see Kautsky (1984: 25).

42 As Kautsky (1988: 111, 112) notes: 'It takes a very obdurate admirer of smallscale landownership to see the advantages derived from forcing small cultivators down to the level of beasts of burden, into a life occupied by nothing other than work – apart from time set aside for sleeping and eating… The overwork of the small independent farmers and their families is therefore not a factor which should be numbered amongst the advantages of the small farm even from a purely economic standpoint, leaving aside any ethical or other conditions.'

43 See Kautsky (1984: 14). The dynamic structuring this seemingly 'autonomous' peasant economy is made clear in the following manner (Kautsky, 1984: 19, original emphasis): 'The capitalists favour this settlement of their workers on the land because they can make sure of their labour-power in this way, and make the workers more dependent on them…Thus the number of dwarf-enterprises can grow under certain circumstances within the capitalist mode of production, alongside the latter, and as part of the latter's growth, of the growth of the large-scale enterprise, of the growth of the proletariat. The dwarf-enterprise does not draw its vital force from its *ability to compete* but from *the worker's wage*.'

44 See Kautsky (1988: 163), where he writes as follows: 'The best conditions for bringing up a plentiful supply of able-bodied labour are found among the owners (or tenants) of small farms on which an independent household is linked with independent farming. Not only does this group supply labour-power for itself, but also turns out a surplus [in the form of] workers via their children, for whom there is no room on the family farm, and who can therefore be taken on as house-servants or day-labourers by large farms.'

45 Observing that historically 'the large-scale agricultural enterprise became impossible to keep up, and peasant and tenant farms took the place of the plantations,'

economy by large commercial farms so as to retain a labour reserve is insufficient to prevent such workers from seeking better-paid employment in industry, and for this reason coercion is necessary to keep them on large enterprises.[46] Kautsky makes clear not only the unfree nature of the workforce retained/employed in agriculture at this conjuncture, but also how this is achieved: state compulsion, punishing breach of contract, enforcing the Masters and Servants Ordinance ('to ensure that farmers can keep their servants'), and preventing the 'free movement' of migrants (= foreign workers).[47]

In other words, a large farm had also to prevent the workers forming the labour reserve it had created from personally commodifying or recommodifying their own labour-power in the manner of a proletariat;

Kautsky (1984: 14–5) adds: 'This is also one of the reasons for the phenomenon that on the continent of Europe it is precisely in the most economically and politically developed states, states which were the first to suppress compulsory feudal labour services, that peasant economy is most strongly entrenched'. Elsewhere in Europe the large-scale unit continues to be commercially viable precisely because 'since the abolition of forced labour [this has rested] first and foremost on a new kind of slavery, *the slavery of indebtedness*' (original emphasis). Such a view was prevalent right across the political spectrum at that conjuncture, as is evident from what A.J. Balfour, the British Conservative Member of Parliament, stated in an address to the Industrial Remuneration Conference in 1885. On this subject, he wrote as follows (Dilke, 1968: 342–3): 'This view which, with very great reluctance I am compelled to accept, asserts that a peasant proprietary may, and in all old countries where it extensively prevails actually does, co-exist with great poverty in the large towns, with low wages and sometimes with harsh treatment of the labourer in the country districts. That while peasant proprietors are hard masters, and, where they have the chance, hard landlords, they themselves are too frequently subjected to a condition of dependence more cruel than that of any tenant or any landlord, or any labourer or any employer – the dependence, namely of a small debtor on a professional moneylender.' Balfour went on seemingly to commend the work of Marx on this subject (Dilke, 1968: 344), saying that – although he himself was no socialist – in his view it possessed 'intellectual force,' 'consistency,' and 'economic reasoning'.

[46] Hence the observation (Kautsky, 1988: 225) that 'large-scale landownership set about the artificial creation of small farms wherever the land has been cleared of them. And the stronger the pull of the town, the more landowners will try to bind the workers they need to the land. But often the mere creation of small peasant plots is not sufficient to overcome the attraction of industry: legal compulsion also has to be used to keep workers on the large estates.'

[47] Where flight from the land continues, observes Kautsky (1988: 231), 'state compulsion steps in to assist. Tightening up the Servants Ordinance, punishing breach of contract…are all meant to ensure that the farmers can keep their servants. The elimination or obstruction of free movement by banning [internal] migration, measures making it more difficult for migrants to settle in towns…and similar moves, are meant to keep migrants at home.' That is, economically immobile, on the land. This, Kautsky agrees, 'will merely make rural life even more unbearable for the servants and contract workers [and] would rob numerous small peasants of the only opportunity they have for supplementary employment and throw them into acute poverty.'

that is, it was necessary to deproletarianize them. His twofold conclusion is significant. First, that what populists misinterpreted as the 'blossoming' of peasant economy – its seeming capacity to reproduce itself in the face of capitalism – was much rather a sign of its distress, one characteristic of which was that 'feudal forms of labour contract are re-emerging.'[48] And second, the latter underlined the extent to which agrarian capitalist development in Germany during the 1880s was being accompanied by the intensification, not the elimination, of unfree labour.[49]

III

Lenin, too, understood the connection between on the one hand the presence of debt bondage and on the other the centrality of class struggle leading to the restructuring the capitalist labour process, using out-workers composed of unfree labour drawn from the industrial reserve army. Where issues of systemic and relational transition are involved, the work of Trotsky, Hilferding and others also provides a useful guide to a Marxist understanding of the apparently contradictory way in which capital deploys/reproduces both free and unfree labour-power in the course of agrarian transformation.

---

[48] Empirical data suggesting that peasant economy was reproducing itself economically, argued Kautsky (1988: 233), 'warm the hearts of all good citizens who see the peasantry as the sturdiest bulwark of the existing order. Look, they exclaim, there is no movement – in agriculture that is: Marx's dogma does not apply *here*... The peasantry [in the 1880s] appears to be blossoming anew – to the detriment of all those socialist tendencies produced by industry. But this blossom has its roots in a swamp. It is not a product of the *well-being* of the peasantry, but of the *distress* of the whole of agriculture...feudal forms of labour contract are re-emerging' (original emphasis).

[49] For more on this, see the case study presented in Chapter 6. The continued significance of unfree labour at this conjuncture is evident from the fact that it is enshrined in German legislative ordinances. Thus the 1891 Industrial Code Amendment Bill (Germany) contains the following clauses (Schäffle, 1893: 232, 233): 'If the apprentice quits his instruction...without consent of his master...the police magistrate may, on application of the master, oblige the apprentice to remain under instruction so long as apprentice relations are declared by judicial ruling to be still undissolved...In case of refusal [by the worker], the police magistrate may cause the apprentice to be taken back by force, or he may compel him to return under pain of a fine, to the amount of fifty marks, or detention for five days...The apprentice shall not be employed in the same trade by another employer, without consent of the former master, within nine months after such dissolution of apprentice relations' (Clauses §130 and §132).

Lenin and Trotsky on Unfree Labour

About restructuring Lenin notes that in Russia the outwork system which takes the form of domestic industry 'by no means eliminates the concept of capitalist manufacture, but on the contrary, is sometimes even a sign of its further development'.[50] The importance of these small establishments is that they are connected with big ones to form what he calls 'a single system of industry', an arrangement described as typical of capitalist manufacture.[51] Many of those who became 'master-industrialists', observed Lenin, were in fact better-off peasants.[52]

In late nineteenth century Russia, the sweating system not merely drew in but depended upon the unfree and thus cheap labour-power of women and children, a phenomenon Marx had earlier identified in the case of Britain.[53] And again like Marx, Lenin noted the prevalence of unfree production relations (bonded labour, the truck system)

---

[50] See Lenin (1964a: 413). Opposing the Narodnik view that domestic industry was an autonomous economic form of production unconnected with capitalism, Lenin (1964a: 450, 452) argued that outworkers wrongly classified as part of 'handicraft industry' should more realistically be categorized as 'capitalistically employed workers' – that is, as part of a specifically capitalist system of production, and its social relations consequently seen as desired and reproduced by it. His conclusion (Lenin, 1964a: 541) is equally emphatic: 'The facts utterly refute the view widespread here in Russia that "factory" and "handicraft" are isolated from each other. On the contrary, such a division is purely artificial. The connection and continuity between the forms... is of the most direct and intimate kind.'

[51] See Lenin (1964a: 414, 438). Criticizing the Russian populists for missing this connection ('The fundamental error of Narodnik economics is that it ignores, or glosses over, the connection between the big and the small establishments...'), he goes on to point out that (Lenin, 1964a: 441) 'capitalist domestic industry is met with at all stages of the development of capitalism in industry, but it is most characteristic of manufacture'.

[52] 'We have seen,' notes Lenin (1964a: 446), 'that the big master-industrialists, the buyers-up, work-room owners and subcontractors are at the same time well-to-do agriculturalists.' In the construction industry, the labour contractor is described as the one who becomes 'a real capitalist' (Lenin, 1964a: 530 ff.). The same kind of phenomenon was noted earlier by Marx in relation to the gang system in nineteenth century English agriculture, where the labour contractor was a gangmaster who recruited and controlled groups of workers. 'Some gangmasters,' he observed (Marx, 1976a: 851 note 10), 'have worked up to a position of farmers of 500 acres, or proprietors of whole rows of houses.'

[53] Referring to manufacturing apprenticeship, Lenin (1964a: 427–8) argues that it 'is well known that under general conditions of commodity economy and capitalism this [apprenticeship] gives rise to the worst form of dependence and exploitation'. He then compares the practice of apprenticeship to the conditions structuring the employment of child labour in manufacturing industry. Children continue to work, Lenin notes, even with 'the advent of large-scale industry', concurring with the analysis by Marx himself of this same trend in British industry some three decades earlier.

accompanying this process of capitalist restructuring.[54] Observing that the latter gives rise to a worker who is 'not only a wage-slave, but also a debt-slave', Lenin confirms thereby that in his opinion accumulation results in labour-power that is paid and simultaneously unfree.[55]

In line with almost all other Marxists, Lenin was aware of not only the importance of class struggle as waged by capital so as to cheapen/discipline labour, but also the resort by an employer to unfreedom when his (or 'his') workers attempt personally to commodify/recommodify their own labour-power and sell it to the highest bidder.[56] Accordingly, those categorized by Lenin as capitalist wage-labourers are also described as being subordinated by all the mechanisms familiarly associated with unfree production relations: employer collusion, retaining workers passports, and prohibiting farmers from employing 'absconding' agricultural labourers.[57] The employment of child labour in agriculture is perceived as a way in which peasant competes with capitalism, and in industry – specifically, the outwork system – it is seen as a way in which enables some capitalist enterprises to compete with other capitalist ones.[58]

---

[54] 'Alongside the sweating system, and perhaps as one of its forms, should be placed the truck system,' which, Lenin (1964a: 443) accepts, is commonplace in outwork arrangements, adding that the 'drawing of women and children of the tenderest age into production is nearly always observed in domestic industry.'

[55] Hence the following (Lenin, 1964a: 445): 'The isolation of the home workers and the abundance of middlemen naturally leads to widespread bondage…which usually accompany "patriarchal" relationships in remote rural districts. Workers' indebtedness to employers is extremely widespread in the "handicraft" industries in general, and in domestic industry in particular. Usually the worker is not only a Lohnsklave [wage-slave] but also a Schuldsklave [debt-slave].' Having described the squirrel-fur industry as 'a typical example of capitalist manufacture', Lenin (1964a: 408–9) accepts that 'relations between masters and workers are "patriarchal"', an employment situation where 'masters knock them [labourers] about'. The same is true of relations in the button industry (Lenin, 1964a: 411).

[56] Lenin (1964a: 440) accepts that even the development of industrial capitalism – as distinct from merchant capital – does not lead to the eradication of bonded labour ('The mass of peasants…are in a similar state of bondage. Can one, under such circumstances, rejoice over the slight development of industrial capital?').

[57] Lenin (1964a: 246) cites the following example from the Kuban region: 'The Cossack resorts to every possible method to force down the price of labour, acting either individually or through the community…cutting down the food, increasing the work quota, docking the pay, retaining workers' passports, adopting public resolutions prohibiting specific farmers from employing workers, on pain of a fine, at above a definite rate, etc.'

[58] On the employment of child labour in Russian agriculture, see Lenin (1963b: 209–13). Significantly, even when he differentiates backward forms of capitalism from more advanced kinds, it is clear that unfree labour is common to both. Thus, for example, the mining industry in the Urals is characterized as a 'backward' form of

Nor was it the case that constraints on outmigration posed by the existence in rural areas of unfree relations prevented the access by capital to an industrial reserve army of labour.[59] In cases where rural inhabitants were unable to leave their communities, therefore, factories were sited in the villages. This, as Lenin observed, meant that '[w]hile the erection of factories in the countryside involves quite a few inconveniences, it does, however, guarantee a supply of cheap labour. The muzhik is not allowed to go to the factory, so the factory goes to the muzhik.'[60] The contemporary resonance of this kind of capitalist relocation, plus the reason for undertaking it, and the working arrangements licensed thereby, are too obvious to need much elaboration.[61]

---

capitalism where bonded labour persists, whereas mining in the South is described as a 'purely capitalist industry' (Lenin, 1964a: 488 ff.). He then goes on to accept that unfree relations *do* exist even in the South, which earlier he held up as the epitome of 'advanced capitalism', stating (Lenin, 1964a: 495): 'Can one be surprised, for instance, at Southern mine owners being eager to tie the workers down and to secure the legislative prohibition of competition by small establishments, when in the other mining area [i.e., the 'backward' Urals] such tying down and such prohibitions have existed for ages, and exist to this day, and when in another area the iron-masters, by using more primitive methods and employing cheaper and more docile labour, get a profit on their pig-iron, without effort...?'

[59] About the lumber and building industries, Lenin (1964a: 525 ff.) asks 'How is this industry organized?', and answers 'On purely capitalistic lines'. He goes on to delineate the relational forms characterizing such capitalist enterprises: 'Lumbering is one of the worst paid occupations...Left to toil in the remote forest depths, these workers are in a totally defenceless position, and in this branch of industry bondage, the truck system, and such-like concomitants of the "patriarchal" peasant industries prevail...Moscow statisticians mention the "compulsory purchase of provisions," which usually reduces to a marked degree the lumber workers' earnings.' Further on he (Lenin, 1964a: 528–9, original emphasis) notes that the 'peasants are in "perpetual bondage" to the lumber industrialists', and goes on to observe that lumbermen 'represent that form of the reserve army (or relative surplus-population in capitalist society) which (Marxist) theory describes as *latent*; a certain (and, as we have seen, quite large) section of the rural population must always be ready to undertake such work, must always be in need of it. That is a condition for the existence and development of capitalism.'

[60] See Lenin (1964a: 524), where the reason for this is explained as follows: 'The muzhik lacks complete freedom (thanks to the collective-responsibility system and the obstacles to his leaving the community) to seek an employer who gives the greatest advantage; but the employer has a perfect way of seeking out the cheapest worker.'

[61] This pattern of relocation in search of ever-cheaper and more easily subordinated forms of labour-power – an industrial reserve army that is global in scope, in other words – corresponds to what currently takes the form of the new international division of labour (Fröbel, Heinrichs and Kreye, 1980). It corresponds closely to the dynamic identified a century ago by Lenin (1964a: 525, original emphasis): 'By converting the backwoodsman-muzhik into a factory worker *at one stroke*, the factory may for a time ensure for itself a supply of the cheapest, least developed and least exacting "hands"'.

That Trotsky subscribed to the view that capitalism strives to replace free wage labour with unfree production relations is clear from a number of things. From the fact of his opposition to the conceptual apparatus structuring the concept 'semi-feudal' and 'feudal', from his belief that the agrarian question would be resolved not by the bourgeoisie under capitalism but by the proletariat under socialism, and – most importantly – from what he wrote in 1925 about the way in which accumulation made it necessary for advanced capitalist production to negate the very conditions of its own existence. On the latter point, therefore, Trotsky observed that advanced capital undermined not only competition (or the free market) but also 'the freedom of labour'.[62]

Trotsky recognized, as did Lenin, that even in late nineteenth century Russia capital 'in the financial and industrial form, poured down on us during that period when Russian handicraft had not in the mass divided itself from agriculture.'[63] He went on to describe how in these circumstances accumulation involved 'the appearance amongst us of the most modern capitalist industry in an environment of economic primitiveness'. This process, labelled 'combined and uneven development', corresponded to the kind of relocation/restructuring identified by Lenin as one whereby 'the factory goes to the muzhik'.

Hilferding and other Marxists on Unfree Labour

Hilferding also placed the reproduction unfree production relations within a context of class struggle waged by capital against labour. For him, this entailed a more or less continuous stand-off between workers and employers over the terms and conditions of the labour contract. As capitalism developed, therefore, contract increasingly became the focus of class struggle, workers demanding its legal regulation.[64] According to Hilferding, such conflict went through three stages: originally it took the form strife between the individual employer and

---

[62] His observation about this is as follows (Trotsky, 1976: 49, emphasis added): 'Standardization is socialization carried into the technical side of production. We see how in this direction technical science in the leading capitalist countries is tearing through the cover of private property, and embarking on what is, in essence, *a negation of the principle of competition, "the freedom of labour" and everything connected with it*.'

[63] See Trotsky (1934: 476), where in an Appendix this argument is deployed to defend the theory of permanent revolution from the attack made on it in 1922 by Pokrovsky. Additional points raised by this interpretation are considered below in Chapter 3, in relation to the theoretical and political differences between Trotskyism and semi-feudal thesis.

[64] See Hilferding (1981: 335).

the individual worker; then, a confrontation involving the individual employer and a workers' organization; and, finally, a struggle pitting organizations of workers' against those of employers.[65]

Noting that as capitalism develops in colonial areas, commercial employers resorted to four methods of obtaining labour-power. The first two – familiar enough to Marxist theory – were designed to drive existing smallholders into the labour market, either by depriving them of land (= depeasantization) or by imposing taxation on them, money payment of which required the sale of labour-power to commercial enterprises.[66] Neither of these two methods necessarily resulted in production relations that were unfree.

This, however, is not true of the last two – the resort to slavery and worker immigration – each of which historically has given rise to the phenomenon of capitalist unfree labour. A dual system of unfree labour is reintroduced. On the one hand, Hilferding notes, 'slavery is reinstated as an economic ideal'.[67] On the other, immigrant or 'coolie' labour is recruited, 'an ingenious system of contract slavery' the object of which is to prevent workers from selling their labour-power to the highest bidder, and consequently to keep wage levels in such contexts from increasing (= 'the laws of supply and demand do not exert any undesirable effects on the labour market').[68]

For Hilferding, therefore, contract is unequal, based on coercion, and thus a source of conflict based on class. This is the antithesis of the way it is seen by neo-classical economic theory: as evidence for worker/

---

[65] See Hilferding (1981: 351 ff.), who outlines how both parties to the struggle try to prevent the market from favouring their opponents. Thus trade unions attempt to eliminate competition among workers – foreign immigrants and domestic unemployed – from entering the market, to the detriment of those currently in jobs. Historically, this is a familiar enough 'from below' strategy. That employers should also intervene in the market, by placing obstacles so as to prevent workers from selling their labour-power to the highest bidder, is a 'from above' strategy rather less well-known.

[66] See Hilferding (1981: 319).

[67] 'Slavery is reinstated as an economic ideal,' notes Hilferding (1981: 320), 'and along with it that spirit of brutality which is then transferred back from the colonies to the champions of colonial interests at home and celebrates here its disgusting orgies.'

[68] Hence the observation (Hilferding, 1981: 320, emphasis added): 'If the native population does not suffice to produce the desired volume of surplus value, either because excessive zeal in expropriating them has deprived them of their lives as well as land, or because the population is in any case small, or the natives are not sufficiently robust, capital attempts to solve the labour problem by introducing foreign labour. The import of coolie labour is organized, and *an ingenious system of contract slavery is devised to ensure that the laws of supply and demand do not exert any undesirable effects on the labour market*.'

employer equilibrium, based on assent and thus reciprocal. As in the case of other Marxists, the reproduction of working arrangements that are unfree is seen by Hilferding to be a crucial weapon deployed by capital in its struggle to control/cheapen/discipline labour-power. In other words, he too recognized the presence and role of a process that is interpreted here as one of deproletarianization.

Much the same point was made subsequently by a number of historians who were also Marxists, among whom were Jürgen Kuczynski, Maurice Dobb, Daniel Guérin and Ernest Mandel. Each recognized that, even in an advanced capitalist economy, unfree labour could be an outcome of class struggle. All of them accepted that capital did not always try to eliminate unfreedom and replace it with free labour, nor indeed did accumulation necessarily depend on this kind of transformation.[69] In fact, Dobb – like Mandel – had no difficulty in recognizing that, even in metropolitan contexts, capital imposed unfreedom on labour when market conditions favoured workers and not employers.[70]

[69] 'The freedom of mobility has been taken away from labour to a degree which makes one question whether one can really still speak of a proletariat such as we have known since the Industrial Revolution', noted Kuczynski (1939: 42), adding that '[o]ne can speak of the German worker only in a very limited sense as a "free-wage worker", free to sell his labour where he gets the least lowly price for it.' Dobb made much the same kind of point. Designed 'to lessen the "labour turnover" and to tie a worker to a particular firm', restrictions on economic freedom include a lack of information about alternative employment, tied and company housing, and the truck system (Dobb, 1946a:13–5). In a similar vein, Guérin (1956: 27) maintained that the acceptability to capitalism of unfree labour should be understood with reference to the fact that '[s]lavery flourished as long as it was *profitable*' (original emphasis).

[70] Talking about war-time Britain, Dobb (1940: 332) observes: 'The crucial limit seems to be…full employment in the labour market to raise wages to such an extent as to precipitate a sharp shrinkage of surplus-value, and consequently to change the value both of existing capital and of new investment. So abhorrent and unnatural does such a situation appear as to cause exceptional measures to be taken to clip the wings of labour - even…*to curtail the normal working of competitive forces* - whenever labour scarcity shows signs of becoming an enduring condition of the labour market' (emphasis added). Talking about war-time Germany, Mandel (1975: 162) observes in a similar vein: '[E]ven under conditions where the working class is completely atomized, the laws of the market which determine short-term fluctuations in the price of the commodity labour-power do not disappear. As soon as the industrial reserve army contracted in the Third Reich, workers were able to try, by means of rapid job mobility - for instance into the spheres of heavy industry and armaments which paid higher wage-rates and overtime - to achieve at least a modest improvement in their wages, even without trade union action. Only a violent intervention by the Nazi state to sustain the rate of surplus-value and the rate of profit, in the form of the legal *prohibition* of job changes, and the *compulsory tying* of workers to their job, was able to prevent the working class from utilizing more propitious conditions on the labour market.

Similarly, in the 1960s Mandel contrasted two extreme forms of capitalism; whereas the object of public expenditure under the then dominant welfare state was 'improving the position of low-income families and to purposes of public utility', under the recently defeated fascism the same economic activity had been designed to reduce living standards of workers in order to maintain or boost capitalist profitability.[71] Central to the latter, he argued, is the replacement of free labour with workers that are unfree, the object being to lower the cost of labour-power by depressing yet further the subsistence minimum, so as to enhance the level of surplus extracted in the course of the accumulation process.[72] This is not to say that the resort by capital to unfree labour-power either prefigures fascism or is evidence for the presence of the latter, only to recognize that in periods of acute class struggle with labour, where its own survival may be at stake, capital does not rule out any option available to it. And deproletarianization is just such an option.

IV

Deproletarianization involves the reproduction, the introduction, or the reintroduction by capital of unfree labour, and corresponds to a form of workforce decomposition/recomposition frequently resorted to by employers in their struggle with labour.[73] In contexts/periods

This abolition of freedom of movement of the German proletariat was one of the most striking demonstrations of the capitalist class nature of the Nationalist Socialist State' (original emphasis).

[71] Hence the view (Mandel, 1968: 537): 'The significance of this policy is clear – to bring about a recovery in the rate of profit at the expense of the working class, which is deprived of its political and trade-union means of defence... In the extreme form which it assumed, above all in Germany, during the Second World War, fascism goes beyond the militarisation of labour, to the abolition of free labour in the strict sense of the word, to a return to slave labour on an ever larger scale.'

[72] 'What is characteristic of forced labour,' Mandel (1968: 537, third footnote) points out, is 'precisely that the mere idea of a necessary product, of a subsistence minimum, is completely deprived of meaning. The "payment" of labour is lowered so as not merely no longer to ensure survival in good health but even to imply certain death within a brief period of time.'

[73] Details about the interrelationship between on the one hand the decommodification of labour-power, the employment of unfree labour, capitalist restructuring, and workforce decomposition/recomposition, and on the other the process of deproletarianization are outlined in Brass (1999). The latter outlines also the many examples of strong worker opposition to restructuring, and equally forthright attempts by employers to proceed with this, in order to cut production costs. Numerous contextually and

where/when further accumulation is blocked by overproduction, therefore, economic crisis may force capital to restructure its labour process in one of two ways: either by replacing free workers with unfree equivalents, or by converting the former into the latter.

The economic advantage of such restructuring is that it enables landholders/planters first to lower the cost of local workers by importing unfree, more easily regulated, and thus cheaper outside labour, and then to lower the cost of the latter if/when the original external/local wage differential has been eroded. In this way it is possible for commercial producers either to maintain wages at existing (low) levels or even to decrease pay and conditions of each component of the workforce, thereby restoring/enhancing profitability within the capitalist labour process.[74]

Deproletarianization and/as Mature Capitalism

Deproletarianization as a concept is based on Marxist theory about labour-power as the personal property of the worker, indeed his/her only one. It is clear that when Marx talks of labour-power being 'free', he is simply contrasting the feudal serf with the capitalist wage labourer. Whereas the former was still not separated either from means of production (land) or from the control of its owner (feudal lord), the latter is now compelled to provide the capitalist with labour-power. As described by Marx, this transition did not necessarily generate a workforce that is free.[75]

---

historically-specific instances exist of the central role played by unfree labour in the process of capitalist restructuring, a procedure whereby employers used it to replace free workers bargaining over pay and conditions or engaged in strike action. Over the past two decades, Marxist theory about deproletarianization has been defended from critiques emanating largely from (mainly) anti-Marxist frameworks. The latter include not only neo-classical economic historiography (Steinfeld, Shlomowitz, Fogel and Engerman,), postmodernism (Prakash, Taussig) and exercises in eclecticism (Banaji), but also interpretations linked to the semi-feudal thesis (Byres, Patnaik, Breman).

[74] This is the reason why the capitalist state is frequently called upon to ensure that those separated from their means of production are not just available to employers but also remain so. Hence the battery of legislative ordinances (peonage, pass laws, master and servant laws, vagrancy laws) designed to keep those without the means of labour in employment that may not be either of their choosing or to their liking. Whereas making those separated from their means of production sell their labour-power on the market is compatible with free work relations, requiring them to stay within such employment once entered into is not.

[75] About this Marx (1976a: 875) noted: 'The starting point of the development that gave rise both to the wage-labourer and to the capitalist was the enslavement of the worker. The advance made consisted in a change in the form of this servitude, in the

In keeping with Marxist theory about the capitalism/unfreedom link, therefore, deproletarianization defines a relation of production in terms of whether or not a worker is able personally to commodify his/her own labour-power. The latter is free by virtue of its owner being able to commodify and recommodify it unconditionally: that is, to be free in the sense understood by Marx and Marxism a worker must be able personally to sell his/her own labour-power on a continuous basis. It is the incapacity of a worker personally to commodify or recommodify his/her labour-power that for Marxism defines the relation as unfree, and distinguishes it from those relations where workers retain this capacity.[76] Accordingly, unfree labourers also get paid and appear in the market, but not as sellers of their own commodity.

In contrast to the negative meaning attached here to deproletarianization, those on the political right who use the same concept see it in benign terms. For both Pieper and Mises, therefore, deproletarianization refers to the capacity on the part of a worker to have the leisure-time that is the basis of culture.[77] Although all these interpretations

---

transformation of feudal exploitation into capitalist exploitation...' Elsewhere, however, it is not labour-power but rather labourers themselves who are categorized as by Marx and Engels as commodities under capitalism, a view which suggests that they perceived little relational distinctiveness between slaves and workers employed by capital. Hence the statement (Marx and Engels, 1976: 490) to the effect that '[i]n proportion as the bourgeoisie, *i.e.*, capital, is developed, in the same proportion is the proletariat, the modern working class, developed – a class of labourers, who live only so long as they find work, and who find work only so long as their labour increases capital. These labourers, who must sell themselves piecemeal, are a commodity, like every other article of commerce, and are consequently exposed to all the vicissitudes of competition, to all the fluctuations of the market.'

[76] That this is the case is evident not just from Chapter 6 ('The Sale and Purchase of Labour-power') in *Capital I* (Marx, 1976a: 272) but also from the manuscript for *A Contribution to the Critique of Political Economy* (Marx; 1988: 37–8), written in the period 1861–63. The latter contains the unambiguous observation (Marx, 1988: 111, 135, emphasis added) that, so as to confront capital as wage labour, '[t]he worker must be free, in order to be able to dispose of his labour capacity as his property, he must therefore be neither slave, nor serf, nor bondsman. Equally, he must on the other hand have forfeited the conditions for the realization of his labour capacity. He must therefore be neither a peasant farming for his own needs nor a craftsman: he must have altogether ceased to be an owner of property... By wage labour we understand *exclusively free labour* which is exchanged for capital, is converted into capital and valorizes capital.'

[77] In the opinion of Pieper (1952: 66–7) deproletarianization means 'enlarging the scope of life beyond the confines of merely useful servile work', a process dependent in turn on combining three conditions: 'by giving the wage-earner the opportunity to save and acquire property, by limiting the power of the state, and by overcoming the inner impoverishment of the individual'. Similarly, von Mises (1949) describes the term as 'an improvement in the living conditions of the manual workers that raises

accept that what is involved amounts to the cessation of a specifically proletarian status, the Marxist view is that such a transformation entails a downwards move to a relational form that is unfree, whereas the political right sees the transformation as a positive move upwards, corresponding to an embourgeoisification of the worker.

Why Deproletarianization Matters

The historical and contemporary significance of deproletarianization, and its implications for the direction taken by class struggle, as capitalism becomes global, is not difficult to discern. Since its form of unfreedom entails both economic and ideological decommodification, preventing workers from selling their labour-power also conceptually devalorizes the wage form.[78] For this reason, the free/unfree distinction is not merely important, but its significance extends beyond the usual restriction of this transformation to a once-off aspect of historical transition – from feudalism to capitalism – and locates it as a process within capitalism itself.

Theorized thus, unfreedom becomes a crucial and twofold part of the class struggle waged by capital to ensure the reproduction of the capitalist system. On the one hand, therefore, workforce restructuring involving the replacement of free workers by unfree equivalents, or the conversion of the former into the latter, enables capital to combat economic crisis by cheapening the cost of labour-power. On the other, this same process of workforce decomposition/recomposition permits capital to restructure class relations in its labour process, the object of deproletarianization being either to undermine or to pre-empt working class consciousness/solidarity and agency based on this.[79]

their standard of living to the customary standards of the "middle classes"'. For them both, therefore, deproletarianization is a benefit realized by the worker in the face of opposition from a 'totalitarian' state. Neither is such a benefit to 'be confused with the struggle against poverty' (Pieper, 1952: 67), thereby rejecting explicitly the causal link made by Marxist theory between worker impoverishment and deproletarianization.

[78] This point was not lost on rural capitalists and their representatives. In the case of late nineteenth century Mexico (Beals, 1932: 307), for example, '[t]he Governor of Coahuila reported the farm-workers, who received three to five dollars a month, as being "too proletarian"'.

[79] Introducing, reproducing or reintroducing unfreedom 'from above' forms a crucial aspect of the ideological class struggle. In such circumstances, unfree labour is a specifically capitalist method of fragmenting a 'from below' consciousness of class. It is achieved by shifting the identity of the worker, away from a sense of collective identity (and agency linked to this), and towards a sense of individual selfhood. This is especially the case where struggle between capital and labour is informed additionally by

To both these ends, capital decomposes the proletariat and simultaneously recomposes its workforce as unfree labour – with or without wages and contract. As Marx himself pointed out, it is precisely in the existence of a space between unfree and free labour and the desirability not just of a transition from one to the other but also the reproduction of proletarian selfhood once achieved, that workers are afforded the opportunity and possibility of a shift in and retention of a specifically working class consciousness, through the realization of the fact of the appropriation from them of value they produce.[80]

It is a truism that capitalism shapes not only the labour process but also its worker in a way that is suitable for the prevailing conditions of production.[81] Previous relational forms are not reproduced exactly,

---

acute conflict at an international level between different enterprises attempting to establish or maintain a monopoly in a particular sector or economic activity. Hence the crucial role of ideological fragmentation as a way of combatting or pre-empting trade unionization, worker solidarity and/or organized labour. This process of ideological individualization, imposed on workers by employers, has led to the mistaken assumption that deproletarianization is a concept drawn from liberal theory, in that the focus is on the worker-as-subject. This category mistake – made by, among others, Banaji (see Chapter 4) – confuses individualization as a political strategy adopted by employers in their struggle with labour (which does indeed happen) with an analytical endorsement of individualization as an end in itself (which obviously is not the case).

[80] Hence the view (Marx, 1973: 464–5): 'What the free worker sells is always nothing more than a specific particular measure of force-expenditure [*Kraftäusserung*]; ... He sells the particular expenditure of force to a particular capitalist, whom he confronts as an independent *individual*. It is clear that this is not his relation to the existence of capital as capital...Nevertheless, everything touching on the individual, real person leaves him a wide field of choice, of arbitrary will, and hence of formal freedom. In the slave relation, he belongs to the individual, particular owner, and is his labouring machine. As a totality of force-expenditure, as labour capacity, he is a thing [*Sache*] belonging to another, and hence does not relate as subject to his particular expenditure of force, nor to the act of living labour. In the serf relation he appears as a moment of property in land itself, is an appendage of the soil, exactly like draught-cattle. In the slave relation the worker is nothing but a living labour-machine, which therefore has value for others, or rather is a value. The totality of the free worker's labour capacity appears to him as his property, as one of his moments, over which he, as subject, exercises domination, and which he maintains by expending it' (original emphasis).

[81] This characteristic is outlined by Marx (1986: 42) in the following manner: 'The example of labour strikingly demonstrates that even the most abstract categories, despite their being valid – precisely because they are abstractions – for all epochs, are in the determinedness of their abstractions, just as much a product of historical conditions and retain their full validity only for and within these conditions. Bourgeois society is the most developed and many-faceted historical organization of production. The categories which express its relations, an understanding of its structure, therefore, provide at the same time, an insight into the structure and the relations of production of all previous forms of society the ruins and components of which were used in the

but aspects of such relations conducive not just to accumulation but also to competition and profitability can be and are adapted by capital to meet existing requirements. Not even free labour-power can expect to remain the same ('all new-formed [relations] become antiquated before they can ossify').[82] This is especially true currently, in a capitalist system that is global in extent and operates mainly or only according to *laissez faire* principles.

Conclusion

In epistemological terms, Adam Smith argued that labour-power was a source of value, while Hegel indicated that labour-power was owned by its subject. These positions found their synthesis in the analysis of Marx, who combined them to show how, since labour-power is both the property of its subject and also the source of value, under capitalism it can and does become a commodity that is sold to commercial employers by workers. Marx then outlined the way in which, as a result of this transaction, surplus-value was extracted by capital from the owner of the commodity labour-power, an appropriation which in turn corresponded to the economic dynamic that fuelled the accumulation process.

Because such a process of appropriation generated conflict between the parties to the exchange, Marx identified the sale/purchase of labour-power in a capitalist context as an act possessing an additional dynamic: that of class struggle, involving owners of means of production who purchased labour-power, and owners of the latter. In the course of this struggle, workers sought to improve pay and conditions while capitalists, by contrast, attempted to force down wage levels and increase the intensity of labour. As long as they remained free, workers

---

creation of bourgeois society. Some of these remains are still dragged along within bourgeois society unassimilated, while elements which previously were barely indicated have developed and attained their full significance, etc.'

[82] This is the gist of the famous passage in *The Communist Manifesto*, where Marx and Engels (1976: 487) state: 'The bourgeoisie cannot exist without constantly revolutionising the instruments of production, and thereby the relations of production, and with them the whole relations of society. Conservation of the old modes of production in unaltered form, was, on the contrary, the first condition of existence for all earlier industrial classes. Constant revolutionising of production, uninterrupted disturbance of all social conditions, everlasting uncertainty and agitation distinguish the bourgeois epoch from all earlier ones. All fixed, fast-frozen relations, with their train of ancient and venerable prejudices and opinions, are swept away, all new-formed ones become antiquated before they can ossify. All that is solid melts into air…'

retained an ability to bargain with employers over the sale of their only commodity, and to withdraw their labour-power if pay and conditions on offer were not to their liking.

It is precisely this context – the struggle between capital and labour – that the free/unfree distinction becomes significant, not least for Marxist analysis of what nowadays is categorized as 'globalization'. As accumulation unfolds and becomes international in scope, capital frequently restructures its workforce by replacing free labour with unfree equivalents. This constitutes a process of workforce decomposition/recomposition termed deproletarianization, or the economic and politico-ideological decommodification of labour-power.

Where the capitalism/unfreedom link is concerned, therefore, Marxism – not just of Marx and Engels, but also of Lenin, Kautsky, Trotsky and Hilferding, as well as of Kuczynski, Dobb, Guérin and Mandel – breaks with two alternative interpretations. The first, and most obvious of these is the non-Marxist theory of Smith, Malthus, Mill, Bright and Weber considered in the previous chapter. A second, and rather less obvious interpretation, however, is to be found within the ranks of what currently still passes for Marxism itself. It consists of two Marxist variants that analyse the same capitalism/unfreedom link in a very different way.

On the one hand, the variant described as the semi-feudal thesis insists that capitalism and unfree labour are incompatible, because the latter is a pre-capitalist relation destined to be replaced by a free worker as capitalism spreads. On the other, the 'disguised' wage labour thesis maintains that, since all production relations are contractually free, these are historically ubiquitous. Each of these two Marxist variants denies the existence of a capitalism/unfreedom link, for reasons – and with what implications – considered in the next two chapters.

CHAPTER THREE

SEMI-FEUDALISM AND MODERN MARXISM

Like most other variants of Marxist theory, the semi-feudal thesis was temporarily eclipsed in the 1980s by the rise of postmodernism, an interlude during which discussions about patterns of economic growth in the so-called Third World were diverted down a culturalist cul-de-sac, in that development itself was called into question and deemed to be neither possible nor desirable. Although postmodernism has waned in terms of academic popularity during the late 1990s, the semi-feudal thesis not only survives but remains influential in certain quarters: in the study of agrarian change in the so-called Third World generally, and especially in the case of India.[1]

In keeping with the non-Marxist theory considered in Chapter 1, therefore, the semi-feudal variant of Marxism views unfree labour as incompatible not just with capitalism but also with advanced productive forces, economic efficiency, skilled workers, and market expansion.[2] Most crucially, the epistemological importance of the claim, by Marxists who are exponents of the semi-feudal thesis and non-Marxists alike, that unfree labour is always and everywhere an economically inefficient relational form, is its corollary.[3] Namely, that

---

[1] That such a view continues to inform debate about the agrarian question in India is evident from two recent analyses. One is by Ajay (2008), who characterizes Haryana as semi-feudal, despite the emergence there of a dynamic commercial agriculture pursued by an economically powerful stratum of rich landowning peasant farmers who recruited/employed migrant workers. Because the latter were composed of bonded labour, the agriculture in which they were deployed could not in his opinion be a capitalist one. The other is by Ramachandran and Rawal (2010), who argue much the same case with respect to India as a whole. Namely, that the struggle in the Indian countryside remains one against foreign capital and its internal ally, the landlord class – the central emplacement of the semi-feudal thesis.

[2] Among other things, the focus by both non-Marxist theory and exponents of the semi-feudal thesis on technical improvements as the motor of economic transformation – allocating primacy to the forces of production, in other words – opens the door to the position that it is possible to increase output *without* altering social relations.

[3] The existence of a considerable epistemological overlap between on the one hand the non-Marxist interpretations considered above in Chapter 1, and on the other the semi-feudal thesis, ought to signal caution where claims to Marxist 'authenticity' are concerned.

capital is seen as opposed to using unfree labour, and in contexts where the latter relational form is found, invariably strives to replace it with free labour-power.

Refusing to contemplate the possibility of socialism, exponents of semi-feudalism argue that the next step is to a 'fully functioning' capitalism. With this kind of politics, socialism is never ever going to get onto the agenda. What exponents of the semi-feudal thesis refuse to confront, therefore, is the impact of outsourcing/restructuring on the production relations available to capital. They still think a group of permanent workers enjoying trade union rights and employed for a good wage under one roof in a big factory is the next step, whereas the reality nowadays is very different.[4]

The pattern currently takes the form of subcontracting of production by large off-shore corporations to many smallscale sweatshops (frequently located in the countryside, out of sight of government regulation) where coercion and bonded labour relations are rife. Coming across the latter, exponents of this Marxist variant declare them to be evidence for semi-feudalism, and thus for the absence of a 'fully functioning' capitalism, rather than what such units actually are: evidence precisely for the existence/operation of a 'fully functioning' – or a mature – capitalist system.

It is for these reasons that the concept 'semi-feudalism', its theoretical assumptions and political effects merit close scrutiny. Of significance is the way in which its view of transition as this applies both to systemic change and a transformation in production relations, licenses an interpretation of Third World development that, both politically (nationalism not socialism) and economically (privileging growth, not redistribution), is shared with much non-Marxist theory.

To this end, the first section of this chapter looks at the post-1945 rise to prominence of the semi-feudal thesis, and how its theoretical focus was on the development not of socialism but of capitalism.

---

[4] For example Byres, an exponent of the semi-feudal thesis (see below), wrongly equates capitalist development with a factory system, or massification based on a male workforce employed on a permanent basis. Hence the view (Byres, 1982b: 136) that the central issue is 'whether…industrialization…has created, or is poised to create, a factory system…that would signal a deeply rooted and healthily functioning capitalism.' By contrast, what happened throughout the 1980s and 1990s was the opposite process: capitalist development entailed restructuring, a strategy based in turn on the decentralization of production, the increased importance of outsourcing and downsizing premised on workforce that was casualized and female.

The second assesses critically the claims made by one exponent of the semi-feudal thesis regarding a transformation in production relations and its connection to systemic transition. In the third section, the extent of the overlap between the semi-feudal thesis and non-Marxist development theory is considered, while the fourth examines its political implications.

I

The trajectory within Marxist theory over the second half of the twentieth century of the concept 'semi-feudalism' and the 'semi-feudal' thesis is clear.[5] Its beginnings and influence can be traced to the success of the 1949 Chinese revolution, as a result of which during the decades which followed a mainly Maoist concept of 'semi-feudalism' became inextricably linked in Marxist discourse not only with opposition to imperialism and colonialism/semi-colonialism, but also (and therefore) with landlordism and its role in the paths of agrarian transition.[6]

Semi-Feudalism and Third World Development

One important consequence of classifying a social formation as 'semi-feudal' is that the principal contradiction is located not between capital

[5] Within Marxism, of course, the debate about paths of agrarian transition has a much longer lineage, going back to the formulation in the 1890s by Lenin (1964a) and Kautsky (1988) of the agrarian question.

[6] For the centrality of 'semi-feudalism' to this link, see Mao Tse-Tung (1954:76 ff.). Written at the end of the 1930s, the latter text was no different from the views of populists as well as socialists at that conjuncture. In the case of India during the 1930s and 1940s, for example, the discourse of Acharya Narendra Deva, N.G. Ranga and Rammanohar Lohia – all of whom were regarded initially as socialists of some sort – was basically populist and nationalist. Hence the exploiter is depicted by them as external, while the Indian peasant is regarded as uncorrupted by colonialism and thus a revolutionary subject. The same is true of Latin America, where there was little to distinguish the views of Peruvian socialists and/or communists such as José Carlos Mariátegui and Hildebrando Castro Pozo from those of Peruvian nationalists and populists such as Víctor Raúl Haya de la Torre. On the basis of a shared epistemology, all of them subscribed to the view that the Spanish Conquest imposed an 'inauthentic' and 'foreign' (= European) feudal tenure structure on what each of them interpreted as being a materially self-sufficient and culturally 'authentic' indigenous Andean peasant community that characterized the pre-Colombian era. More important was the fact that for both Mariátegui and Haya de la Torre, this discourse also possessed a programmatic status: the socialism of the former as well as the nationalism of the latter entailed building on what each perceived as being a still-viable peasant economy, a residue from the golden age of Peru that had survived colonialism. For more details about this issue, see Brass (2000: Chapter 1).

and labour but between on the one hand an external imperialism coupled with its internal ally, the 'feudal' landlord class, and on the other an anti-imperialist alliance composed of peasants, workers, and a 'progressive'/nationalist bourgeoisie, in which the peasantry constitute the dominant element.

Thus in the semi-feudal framework the class struggle takes a specific form. It is located between on the one hand the progressive social forces, consisting not just of workers and poor peasants but also of a national bourgeoisie (= as yet not 'fully functioning' capitalists), and on the other international capital and its feudal representatives within the nation. Both the latter constitute an obstacle to the installation of a 'fully functioning' capitalism', for which reason all the former are ranged against them, with the object of setting in motion the accumulation process.

The crux of the problem with this is, as always, a political one: whether or not socialism should be postponed until after a 'pure' capitalist stage has been ushered in, by an equally 'pure' democratic bourgeoisie using correspondingly 'pure' relations of production. In the case of India, therefore, landlords who employ unfree labour will be replaced in a bourgeois democratic stage by 'pure' agrarian capitalists who employ nothing but free wage labour, a stage in which peasant proprietorship reigns supreme. In other words, the abolition of landlord capitalism (= the Prussian path) will lead to peasant capitalism (= the American path), in the process realizing the classic two stages theory of agrarian transformation whereby one form of capitalism (unbenign, landlord, undemocratic) is replaced not by socialism but by another 'pure' form of capitalism (benign, peasant, democratic). In such a two stages pattern of transformation the duty of socialists is to press not for socialism but rather to support elements of the 'progressive' national bourgeoisie and to argue for the redistribution of land on an individual basis to smallholders (= 'repeasantization').

Not only are Maoism and nationalism interchangeable in this discourse, but the specifically Maoist component also allocates the main role in the defence of the (colonized or semi-colonized) nation against 'foreigners' to an undifferentiated and uniformly subordinated peasantry.[7] Accordingly, in Maoist discourse both the politics and

---

[7] This is also true of Stalin (1928:124ff.,276ff.) whose reformist policy in colonial contexts involved cooperation between communist parties and the national bourgeoisie in an anti-imperialist popular front (peasantry + working class against

economics of nationalism, and thus the corresponding absence of capitalism from rural areas of Third World countries, are linked specifically to the way in which landlords oppress the peasantry by means of pre-capitalist (= semi-feudal) exactions which take the form mainly of unfree labour.

Yet the very concept 'semi-feudal' betrays an air of theoretical uncertainty, even an undecidability, about the phenomena in question, which are neither-feudal-nor-capitalist but a hybrid. In this respect, the concept 'semi-feudalism' represents a notion of 'inbetween'-ness which is synonymous with 'transition', each occupying a similarly ill-defined and liminal theoretical space between what for Marxism are two well-defined systems.[8]

In the process of ceasing to be feudal and becoming capitalist, therefore, relational forms manifest aspects of both, and are accordingly less easy to categorize. However, rather than undertake a rigorous exploration of the concept 'semi-feudal', or abandon it altogether, many of those who employ the term have failed to analyse and delineate it conceptually, using it instead as shorthand for the absence of 'pure' capitalism (and thus 'pure' capitalist relations) and/or 'not (or not yet) capitalist'.

Deployed in an untheorized fashion, 'semi-feudalism' has been applied in a contradictory, inconsistent and confusing manner.[9] At times merely a synonym for (and thus interchangeable with) the term

---

imperialism). Like Maoism, such a policy was based on the notion of an intervening bourgeois democratic stage, the existence of which would be characterized by 'progressive' capitalists and a 'pure' capitalism. As Trotsky (1936; 1973) pointed out at the time, such class collaboration led directly to the massacre of workers in China and Spain during the 1930s, when capital demonstrated to all concerned just how 'progressive' it was prepared to be.

[8] Many exponents of semi-feudalism invoke Lenin as a theoretical precursor, despite the fact that the term has little or no theoretical importance in his analysis of transition. Not only did he use the terms 'feudal' and 'semi-feudal' interchangeably, therefore, but in some places Lenin (1963a:377, 488) appeared to suggest that it was compatible with the accumulation process ('[t]here are various kinds of capitalism – the semi-feudal capitalism of the landowners…') while in others that it was not ('the old, semi-feudal, natural, economy had been eroded, while the conditions for the new, bourgeois economy had not yet been created').

[9] The confusion generated by this concept can be illustrated with reference to its contradictory and indistinct role in the analysis by Kotovsky (1964) of agrarian change taking place in 1950s India. The main characteristic of semi-feudalism is described variously as the absence or low level of the productive forces in agriculture, the leasing of land to peasants, and the extraction from peasants of rental payments or compulsory labour (Kotovsky, 1964: 22–3,37,76–7,136,147,153). However, Kotovsky (1964:38, 153 note 2, 161,163) then states that capitalism has developed on the basis of

'feudalism', 'semi-feudalism' has been a metaphor variously for archaic/traditional (as distinct from modern/forward-looking), non-economic (as distinct from economic), economic backwardness (as distinct from economically dynamic/modern), agriculture (as distinct from industry), and landlordism (as distinct from peasant economy). Those attempts to theorize it have succeeded in revealing only the emptiness of this conceptual package.

As with all hybrids, the semi-feudal thesis itself became reified and took on a life of its own during the mode of production debate of the 1970s. Significantly, much of the theoretical dispute about the existence in the Third World countryside of capitalism and semi-feudalism turned on the presence or absence in such contexts of unfree labour: this was true not only of the initial exchanges about Latin America but also of those which subsequently characterized the mode of production debate in India.[10]

The initial participants in the latter debate who were exponents of the semi-feudal thesis maintained that moneylending and debt bondage in India were – and are – archaic relations; because bonded labour was regarded by them as an obstacle to 'pure' capitalist development, unfree labour in the Indian countryside was categorized as a pre-capitalist remnant to be eliminated by capital at the first opportunity.[11]

'the old technical basis of production', and that tenancies entered into by rich peasants are 'not feudal but capitalist-type leases'. The element of indistinctiveness between capitalist and semi-feudal producer is reluctantly acknowledged. 'In reality', he admits (Kotovsky, 1964:26,165), 'it was hard to distinguish between capitalist and pre-capitalist rent in the rental paid by the rich peasant', and further, that '(b)y the type of their economic activity the rich peasants...are vehicles of capitalist as well as semi-feudal relations'. In a similar vein, the same text (Kotovsky, 1964:164–5) notes that during the 1950s zamindar landlords were virtually indistinguishable from rich peasants, and that '[c]haracteristic of the activity of the Indian landlord...are the closely interwoven capitalist and semi-feudal features'.

[10] The debate about feudalism/capitalism in Latin America is encapsulated in the now-classic exchange between Frank (1967) and Laclau (1971). For useful early surveys of the debate about the mode of production in India, see McEachern (1976), Rudra et al. (1978), Goodman and Redclift (1981), and Thorner (1982).

[11] Among the more influential exponents of the semi-feudal thesis contributing to the Indian mode of production debate were Amit Bhaduri (1973), Utsa Patnaik (see her contributions to Rudra et al. 1978), and Pradhan Prasad (1989: 37ff., 95ff.). In Third World rural contexts where it occurs, debt bondage is an unfree relation which involves loans advanced to a worker by a creditor-employer being repaid in the form of compulsory labour-service.

Semi-Feudalism and Relational Transformation

Because their focus is on the coming of capitalism, therefore, exponents of the 'semi-feudal' thesis tend also to focus on unfreedom as an obstacle to capitalist development. By its very nature, such an approach postpones and thus precludes the necessity of having to focus on the coming of socialism; accordingly, exponents of the 'semi-feudal' thesis also miss the fact that unfreedom is now used in the class struggle – and increasingly so – not by feudal landlords in a context where capitalism has yet to develop but by agrarian capitalists (farmers, rich peasants) in situations where capitalism has already developed, in order to pre-empt/prevent conditions that are favourable to the coming of socialism.

Hence a failure on the part of the semi-feudal thesis to appreciate that, in the course of class struggle, relational emancipation can be reversed and unfreedom reintroduced. One important political result of this inability to distinguish between systemic and relational transition is the endorsement of over-optimistic prognoses concerning the current state and probable outcome of class struggle in the countryside.[12] Another is an epistemological requirement to categorize all working arrangements used by agrarian capitalists as free wage labour.[13]

As Petras pointed out long ago, however, in Latin America the cause of rural poverty, inequality and underdevelopment was not – as claimed – 'feudalism' but capitalism.[14] In contrast to exponents of the

---

[12] In the case of India, for example, this has led one exponent of the semi-feudal thesis (Byres, 1999) to claim that as rural labour currently benefits from a combination of 'improved conditions', 'major gains', and 'emancipatory processes', everything is getting better for the agrarian working class.

[13] Ironically, for Kotovsky (1964:157–8) the employment of hired labour in 1950s India was the principal indicator of capitalist development, notwithstanding the fact that this category includes farm servants, who were unfree labourers.

[14] 'The major tactic of this approach,' he argued (Petras, 1970: 378, 379, 382), 'is to ascribe the problems of Latin American development and motivation to "feudalism," "traditionalism," or "Hispanic culture"... Latin landowners who pay low wages and exploit their workers for profits [exponents of this approach maintain,] are not like their counterparts in California or Texas – they are "feudalists" acting out the Spanish heritage.' Rightly, he aligned himself with the approach of Andre Gunder Frank, who 'effectively destroys the myth of the feudal past so often cited and exploited by U.S. scholars as a means of defending capitalist development as a "democratic alternative" to Latin American stagnation.' This critique remains as relevant today as it was then, with the difference that it no longer applies simply to US academics.

semi-feudal thesis, Petras and Veltmeyer point out that in Mexico at the beginning of the twentieth century, where agricultural production had been penetrated by foreign capital, 'brutal forms of torture and labour control [= debt peonage] were not part of an archaic (or "feudal") dynastic order exercising a benign form of authority over the Mexican countryside and its denizens, but the means of maximizing profits for modern capitalists in Europe, North America and Mexico City.'[15] Because they retain within their framework the crucial element of class struggle, therefore, Petras and Veltmeyer are able to make a connection between accumulation and the continued reproduction of unfree labour.

Not the least of the many theoretical difficulties faced by exponents of the semi-feudal thesis (and any political practice based on this), therefore, is that once a transition to capitalism is identified as having been completed, it then becomes necessary for adherents of this view (free labour = capitalist, unfree labour = pre-capitalist) to proclaim all existing production relations are free, any evidence to the contrary notwithstanding.[16] Those 'feudal' relations which remain, or are encountered where they should not be (e.g. on large capitalist farms), are accordingly classified by exponents of the semi-feudal thesis as anomalies, and relegated to the category of residuals; that is, production relations the continuation of which is 'accidental' and which are destined to disappear as 'pure' capitalism spreads throughout the agrarian sector.

II

It is certainly true that there exists a strand of Marxism (= semi-feudal thesis) which associates the presence/absence of capitalism exclusively with a corresponding presence/absence of labour-power that is relationally free. Equally true, however, is that such a view overlooks or downplays an alternative Marxist interpretation (= deproletarianization) of the potential/actual role of unfreedom, which links its reproduction to the class struggle between workers and employers once capitalism is well established. Given the current divergence in Marxist interpretation, therefore, it is necessary to ask the following question.

[15] See Petras and Veltmeyer (2003: 171).

[16] See, for example, the case of Prussian transition considered in Chapter 6.

Is there much support for the claim made by the semi-feudal thesis concerning the developments leading to the formation of a capitalist labour regime in the twenty-first century?

Byres and Sellers of Labour-Power

The kinds of difficulties confronting the semi-feudal thesis can be illustrated with reference to the contradictory nature of arguments advanced by Byres, an influential and long-standing exponent of such arguments, concerning whether or not a transition to capitalism has been accomplished, and why, in the case of twentieth century Asia, Latin America, and Egypt.[17]

Taiwan and South Korea are in his view, 'unmistakable instances of successful agrarian transition', but in Japan a capitalist transition occurred without wage labour and neither landlords nor peasants there became capitalists.[18] The northwestern Indian states of Punjab, Haryana, and Uttar Pradesh, however, are in Byres' opinion instances of a 'wage-based agriculture', that is, of capitalism, developed 'from below' by rich peasants.[19] Latin American countries, we are then told, are all going down the Prussian road of landlord capitalism; except, that is, for the American or farmer road followed by Mexico after 1934, Peru after 1969, and Chile in the 1967–73 period.[20]

Maintaining that the employment by rich peasants and capitalist farmers of permanent attached labourers was indicative of the capitalist nature of agricultural production in India during the early 1970s, Byres describes them as a rural proletariat, despite the fact that such workers were not free.[21] As virtually all writers on rural India agree, workers in attached labour relations at this conjuncture were bonded

---

[17] A lengthy and sustained defence of the semi-feudal thesis is contained in Byres [1996]. For his presentation of the link between unfree production relations, the agrarian question and the process of transition, see also Byres (1995: 565 ff.; 2003: 54–83). For yet earlier references by him to the feudal and/or semi-feudal character of the post-1947 Indian countryside, see Byres (1974: 223, 246, 247, 248, 251).

[18] See Byres (2003: 61, 66). Japan is accordingly categorized as 'a quite distinct capitalist agrarian transition'.

[19] See Byres (2003: 71).

[20] See Byres (2003: 72–3).

[21] Writing a decade later, however, Byres (1982b: 160) was still insisting that a capitalist agriculture had yet to emerge in India, noting '[i]t is the shift of labour that creates the home market, both in the mass market constituted by the growing wage-earning proletariat in the cities and in the market formed by a thoroughly commercialized, capitalist agriculture. Such a shift has not taken place in India'.

by debt, and thus unfree.[22] In the highly commercialized agriculture of India, therefore, Byres is unable to deny that the 'dominant classes' do indeed utilize 'various tied labour arrangements'.[23]

However, he then goes on to describe as 'contradictions' in the emancipatory process (unfree → free) the fact that the incidence of female attached labour has increased, and qualifies it yet further by casting doubt on this being a widespread a phenomenon.[24] What he fails to question is the extent to which such developments in the capitalist labour process (free → unfree) are typical; instead, he categorizes them as 'anomalies' (= 'contradictions') rather than asking whether in fact they *are* anomalies.

The reason for this is not difficult to discern. Like other exponents of the semi-feudal thesis, Byres is trapped by an epistemology which forbids a link not just between capitalism and unfree labour but also between the latter and more advanced forces of production. Because the focus of his analysis is the development of capitalism in Indian agriculture and the role in this of the new technology, therefore, it is necessary for him to define all workers employed in conjunction with this process as free.[25]

What he overlooks, however, is that such instances amounted to workforce decomposition/recomposition undertaken by agrarian

---

[22] See Byres (1972:105,108; 1982b). For the unfree nature in India of attached labour bonded by debt, see the many different examples referred to in Brass (1999: Chapters 3, 4 and 7).

[23] See Byres (1999: 17).

[24] See Byres (1999: 18–9).

[25] The kinds of difficulties to which this epistemology gives rise emerge most clearly in Byres [1982a]. In the first part of that article, dealing with the era which preceded the Green Revolution, not only is freedom defined in terms of Marx's double criteria ('free of the means of production and free to sell its labour power'), but both the presence and the unfree nature of debt bondage is also recognized (Byres, 1982a:34). Once the Green Revolution and the new technology become the focus of the analysis, however, the second of these two conditions – the freedom to sell its labour power – is discarded, and only landlessness is used as a criterion for characterizing a proletariat (Byres, 1982a:39 ff). The contradictions between the first (bonded labour ≠ free) and second part (bonded labour = free) of this text are highlighted in the third, where it transpires that permanent workers described as a 'new [and] particular kind of rural proletariat' are in fact tied to their employers through debt, and unknowingly solved in the fourth, where it emerges that a the object of bonding such permanent workers through debt is to prevent them from personally commodifying their labour-power and developing a consciousness of class (Byres, 1982a:46 ff.,50 ff). The obvious question to ask here is: if these 'new' permanent workers are tied by means of debt, how can they possibly be categorized as free labourers and thus constitutive of a rural proletariat? *Pace* Byres, his case study illustrates both the way in which deproletarianization operates and also the reasons for its existence.

capitalists in the course of their class struggle with rural labour.[26] Rich peasants in each of the 'capitalism-from-below' case studies cited by Byres – Punjab and Haryana in northwestern India, the eastern lowlands of Peru after 1969 – employed bonded labour in order to lower costs and maintain discipline.[27] This suggests that where a class of rich peasant capitalists has emerged over the latter part of the twentieth century, a pattern corresponding to a supposedly more benign form of capitalism (= the American path), agricultural workers employed by them on a permanent, seasonal or temporary basis were not free, as Byres maintains. In other words, accumulation *did* occur in the agrarian sector, but the social relations of production linking landless workers and capitalist proprietors were *not* those characteristic of a rural proletariat.

Byres' dilemma is all too understandable. Having conceded that, following the Green revolution in India capitalist farmers employed attached labourers to operate machinery, it is then epistemologically necessary for him to categorize such workers as free.[28] Otherwise, two of the main planks of his semi-feudal thesis – that both capitalism and advanced productive forces are incompatible with unfree labour – would demonstrably no longer hold true. The same problem is at the root of his difficulties in comprehending the nature of agrarian transformation in the case of Egypt, but with one difference.

Rather than unfree labour being absent because capitalism is present, therefore, debt bondage in rural Egypt is not only recognized as an unfree relation but its presence is invoked in order to cast doubt on

---

[26] The irony of Byres (1987) taking Chakravarty (1987) to task for excluding class struggle from his analysis of the contribution by Marxist political economy to an understanding of development theory, when this is precisely what Byres himself does with regard to the acceptability to capitalist producers of unfree labour, requires no further comment.

[27] Details about the unfree relations of production utilized by rich peasant capitalists in each of these case studies are presented in Brass (1999). That agrarian capitalists still prefer unfree workers to labour-power that is free, not just in the eastern lowlands of Peru but also in both the Santa Cruz region and the north Amazon of Bolivia, is clear from current research into the operation of the *enganche* system in these areas (Assies, 2002; Bedoya Garland and Bedoya Silva-Santisteban, 2005a; 2005b). For confirmation that in Haryana the incidence of unfree labour is as entrenched as ever, see Mukherji and Sahoo (1992), Chowdhry (1993) and Rawal (2004).

[28] Elsewhere, however, Byres (1994:40) is critical of the semi-feudal thesis, noting that its 'insistence upon the tenacity of semi-feudal structures prevents possible recognition of developing capitalist relationships', an observation which, it could be argued, describes his own views on the subject of agrarian production relations rather well.

the efficacy of a transition to capitalism. Thus Byres disputes the claim advanced by Mahmoud Abdel-Fadil that rural Egypt under Nasser had undergone a transition to capitalism on the grounds that landless casual migrants were bonded by debt.[29] The employment by rich peasants of unfree labour, Byres argues, points to incompleteness of a capitalist transition, a situation 'widespread in the so-called Third World'.[30]

Semi-Feudalism and Systemic Transition

Until the 1980s, the semi-feudal thesis was the most common argument made with regard to systemic transition in India and elsewhere, exponents of which insisted that capitalists would replace unfree labour with free workers, a view that still informs much of the discussion about rural transition and the agrarian question.[31] According to this view, all social relations of production in Third World agriculture will gradually metamorphose into those that characterize agriculture in metropolitan capitalist countries.[32] Since in the semi-feudal framework

---

[29] See Abdel-Fadil (1975) and Byres (1977). As the former makes clear, during the period in question capitalist rich peasants who were the beneficiaries of the 1952 agrarian reform in Egypt not only owned the largest amounts of land on which they cultivated mainly commercial crops using advanced productive forces (tractors, irrigation), but were also those who employed the most quantities of labour-power (Abdel-Fadil, 1975: 31,41 ff.). The main source of the latter took the form of gang labour (*tarahil*) composed of casual workers recruited by and under the control of a contractor. Such labour arrangements are characterized in the following unambiguous manner: '*tarahil* labourers are not free agents,' points out Abdel-Fadil (1975:46,48), because 'they are normally attached to their contractors by various bonds (kinship, debts, money advances during the slack season...) [...] consumption-loans are...the main cause of the perpetual indebtedness of the *tarahil* labourer, and hence of his inability to break free from the *tarhila* system dominated by the contractors. Thus the *tarahil* labourer finds himself caught in a system of perpetual bondage as he is always compelled to supply his labour services to the same man, to whom he is perpetually indebted... Such interlocking markets increases the exploitative power of the labour contractors over the landless labourers, and it would thus be misleading to ignore the pervasive nature of this exploitation, which is inherent in the "relations of production" in the Egyptian countryside'.

[30] Byres (1977: 268–9). For the latter, the presence of these unfree *tarahil* casual labourers in rural Egypt 'suggests...that the transition to capitalism is by no means complete', and demonstrates 'the continued existence, not merely as a "feudal remnant" but as a substantial and integral part of the relations of production in the countryside [of] a "semi-feudal" mode of exploitation'.

[31] On the claims made by and the persistence of the semi-feudal thesis, see Brass (2002; 2007; 2008).

[32] As noted by Lukács (1971: 239, original emphasis), 'the view of history favoured by vulgar Marxists has also been a decisive influence on the actions of the workers' parties and on their political theory and tactics. The point at which the disagreement

unfree relations are regarded as pre-capitalist, their presence in any context invariably signals either the absence or incompleteness of a national transition to capitalism.

At the root of the difficulties faced by the semi-feudal thesis is that it conflates what are actually two distinct forms of transition: systemic and relational transformation. Because relational transformation (from unfree to free labour) is equated with systemic transition (from feudalism to capitalism), there is a corresponding misrecognition of the fact that the latter can be realized without necessarily accomplishing the former.

Since Byres restricts his analysis of the agrarian question, and its process of systemic transition, to individual nations, he consequently discounts the crucial role of the wider context in the development of capitalism. Any process of transition, and the way in which the agrarian question is or is not 'resolved', accordingly takes place within a national framework: capitalist development, surplus extraction, and its transfer from agriculture to industry, are all said to occur within the confines of the same nation state. This, Byres insists, is still the case today.

A lack of capitalist development is equated by him with a stagnant home market, itself an effect of the lack of purchasing power by impoverished workers whose low wages are due to the fact that they are unfree. Because he is operating with a model of a closed economy, defined by national boundaries, Byres misses the point that agribusiness enterprises in an international capitalist system break the link between consumption and production.

This interpretation licenses in turn a specific politics. Equating unfree labour with the absence of a 'fully functioning' capitalism, exponents of the semi-feudal thesis maintain that systemic transformation entails a transition not to socialism but much rather to capitalism. For this reason, their political agenda consists of furthering the following strategic objectives: bourgeois democracy, to be realized by means of an all-embracing alliance between workers, peasants and a

with vulgar Marxism is most clearly expressed is the question of *violence*; the role of violence in the struggle to gain and reap the fruits of victory in the proletarian revolution... The position is that vulgar Marxist economism denies that violence has a place in the transition from one economic system to another. It bases itself on the "natural laws" of economic development which are to bring about these transitions by their own impetus and without having recourse to a brute force lying "beyond economics."'

'progressive' national bourgeoisie in order to install a purportedly absent or an as-yet not 'fully functioning' capitalism.

The problem with this approach is an economic one. Even where the crucial and historically important link between worker-as-producer-of-commodities and worker-as-consumer-of-commodities has been broken, the accumulation project of capital continues independently of the purchasing power of a class of workers in a particular location. Surplus extracted by agribusiness from agriculture is reinvested in industry elsewhere, not least through keeping wages for agricultural labour-power low (by means of unfree relations, among other things).

In this way, additional surplus-labour can be extracted and redistributed throughout global circuits of capital. It is also realized in the form of lower food prices, which in turn permit the bundle of wage goods that register as costs of industrial accumulation in other contexts to be lower, thereby contributing to the process of capitalist development elsewhere.

Simply put, it does not matter to agrarian capitalists exporting commodities produced with unfree workers (composed of landless labourers and poor peasants who are bonded) if these are unable to consume, since the market where the output is sold is located elsewhere. Not dependent solely on its own home market, both national and international capital can as a result employ unfree labour, the presence of which would place limits on any economic growth predicated on the existence only of a domestic market. Capitalist development can and does take place where the rural workforce is unfree and thus impoverished, since both accumulation and profitability are determined not by the home market (which may be non-existent or negligible) but by an international one.

The same kind of difficulty faces Byres' inability to recognize the presence of endogenous capitalism within national contexts. Because they employ labour that is unfree, rich peasants cannot in his view be capitalist producers. Although within the ranks of the peasantry 'constrained tendencies towards capitalism might be dimly perceived', therefore, 'nowhere had a class of rich peasants become a class of capitalist farmers'.[33] For this reason, rich peasants are for Byres always on the verge of becoming agrarian capitalists, but they never succeed in making a breakthrough into this category.

---

[33] See Byres (2003: 57).

As long as the workforce employed by rich peasants is unfree, a 'fully functioning' capitalism is destined not merely to be late in spreading to the countryside but never actually to arrive there.[34] For exponents of the semi-feudal thesis such as Byres, therefore, peasants cannot, by definition, be or become capitalists as long as they employ unfree labour. Hence the possibility that capitalist producers might prefer workers who are unfree to free labour is excluded *ab initio*.[35]

[34] This emerges clearly from a comparison of early texts by him with more recent ones. Hence the following assertion (Byres, 1974; 235): 'Rich peasants were not the "masters of the countryside" at Independence – the landlord class was still very much in command – and they were not to be clearly seen in all parts of India. They were a class of capitalist farmers in embryo, in the womb of the old order.' A quarter of a century on, nothing much has changed in this regard. 'Rich peasants,' we are told by Byres (2000: 266) in a much later text, 'constituted a class of proto-capitalists, that still bore the stigmata of a pre-capitalist order.'

[35] Nowhere is this demonstrated more clearly than in the attempt by Byres to dismiss the argument made by Bowman (1993), an earlier and infinitely better comparative study of the US planter class and the Prussian Junkers. Byres (1996: 125) cites in part a long section from Bowman (1993: 110–11), a fuller version of which goes as follows: 'As growing numbers of rural East Elbians migrated to urban centres in the westerly provinces or emigrated to the United States, and as the expanding cultivation of sugar beets increased the demand for large numbers of seasonal labourers, Junker landowners turned rapidly in the 1880s to the seasonal employment of low-wage migratory workers from the Polish districts of the Russian and Austro-Hungarian Empires... Insofar as these migrant Polish labourers were subject to physical abuse, deemed racially and culturally inferior, enjoyed no political rights, and *were not permitted to change employers during the agricultural season (April to November)*, the label "free labour" seems as inappropriate for them as for contemporaneous black sharecroppers. It was not until the German revolution of 1918–19 and the Weimar Republic that agricultural workers achieved a civil and political status equal to that of industrial workers' (emphasis added). Against this view Byres makes the following objection: 'That is simply to confuse concepts nd misunderstand the meaning and nature of free wage labour. Such migrant labour was free of the means of production, and, *despite restrictions during the agricultural season* (*a phenomenon not uncommon among agricultural labourers, and indeed other forms of labour, where capitalist relations prevail*) free to move between seasons' (emphasis added). Unfortunately, it is Byres, not Bowman, who misunderstands the conceptual distinction between free and unfree labour. What Byres forgets is that, for a worker to conform to the Marxist definition of free labour, s/he must have and retain permanently the capacity to commodify or recommodify his/her own labour-power. Where such workers are unable personally and unconditionally to sell their only commodity, labour-power, the social relations of production are not (and cannot be considered to be) free. That Polish workers employed on a seasonal basis in German agriculture were not a proletariat is clear from the trajectory of their employment history (see Chapter 6). In short, Polish workers had been deproletarianized: they were free but became unfree. The italicized portion of the quotation from Byres underlines neatly the dilemma he cannot avoid facing: those using these 'restrictions' (as he admits, 'a phenomenon not uncommon among agricultural labourers') are *capitalists*. Hence the need for Byres to have to define these production relations as 'free', any evidence to the contrary notwithstanding.

Accordingly, the major weaknesses in – and thus objections to – Byres' view of agrarian transition are twofold. First, that it is restricted to an untenable notion of capitalist development as simply and everywhere an endogenous (= national) process.[36] And second, that capitalism is itself defined untenably, as existing only where free wage labour is also present.

On the first point, therefore, the attempt to confine the agrarian question within the boundaries of contemporary nation states ignores the fact that nowadays surplus extracted from agriculture can fuel accumulation and industrialization in national contexts other than that where cultivation initially takes place. Indeed, this is norm throughout much of the so-called Third World, where the financial and investment strategies of agribusiness enterprises are international in scope. This is not, as Byres claims, a 'descent into a kind of "world system" determinism' – that is, determination by globalization – but rather determination by *capitalism*, as located within a global *system* that contains both national and international capital.[37]

---

[36] This is linked in turn to a very old fallacy circulating in the domain of bourgeois political economy (mainly in Germany towards the end of the nineteenth century), and one criticized almost a hundred years ago by Rosa Luxemburg (1954). Even at the start of the twentieth century, therefore, Luxemburg (1954: 10–11) points out that '[a]ll of these advanced countries [with which Economics so exclusively concerns itself] produce for one another, partly also for the most distant parts of the world, and the products of every continent are utilized by them at each step, in consumption as well as production. In the face of such enormously developed mutual exchange, how can we separate the boundaries of the "economy" of this nation from those of another? How can we speak of so and so many "national economies," as if they were economically closed areas which we could analyze each by itself?'. Her conclusion is salutary (Luxemburg, 1954: 24): 'We are discovering that these days [c. 1916] a "commodity" is being exported and imported which King Nebuchadnezzar did not know, nor did his contemporaries, nor did Antiquity, or the Middle Ages. This commodity is *capital.* This "commodity" is not used for the purpose of filling in "certain gaps" in foreign "national economies," but, on the contrary, it produces gaps, creates cracks and fissures in the structures of antiquated types of economies. It penetrates them, and like a charge of dynamite, sooner or later, it reduces these economies to a heap of rubble. Together with this "commodity", capital, even stranger "commodities" are being exported to the entire globe by a few older countries – and in constantly increasing quantities: modern means of transport and the annihilation of entire peoples, money economy and the economic ruin of the peasantry, wealth and poverty, the proletariat and exploitation, insecurity of existence and crises, chaos and revolutions.' (original emphasis) This view – that from the early twentieth century onwards capitalism was an increasingly non-national systemic form, and consequently opposition on the part of workers should be correspondingly international in scope – was undermined by the rise of Stalinist theory. Like bourgeois political economy, it recuperated the epistemology structuring nationalism, and restored the nation to its politically central role in struggles that were henceforth about a transition not to socialism but to capitalism.

[37] See Byres (2003: 58).

III

Because exponents of the semi-feudal thesis perceive the agrarian question principally as a one-off historical stage, confined to a transition from feudalism to capitalism, whereby surplus is transferred to industry, they miss a crucial dimension of the economic development which ensues. Having brought into being a free worker, the subsequent class struggle generated by an accumulation project in Third World agriculture on occasion requires an employer to replace this kind of production relation with one that is unfree.

As is well known, the desirability of a dynamic agriculture, and the obstacles to this, have always been at the centre of non-Marxist discussions about the absence or slowness of economic growth in most less developed countries.[38] However, the reasons for the fusion of non-Marxist and Marxist views about the necessity of Third World development and the role in this of agrarian transformation must be sought in the period after World War II, when bourgeois economic theory attempted to formulate solutions to (and thus avoid a return of) the 1930s capitalist crisis.

Semi-Feudalism and Non-Marxist Development Theory

In order to prevent a recurrence both of the 1930s capitalist crisis and also its political effects (the spread of communism), therefore, Keynesian economics advocated the adoption by bourgeois governments in metropolitan capitalist countries of a dual strategy. First, opposition to cutting real wages, since during the 1930s it was this which led to economic stagnation: that is to say, a reduction in the level of consumption necessarily entailed a decline in capital investment premised on its continued existence. And second, state intervention in the economy, with the object of maintaining full employment, thereby

[38] There are numerous instances, dating from the first half of the twentieth century, of the advocacy by non-Marxist economists, or bourgeois and/or landlord representatives, of rural reconstruction in order to generate economic growth. In the case of Peru, for example, see the work of Klinge (1935; 1944; 1946), an agronomist who was an advisor to the Peruvian landlords' association (SNA, or *Sociedad Nacional Agraria*) and González Tafur (1952); in the case of India, see among many others Voelcker (1897), Sapre (1926), the Linlithgow Commission (Government of India, 1927), Moreland (1929), Mann (1929; 1967), Gangulee (1935), and Huque (1939). Some official documents from this period – for example, that by Keen (1946: 13–4) on the desirability of post-war agricultural improvement in the Middle East – go so far as to identify and attack 'the feudal system' as an obstacle to economic development.

guaranteeing capital the effective demand it needed as an incentive to invest.

A similar strategy was subsequently extended to Third World countries, where the same problem of economic stagnation was met with bourgeois development policies structured by Keynesian demand management, premised in turn on the desirability and interrelatedness of domestic capital accumulation, rural institutional change and the implementation of agrarian reform programmes. Both the 1949 Chinese revolution and the Cuban revolution a decade later served to confirm metropolitan capitalist fears about the political dangers of inaction, and each infused bourgeois development theory with new urgency.

This urgency took the form of a perception by mainstream economics of pre-capitalist relations as obstacles to growth, and thus as a principal cause of underdevelopment and a corresponding weakness (or even absence) of a domestic bourgeoisie in what were mainly rural Third World nations. Accordingly, the post-war rise to academic prominence of the semi-feudal thesis has to be seen as due in no small part to a confluence between it and mainstream economics regarding the desirability of capitalist development in the Third World generally and its agriculture in particular.[39]

Throughout the 1950s the development debate was conducted mainly by historians with reference to case-studies of transition long past.[40] Examining how and why in particular contexts (Europe, Japan)

[39] The list of Marxist and non-Marxist economists (and non-economists) for whom post-war economic growth in the Third World was the *sine qua non* of development theory is a long one, and would include Panikkar (1959), Lewis (1951; 1961), Ward (1961), Kotovsky (1964), Kaldor (1964), Pinto (1965), Balogh (1966), Dobb (1967:50 ff.), Myrdal (1968), Ulyanovsky (1974), Kalecki (1976), Ladejinsky (on whom see Walinsky 1977), and Rastyannikov (1981). Priority allocated to economic growth led some socialists (e.g., Bateson 1946) to downgrade or abandon a change in production relations as part of the transition process. In a strategy described as 'intelligent anti-communism', one American Cold Warrior (Rostow, 1955:12–3) conceded that there were 'lessons to be learned from Indian planning experiences' and asserted that '[t]he American interest in Asian economic growth is an acknowledged part of national policy'. Indeed, the 1959 Cuban revolution demonstrated clearly what might happen throughout the Third World if economic growth did not take place.

[40] The debate at this conjuncture, which included contributions by historians such as Maurice Dobb, Rodney Hilton, Christopher Hill, Georges Lefebvre, Kohachiro Takahashi, and Eric Hobsbawm, is collected in Hilton (1976). In the classical texts of Marxism, the process of accumulation that constitutes capitalist development is itself premised on an agrarian transition that licenses the generation of a surplus which is then transferred from agriculture to industry.

feudalism had been replaced by capitalism, the discussion focused on issues such as the relative importance to these transitions of endogenous versus exogenous variables such as trade and class. Although the parameters were defined by historical materials, some – such as Maurice Dobb – who participated in the debate about historical transitions also took part in subsequent debates about economic growth in the Third World.[41]

Accordingly, the debate about development (and thus transition) underwent a twofold shift, both in terms of emphasis and the kind of case-studies involved. Instead of being concerned with specifically historical instances of transition from feudalism to capitalism, therefore, it was conducted now largely within the domain of the social sciences, and focused on obstacles to contemporary capitalism in underdeveloped social formations.

Semi-Feudalism, Land Reform and Economic Growth

The epistemological confluence became more marked from the 1960s onwards, as non-Marxist development strategy for both Asia and Latin America was premised on the extension of the internal market so as to raise consumer demand for industrial products, which in turn would provide local capitalists with an incentive to invest in productive capacity.[42] Since the theoretical priority of both Marxist and non-Marxists

---

[41] The reasons for this are clear: 'As soon as academic interest shifted [to] economic development and planning,' notes Hobsbawm (1967:7–8), 'the Marxists' theoretical interests became much more obviously relevant. The trend of Dobb's own writings in the postwar period encouraged this *rapprochement* [and] helped to reopen the discussions on the origins of capitalist industrialization, which has increasingly occupied economic historians.' The extent to which this *rapprochement* operated during the post-war period is evident from the fact that an influential spokesperson for British Colonialism (Griffiths, 1946:149) observed in the mid-1940s that 'for many years to come, improved agriculture must be the foundation of India's national prosperity,' while in the mid-1950s United States even non-Marxist anthropology (e.g., Salz, 1955) - that most conservative of academic disciplines in what was anyway a reactionary political climate – was beginning to focus on existing agrarian relations as obstacles to economic development in the Third World, and to realize that industrialization required the transformation of rural estate tenants into workers.

[42] A general statement of the theoretical issues involved is contained in Nurkse (1961:41 ff.). For Asia, see Ward (1961), Myrdal (1968), and Walinsky (1977); for Latin America, see Baer and Kerstenetzky (1964), Chonchol (1965), and Barraclough (1973); for summaries, see O'Brien (1975), and Goodman and Redclift (1981). Since unproductive/feudal landlords were regarded at this conjuncture as the main hindrance to the creation of a mass market, which involved increasing the purchasing power of a mainly rural population on which domestic accumulation depended, bourgeois

approaches at this conjuncture was on how to generate economic growth, a major focus of each became to identify those institutional forms in an agrarian sector of less developed countries which – because they were thought to impede productive efficiency – blocked investment and planning, and thus hindered accumulation by a domestic bourgeoisie.[43]

Although a transition to socialism continued to stay on the political agenda of those such as Dobb, this outcome increasingly ceased to be the focus of Marxists who were exponents of the semi-feudal thesis, whose theoretical gaze remained steadfastly on the presence/absence of conditions favouring capitalism.[44] For non-Marxist and Marxist economists alike, economic growth was regarded by as incompatible with feudal latifundia, a defining characteristic of which was the presence of unfree labour. The presence of the latter relation came to be seen by non-Marxist and Marxist economists as an obstacle to accumulation, while its absence by contrast signalled the realization of a transition to capitalism.

Although the main hindrance to capital accumulation in Third World agriculture was perceived by both as being the unreformed land tenure system controlled by a traditional landowning class, because

---

development strategy was premised on the implementation of agrarian reform programmes. Underutilized large estates owned by unproductive/feudal landlords would be expropriated by the state and redistributed to productive peasant smallholders, thereby raising agricultural output. Not only would the provision of low-cost foodstuffs for the urban workforce save the expenditure of foreign exchange on food inputs, therefore, but increased peasant income would also generate consumer demand in rural areas, and thus stimulate domestic industrialization.

[43] Hence the view (Hobsbawm, 1967:7) that, on the subject of underdevelopment, Dobb's critique 'of the economic orthodoxy of the time ran parallel to the Keynesian one'. It cannot be without significance that four of the participants in the Indian mode of production debate (Ashok Rudra, Amit Bhaduri, Pradhan Prasad, Daniel Thorner) were also contributors to a collection (Mitra, 1974) exploring the role of capital investment and planning in development strategy and the institutional obstacles to this. In his contribution to the latter, Prasad (1974: 262–72) attributes the lack of capital investment in agriculture and the resulting low productivity on peasant smallholdings to the persistence of semi-feudal production relations.

[44] For the continuing importance to him of a socialist transition, see for example Dobb (1940:270 ff.; 1963). There are numerous instances of Marxist texts adhering to a semi-feudal framework which consciously rule out any consideration of a transition to socialism. In their analyses of the agrarian structure/reforms in India during the 1950s and 1960s, neither Kotovsky (1964) nor Rastyannikov (1981) mention the possibility of (let alone the conditions favouring) a socialist transition, their sole concern being the degree to which a capitalist agriculture had developed in the period following Independence.

the power of the latter was based on labour-rent coercively extracted from tenants, unfree relations of production in such contexts were as a consequence equated solely with landlord/tenant relations.[45] Since unfreedom was confined epistemologically to a traditional and thus economically backward landowning class interested only in perpetuating an economically anachronistic (= semi-feudal) agriculture, therefore, it was by definition excluded from agrarian relations involving employers who were forward-looking (= 'progressive'/'pure') capitalist farmers or rich peasants and their landless workers.

Illustrations confirming that the emphasis placed by exponents of the semi-feudal thesis on economic growth, and the consequent perception of unfree labour as an obstacle to this, were also shared by non-Marxists, are not difficult to find. Like the semi-feudal thesis, therefore, neo-classical economic historiography (= 'cliometricians') which rose to prominence in the mid-1970s was informed by the view that unfree labour and capitalism were incompatible, and consequently the search by exponents of the semi-feudal thesis for 'pure' capitalism in Indian agriculture paralleled a similar kind of quest by neo-classical economics for evidence of perfection in markets, prices, competition, and knowledge.

In the case of the debate about chattel slavery in the American South, for example, it was because antebellum cotton plantations were economically efficient that Fogel and Engerman categorized such units as capitalist, as a result of which it was necessary to claim that slaves chose to remain on them in what could only be non-coercive working arrangements and conditions.[46] Much the same was true of subsequent debates about Latin American debt peonage (the *enganche* system) in the period 1870 to 1920 and attached labour in India following the Green Revolution, when unfree labour was similarly delinked from accumulation by neoclassical economists such as Cotlear, Bardhan and Platteau.[47] In all these neo-classical economic analyses of agrarian relations in different contexts at different conjunctures, therefore, coercion is equated with economic inefficiency and thus constitutes evidence of a backward agriculture, while any working arrangements connected

[45] See, for example, Panikkar (1959:50), Myrdal (1968:1039 ff.), Balogh (1963: 37; 1966: 52), Kotovsky (1964), Barraclough (1973: 7–9,33 ff.), and Walinsky (1977).

[46] See Fogel and Engerman (1974: 67–8) and Fogel (1989: 64 ff.).

[47] See Cotlear (1979), Pranab Bardhan (1984), and J.-P. Platteau et al. (1985).

with capitalism are by contrast perceived as non-coercive, and thus freely entered into by the workers concerned.

Both the contradictions inherent in bourgeois development economic theory about unfree labour, and also the extent of the assumptions it shares with the semi-feudal thesis, can be illustrated with reference to the case of Amartya Sen. Accordingly, the latter endorses not only the revisionist 'findings' by neo-classical economic historiography concerning the economically advantageous material conditions enjoyed by plantation slaves in the antebellum American south, but also the semi-feudal view of bonded labour as a pre-capitalist relation.[48]

Since the object of the development debate that took off during the 1960s was simply to augment economic growth, therefore, no difference existed between on the one hand bourgeois economists pressing for capitalist development in the so-called Third World and on the other exponents of the semi-feudal thesis. All sought the holy grail of increased agricultural productivity, and thus what they took to be the obstacles to this.[49]

Common to the semi-feudal thesis and to neo-classical economics was the extirpation of unfree relations of production that each wrongly held was incompatible with the accumulation process in the countryside. When unfree workers were encountered where they should not be – employed in a labour process that was capitalist – one of two theoretical 'solutions' was adopted. Either the labour process in question was declared to be pre-capitalist, and awaiting a transition to capitalism, or the fact of accumulation was accepted and the workers employed there were relabelled as free labour.[50]

---

[48] The weight of evidence to the contrary notwithstanding, Sen (1999: 28–9) accepts at face value the much-criticized 'findings' by Fogel and Engerman (1974) that slaves on the antebellum plantation in the American south enjoyed a higher living standard of living than free workers in the industrial north.

[49] For the centrality to the semi-feudal framework of the systemic conditions licensing increased agricultural productivity, see Byres (2000: 239). It is, in his words (Byres, 2003: 55), a question of 'what is it that has allowed the unleashing of capital accumulation, in both town and country, that has lain at the heart of capitalist transformation'.

[50] For the view that unfree relations of production (= 'semi-feudal features') are incompatible with capital accumulation in agriculture, see Byres (1996: 29, 78). For the relabelling by him of bonded labour employed by capitalist producers as 'free wage labour', see Byres (1996: 38). For examples of the same views – the attempt to redefine as free those unfree workers employed in capitalist agriculture – but this time held by neo-classical economic historians, see Fogel and Engerman (1974) and Steinfeld and

IV

The difficulty with this shared epistemology is obvious. At best, the assumption of non-Marxist political economy was that economic growth would eventually lead to a more egalitarian redistribution of wealth. At worst, that it did not matter if such redistribution failed to occur, since the object of mainstream development theory was simply to promote accumulation. Once bourgeois political economy had succeeded in making industrial growth the centrepiece of the development agenda, its ideological task was accomplished. That of Marxism, however, was not, its object being to formulate theory about the next step: the link between capitalist development and a transition to socialism. This the exponents of the semi-feudal thesis notably failed to do.[51]

Semi-Feudalism and Trotskyism

However, not all forms of Marxist theory fell into this trap. Among those on the left who challenged the view that a 'pure' form of capitalism is the next necessary step in agrarian transition, that capitalists would be 'progressive' under such a bourgeois democratic stage, and that as a consequence unfree labour would then be eliminated, were Trotskyists.

The latter maintained that capitalism was already well-established in the countryside of many Third World contexts, and the principal contradiction was thus between capital and labour and not between capital and labour in one national context and that in another.[52] Trotskyists

---

Engerman (1997). Not the least of the many ironies about this epistemological overlap is that, over the years, Byres has always insisted that a vast theoretical gulf separated his own (semi-feudal) analytical framework from that of neo-classical economists such as Michael Lipton.

[51] Details about this are outlined in Brass (2002). Socialism is not merely nowhere on the semi-feudal agenda, therefore, but never has actually been a part of this (see, for example, Byres 1982a:136; 1991:3; 2005: 85). It is with some relief, one imagines, that Byres (2003: 54) is able finally to join all the other ex-socialists in proclaiming capitalism as the 'saviour' of the holy grail of agricultural productivity. About this shift there can be no question, since he makes it clear in the following observation: 'Whether, with the demise of a socialist path seriously pursued and the disappearance of collective agriculture, one should continue to use the notion of a "third world" and suggest thereby a possible socialist solution to economic backwardness, is, perhaps, doubtful. We may proceed, rather, in terms of "rural societies" in contemporary economically backward, or poor countries, in which, unambiguously, it is capitalism that must be the focus of our attention. It is capitalism that drives such transformation.'

[52] Trotskyists who have argued along these lines include A R Desai (1984).

pointed out that not only does such a view play into the hands of nationalists but also that the two stages theory of agrarian transformation underpinning the semi-feudal thesis ignores the existence and effect of capitalist restructuring.[53]

Hence the semi-feudal thesis identifies while restructuring denies the existence of an economic and political distinction between landlord and peasant capitalists. In contrast to the two stages theory, therefore, the Trotskyist argument is that, for reasons of cost and discipline, rich peasants no less than landlords engage in restructuring the agrarian labour process and thus also seek to replace free labour with its unfree equivalent.[54] Consequently unfreedom is as acceptable to those elements of the 'progressive' national bourgeoisie who, according to exponents of the semi-feudal thesis, would emerge in the democratic stage as representatives of 'pure' capitalism employing only free labour.

Trotsky clearly regarded agrarian relations identified as 'semifeudal' and reproduced by a declining landlord class as in fact capitalist, and thus reproduced by a rural bourgeoisie. This is my view, and accords precisely with my interpretation of unfree labour as deproletarianization undertaken by capital.[55] During the 1970s, a number of commentators

---

[53] That exponents of the semi-feudal thesis are hostile to Trotskyism and Trotskyist views of India as already capitalist is evident from, for example, Patnaik (1995: 79) and Byres (1994: 37–8).

[54] It is precisely because rich peasants would oppose not only any further socialization of the means of production but also the emancipation of unfree labour that Trotskyism advocates the theory of permanent revolution, or an immediate transition to socialism following the expropriation of a ('semi-feudal') landowning class.

[55] Writing in 1931 about the agrarian question in Spain, Trotsky (1973: 77) observed: 'The relationships in the Spanish countryside present a picture of semifeudal exploitation. The poverty of the peasants...the oppression by the landowners, authorities, and village chiefs have already more than once driven the agricultural workers and the peasant poor to the door of open mutiny. Does this mean, however, that even during a revolution bourgeois relations can be purged of feudalism? No. It only means that under the current conditions in Spain, capitalism must use feudal means to exploit the peasantry. To aim the weapon of the revolution against the remnants of the Spanish Middle Ages means to aim it against the very roots of bourgeois rule.' Five year later, in 1937, Trotsky (1973: 307) notes: 'According to [the Stalinists], the Spanish revolution was called upon to solve only its "democratic" tasks, for which a united front with the "democratic" bourgeoisie was indispensible...Fascism, however, is not a feudal but a bourgeois reaction.' Trotsky then goes on to state that the attempt not to 'transgress the bounds of bourgeois democracy' is made in ignorance of the fact that 'the landowners are intimately bound up with the commercial, industrial and banking bourgeoisie, and the bourgeois intelligentsia that depends on them.' He concludes (Trotsky, 1973: 307–8) that 'The agrarian revolution could have been accomplished only *against* the bourgeoisie, and therefore only through measures of the dictatorship of the proletariat. There is no third, intermediate regime.'

took issue with Deutscher's view that Trotsky was a Marxist internationalist who, because his interest was in world revolution, possessed an outlook that extended beyond Russia.[56]

For these commentators, therefore, Trotskyism was essentially about how Marxist theory coped (or failed to cope with) the conditions generated by economic backwardness: hence the view that 'far from being mired in internationalist concerns, [Trotsky] was throughout his life preoccupied with the problem of the relationship and applicability of Marxism to Russia, or, more generally, to backward, non-capitalist societies, and the idea of "world revolution" was an *aspect of this*, not *vice versa*'.[57]

In contrast to the semi-feudal thesis, Trotsky was not interested simply in the Marxist theory about backwardness, much rather the opposite. Precisely because his political objective involved world revolution, and his analytical focus was correspondingly on how capitalism operated and reproduced itself as a (world) system, Trotsky insisted that any meaningful examination of the latter process required an understanding of the way in which accumulation occurred *both* in advanced *and* in backward societies simultaneously, as part of the same systemic unity.[58] In short, his argument was not about economic backwardness *per se*, as claimed, but rather about the contradictions generated by economic *maturity*, or how what happens in seemingly backward societies where apparently non-capitalist (= 'feudal' or 'semi-feudal') relations are supposedly dominant, is actually determined by the unrecognized presence there of advanced capitalist elements.

The Politics of Semi-Feudalism

The political difference between this Trotskyist interpretation and that of the semi-feudal thesis is clear. Having collaborated theoretically and ideologically with bourgeois political economy, by supporting the push for Third World accumulation, exponents of the semi-feudal thesis then continued to repeat the mantra that the agrarian sector of these

---

[56] Among those who subscribed to this kind of critique of Trotskyism were Day (1973), Hodgson (1975), and Knei-Paz (1977). On Trotsky's internationalism, see the justly celebrated trilogy by Deutscher (1954; 1959; 1963).

[57] This is the view of Knei-Paz (1977: 67, emphasis added), who goes on to categorize Trotsky's theory of 'permanent revolution' as the 'revolution of backwardness'.

[58] For more on this interpretation by Trotsky of the way in which capitalism reproduced itself systemically as a process of 'combined and uneven development', see Chapter 2.

countries was 'not yet capitalist' or 'not capitalist enough'. Its proponents still argue, even now, for the necessity of boosting agricultural performance in India, so that the ever elusive agrarian capitalist – the absent 'other' of the semi-feudal framework – may finally emerge onto the historical stage and begin to provide a surplus for what in their view is an as-yet insufficiently realized drive to industrialization.

This, it seems, will continue to be their view as long as the production relations regarded by exponents of the semi-feudal thesis as capitalist – 'pure' wage labour that is free, in other words – are not encountered in agriculture. Since in many parts of the so-called Third World unfree labour is the relation of choice where agrarian capital is concerned, this means in effect postponing opposition to capitalist development there until the Greek Calends.[59]

Rather than occupying an heretical position, therefore, the semi-feudal thesis has found itself in the increasingly dominant mainstream of bourgeois development theory. In this regard there has been a political and ontological departure from the texts not just of Lenin, Trotsky and Kautsky, but also of Mao and Dobb, for whom any talk of a transition that excluded socialism was unthinkable. The significance of this is simply put: some of the participants in the debate about the mode of production in India still maintain that the continued existence of debt bondage relations in agriculture is evidence of semi-feudalism and thus an obstacle to economic growth.[60]

In keeping with such a view, another exponent of the semi-feudal thesis has defended this position, and declared further that '[t]he mode of production debate is by no means spent'.[61] In short, the political role of the semi-feudal thesis is still regarded as politically progressive and a theoretically relevant contribution to the struggle for socialism.

---

[59] The extent of the current overlap between the semi-feudal thesis and neoclassical economic theory regarding the necessity of yet more capitalist development in the so-called Third World is evident from a comparison of Byres' epistemology with that informing the marginalist approach of Lal (2004). The latter, like Byres, argues both that economic growth *per se* is a desirable end and that it is capitalism that will deliver this throughout the Third World. Where such an argument leads is equally clear. Lal concludes that, as empires guarantee economic development, imperial conquests are 'natural', they result in mutual gains and have 'promoted peace and prosperity'. That a neoliberal economist holds this view about the continuing and benign role of the market as a solution to the problems of underdevelopment is unremarkable; that much the same kind of argument underpins the view of a self-proclaimed Marxist is, to put it mildly, surprising.

[60] See, for example, Patnaik (1986: 791) and Prasad (1989).

[61] See the review by Byres (1992: 345,346–7) of Patnaik (1990).

Accordingly, a two stage concept of transition licenses the kind of political conservatism traditionally associated with the non-Trotskyist left, for whom the Third World continues to be composed of 'semi-feudal' nations in the agrarian sector of which there are similarly no 'pure' capitalist relations, and the absence of which precludes a transition to socialism. The legacy of this mistaken political strategy has its roots in the semi-feudal thesis, and remains with us even today; not only are there lessons for the future direction of political practice by those on the left, therefore, but when a history of socialist development theory over the second half of the twentieth century is finally written, a pervading theme will (or should) be a sense of missed opportunity.

Conclusion

For almost three decades now the adherents of the 'semi-feudal' thesis have argued that, as capitalism develops, agribusiness will replace unfree labour with a workforce that is free. Against this it has been argued strongly that there is no inherent tendency on the part of capital to replace unfree production relations with free equivalents, particularly when cost/control considerations – vital in the class struggle – favour the continued employment of labour that is unfree. What exponents of the semi-feudal thesis thought – and think – is that all social relations of production in Third World agriculture will gradually metamorphose into those that characterize agriculture in metropolitan capitalist countries.

By contrast, it is argued here that the exact opposite is the case: agrarian relations in advanced capitalism are increasingly coming to resemble those in Third World agriculture. This arises from the decomposition/recomposition of the global capitalist labour process, a transition that has to be understood in terms of relational and not systemic change. It involves either the replacement of free labour by unfree equivalents, or the conversion of the former into the latter.

Such agrarian transformation is a form of capitalist restructuring that corresponds to deproletarianization, a concept which refers not just to permanent and/or local debt bondage relations but also to ones that extend to include migrant, seasonal and casual workers. In the course of restructuring the labour process, therefore, capitalist producers have not only replaced permanent labour with temporary workers but also shifted the element of unfreedom, from long-term employment to casual/migrant jobs.

Following its theoretical resurgence in connection with Maoism and the success of the 1949 Chinese revolution, the concept 'semi-feudal' was present – mainly by inference – throughout the academic debate of the 1950s and early 1960s about systemic transition. In the course of the development decade, the concept led to the formation of what became known as the semi-feudal thesis, which began to dominate academic interpretations about the causes of growth, stagnation and underdevelopment in the Third World, a framework which achieved intellectual prominence in the 1970s mode of production debate. Throughout this era, this was a position that exponents of the semi-feudal thesis shared with most bourgeois development theory: even neo-classical economics regarded 'pre-capitalist' unfree labour as an obstacle to growth.

There is, however, nothing intrinsically Marxist about economic growth: many non-Marxist development economists have long advocated just such a process. What *is* specifically Marxist about this is its epistemological link with a transition to socialism; without economic growth there can be no capitalism, and without capitalism no socialism. The problem is that Marxists who are exponents of the semi-feudal thesis – like all non-Marxists and most non-Marxist development theory – focus exclusively on economic growth leading to capitalist development. Nothing is said about the transition to socialism, unsurprisingly in the case of bourgeois development theory and rather more surprisingly in the case of those who claim to be Marxists.

Since those who write from with the semi-feudal framework are unable to recognize the central and important role of unfree labour in class struggle generated by the process of capitalist development, the outcome for their analyses in terms of theory is in both cases the same. Epistemologically unable to make this capitalism/unfreedom connection, they mistakenly conclude that, as the countryside in Third World nations is still characterized by archaic relational forms, agriculture continues to be in a pre-capitalist stage. In part, this misinterpretation stems from confining his analysis of capitalist development and markets to national economies, rather than locating them both in an international context. A corollary is that for them capitalism is still a progressive force, to be promoted economically and supported politically. The implications of this, both for development theory and for political practice, are profound.

Because their problematic is restricted to the coming of capitalism, therefore, exponents of the semi-feudal thesis have tended to focus on unfreedom simply as an obstacle to capitalist development. By its very nature, such an approach postpones a consideration of socialism, and thus precludes the necessity of having to examine conditions favourable or antagonistic to *its* development. Accordingly, the semi-feudal thesis also misrecognizes the fact that the role of unfreedom in the class struggle has undergone a dramatic change: in so-called Third World countries, it is now used not by semi-feudal landlords in a context where capitalism has yet to develop but increasingly by agrarian capitalists (farmers, rich peasants) in situations where capitalism has already developed, in order to pre-empt/prevent conditions that are favourable to a socialist transition.

CHAPTER FOUR

'DISGUISED' WAGE LABOUR AND MODERN MARXISM

Like the semi-feudal thesis, the second variant of Marxist theory – the 'disguised' wage labour framework – also regards unfree labour as incompatible with capitalism, but for a different reason. The central flaw of each of these two approaches is easily discerned. In the case of the semi-feudal thesis, it is the assumption that unfree production relations will necessarily give way to free labour-power. The 'disguised' wage labour argument maintains that, since all production relations are free, these are historically ubiquitous. Because it cannot see anything other than feudalism/semi-feudalism, one interpretation (the semi-feudal thesis) maintains that the conditions are still not yet ripe for socialism. By contrast, the other interpretation (the 'disguised' wage labour thesis) cannot see anything other than capitalism, since it regards the wage-form as an 'eternal'/'natural' – and thus a-historical – phenomenon.

In many ways, the epistemology structuring claims about 'disguised' wage labour advanced by Jairus Banaji is the mirror image of that informing deproletarianization. Whereas the latter maintains that in the course of class struggle capital attempts to replace free labour with workers that are unfree, the former by contrast argues that the free/unfree distinction is non-existent, and that all workers in receipt of a wage are simply hired labour. What Banaji has done, in short, is to fetishize the wage, the presence or absence of which for him determines the nature of every and any historical and contemporary relation. Hence the claim he makes about the prevalence of free labour in the eastern Mediterranean during late antiquity.

The reason for dwelling on the study by Banaji of classical antiquity is simply put. Over the years many Marxists have found it necessary to examine the agrarian structure of ancient society (land tenure, mode of production, systemic transformation, peasant economy, free/unfree labour regimes, surplus generation/appropriation, etc.) in order to address the same issues as these occur in contemporary capitalism.[1]

[1] All Marxists are aware of the main trap awaiting those who undertake this retrospective historiographical journey: namely, the conclusion that classical antiquity is in

Of these issues, by far the most important – and theoretically/politically the most contentious – is the nature of the labour regime, and especially the presence/absence/meaning of production relations corresponding to unfree labour.

This is in an important sense fallout from the mode of production debate that took place some four decades ago, in that claims about 'disguised' wage labour form an attempt to reassert the validity of its dominant theoretical framework: namely, that wage labour = hired labour = capitalist relation, therefore paid labour = free wage labour. During the early 1970s Banaji contributed to the debate about the mode of production in Indian agriculture, an important discussion (largely within the domain of Marxist theory) about the causes of development and underdevelopment in Third World countries.[2]

Coercion is ubiquitous, Banaji maintains, and has been applied historically to all known forms of working arrangement. For this reason, he argues, no distinction has existed – or can exist – between free and unfree labour. Consequently, the link between free production relations and a class response by the proletariat to capitalism is dissolved, and with it the impetus for a transition to socialism. Such interpretations contrast absolutely with the one informed by deproletarianisation, which insists that because unfreedom does not lie on a continuum at the end of which is a transition to free labour-power, the free/unfree distinction applies equally to production relations that are capitalist.

This chapter is divided into four sections, of which the first traces the origins of 'disguised' wage labour to debates about the mode of production. Rooted in a discourse about contract, the links between this concept and Marxist and marginalist theory are examined in the second part. The third section considers the application of 'disguised' wage labour to working arrangements in late antiquity, while the fourth looks at its theoretical implications in terms of arguments about systemic transformation.

I

The origins of the problem facing Banaji lie in the notion of class that he inherits from his earlier theoretical flirtation with the semi-feudal

many respects no different from modern capitalism. Most manage to avoid this pitfall: as will be seen below, Banaji unfortunately does not.

[2] See Banaji (1972; 1973; 1977; 1978).

thesis and the 'colonial' mode of production, a difficulty which surfaces in the way he categorizes the colonial workforce.[3] The latter, according to Banaji, consisted of what he termed 'disguised' wage labour, a working arrangement whereby smallholders in the colonies continued to operate their own labour process, but no longer as independent units of production.

Disguised Wage Labour and Peasant Economy

The reproduction of these smallholding units, argues Banaji, was governed by capital, and when the simple commodity enterprise operated in this fashion, it no longer had its 'own laws of motion' but was instead 'a quasi-enterprise with the specific social function of wage labour'.[4] The price which the producer received for the enforced sale of his/her crop was now 'a concealed wage', since 'disguised' wage labour worked mainly on its own land and not that of – or for – others.

For Banaji, therefore, rural households are not differentiated internally along class lines (= peasants-as-workers), composed of family members who in the main *actually* sell their personal labour-power to others. Rather, he perceives the rural household mainly as a unitary form (= peasant-as-cultivator), composed of family members all of whom receive a 'hidden' wage for growing crops on their *own* land.[5] In nineteenth century colonized 'peasant nations', therefore, capital integrated peasant economy into commodity production 'by a process called "forced commercialization"', which did not require dispossession of the direct producer, since s/he continued to work on his/her

[3] References to what is termed the 'colonial' mode of production are found in Banaji (1972; 1973; 1977; and 1978). Class and class struggle were categories absent from the very start. Symptomatically, when considering the rival approaches of Beidelman and Dumont to the *jajmani* relation, widely recognized as the *locus classicus* of bonded labour in rural India, Banaji (1970a) does this in terms of hierarchy and status, and fails even to mention class and class struggle. Nor is the absence of the latter from British social anthropology mentioned by him (Banaji, 1970b) as being among the causes of its crisis.

[4] Banaji (1977: 34).

[5] See, for example, Banaji (1973: 394), where it is stated that '[i]n the colonies which capitalism subjugated [it] did not eradicate tribal modes of production…[t]he populations it encountered consisted largely of peasants and far from uprooting their existing forms of production through their expropriation and conversion into wage labourers, so as to lay the foundations for an internal expansion of its own mode of production, capitalism imparted a certain *solidity* to those forms and even *extended* them…' (original emphasis).

own land.[6] The resulting problems Banaji has with the existence of historically-specific components of a working class, and where capitalism is present his reduction of them all to 'disguised' wage-labour, are fourfold.

First, because he perceives rural households as cultivators who are not in the main dispossessed, and as such cultivate produce for capital, Banaji dismisses the need for capital either to dispossess producers or to form a labour market.[7] Second, he fails to recognize that 'forced commercialization' of peasant cultivation is not the same as bonded labour.[8] Whereas debt bondage entails the appropriation by capital from indebted workers of surplus-value, forced commercialization can involve the appropriation of surplus product by agribusiness from what are in fact other small agrarian capitalists.[9]

Third, notwithstanding that the 'disguised' wage labour is that of smallholding peasants, such cultivators are termed by him a 'proletariat', despite the fact that they are separated neither from the control of a particular employer – they are unfree as a consequence of being indebted to 'monied capitalists' – nor from their means of labour (land).[10] And fourth, because he is unsure as to whether or not debt

---

[6] See Banaji (1972: 2499; 1977: 35; 1978: 381–2, 385) where it is stated clearly that 'this represented the necessary forms of appearance of capitalist relations in the conditions of a small production economy where *the process of labour remained the process of the small producer*' (emphasis added).

[7] Banaji (1977: 36). As always, it is necessary to introduce a caveat, since in the case of nineteenth century Deccan he maintains (Banaji, 1978: 377, 393, 395, 396, 401–2, 404) that peasant dispossession, land transfers and labour market formation all occurred.

[8] Further details about this are contained in Brass (1999: 16, 31–2 note 10).

[9] Hence the forced commercialization of tenant produce by landlords in the Peruvian province of La Convención during the late 1950s resulted in the unfreedom not of the tenants themselves, who were rich peasants, but rather of poor peasant subtenants and/or agricultural labourers employed by these same rich peasants to meet their own labour-service obligations. This case study is examined in Brass (1999: Chapter 2).

[10] For the equation of peasant smallholders and artisans with a proletariat, see Banaji (1978: 365–6, 368, 385, 401, 406–7). The kinds of theoretical contortions to which this gives rise are evident from his confusion in categorizing the *geōrgoi* of late antiquity both as landless workers and as 'substantial peasants' (Banaji, 2001: 192). That a proletariat is composed of the 'disguised' wage labour of peasants, and the resulting idea that all production relations are capitalist, is firmly anchored in his original conceptualization of the mode of production as 'colonial'. According to Banaji (1972: 2500), the difference between the capitalist mode of production in metropolitan and colonial contexts is that, unlike the latter, in the former accumulation was based on advanced productive forces. In the colonies, therefore, accumulation took place on

bondage is actually a capitalist relation, Banaji's theory is unable to account for the fact that rich peasant households can and do become accumulators of capital using intra-kin coercion.[11] Rather than originating externally and affecting all household members uniformly, therefore, such compulsion operates from within the peasant household itself, and affects only the landless members of these same units.

The difficulties to which his kind of theorization (= a proletariat composed of peasants) give rise are evident from Banaji's uncertainty about the historical development of capitalism in India and its connection with the expansion of the working class. Having proclaimed that a 'rapid growth of [India's] working class during the First World war and its aftermath was co-terminous with an expansion of national capital', Banaji subsequently admitted that 'a substantial modern proletariat would emerge only after Independence, with the new period of capital expansion that started in the [nineteen] fifties'.[12]

---

the basis of 'an immense super-exploitation of variable capital' – i.e. not machinery but labour-power. There are enormous difficulties with this view. To begin with, it implies that in metropolitan capitalist context no equivalent process of super-exploitation of labour-power is to be found, which is wrong. As the examples of agriculture in the southern United States and Germany during the 1930s (see Chapter 6), and the current economic importance in Europe and America of the informal sector (= sweatshop industries), all attest, accumulation in metropolitan contexts also involves super-exploitation. Equally problematic is the fact that the metropolitan/colonial dichotomy, overlaid as it is with an additional mechanized/labour-intensive polarity, creates a space for the argument made by exponents of the semi-feudal thesis that unfree labour occurs in colonial contexts because it is incompatible with advanced productive forces, which of course is also wrong.

[11] On the question of whether or not bonded labour is a capitalist relation, Banaji (1978: 387–8, 392, 410, original emphasis) offers diametrically opposed views, both in the same text. At one point, therefore, he states: 'The peasants whom Norman saw [in 1874] were not "bonded labourers" of any variety...the compulsion or element of unfreedom that this assistant collector saw pertained *specifically to the fact* that the small peasants...were not free to dispose of their crop as they chose, so long as they were bound by a capitalist who year after year paid their subsistence-costs (their wages) and to one extent or another controlled their means of production. That is to say, in these relationships there was "no fixed political and social relationship of supremacy and subordination" of the sort that characterizes the feudal economies of Europe'. Later on, however, we are informed both that rich peasants 'regularly utilized permanent farm-labourers on the labour-mortgage system [= bonded labour]', and that 'the tying of labour to this or that individual capital (landowner) does not in the least alter the content of the social relation as one of capitalist domination...such forms of bondage are precisely a characteristic of the *formal* subordination of labour to capital, that is, of a system in which capital retains its individual capital'.

[12] Cf. Banaji (1980b: 214, 264).

Disguised Wage Labour, Feudalism and Capitalism

Significantly, the concept of peasant-as-cultivator is also a legacy of the semi-feudal thesis: for exponents of the latter, therefore, although capital reproduces the peasant household economically, it nevertheless remains external to it. Another legacy, shared by semi-feudalism and the 'colonial' mode of production alike, is the view of the colonial state as the main exploiter of the Indian peasant, albeit 'mediated' by 'monied capitalists'.[13]

What all this suggests is that Banaji has still not broken completely with the main assumption of the semi-feudal thesis to which he originally adhered, in that his 'disguised' wage labourer remains a cultivator working on his/her own land, albeit at the behest of capital. During the course of the earlier mode of production debate, Banaji changed his mind not once but twice. Having been an enthusiastic supporter of Utsa Patnaik (then as now an exponent of the semi-feudal thesis), he then changed his mind and became an opponent of her views.[14] The same is true of his initial endorsement of the concept 'colonial mode of production', which he also jettisoned subsequently.[15]

In reality, the theoretical gap between on the one hand Banaji's smallholder as a 'disguised' wage labourer, and on the other Patnaik's 'pauperized' peasant is vanishingly small. An apparent distinction does, however, exist. Exponents of the semi-feudal thesis define systemic differences in terms of production relations: bonded labour therefore feudalism, wage labour therefore capitalism. Banaji maintains the opposite, and defines production relations by means of the economic system: if capitalism, then all relational forms necessarily correspond to wage labour, which itself designates the workforce as a proletariat.

In the end, both these approaches are not only the same, in that the wage form signals the presence of capitalism, but break with Marx, who maintained that capitalism could and would utilize a variety of

---

[13] Banaji (1978: 364, 379).

[14] As one noted commentator (Thorner, 1982: 1998) on the mode of production debate observes, '[w]here Banaji had earlier intervened as a supporter of Utsa Patnaik, he now classes her…as a practitioner of "extreme formalism"'.

[15] Having noted his earlier enthusiasm for the 'colonial mode of production', the same commentator then observes of a subsequent contribution by Banaji to the debate that 'this time he also eschews any reference to a colonial mode of production'. On this particular *volte face*, see Thorner (1982: 1965, 1998).

relational forms for the purpose of accumulation, a position consistent with the view about deproletarianization, or accumulation on the basis of unfree labour.[16]

II

Rather than attempting an in-depth examination of arguments about unfree labour and the data presented in support of them, Banaji merely restates a position developed some three decades ago.[17] There he attempted to differentiate what he claimed was the 'authentic' meaning of wage-labour, the one that Marx used, from those definitions he dismissed as 'inauthentic' and 'vulgar marxist'. Criticizing the latter for arguing that the mode of production is deducible from relations of production, Banaji accused such interpretations of equating coercion simply with feudalism and serfdom. The inference was that such 'inauthentic' Marxism was unable to make the epistemological connection between unfreedom and accumulation.[18]

Disguised Wage Labour and Marxism

The definition to which Banaji objected then, and objects still, is the view of wage-labour as a commodity, a conceptualization he dismisses as a 'simple category' and thus un-Marxist.[19] In its place, he proposes a concept which is his view not only operates at 'a deeper level of abstraction', where 'wage-labour [is] capital-positing, capital-creating labour', but is one to which Marx himself adhered. In support both of his own conceptualization, and also of his criticisms of what he deems the

[16] That Banaji (2003a: 66) still shares with exponents of the semi-feudal thesis the view that the wage form necessarily signals capitalism is evident from his assertion that 'the real issue here is whether we can sensibly visualise the accumulation of capital being founded on unfree labour... And the obvious response is, no'. The same is clear, for example, from his claim (Banaji, 1978: 387–8) that in mid-nineteenth century Deccan the domination by 'monied capital' over smallholding peasants did not correspond to bonded labour, because for him the latter relation is a characteristic of European feudalism.

[17] Hence the reference by Banaji (2003a: 66 note 56) to his earlier argument contained in Banaji (1977), and the redeployment of the latter in Banaji (2003a: 66 *passim*). Among those who have criticized the views to which Banaji adhered during the 1970s are Chattopadhyay (1978a; 1978b), Wolpe (1980), and Rudra (1990).

[18] Banaji (1977: 6).

[19] Banaji (1977: 6–7). Those dismissed as adherents of the 'inauthentic' view include not just Dobb but also Sweezy.

incorrect view, Banaji invokes the authority of what Marx himself wrote in the *Grundrisse*.[20]

There, however, Marx states quite clearly that free labour is in terms of a consciousness of labour as the property of the self an improvement (= 'advance') over the way this relation is perceived by unfree workers.[21] Neither is it true – as Banaji asserts – that Dobb equates compulsion with pre-capitalist relations of production, since the latter recognizes that, even in metropolitan capitalist contexts (the US, Europe) during the mid-twentieth century, capital has imposed unfreedom on labour where market conditions favoured workers and not employers.[22] Similarly, in invoking the authority of Lenin, Banaji fails to mention that he, too, subscribed to the free/unfree labour distinction.[23]

Not the least of the many difficulties that result from Banaji's failure to problematize unfreedom is his mistaken assumption that any/every kind labour-power that receives wages must as a consequence be free, thereby failing to realize that unfree labourers also get paid and appear in the market, but not as sellers of their own commodity. In doing this, Banaji overlooks the fact that Marx did indeed say that capital used previous relational forms in the accumulation process, but he did *not*

[20] Not the least of the many oddities structuring this attempt by Banaji (1977: 6–7) both to reconceptualize wage-labour and to attribute the result to Marx is the scattered nature of the textual evidence invoked. Whereas references to 'capital-positing, capital-producing labour' are found on page 463 of the *Grundrisse*, evidence for the concreteness of the resulting category is sought from a section of the text some 363 pages earlier!

[21] The relevant text (Marx, 1973: 463) is as follows: 'The recognition [*Erkennung*] of the products as its own, and the judgement that its separation from the conditions of its realization is improper – forcibly imposed – is an enormous [advance in] awareness [*Bewusstsein*], itself the product of the mode of production resting on capital, and as much the knell to its doom as, with the slave's awareness that he cannot be the property of another, the existence of slavery becomes a merely artificial, vegetative existence, and ceases to be able to prevail as the basis of production'.

[22] 'In American mining towns', notes Dobb (1946a: 14), 'it is common for the company to own practically the whole town, sometimes not excluding the magistrates and police. Where this occurs, *the employee may be prevented from transferring to alternative employment* or refusing to accept the employer's contract for fear of losing his home, or in the other case he will be prevented from spending his wages in the cheapest market by the manner in which he is paid. Many of the schemes to lessen the "labour turnover" and *tie the worker to a particular firm*, of which much is heard in America, tend to have a similar effect' (emphasis added). For a similar view about Britain during the 1939–45 war, see Chapter 2.

[23] Thus the resort by capitalist producers to bonded labour is described by Lenin (1960a: 216; 1960b: 484) not only as 'preventing him from changing his "master"' – that is from personally commodifying his/her own labour power, but also as a situation whereby 'the producer is…tied to a definite place and to a definite exploiter'.

say that these forms became free wage labour as a result. As noted in Chapter 2, plantations in the southern US and the Caribbean were indeed capitalist enterprises, but the workforce deployed on them was not composed of 'wage labour' that was free, 'disguised' or otherwise.

It is precisely this aspect – the incapacity of a worker personally to commodify or recommodify his/her labour-power – that for Marxism defines the relation as unfree, and distinguishes it from those relations where workers retain this capacity of commodification/recommodification. The assertion by Banaji, that Marx did not conceptualize wage labour as free or labour-power as a commodity at the level of the individual worker, fails to survive even the most cursory examination. Marx himself insisted that the two defining and interrelated characteristics of wage labour under capitalism are that it must be free, for which its owner must have *and keep* the ability personally to commodify his/her labour-power.[24]

Not only did Engels hold the same view, but he made it clear that he did so in the very same review of *Capital I* that Banaji cites as evidence for the contrary.[25] The centrality to the wage labour relation both of the freedom on the part of the worker concerned to sell labour-power, to sell it personally, and to retain this ability (= 'the absolute right of commodity owners to dispose of their commodities'), is also evident from what other Marxists have written.[26] In cases where labourers possess

[24] That to be free, a worker did not just have to have but had to retain – i.e. to be able to *re*commodify – the capacity to sell his/her labour-power, is clear from Marx (1976a: 271): 'He [= the free worker] must *constantly* treat his labour-power as his own property, his own commodity...[in] this way he manages to alienate (*veräussern*) his labour-power *and to avoid renouncing his rights of ownership over it*' (emphasis added). It is precisely these aspects – the 'constant' ability to recommodify labour-power, and the non-renounciation of personal ownership rights to the latter – that break with bourgeois legal and neoclassical economic notions of 'contract'.

[25] Banaji (2003a: 57 note 18) cites Engels (1985a: 255) in support of the contention that wage labour is not and cannot be free. However, in that same review Engels (1985a: 244–5) – citing Marx (1976a: 270–1) – writes as follows: 'But in order to enable the owner of money to meet the labour-power as a commodity in the market, several conditions have to be fulfilled...*labour-power can appear as a commodity, in the market, so far only as it is offered for sale, or sold, by its own owner, the person whose labour-power it is.* In order to enable its owner to sell it as a commodity, *he must be the free proprietor of his labour-power,* of his person. He and the owner of money meet in the market, and transact business, as each other's peers, *as free and independent owners of commodities*, so far different only that the one is the buyer and the other the seller' (emphasis added). For more along the same lines, see Engels (1985b: 289).

[26] Thus, for example, Kautsky (1936: 59–60) notes: 'Labour-power has to appear in the market as a commodity. What does this mean? ...*the exchange of commodities is*

this capacity, and indeed exercise it by entering a relation from which they are unable to exit, such workers have in Marxist terms been deproletarianized: they *were* free, but *are* unfree.

Disguised Wage Labour and Marginalism

A major difficulty faced by Banaji is a failure to question either the theory or the methodology of the sources he invokes in support of his claims about disguised wage labour. Consequently, he accepts at their face value the arguments of those such as Steinfeld, an anti-Marxist exponent of neo-classical economic historiography, without asking about the way in which these are constructed and what theoretical assumptions inform and political discourse accompany their epistemology. Accordingly, Banaji's a-historical concept of ('disguised') wage labour is not unlike that deployed by neoclassical economic theory: hence the enthusiastic citation by him of Steinfeld.[27] The extent of overlap between their arguments about wage labour and unfreedom is indeed remarkable.

Like Banaji, Steinfeld maintains that, as during the nineteenth century 'neither wage labour nor contract labour had a fixed content', wage labour was essentially no different from contract labour, and consequently no real difference existed between wage (= free) labour and contract (= unfree) labour.[28] Again like Banaji, Steinfeld both complains that wage labour is not viewed as unfree, and erases the difference between free and unfree labour on the grounds that all employment is to some degree regulated.[29]

Steinfeld then goes on to argue that the free/unfree labour polarity is a false (= non-existent) dichotomy, since both free and slave labour

---

based on the absolute right of commodity owners to dispose of their commodities. The owner of labour-power, the worker, must therefore be a free man, if his labour-power is to become a commodity. His labour-power must remain a commodity; consequently, he must not sell it outright, but only for definite periods, else he would become a slave, and be transformed from a commodity owner into a commodity' (emphasis added).

[27] For endorsing citations of Steinfeld (1991; 2001), see not only Banaji (2003a: 56 notes 2, 5 and 6, 57 note 20, 65 note 52, 74 notes 107 and 111), but also Banaji (2001: 208 notes 108 and 113). Ironically, Steinfeld (2001: 13 notes 22–6) attacks Marx for adhering to the free/unfree distinction.

[28] Steinfeld and Engerman (1997). Steinfeld's views are no different from those of his co-author Engerman, whose marginalist economic framework informed the conservative and highly influential revisionist account of *antebellum* plantation slavery as non-coercive/'benign'/'mild'.

[29] Steinfeld (2001: 12).

possess the same ability to choose to work.[30] Not only does this difference-dissolving claim overlook abundant evidence to the contrary, but the categorization of both free and unfree labour as 'choice-making' is redolent of the concept 'subjective preferences' at the centre of neoclassical economic theory. And yet again like Banaji, Steinfeld argues that whether or not coercion exists is ultimately a question of law (economic coercion is governed by law).[31]

That the wage 'contract' once entered into must by definition be free ('entry into' = 'choice') is accordingly central not to Marxism but to the anti-Marxist framework of bourgeois economic theory. Hence the view of Steinfeld – internally consistent for a neoclassical economist but from a Marxist perspective contradictory – is that it was by means of contract enforcement that nineteenth century employers made 'freer labor markets' work.[32] For exponents of bourgeois economics, such as Steinfeld, 'contract' is not just voluntary, but a reciprocal exchange agreed between capital and labour, each of which is perceived as equal.[33] It is in *this* conceptualization, *not* that of Marx, that free labour is imbued with the additional notion of 'consent'.

Marxists, by contrast, see no such thing, and argue that the wage relation is not given (= 'contract-as-*agreement*') – let alone 'eternal',

---

[30] That the epistemology informing neo-classical economic historiographic view about unfree labour – it is 'voluntary', and therefore in a sense 'free' – finds echoes in the justification of slave labour advanced by defendants at the 1945 Nuremberg Trial (HM Attorney-General, 1946: 189) may or may not be significant. Hence the view that '[w]hilst admitting the deportation to Germany and the utilization for the war industries...of millions of workers from the occupied territories, [Plenipotentiary-General for the employment of labour] Saukel denied the criminal character of this action, affirming that the recruitment of labour was allegedly carried out on a voluntary basis.'

[31] Steinfeld and Engerman (1997). Significantly, Banaji (2003a: 56 note 8, 58 notes 21 and 22) eschews specifically Marxist analyses of legal theory, such as Renner (1949) and Pashukanis (1978), preferring instead to base his case about contract on impeccably bourgeois sources such as the *Yale Law Journal* and *Harvard Law Review*. The extent of this influence is evident from the fact that many of the legal sources and case studies that appear in Banaji (2003) are found originally in Steinfeld (2001): thus, for example, Duncan Kennedy, and Robertson v. Baldwin – cited endorsingly in Banaji (2003a: 56 note 5, 57 note 19, 58 note 21) – are also encountered in Steinfeld (2001: 22 note 44, 25 note 52, 72 note 113, 189 note 65, and 270ff.).

[32] Steinfeld (2001: 318).

[33] The bourgeois legal theory structuring neoclassical economic claims about the wage relation as 'contract' being 'free' despite the inability of an indebted worker to exit from it is outlined in Pawate (1953: 6): 'Thus in a contract the assent of the promisor is at the root of the matter and the apparent fetter or bondage that has sprung from the root of free assent cannot be anything but an aspect of the promisor's own freedom. The promisor would be lacking in freedom were he not free to bind himself by his own will'.

'reciprocal' or 'equal' – but rather the object of struggle (= disagreement), and under capitalism the object of class struggle. This neoclassical economic historiography denies, since it does not recognize the existence of class, let alone class struggle, each of which is politically incompatible with discourse about 'contract' based on 'reciprocity', 'equality' and 'consent'.[34] Formal conditions governing 'contract' say nothing about the reality on the ground, which focuses on class and class struggle, or the differential capacity of each party either to disregard or to enforce contractually binding legal conditions. Not only is class and class struggle abolished by the neoclassical concept of an employer/worker equilibrium, but wage labour becomes – like capital (= 'saving') itself – an ever-present (and thus 'natural') category, a pan-historical form that underlies all known working relations/arrangements, and now features in the economic transactions of the trinity formula merely as one 'factor of production'.[35]

III

The pan-historical category of wage labour (= 'contract') which Banaji shares with neoclassical economic historians such as Steinfeld– together with its theoretical implications – can now be found in late antiquity,

---

[34] At times Steinfeld (2001: 317, 320, 321) comes close to recognizing this. Without mentioning class struggle, therefore, he accepts that employers 'were using forms of legal compulsion to tie workers to jobs for longer or shorter periods because they hoped to reduce labor costs by taking these steps… Only when American labor became better organized after the Civil War…was legislation passed that cut back contract remedies even further… In both England and the United States a broad suffrage, together with a well-organized labor movement and a set of arguments that resonated widely because they drew on fundamental values, seem to have been crucial for establishing a contracts policy that imposed strict limitations on [employers]'.

[35] It is impossible to improve on Sweezy's (1946: 6–7) description of the a-historicism structuring marginalist economics: '[T]he particular concept "wages", which plays a role in all modern [bourgeois] economic theories…is taken from everyday language in which it signifies the sums of money paid at short intervals by an employer to hired workmen. Economic theory, however, has emptied out this social content and has redefined the word to mean product, whether expressed in value or in physical terms, which is imputable to human activity engaged in a productive process in general. Thus Robinson Crusoe, the self-employed artisan, and the small peasant proprietor as well as the factory labourer all earn wages in this sense, though in common parlance, of course, only the last-named is properly to be regarded as the recipient of wages. In other words, *"wages" becomes a universal category of economic life (the struggle to overcome scarcity) instead of a category relevant to a particular historical form of society*' (emphasis added). A similar critique of marginalist economic theory is found in Bukharin (1927).

which is precisely where Banaji encounters it.[36] It comes as no surprise that his claims about the prevalence of free labour in the eastern Mediterranean countryside in the period between the fourth and seventh century project backwards – and simultaneously replicate the mistaken assumptions – of neoclassical economic historiography. When observing that slaves worked as hired labourers, on nineteenth century cotton plantations no less than in ancient society, therefore, Banaji makes a common methodological error, and assumes that the sale of labour-power by slaves was no different from that by other wage workers.[37]

Hired Workers in/as Ancient History

Every kind of production relation Banaji encounters in late antiquity is re-categorized by him as wage labour that is 'free'. Although members of the 'small' aristocracy relied on sharecropping, therefore, according to Banaji the sharecropper was essentially a labourer.[38] Similarly, permanent workers or farm servants were not serfs, and – because they were landless – peasants employed on estates were 'a largely proletarianized labour force'.[39] Equally, labour-service tenants are regarded merely as one kind of worker, along with other skilled labour (carpenters, smiths, potters, etc.) 'employed on a range of contracts'. The reason for this is that, in his opinion, 'no evidence survives as to the kind of contracts through which these rural labourers were "attached" to their employers', that 'binding peasants to the soil' was unnecessary and unconnected with agricultural production, and that workers employed in the latter activity were free.[40]

---

[36] The questionable claim made in Banaji (2001) is that late antiquity not only saw the emergence of a 'new' aristocratic elite that invested in agricultural production, but – and more problematically – that such landlords utilized a workforce composed of hired workers ('free wage labour', in other words).

[37] See Banaji (2001: 217 and note 21).

[38] See Banaji (2001: 167, 181, 200).

[39] See Banaji (2001: 181). In arguing that permanent workers were free, Banaji replicates the claim advanced earlier by Rathbone (1991: Chapter 3) who, because he utilizes a crude slave/non-slave dichotomy, deems that all rural working arrangements in third century Egypt not involving slaves are automatically 'free'. Since he was not a participant in the debate about the mode of production, Rathbone can be excused for making this basic theoretical error; because he did participate in that debate, Banaji has no such excuse.

[40] See Banaji (2001: 5, 90, 93, 186).

He then commends a source that 'rejects the usual interpretation of the *enapographoi geōrgoi* [= estate workers] as a semi-servile labour force', noting that such workers were paid monthly, and were not tenants.[41] Not only did the 'small' aristocracy engaged in wine cultivation employ hired labour (paid in gold coin) on their estates, mainly for the purposes of irrigation, but 'skilled workers were paid high rates of money wages, cash payments were widespread suggesting...a continuing demand for labour'.[42] It is the existence of money in rural transactions that, according to Banaji, constitutes evidence for the widespread presence of hired labour in the countryside, thereby revealing the structure of his teleology (money = wages = hired labour = free workers). This teleology extends to other issues as well: the 'fact' of 'free' wage labour is itself dependent on the increased ('free') availability of workers, which in turn rests on population growth in the Mediterranean during the sixth and seventh centuries.[43] On the latter rests additionally the argument about production increases by landlords. Needless to say, all these claims are either empirically unproven or theoretically unsustainable (and frequently both).

To begin with, the claim that 'I break with the widespread orthodoxy that wage labour has been of only marginal importance in so-called "pre-capitalist" forms of economy', and that by inference he is the first to argue for the existence in ancient society of free labour is quite simply wrong, a point subsequently conceded.[44] Not only is this argument itself an old one, and the criticisms made of it equally well-known, but scattered throughout the historiography of ancient society are periodic assertions that wage labour was a crucial (not to say the dominant) relational form in specific contexts at particular conjunctures.

---

[41] See Banaji (2001: 97, 108).

[42] See Banaji (2001: 164, 165–6). Again like Banaji, Starr (1977: 148) cites the installation and maintenance of irrigation as a reason for the employment of wage labour ('in the Near East irrigation and drainage required the cooperation of great masses of rural labourers who worked under common direction').

[43] Hence the view (Banaji, 2001: 168) that '[t]he use of paid labour for irrigation was widespread...indicating both an increased demand for such labour and perhaps an increased supply of wage labour more generally'. That labour was 'freely available' (Banaji, 2001: 181) then becomes additional 'proof' for on the one hand the existence of abundant workers and on the other the claim that the latter were 'free' wage labourers.

[44] See Banaji (2001: 5), who then accepts that in antiquity the economy 'had always depended to some degree on reserves of free labour' (Banaji, 2001: 188), a view which contrasts with his earlier claim that no one but himself recognized this.

Towards the latter part of the nineteenth century, Mommsen, Cicciotti and Bücher, for whom free wage labour was a common feature of employment patterns in ancient Greece and Rome, advanced this very position.[45] Some sixty years ago the same argument was made by Thomson, who maintained that cheap hired labour was employed on a seasonal basis, and that because the slave population in Attica during the sixth century BC was small and the demand for agricultural labour was seasonal, the latter was met by free wage labour.[46]

In the late 1940s and early 1950s Siegel, Westermann, Starr, and Hammond advanced a similar view about ancient society.[47] Although his analysis was about slavery, Westermann maintained – wrongly – that unfree workers were in many instances hired labourers, a misinterpretation noted by de Ste Croix.[48] For his part, Hammond noted that in Greece '[s]laves in most states worked alongside of free men…as harvesters winnowing grain… [u]sually an owner put slaves to work

---

[45] Noting that in the rural workforce of ancient Rome slaves were 'far less numerous' than other forms of labour, Mommsen (1864, I: 200) observes that free workers outnumbered slaves. He continues: 'In Greece "day labourers" in various instances during the early period occupy the place of slaves of a later age, and in some communities, among the Locrians for instance, there was no slavery…'. On Ciccotti's *Il tramonto della schiavitù nel mondo antico* (1899), see Finley (1983a: 42). About the prevalence of free workers in ancient society Bücher (1901: 96 note 7) – whose work on antiquity is cited by Banaji (2001: 24, 31, 32, 91, 221) – makes the following observation: 'In my work on the the insurrections of the unfree labourers between 143 and 129 B.C. (*Die Aufstände d. unfreien Arbeiter, 143–129 v. Chr.*, Fr.-a.-M., 1874), I have shown that before the rise of slave-work on a large scale the economic life of antiquity furnished considerable scope for free labour, the formation of separate trades, and the exchange of goods.'

[46] See Thomson (1941: 71, 154–5). The similarities do not end there. Like Banaji, Thomson (1941: 345) insisted that slaves were a proletariat, despite the fact that they were not free.

[47] These views were presented in an article by Siegel (1947); in book form by Westermann (1955) and Hammond (1959); and in an influential 1958 article by Starr (1979a). The latter reproduced the same argument in a subsequent book (Starr, 1977: 155), where he concluded that 'a very considerable part of the Athenian populace either had no land or else their plots were too small for a secure livelihood, and they provided a large reservoir of labor for the seasonal demands of their richer neighbors'.

[48] See, for example, Westermann (1955: 18, 91). Where the free/unfree distinction is involved, de Ste Croix (1957: 55) pointed out that '[t]here are also very many errors of fact and interpretation, as when the slaves referred to by Pliny…are presented [by Westermann] as hired labourers, and we are given an entirely false picture of Pliny and his neighbours as "employing outside hired labour rather than using slaves of their own"'. Westermann also failed to note both the fact that edicts freeing Athenian slaves were cancelled immediately, and the presence of slaves owned by aristocrats in the Later Empire (de Ste Croix, 1957: 55).

on his own account, or else he hired them out to others and took part of the proceeds (*apophora*).'[49] In a similar vein, Starr insisted that '[e]ven in the field of agriculture, I suspect – though this criticism cannot be statistically proved – that in Italy as a whole the place of slaves is usually overemphasized. It is commonly agreed that the rich Po valley was farmed by free men, and the same may be assumed of the poor farming valleys in the hills'.[50]

More recently, both the presence and economic significance of hired labour in ancient society has been noted by many others, including Dandamaev, Welskopf, Skydsgaard, Whittaker, Garnsey, Kreissig, Powell, Klengel, Rathbone and Wood.[51] Hence the prevalence of hired labour is not – as Banaji insists – a departure from existing orthodoxy.

---

[49] On this point, see Hammond (1959: 527), who emphasizes the practice by slave-owners of leasing out their unfree workers to other employers.

[50] See Starr (1979b: 54), who attempted to demonstrate the importance of free labour by focusing on the numerical insignificance of slaves in the workforce. Slave labour could then be said not to be as important economically as free workers. This, as Degler (1959: 273) pointed out at the time, meant that Starr ended up posing the wrong question. The right question was not 'did slaves do most of the work?' but rather 'what role did they play in the economic process?'. It was the latter question that informed the subsequent analysis by de Ste Croix (1981), whose focus was on the economic role of unfree labour in Classical Antiquity, and for whom 'the most distinguishing feature of a given mode of production is not so much *how the bulk of the labour of production is done*, as *how the dominant propertied classes*, controlling the conditions of production, *ensure the extraction of surplus*' (de Ste Croix, 1988: 20, original emphasis). According to Brunt [1971: 196], in Italy between 225 B.C. and A.D. 14 '[l]arge estates may not have excluded the use of free labour...*latifondisti* may have recruited and brought free labourers from the south'. He adds (Brunt, 1971: 703) that 'the ratio of slaves to free in Roman Italy falls far short of that in the British West Indies, where they formed 86 per cent of the population about 1790'.

[51] Dandamaev (1986) notes the widespread availability of hired labour in Babylonia in the period between the fourth and seventh centuries B.C. Welskopf ('Free Labour in the City of Athens'), Skydsgaard ('Non-slave Labour in Rural Italy during the Late Republic'), Whittaker ('Rural Labour in Three Roman Provinces'), and Garnsey ('Non-slave Labour in the Roman World') all contribute to the collection edited by Garnsey (1980). For analogous findings, see Kreissig (1978), Powell (1978) and Klengel (1978). Similarly, Rathbone (1989; 1991) outlines at length and in some detail the presence of paid workers in rural Egypt during the third century A.D. The following observation by Wood (1998: 3) confirms the extent to which the argument claimed by Banaji as new and his is in fact neither: '[w]hile disputes still rage about the extent and function of slavery, scholarly opinion is all but unanimous in the view that many Greek citizens, and more particularly the majority in the most culturally vigorous polis, Athens, worked for a living as peasants, craftsmen, and even casual labourers'. Even history textbooks about late antiquity designed specifically for a non-specialist audience observe both that 'hired labour had been used alongside slaves for centuries, especially at peak times like harvest...' (Cameron, 1993: 120), and that 'it can be supposed that on the evidence of certain estates in Asia Minor that slaves only formed ten to twelve per cent of the agricultural workforce' (Fossier, 1989: 29).

Contrary to his assertion, this view is far from novel, and the more interesting issue, in terms of the political implications, is who opposes arguments about unfree labour, and why.[52] To say that hired labour was present in ancient society (as many historians have done) is not the same as claiming – as does Banaji – that it was 'free', and consequently no difference exists between it and unfree labour.[53]

Evidence advanced by Banaji that a 'new' workforce is composed of 'free' wage labour is methodologically problematic.[54] Hence the contradictory statement that 'the papyri are a far better clue as to how employers used labour, *at least in the limited regions and areas of production which mainly figure in these documents (that is, a handful of districts among well over seventy, and chiefly agriculture)*' (emphasis added).[55] The degree to which such flimsy evidence is itself stretched is apparent, for example, from the claim that 'labour cost considerations' imply a 'dependence on hired labour'; they imply nothing of the sort, of course, since 'labour cost considerations' might just as easily refer to the purchase of slaves.[56]

In support of his argument, he cites as 'free labour' the terms *ouvriers agricoles* and *ouvriers salariés* used by a source, forgetting that in the latter these are conceptualized simply as agricultural or hired workers, which says nothing about whether such workers were free or unfree.[57] Similarly, it is inferred that the reason one employer manumitted his entire slave workforce was because he was a 'new' kind of producer,

---

[52] The relay-in-statement to which Banaji subscribes (contract = free labour = early capitalism), plus the political identity of those who share this view, are issues examined below.

[53] Among the historians of ancient society who have in the past resisted any attempt to conflate free and unfree labour, thereby eradicating the free/unfree distinction, are Austin and Vidal-Naquet (1977: 45) and Finley (1983a: Ch. 2). Even when disagreements occur – as they do between Finley (1983b: 97 ff.) and de Ste Croix (1988: 21) over the role and incidence of unfree labour in ancient Greece – the fact of unfree labour, together with its relational specificity, is not disputed.

[54] Hence the view (Banaji, 2001: 93) that in Egypt the 'large estate regulated its work relationships by written agreements, using the contract as a general means of control over obligations…' conveys the impression that members of the workforce gave written consent (= 'written agreements') to working arrangements (= contract) into which they entered. Were all the wage labourers who were party to these contracts literate, and if not, what are the implications of this for any notion of 'consent' (= freedom) informing such 'agreements'?

[55] See Banaji (2001; 197–8).

[56] See Banaji (2001; 203).

[57] See Banaji (2001; 92). This criticism is also true of the same kind of claim made elsewhere by Banaji (1999: 200), where he cites a source ('les ouvriers attachés pendant l'année aux travaux de l'exploitation') in support of his view that Egyptian tenants were

interested only in hiring wage labour.[58] This idealized view overlooks the fact that – where/when they occur – such 'benign' acts have been and are motivated not by the desire to eliminate unfreedom, but to replace old, worn-out unfree workers with younger, more productive equivalents.[59]

Hired Workers = Free Wage Labour?

Given these methodological problems, it is in a sense unsurprising that all the production relations classified by Banaji as 'free' wage labour were much rather unfree, structured by debt bondage, cash advances and coercion.[60] Thus the assertions made by him initially, about there being no evidence either of attached labour or of peasants bound to the soil, are subsequently shown to be incorrect. As will be seen below, however, the fact that production relations classified by Banaji as 'free' turn out to be unfree derives mainly from theoretical causes, and in particular his equation of hired labour with contract, an analytical approach to work relations he shares not with Marxism but rather with anti-Marxist neo-classical economic historiography. Where rural Egypt in classical antiquity is concerned, Banaji bases his argument about labour contract on the earlier work of Rathbone, in the process reproducing all the assumptions of the latter (rural labour was free)

---

simply permanent labourers who were paid. As the source itself suggests, however, the workers in question were attached labourers employed on a yearly basis who – like their counterparts in rural India – were (and are) unfree.

[58] See Banaji (2001; 125).

[59] It is important to be aware of the precise dynamic underlying the act of manumission: that unfreedom ends for a specific individual when s/he is no longer economically useful, who is then replaced by another individual to whom the same relational constraints apply. In other words, for the duration of his/her economically active life, the worker concerned was unfree, and it was only after this came to an end that the subject was emancipated. To claim that the incidence of manumission is somehow always an indicator of free *labour* is therefore wrong. The economic benefit slave-owners in ancient society derived from manumission is clear. Hence the money paid by slaves to their master in order to purchase their freedom enabled the latter to replace older slaves with younger ones (Edmunds, 1873: 143–4; Kautsky, 1925: 156; Hopkins, 1978: 128, 131–2). Much the same is true of nineteenth century Brazil, where plantation slaves who became too old for work were manumitted by their 'generous' masters (Degler, 1976), and also of Bihar during the 1980s, where producers encouraged older bonded labourers (whose usefulness as agricultural workers had ended) to free themselves, yet strongly resisted attempts at self-emancipation on the part of younger bonded labourers (Tiwary 1985).

[60] On the unfree character of working arrangements classified as 'free', see Banaji (2001; 186 note 108, 191, 204, 205).

and consequently all his mistakes (production relations were actually unfree).[61]

Not only did big landlords want 'lifelong control over [labour with] skills which may have been in short supply', but 'the reason why landowners felt it was necessary to bind workers through a [contractual] clause of this type may well have been their…mobility between several jobs (different estates) in the course of the year'. Moreover, '[i]t seems likely that these were bonds which employers used to tie labour down or strengthen their own control over its exertion – a common feature of rural labour markets', and further, that '[d]ebt was the essential means by which employers enforced control over the supply of labour, fragmenting the solidarity of workers and "personalizing" relations between owners and employees'.[62]

Exemplified by the *paramonē* arrangement – classified by de Ste Croix as the commonest form of debt bondage throughout the ancient world – unfreedom is for Banaji merely a relationally non-specific form of 'standard employment contract', amounting in his opinion to no more than 'intense landlord control'.[63] Not only is the latter term a-historical, eliminating as it does both production relations and the element of systemic specificity linked to them, but slavery itself could be dismissed as simply one more form of 'intense control'.

Neither is it the case that employment of hired labour (*geōrgoi*) to irrigate crops is of itself evidence for the existence of 'free' wage labour.[64] Migrants employed for exactly the same purpose – tasks connected with irrigation – in the northwestern states of India currently are not free workers but much rather bonded labour. That the same is true of

---

[61] Rathbone (1991: 89ff., 107, 111, 115, 116, 391) categorizes permanent workers (*paidarion, oiketes, metrematiaios*) in third century rural Egypt as 'free contracted labourers' because they were juridically free, received payment, and – unlike slaves – had wives and families.

[62] The latter are just a few of the many examples found in Banaji (2001: Chapter 8) that confirm labour-power was unfree.

[63] For working arrangements described as 'intense landlord control', see Banaji (2001: 200, 210). On the subject of unfree labour in ancient society, and how historiography has tended to underestimate this, de Ste Croix (1984: 108) observes that 'debt bondage existed…on a far larger scale than the vast majority of ancient historians have recognized'. Significantly, Marx (1976a: 233) argued that '[t]he class struggle in the ancient world…took the form mainly of a contest between debtors and creditors, and ended in Rome with the ruin of the plebeian debtors, who were replaced by slaves', thereby confirming the interpretation of de Ste Croix concerning the importance of debt.

[64] Thompson (2003: 211, 214) provides evidence of irrigation systems in classical antiquity operated by slave labour.

geōrgoi in late antiquity emerges when the characteristics of the workforce classified by Banaji as 'free' wage labour finally emerge. Thus it turns out that what has hitherto been termed 'wages' paid to hired workers are actually cash advances, the classic method of bonding labour.[65]

As long as permanent workers on an estate were unable to reimburse such cash (or kind) advances, regarded by the landowners as a loan, they were permitted neither to quit existing employment nor to work for another employer.[66] Confronted by the fact that landowners withhold wages from their permanent workers – another familiar way of immobilizing labour – Banaji explains this away by arguing that, as such coercive mechanisms occur everywhere, their presence in classical Rome is somehow unexceptional.[67] This misses the point entirely, which is not that these same relations are found currently, an observation that is incontrovertible, but rather what kind of relations they are, wherever and whenever they may be encountered.

Perhaps sensing the degree to which his earlier classification of such workers as 'free' is no longer tenable, Banaji offers contradictory accounts of the implications of indebtedness for worker mobility.[68] On the one hand, therefore, he states that no element of constraint on the freedom of the worker was involved ('it is not clear...whether such *geōrgoi* were either barred or discouraged from working for other employers during the period of the agreement'), and on the other that the intention of landowners were precisely to bond the worker ('the reason why landowners felt it was necessary to bind workers through a clause of this type may well have been their...mobility between several

[65] See Banaji (2001: 183, 198, 200).

[66] The object of advance payment, Banaji (2001: 205, note 98) concedes, was that a worker 'would "serve continuously" with the creditor' – becoming as a result a labourer who was bonded to a particular landowner. That a labourer who owed his current employer a debt as a result of having accepted from him/her a cash advance was not permitted to seek alternative employment, or withdraw from employment altogether, without first repaying the sum is evident from the fact that an indebted worker 'agreed he would return the advance if he showed any intention of abandoning the job before the expiry of his contract' (Banaji, 2001: 169). The latter is repeated verbatim later on in the book, perhaps to reinforce the point: 'the worker would "return" the amount advanced...just in case he abandoned his contract before its date of expiry' (Banaji, 2001: 191). The fact that *geōrgoi* who were sharecroppers were deprived of their share 'through debt relations' (Banaji, 2001: 204) hints at the difficulty – not to say impossibility – of debt repayment.

[67] See Banaji (2001; 198).

[68] For these accounts, see Banaji (2001: 191).

jobs (different estates) in the course of the year').[69] Exactly! The object of the debt bondage mechanism – for that is what Banaji has in effect described – was precisely to curtail the freedom of a worker thus indebted to change jobs: to sell his/her labour-power elsewhere, in other words.

Late Antiquity as Early Capitalism?

One could be forgiven for thinking that, of the many historiographical traditions, the investigation of ancient society would be the least likely to bear the marks of current political anxieties faced by its practioners. More than most, classical scholars generally, and particularly those who carried out philological research during the nineteenth century, manage to convey the impression of a detached 'other-worldliness' that precludes – forbids, even – an intrusion of contemporary issues and debates.

The exact opposite turns out to be the case, in that discourse concerning antiquity throughout the nineteenth and twentieth centuries tends not merely to embody but accurately to reflect the ideological and political battles being waged in the society to which its historians belonged.[70] Chief among these was the way in which a fear of socialism

---

[69] This claim – that indebtedness possessed no implications for worker freedom – is anyway a surprising one to make, since elsewhere in the ancient world indebtedness by the propertyless invariably resulted in the imposition of constraints on economic mobility. Thus, for example, some five hundred years before the period considered by Banaji, debtors in Alexandria who owned property used it to cancel loans, while those who were propertyless repaid debts in the form of work, becoming as a result debtor-slaves (*hypochrea somata*) or bonded labourers (Westermann, 1929: 48–9). Rather than the acceptance of possessions belonging to a free person in lieu of debt, therefore, such arrangements entailed the seizure by a creditor of the labour-power belonging to the debtor. The latter was consequently unable to work for someone else (or on his/her own account) for as long as the debt in question remained undischarged.

[70] For accounts from different theoretical viewpoints of these debates about ancient society, see Vogt (1974: 170 ff.), Starr (1979c: 301–12) and Finley (1983a). The extent to which contemporary issues informed the historiography of classical antiquity is clear from the following observation by Carr (1961: 30–1) about the political sub-text to Grote's *History of Greece* and Mommsen's (1864–67) *History of Rome*: 'Grote, an enlightened radical banker writing in the 1840s, embodied the aspirations of the rising and politically progressive middle class in an idealized picture of Athenian democracy, in which Pericles figured as a Benthamite reformer, and Athens acquired an empire in a fit of absence of mind. It may not be fanciful to suggest that Grote's neglect of the problem of slavery in Athens reflected the failure of the group to which he belonged to face the problem of the new English factory working class. Mommsen was a German liberal, disillusioned by the muddles and humiliations of the German revolution of

in late nineteenth century and early twentieth century Europe structured the highly influential interpretations of ancient society by anti-Marxist historians such as Meyer, Pöhlmann, Guirard, and Rostovtzeff.[71] All the latter not only objected to Marxist interpretations of ancient slavery but also 'read' antiquity in terms of a warning against what might happen in their own societies were certain developments to remain unchecked.[72]

The same is true of subsequent ancient historiography, particularly as this concerned slavery and its interpretation. Thus, for example, Starr accused 'Marxist popularizers' of having 'magnified the effects of slavery in the ancient world', deriding them for arguing that 'slavery was the basic flaw of classical civilization [and that] the ancient world was doomed – a tidy lesson for those benighted modern men who refused to hasten the victory of Marxian socialism'.[73] His conclusion

---

1848–49. Writing in the 1850s...Mommsen was imbued with the sense of need for a strong man to clear up the mess left by the failure of the German people to realize its political aspirations; and we shall never appreciate his history at its true value unless we realize that his well-known idealization of Caesar is the product of his yearning for the strong man to save Germany from ruin, and that the lawyer-politician Cicero...has walked straight out of the debates of the Paulkirche in Frankfurt in 1848. Indeed, I should not think it an outrageous paradox if someone were to say that Grote's *History of Greece* has quite as much to tell us today about the thought of the English philosophical radicals in the 1840s as about Athenian democracy in the fifth century B.C., or that anyone wishing to understand what 1848 did to the German liberals should take Mommsen's *History of Rome* as one of his text-books'.

[71] For the anti-Marxist views of some of these ancient historians, see Finley (1983a: 45 ff.) and Kautsky (1925: 62–4).

[72] Thus for Meyer '[s]ocialism was the worst symptom of everything that was going wrong with his world, not only socialist politics but any kind of socialist thinking. In that respect his views were generally shared in the conservative German academic world'. Similarly, 'in the closing years of the nineteenth century [Pöhlmann] wrote the classic polemic against socialism in the name of ancient history', while Guiraud concluded that '[i]f Greece perished because of agrarian socialism, it does not follow that we are condemned to suffer a similar fate'. For his part, Rostovtzeff was 'contemptuous of economic theory, particularly Marxism', dismissed by him as 'the grossly exaggerated and untenable Marxian doctrine'. For all these views, see Finley (1983a: 49, 51, 53).

[73] See Starr (1979a: 45). At the end of the 1950s, the same author (Starr, 1979b: 311) uttered in unmistakeably cold war terms the following opinion: that 'the study of the Roman Empire today [1960] appears to lack the stimulus of major new concepts. This condition is true at least in the Western world: and *few of us would consider that the doctrine of Marx and Engels has yet proved itself an adequate underpinning for re-evaluating the Empire*' (emphasis added). In a similar vein, he commends a 1950s retranslation of the Theodosian Code on the grounds that its introduction draws attention to 'the horrible results of state socialism' (Starr, 1979b: 303). Other, equally dismissive, references by him to Marxists (= 'seriously blinkered', 'imposing a strait-jacket of modern ideology', etc.) for emphasizing class struggle, the exploitative aspects of

about the way in which both ancient society and slavery should be investigated was symptomatic: namely, that one should view 'ancient slavery without the blinkers of…twentieth century Marxist totalitarianism. In the most advanced economic centers slavery certainly was a means of providing additional power and so increased production: it was of real importance in furthering the advance of such areas'.[74]

Of especial interest is the way in which this view anticipates both the defence of unfree labour and the political discourse informing the attempt during the mid-1970s to revise negative perceptions of antebellum cotton plantation slavery in the nineteenth century American south.[75] Like many historians of ancient society, therefore, neoclassical economic historians of the antebellum plantation focussed mainly on the issue of economic growth (plantation = capitalist), maintaining that where it ocurred, plantation slavery was as a result not only not as oppressive as depicted, but in many respects actually indistinguishable from non-slave labour.

IV

Broadly speaking, approaches to the analysis of slavery in ancient society by Marxists can be divided between those who regard slaves as proletarians because of the way both struggle against exploitation, and those for whom unfree labour is an obstacle to economic development, because it is seen as inefficient, undercuts free labour, and is thus incompatible with advanced productive forces.[76] Although not mutually exclusive, the work of Ciccotti, Thomson and de Ste Croix belong

labour relations, and/or Roman imperialism, are encountered elsewhere in his published writings (Starr, 1977: 15, 19, 199–201 notes 23 and 31, 224 note 34; 1979c: 217–8, 219–20, 302).

[74] Starr (1979a: 57). His anti-Marxism cannot have been far from his mind when observing both that '[t]he study of any part of past human development which is directly motivated by present concerns often lies on, or close to, the lunatic fringe of scholarship' (Starr, 1979b: 303), and in the Preface to his book (Starr, 1977: vii) that 'I am seeking to understand the development of early Greece, not to draw lessons for the modern world or to buttress doctrines which are widely held today'.

[75] See also the claim by Westermann (1960: 31) that slave labourers in ancient Greece were better-off than their free counterparts, a claim made subsequently by Fogel and Engerman (1974) with regard to the nineteenth century cotton plantation in America.

[76] It is to the equation of slave revolt with working class agency that non- and anti-Marxists, such as Starr (1979a: 53) and Vogt (1974: 83 ff.), object.

to the former category, while that of Salvioli and Kautsky falls into the latter.[77] Despite regarding himself – and perhaps even being regarded by others – as a Marxist, Banaji belongs in neither of these categories. Where the characterization both of unfree labour and of capitalism are concerned, his theoretical affinity is, much rather, with a very different kind of epistemology: neo-classical economic historiography.

Marxism and Ancient Society

The argument that unfree labour constitutes a proletariat is the first step on a long and well-travelled road that leads back to classical antiquity, where others too – mainly non-Marxists – have located capitalism.[78] At the beginning of the twentieth century, for example, the influential thesis advanced by Meyer not only dismissed the historical significance of slavery but argued that Athens during the fifth and fourth centuries was capitalist, 'just as much as England since the eighteenth and Germany since the nineteenth'.[79] Earlier still, in the mid-nineteenth century, Mommsen had not only described the economy of ancient Rome as 'a pure capitalist system' dominated by the 'one-sided power of capital', but maintained that the countryside was penetrated by agrarian capitalists that – like Banaji's 'new' imperial aristocracy –

[77] See Kautsky (1925), Thomson (1941), de Ste Croix (1981; 1984; 1988), Finley (1983a: Ch. 2), and – for the introduction by Kautsky to the analysis of ancient society by Salvioli – Gaido (2003).

[78] The case made in this regard by Rostovtzeff (1926) is in many ways remarkably similar to that of Banaji (2001: 220 n47) who accepts the existence of an epistemological overlap between his own view of the accumulation process in late antiquity and that of Rostovtzeff. Like Banaji, therefore, Rostovtzeff (1926: 255, 259, 263, 269–70, 302 ff., 482 ff.) not only criticized Weber (as well as Salvioli and Bücher) for the view that peasant smallholding (= 'primitive house-economy') was ubiquitous, questioning the development of an autarchic household economy, but also pointed out that market relations were widespread, and that the eastern Mediterranean area remained economically dynamic. His account of Egypt at an earlier conjuncture, where 'a well-to-do Greek *bourgeoisie* gradually grew up all over the country, a bourgeoisie of officials and tax-farmers' who also became provincial landowners, anticipates Banaji's 'new' imperial aristocracy. It is perhaps significant that in developing this interpretation of ancient society Rostovtzeff intended to do two things. First, to oppose the materialistic interpretation advanced by Marxists for the economic decline of the Roman Empire, arguing that the latter process was due instead to social and political causes. And second, to warn that – as the Bolsheviks in Russia demonstrated – even economically advanced civilizations could be undermined by those at the grassroots ('Did not the peasants of the Roman Empire act subconsciously on the same principle?').

[79] See Finley (1983a: 44, 46). Similar claims about the existence of 'capitalism' in Greece during the period 400–354 BC are found in Hammond (1959: Chapter 4).

were powerful in the state apparatus.[80] His account of economic (and moral) decline, which charts the ruin of a virtuous smallholding peasant farming based on family labour by rapacious landlords employing slaves on their *latifundia*, is an early version of urban bias, itself a consequence of grain prices kept artificially low in order to appease plebeian Rome.[81]

For such interpretations, Marx reserved his most scornful remarks. This is evident from the following observation from Volume 1 of *Capital*: 'In encyclopedias of classical antiquity one can read such nonsense as this: In the ancient world capital was fully developed, "except for the absence of the free worker and of a system of credit". Mommsen, too, in his *History of Rome*, commits one blunder after another in this respect'.[82] Much the same is said in Volume 3, where Marx once again criticizes Mommsen for having discovered 'the capitalist mode of production in every monetary economy...to be found nowhere in mainland Italy in ancient times'.[83] Banaji, it seems, has now supplied those self-same 'encyclopedias of classical antiquity' with their missing 'free' worker (and, where the expanding circulation of gold is concerned, perhaps its missing 'system of credit' as well).

---

[80] See Mommsen (1864, II: 383, 386, 387).

[81] This policy of keeping grain prices low, designed to favour the urban workforce at expense of peasant farmers, meant the latter were increasingly unable to compete with 'slave-corn' imported from Sicily (Mommsen, 1864, II: 371 ff.). Agriculture 'was in this way systematically ruined, and the welfare of the nation as a whole was sacrificed in the most shameful fashion to the interests of the essentially unproductive population of the capital, to which in fact bread could never become too cheap'. The morally corrupting result of such capitalist development on peasant farming in ancient society was, according to Mommsen (1864, II: 388, 389–90), equally predictable: '...above all the deep-rooted immorality, which is inherent in an economy of pure capital, ate into the heart of society and of the commonwealth, and substituted an absolute selfishness for humanity and patriotism... [u]nhappily it is a truth as remarkable as it is painful, that this husbandry, commended so much and certainly with so entire good faith as a remedy, was itself pervaded by the poison of the capitalist system'.

[82] This dismissive comment is encountered in Marx (1976a: 271, note 2). As he makes clear elsewhere (Marx, 1986: 430), the presence in ancient society of money and wealth does not amount to evidence for the presence there also of capital: 'Monetary wealth is itself one of the agents of that dissolution [of earlier modes of production], just as that dissolution is the condition of its transformation into capital. But the *mere existence of monetary wealth* [in ancient Rome, Byzantium, etc.], even its conquest of a sort of supremacy, is not sufficient for this *dissolution into capital* to occur'. (original emphasis)

[83] See Marx (1981: 923), where it is noted that '[i]n his *Römische Geschichte* Mommsen uses the word "capitalist" in no way in the sense of modern economics and modern society, but rather in the manner of a popular idea...as an outdated tradition from past conditions'.

Although he disavows any connection between modern capitalism and the ancient economy he describes, it is clear that Banaji experiences considerable difficulty in sustaining this notion of systemic distinctiveness.[84] To begin with, the central component of his thesis – that in the late empire gold was 'a powerful medium of accumulation' – licenses the view that all sectors 'saw a substantial investment of private capital based on the individual pursuit of profit', and in particular that 'the countryside clearly absorbed a great deal of investment, starting or restarting in the fourth century'.[85] Banaji is consequently unable to avoid the conclusion that, in terms of their economic dynamic, clearly *some* 'businesslike entities' in the eastern Mediterranean during late antiquity were in fact no different from modern capitalist enterprises.[86]

Accordingly, the picture he paints of economic activity in the late empire – profit-oriented accumulation by a 'middle' aristocracy that employs 'free' wage labour, invests in land and productive technology, and produces for the market, plus the extensive use of money and presence of a labour market – could just as easily be a description of economic activity in modern capitalism. Banaji is, one suspects, aware of the looming conflation, and attempts to evade this by claiming that the economic process he outlines is, much rather, akin to the 'business economy' of Sombart.[87] The historical 'explanation' offered by the latter

[84] See Banaji (2001: 218 ff.).

[85] See Banaji (2001: 213, 219). For other, similar, references to the accumulation process in the countryside and the presence there of rural capitalism, see Banaji (2001: 150, 196).

[86] '[I]t is clear', Banaji (2001: 218, emphasis added) concedes, 'that enterprises were run only if they were profitable, which is not to say that *all* owners or businesslike entities strove to expand profitability from year to year in the way modern capitalist firms do as a condition of their survival'. Clearly, then, *some* did. Elsewhere, and in a similar vein, he observes (Banaji, 1999: 212–3): 'this landscape was a product of the evolving agrarian capitalism of the late nineteenth century, with its formation of large privately held estates and the spread of perennial irrigation [a] pattern [that] was at least partially replicated in the history of sixth century estates…surely we must extend these characterizations [= large Egyptian estates in the nineteenth century] to the rural society of the sixth century and see in the large estates of that period a curious prefiguration of something intrinsically modern'.

[87] The revisionism of Sombart was such that it amounted in effect to a negation of Marxism; his 'defence' of the latter entailed an abandonment of virtually every single theoretical claim made by historical materialism. Not only did he (Sombart, 1909: 65 ff.) claim that – at best – systemic change was evolutionary, not revolutionary, but he also denied the existence of a trend either towards the concentration of capitalist enterprises (particularly in agriculture), towards monopoly capital, or towards working class immizeration. Given the absence of pauperization, working class struggle was

is unpersuasive, and proves no more capable theoretically of differentiating ancient/modern capitalism than Banaji himself.[88]

Cliometricians, Capitalism, and Contract

Not only does Banaji essentialize wage labour, but he then relabels it '*free* wage labour', notwithstanding abundant evidence to the contrary. Because of this, he mistakenly assumes that any/every kind labour-power that receives wages must as a consequence be free, thereby failing to realize that unfree labourers also get paid and appear in the market, but not as sellers of their own commodity. Historically (and contemporaneously), therefore, many different kinds of worker – slaves, indentured labourers, sharecroppers, labour-service tenants, convicts, smallholders – have been (and are) paid a wage, which of itself indicates neither that the workers concerned are the actual recipients of the payment made, nor that they are free, and become thereby a proletariat.[89] Fetishizing the wage in this manner in effect collapses the

---

in his opinion non-material in origin, and prompted by envy. Most significantly, this benign view of capitalism led Sombart to question whether the seeds of socialism were indeed to be found in capitalism, thereby aligning himself with those anti-Marxists who argued against either the need for or the possibility of a transcendence of capitalist production. Without perhaps quite realizing it, Banaji has endorsed the central tenet of Sombart's revisionism. Namely, that there is nothing in Marxist theory that leads one to believe that capitalism contains within itself the causes of its own destruction (its systemic 'other'). If one accepts this, as Banaji appears to do, then it is indeed possible to locate capitalism in late antiquity, because there is no necessary connection between its reproduction as an economic system and a transition to socialism.

[88] Invoking Sombart's concept of 'business economy' in support of arguments about early capitalism in late antiquity is problematic, for the following four reasons. First, not only was Sombart a revisionist opponent of Marxism (see previous endnote), but he also conceptualized (Sombart, 1967) the development of capitalism largely in terms of consumption (= luxury), rather than production – as did Marx and all Marxists. Second, in attributing capitalist development specifically to the consumption of luxury in Europe, he failed to explain why this causal process (luxury $\Rightarrow$ capitalism) occurred historically only in Europe, and not in India or China, where luxury consumption by non-capitalist ruling classes was also prevalent. Third, Sombart (1909: 5; 1967: 142) – unlike Banaji – does not reconceptualize the unfree rural labour employed in producing luxury goods on what he refers to as 'largescale capitalistic enterprises' as 'free' wage labour. And fourth, given Banaji's claim to be a Trotskyist, the highly critical dismissal by Trotsky (1946: 14) of Sombart's revisionism – 'Werner Sombart... later revised all the more revolutionary aspects of Marx's teaching, [and] countered Marx's *Capital* with his own *Capitalism*, which probably is the best known exposition of bourgeois economic apologetics in recent times' – is both interesting and significant.

[89] According to Hopkins (1978: 126), masters in ancient Rome paid their slaves a 'regular monthly wage', while Dandamaev (1986: 246) observes similarly that – like

differences between the workforce in ancient society and the industrial proletariat employed under contemporary capitalism. In one important sense, however, Banaji breaks with earlier analyses that locate capitalism in ancient society.

Whereas anti-Marxist historians such as Rostovtzeff and Mommsen evinced a negative view about capital, seen by them as generating social antagonism, and condemned what they saw as its responsibility for creating/reproducing the much-feared Roman plebeian (= 'mob in the streets'), Banaji follows the equally anti-Marxist cliometricians of the mid-1970s in constructing an altogether more benign image of agrarian capitalism.[90] Not only does the latter historiographical approach project a tension-free process of accumulation in a positive light, and banish the concept of struggle, but it also conceptually abolishes unfreedom by downgrading or eliminating coercive aspects structuring the social relations of production.[91]

Banaji's argument about labour in late antiquity being free despite the presence of coercion only works if one accepts his legalistic definition of contract.[92] Freedom of contract for him means quite simply the ability of workers *to enter* working arrangements: that they are subsequently unable *to withdraw* from them without the consent of their employer does not affect his meaning. In this he is no different from neoclassical economists, such as Steinfeld, and ancient historians, such

free workers – slaves in ancient Babylonia also received payment. Westermann (1960: 20 ff.) utilizes the concepts 'unfree "pay-earners"' and '"pay-bringers"' to describe the arrangement in ancient Greece whereby slaves handed a portion of the wages they earned to their masters.

[90] In a section revealingly titled 'Rise of a city rabble', therefore, Mommsen (1864, II: 343–4) makes the following points: 'At length the rabble of clients assumed a position, formally, and often even, practically, of superiority, alongside of the class of independent burgesses…the issue of the elections shows clearly, how powerfully the dependent rabble already at this epoch [i.e., 204 B.C] counteracted the influence of the independent middle class… not only did these natural causes operate to produce a metropolitan rabble: neither the nobility nor the demagogues, moreover, can be acquitted from the reproach of having systematically nursed its growth'.

[91] Symptomatically, the neoclassical economic account of antebellum plantation slavery in the southern US by Fogel and Engerman (1974) is endorsingly described by Banaji (1980b: 516) as one of 'the best studies' on the subject.

[92] For earlier references to the existence in nineteenth century India of what are termed variously 'wage contracts' and 'labour contracts', see Banaji (1978: 393, 409). The same is true of the eastern Mediterranean during late antiquity, where according to Banaji (2001: 198) '[o]ne can speak of a "labour market" wherever labour was recruited through contracts, *regardless of the nature of those contracts or the terms and conditions of employment embodied in or entailed by them, and thus of the coercion and domination of labour which such agreements may have represented*' (emphasis added).

as Rathbone, who similarly apply the term 'contract' to wage labour, and classify such relations as 'free' solely because workers may enter them 'voluntarily'.[93] Like that of Steinfeld and Rathbone, Banaji's assumption is that workers against whom contractually binding stipulations were enforced once employed somehow *remained* free (and retained their identity as a proletariat), when the latter term covers only their entry into and not the possibility of exit from the relation in question.[94]

It is from this epistemologically inconsistent approach – restricting the conceptualization of the working arrangement to the manner of its inception (= entry into), and consequently excluding the conditions governing the reproduction of the *whole* relation (entry into + *exit from*) – that all his difficulties and resultant confusions stem. What Banaji forgets, therefore, is that the presence of a debt relation between employer and worker compels the latter to borrow from the former in order to survive, thereby extending involuntarily the duration both of

---

[93] All these claims are found in a symptomatic series of observations by Steinfeld (2001: 9, 13) that: '...the criminal enforcement of labor agreements was an integral aspect of the first blossoming of free contract in labor markets. Freedom of contract implied that workers should not be constrained to enter only revocable agreements but should be free to bind their labor irrevocably as well... In the case of wage workers under short contracts, criminal punishment was...nothing more than a contract remedy to enforce certain kinds of voluntary agreement' It is similarly clear from the account by Rathbone (1991: 91, 111, 112–3, 115) of third century rural Egypt that permanent rural workers described by him as 'free contract labour' were not only tied to the estate, 'their time and labour...[being] entirely at the estate's disposal', but their 'wages' turn out to be debts to the estate store, an immobilizing mechanism known to all those familiar with rural labour relations on the nineteenth century plantation. Subsequently he reveals that these same workers were bonded by debt, that the 'key feature of these contracts was the obligation on the worker to "remain within" (*paramenein*) the employer, of whose household he had in effect become a member', that such arrangements 'reflect the nature of the traditional *paramone* contract whereby the employee surrendered his freedom of movement', and consequently rural labour was only 'nominally free' (Rathbone, 1991: 116–7, 119, 146). Much the same is true of rural casual labourers, whose 'wages' were also paid in the form of accounts at the estate store (Rathbone, 1991: 162–3, 397).

[94] Among the neoclassical economists adhering to the same view of contract are Drèze and Mukherjee (1987), two of the many bourgeois economists whose views Banaji (2001: 200, 203, 208 notes 63, 88, 108, 113), cites with approval. That Banaji (2001: 197, 198) separates the entry into work relationships from a capacity to exit from these subsequently is embodied in his distinction between 'the forms in which employers *recruited* labour' and 'the methods of *control* which they used to regulate [workers once recruited]' (original emphasis). The labour market, he then adds, is defined simply by the act of recruitment, or 'entry into' work relations.

debt and – consequently – of employment.[95] In short, whilst a worker may have entered a contract voluntarily, he or she ceases to be able to exit from the relation. This voluntary entry into but involuntary retention within a production relation does not permit the categorization of the resulting arrangement as free: were this so, the act of 'self-sale' into slavery (during times of famine, for example) would not be regarded as such.[96] Nor would it be possible to understand how (let alone why) many relations that start free then become unfree.[97]

Not the least of the many ironies is that Banaji's argument about the preponderance and economic role of 'free' labour in late antiquity, and the consequent presence there of capitalism, is vulnerable to precisely the same criticism that he himself made against Dobb and Gunder Frank a quarter of a century ago. According to Banaji, therefore, because of a 'failure to understand "wage labour"', Dobb would 'be compelled to argue that when some of the most deeply entrenched feudal estates of thirteenth century England often based their production mainly or entirely on paid labour ("wage-labour" in Dobb's sense), specifically capitalist relations of production were established'.[98] Much the same accusation was levelled by him against Gunder Frank, who was taken to task for 'collapsing together' capitalism and pre-capitalism because commodity production was a common feature of both, which is precisely what Banaji himself does in the case of hired labour.[99]

---

[95] A variation on this was the sale by indebted parents of children into slavery, for the occurrence of which in the Byzantine world see Phillips (1985: 37). The point is that for the rural poor borrowing led to debt and debt led in turn to unfreedom, whether this involved the labour-power of the indebted parents themselves or that of their children.

[96] The historical link between famine conditions and self-sale into slavery, a 'voluntary' act that does not negate the unfreedom of the subsequent relation, is found not just in ancient Rome (de Ste Croix, 1981: 169) but also in Africa, Russia, Latin America, and India, where specific categories of famine slave – such as *anákála bhritta* (= a person 'maintained in famine') – exist.

[97] Hence the categorization of a particular production relation as either free or unfree, solely on the basis of its form at a given conjuncture, also risks overlooking the dynamic between them, and the extent to which given relations that begin as free ones are transformed into unfree equivalents (and *vice versa*).

[98] This criticism of Dobb is found in Banaji (1977: 7).

[99] See Banaji (1977: 11–2). Indeed, a comparison of texts written by Banaji (1973) and Gunder Frank (1977) roughly at the same time on the same subject underlines the veracity of this interpretation, since politically and theoretically their analyses are virtually indistinguishable. This similarity between the views of Banaji and Gunder Frank has not escaped the notice of others (Goodman and Redclift, 1981: 89; Thorner, 1982: 1998).

Conclusion

The theoretical problem with the concept 'disguised' wage labour, deployed by Banaji in debates about the mode of production and late antiquity, is clear. Because it reifies the wage, this term confuses the fact of payment made to a worker (= wage labour) with labour-power that is free. The two aspects are, of course, distinct: one has to do with the kind of production relation linking a worker to his/her employer, while the other concerns the form taken by the remuneration for labour expended.

Epistemologically, the problem generated by conflating payment of a wage with labour-power that is free is obvious. Throughout history many different kinds of worker who were relationally unfree nevertheless received payment whilst in the employ of another. That they were paid did not of itself signal the presence of labour-power that was free, as many examples of payments made to workers who were also chattel slaves, indentured labourers, debt peons and attached or bonded, all attest.

In conceptualizing wage labour as 'contract', Banaji imbibes from bourgeois legal and economic theory the view that a work arrangement is defined simply by the act of recruitment ('entry into'). This contrasts with Marxist theory, for which a work arrangement is defined by a process: the reproduction of the relational form ('entry into' + 'exit from'), as embodied in the ability of a worker personally to commodify and recommodify his/her own labour-power. Because it has nothing to do with Marxism, bourgeois 'contract' theory licenses the claim made about the free/unfree distinction by neo-classical economic historiography.

The latter, like Banaji, abolishes the free/unfree distinction, in order to be able to argue – wrongly – that every form of paid labour is and always has been the same, is based on 'consent' and is therefore 'free', and thus empowers the subject concerned. As no work relation is disempowering, it follows that consequently there is no need (and no desire on the part of the workforce) for socialism. In effect, Banaji ends up by standing Marx on his head: whereas Marx argues that the wage relation under capitalism must be free, Banaji by contrast maintains that wherever the wage relation occurs it must also be free, and thus historically there too is found capitalism. Whether or not he recognizes this, Banaji is now in the camp of those who assume the permanence and immutability of capitalism, its 'eternal' and non-transcendental character.

The resulting difficulties faced by him are familiar ones, and stem from a process of infinite regression, whereby both accumulation and 'free' wage labour are projected backwards into ancient society, an effect of which is that feudalism was *preceded* by early capitalism in late antiquity. What seems to have occurred is that, in challenging claims made by others in the course of the 1970s debate about the mode of production in underdeveloped rural areas about the continued existence in Indian agriculture of feudalism, Banaji has ended up banishing this particular systemic form from history altogether. Just as exponents of the semi-feudal thesis cannot see anything but feudalism, so Banaji (like marginalist economists) is now unable to conceive of a mode of production anywhere that is not capitalism. Consequently, he leaves unasked (and thus unanswered) crucial questions about systemic change.

What, finally, are the political implications of locating in late antiquity a pan-historical category of 'contract' that is 'free' wage labour? How can workers fight to *become* free labour, a proletariat in the full sense of the term, if that is what they already are and always have been? Conversely, any struggle undertaken by the relationally distinct components of a rural workforce (tenants, sharecroppers, artisans, lumpenproletarians) subsumed by Banaji under the historically ever-present category of 'free wage labour' is not conducted by a proletariat (class-in-itself) to realize itself as such (class-for-itself) but rather by diverse elements of a socio-economically heterogeneous workforce unconnected with working class political objectives (e.g. tenants wanting to convert usufruct rights into landownership, rich peasants wanting lower input and labour costs, reduced taxes, and/or higher crop prices). If there is no longer a concept of class, other than one that is so all-encompassing as to be meaningless, then the concept of struggle to realize class identity so as to transcend capitalism is correspondingly impossible.

CHAPTER FIVE

UNFREEDOM AS *PRIMITIVE* ACCUMULATION?

Although the implausibility of continuing to deny the existence of deproletarianization is now evident, the Marxist argument about the capitalism/unfreedom link has shifted of late. Some of those who earlier questioned the acceptability to capital of unfree labour have relativized their position, and these days tend to claim one of two things. Either that the use by employers of unfree labour in the midst of capitalism amounts to 'primitive accumulation', or that capital uses – but does not actually seek out or reproduce – this kind of relation.

Others dissolve the specificity between primitive accumulation as the 'pre-history' of capitalism and the current *laissez faire* capitalist system. Actually-existing capitalism is for them subsumed under a variety of alternative designations, such as 'empire' or the 'new' imperialism, and its dynamic labelled as a predatory form of 'enclosure' or 'accumulation by dispossession'. Ironically, these reinterpretations identify violence/coercion as the systemic logic informing this development, yet maintain that the workforce employed by commercial producers is composed of a proletariat. Rather than class struggle aimed at a socialist transition, resistance by a 'multi-class' (= 'multitude') alliance has as its object not transcending capitalism but a more benign form of the latter.

Hence the problem remains: whether or not unfreedom constitutes a central aspect of a 'fully functioning' capitalist system, as distinct from merely its 'pre-history'. Central to this problem is the change – mainly, but not only, at the rural grassroots – in the role of debt, from being a method of separating peasants from land they owned (= depeasantization) to one of separating workers from ownership/control of their labour-power (= deproletarianization). In both cases a transformation in property relations is involved, in both cases it is capital that is the beneficiary and in each instance it is the rural poor that are the victims.

But the outcome is in one crucial sense distinct. In the context of primitive accumulation as the 'pre-history' of capitalism, what emerges from the change is a worker who is personally able to commodify/

recommodify his/her own labour-power (= proletariat). In the context of a 'fully functioning' capitalism, by contrast, it is the worker that is deprived of the capacity personally to sell (or resell) the only commodity he/she owns (= deproletarianization).

This chapter is divided into four sections, the first of which outlines the role in Marxist theory of primitive accumulation as capitalist pre-history. The second examines approaches that, either by coupling unfree labour to primitive accumulation, or banishing the latter categories, remove a socialist transition from the political agenda. A similar outcome results from the analyses considered in the third part, all of which interpret primitive accumulation as a contemporary phenomenon. The main reason for this – equating primitive accumulation with depeasantization rather than with deproletarianization – is looked at critically in the fourth section.

I

According to Marx, primitive accumulation not only 'precedes capitalist accumulation' but is also 'an accumulation which is not the result of the capitalist mode of production but its point of departure'.[1] Such accumulation is labelled 'primitive' because, in his words, '[i]t forms the pre-history of capital, and of the mode of production corresponding to capital'.[2] Although Marx noted the existence of continuities between primitive accumulation and the capitalist mode of production, he nevertheless emphasized the prefiguring role of the former. This was a view to which most other Marxists subscribed.

---

[1] See Marx (1976a: 873). As is well known, the concept 'primitive accumulation' was designed to undermine the prevailing view held by economists about the origins of capitalism. According to the latter, capitalism emerged as a result of virtuous and/or industrious thrift, enabling some to save and prosper. Those who did not prosper were the ones that did not work hard and save, a morality tale which blames the victim, who is deemed responsible for his/her own economic plight. Against this idealized view, Marx (1976a: Chapter 26) showed that accumulation was the result, much rather, of expropriation combined with appropriation of surplus labour, a process built on the separation of some from the means of production and its simultaneous consolidation by others.

[2] See Marx (1976a: 874–5), where he makes the following observation: 'So-called primitive accumulation, therefore, is nothing else than the historical process of divorcing the producer from the means of production. It appears as "primitive" because it forms the pre-history of capital, and of the mode of production corresponding to capital. The economic structure of capitalist society has grown out of the economic structure of feudal society. The dissolution of the latter set free the elements of the former.'

Among the many ways of avoiding a theoretical – and thus also a political – engagement with contemporary capitalism are to maintain that conditions favouring a revolutionary transition to socialism are either not yet ripe, not ripe enough, or forever banished from the political agenda. Where a socialist transition is concerned, these forms of avoidance constitute what might be termed a political discourse of either postponement or of cancellation. As in Samuel Beckett's play *Waiting for Godot*, therefore, salvation is made dependent on an absent central character destined never to appear on stage.

Primitive Accumulation and Systemic Transition

Of these two avoidance mechanisms, the first insists that conditions necessary for a socialist transition have yet to be realized, whilst the second maintains that, for a variety of reasons it is no longer possible to transcend capitalism as a system of production. These positions amount, respectively, to a relative and an absolute denial of socialism, a transition to which is either for the time being impossible, or indeed should no longer be considered to be on the political agenda.

In some Marxist contributions (world-systems theory, the 'new' imperialism and 'empire') to the debate about the future theoretical direction of development studies, the discourse of cancellation/postponement currently relies in turn on an elision of two concepts which, although in their different ways central to Marxist political economy, have not hitherto been combined in quite this fashion. These are primitive accumulation and unfree labour, concepts now united epistemologically due to a common emphasis on the centrality to the capitalist system of violence and coercion.

A wide variety of interpretations perceived as being on the left politically – for example, by exponents of the semi-feudal thesis – argued earlier that, where/when it was encountered currently, the continued presence of unfree labour-power signalled the absence of a 'fully-functioning' capitalism. Simply put, such views rest on the premiss that unfree production relations exist because capitalism proper has yet to develop. Once it has, so the argument goes, then commercial agrarian producers in so-called Third World countries will rush to eradicate all forms of unfreedom.

This licensed the conclusion – either implicitly or explicitly – that it was necessary politically to advocate a transition to capitalism proper, and not to socialism. Now that this kind of argument has been shown to be untenable, its exponents have as a consequence shifted their ground. Instead, unfree labour-power is equated with primitive accumulation, a result being that the political outcome is very much the same as before: the discourse of cancellation/postponement is merely reproduced, albeit in a different form.

Since in their view primitive accumulation is characterized by production relations that are not free, and primitive accumulation itself chronologically prefigures capitalism proper, so therefore does unfree labour-power. In this way, the latter relational form remains anchored epistemologically and systemically to the pre-history of capitalism. As before, therefore, what is on the political agenda is a transition not to socialism but – still – to a 'fully-functioning' capitalism.[3]

Primitive Accumulation and/as Capitalist Pre-History

Marx regarded capitalism as the 'normalization' of primitive accumulation: conditions and processes which seem anomalous historically in the case of primitive accumulation emerge as central to the reproduction of capitalism proper.[4] Seen thus, unfree relations of production that characterize primitive accumulation can therefore be said to become 'normal' under capitalism. In the opinion of Marx, therefore, '[i]n Western Europe, the homeland of political economy, the process of primitive accumulation has more or less been accomplished'.[5] That the process of primitive accumulation was confined to the 'pre-history of capital' is a view supported also by Lenin, Kautsky and Dobb in their commentaries on Marx's ideas.[6]

---

[3] For more on the way a discourse about primitive accumulation as the 'pre-history' of capitalism licenses a postponement/cancellation of a socialist transition, see Brass (2009; 2010; 2011a; 2011b).

[4] See Marx (1972: 272).

[5] See Marx (1976a: 931), whose view about primitive accumulation being the 'pre-history of capital' has found acceptance even in non-Marxist analyses. Thus, for example, in his critique of Marxist theory Lichtheim (1961: 157) nevertheless maintains that 'Marx was really an economic historian [and] large stretches of his chief work can in fact be subsumed under the general heading of economic history, notably those sections of *Capital*, vol. I, where he goes into the genesis of what he termed "primitive accumulation"'.

[6] See, for example, Lenin (1964c) and Kautsky (1936: Ch. VI). The latter even entitles his Chapter on primitive accumulation 'The Dawn of the Capitalist Mode of Production'. Much the same point was made by Dobb (1946b: 178, 209), who states unambiguously that '[i]f any sense is to be made...of the notion of "primitive accumulation" (in Marx's sense of the term) *prior in time* to the full flowering of capitalist production... [...] In short the Mercantile System was a system of State-regulated

For Marx, therefore, primitive accumulation is distinctive in two specific ways: in terms of historical conjuncture, and the use of force. It occurred at 'the dawn of capitalism', and was characterized by the forcible separation of the direct producer from his/her means of production, a process of dispossession which – as he made clear – could only be achieved by considerable violence.[7] This point was underlined subsequently by Preobrazhensky, when observing that 'Socialist accumulation can begin only after the proletarian revolution, whereas the process of primitive capitalist accumulation begins and goes on *before* the bourgeois revolutions.'[8]

As is well known, the problem of decoupling the capitalist mode of production from the conditions and context associated with primitive accumulation was identified originally by Luxemburg.[9] Although

---

trade which played a highly important role in the adolescence of capitalist industry: it was essentially the economic policy of an age of primitive accumulation' (original emphasis). The close of the nineteenth century in English history is described by Dobb (1946b: 273) as a period when 'the epoch of "primitive accumulation" [had] long since passed'.

[7] As Marx (1976a: 875, 876) points out, 'this history, the history of their expropriation, is written in the annals of mankind in letters of fire and blood... The expropriation of the agricultural producer, of the peasant, from the soil is the basis of the whole process.

[8] See Preobrazhensky (1965: 116, emphasis added).

[9] Anticipating some of the theoretical problems that arise from associating primitive accumulation with the 'pre-history of capital', Luxemburg (1951: 364–65) notes that 'Marx dealt in detail with the process of appropriating non-capitalist means of production as well as with the transformation of the peasants into a capitalist proletariat... Yet we must bear in mind that all this is treated solely with a view to so-called primitive accumulation. For Marx, these processes are incidental, illustrating merely the genesis of capital, its first appearance in the world; they are, as it were, travails by which the capitalist mode of production emerges from a feudal society. As soon as he comes to analyse the capitalist process of production and circulation, he reaffirms the universal and exclusive domination of capitalist production.' The central difficulty is identified by her (Luxemburg, 1951: 365, emphasis added) as follows: 'Yet...capitalism *in its full maturity* depends in all respects on non-capitalist strata and social organizations existing side by side with it. It is not merely a question of a market for the additional product, as Sismondi and the later critics and doubters of capitalist accumulation would have it. The interrelations of accumulating capital and non-capitalist forms of production extend over values as well as over material conditions, for constant capital, variable capital and surplus value alike. The non-capitalist mode of production is the given historical setting for this process... Capital needs the means of production and the labour power of the whole globe for untrammelled accumulation; it cannot manage without the natural resources and the labour power of all territories... And in fact, primitive conditions allow of a greater drive and of far more ruthless measures than could be tolerated under purely capitalist social conditions.' On the nature of the capitalism/non-capitalism link, and how this renders problematic the whole concept of an historically-specific process of primitive accumulation that is common to all social

recognizing the importance of what she then understandably categorized as non-capitalist social formations and production relations to the reproduction of 'capitalism in its full maturity', nowadays it is difficult to see either of the former as in any way external to the latter.[10]

The recognition, initially by Luxemburg and subsequently by others, of contexts/relations that are ostensibly anomalous where the capitalist mode of production is concerned, however, has facilitated an discursive slide on the part of those now studying present developments in the agrarian sector of so-called Third World nations. It is easy to see how, associated as it is with the forcible expropriation of the peasant smallholder, primitive accumulation can be extended temporally and conceptually to account for the existence of other kinds of coercion in the present. That is, when applied currently to explain the continuing presence in a global capitalist system of relational forms – such as bonded labour – that have hitherto been classified as anomalous pre-capitalist work arrangements.

II

The main theoretical relocation of the concept 'primitive accumulation', and its resulting extension from an historical point at the inception of capitalism to an aspect of capitalism proper, occurred during and after the 'development decade' of the 1960s.[11] Because of the

formations, Luxemburg (1951: 366) concludes: 'Whatever the theoretical aspects, the accumulation of capital, as an historical process, depends in every respect upon non-capitalist social strata and forms of social organization… The solution envisaged by Marx lies in the dialectical conflict that capitalism needs non-capitalist social organizations as the setting for its development, that it proceeds by assimilating the very conditions which alone can ensure its own existence.'

[10] The point about 'primitive accumulation' in Third World agrarian contexts was made most succinctly by Gunder Frank (1977: 88–9): 'If "pre"-capitalist means previous to capitalist, then, by definition it is also "non"-capitalist. If "pre"-capitalist means the beginning of capitalist, then it is part capitalist, part non-capitalist. But in either event, "non"-capitalist need not be "pre"-capitalist, since it can also be simultaneous with, or even post-capitalist. Thus, insofar as "primitive" accumulation refers to accumulation on the basis of production with non-capitalist relations of production, it need not be prior to, but can also be contemporary with capitalist production and accumulation.'

[11] Among those who have subsequently questioned the conjunctural specificity of primitive accumulation, and the its anchoring in the 'pre-history' of the capitalist mode of production, are Althusser and Balibar (1970: 276ff.). Categorizing as the 'second great discovery' made by Marx the 'incredible means used to achieve "primitive accumulation"', Althusser (1971: 85, original emphasis) went on more cautiously to

centrality at that conjuncture to debates about development of economic growth in Third World agriculture, therefore, whether or not capitalism was present in the latter context, and – if so – did it amount to 'primitive accumulation', became paramount considerations.[12] Of late, the concept 'primitive accumulation' has crept back into analyses of neoliberal economic development, in the course of which it has been repositioned in relation to the history of capitalism.

For advocates of the semi-feudal thesis, who have been wrong-footed over claims that capital always and everywhere seeks to replace unfree workers with free equivalents, therefore, 'primitive accumulation' in the midst of neoliberal capitalism has become a theoretical refuge. Such advocates invoke primitive accumulation in order to bolster their claim that a 'fully-functioning' capitalism is still absent. Although some exponents of the 'disguised' wage labour argument follow the logic of the semi-feudal thesis, others take a different line. The latter seek to banish primitive accumulation altogether, since they maintain that all production relations are merely forms of hired labour, and capitalism is consequently ubiquitous.

Relocating Primitive Accumulation

The semi-feudal approach of Byres is an illustration of the way in which primitive accumulation has become a theoretical refuge. In the face of substantial evidence to the contrary, he has long insisted on the unacceptability to capitalism in India and elsewhere of workers who are

---

observe that it was 'thanks to which capitalism was "born" and grew in Western societies, helped also by the existence of a mass of "free labourers" (i.e. labourers stripped of means of labour) and technical discoveries. This means was the most brutal violence: the thefts and massacres which cleared capitalism's royal road into human history. This last chapter contains a prodigious wealth which has not yet been exploited: in particular the thesis (which we shall have to develop) that capitalism has always used and, in the "margins" of its metropolitan existence – i.e. in the colonial and ex-colonial countries – is still using well into the twentieth century, *the most brutally violent means*.' Like Luxemburg, therefore, Althusser and Balibar recognized that the characteristics ascribed to 'primitive accumulation' continued unabated even when capitalism proper had been established.

[12] Some accurately saw the kind of problems that would arise from confusing modern capitalism with primitive accumulation. Criticizing the description of land occupation in Brazilian Amazonia as 'permanent primitive accumulation', Goodman, Sorj and Wilkinson (1984: 209) noted correctly that such a term downplayed the central role of agribusiness enterprises in ordering the labour process with the object of surplus extraction. Identifying the latter simply with primitive accumulation overlooked the extent to which the dynamic informing such appropriation was consistent with modern capitalist reproduction.

unfree – a central theoretical emplacement of the semi-feudal thesis.[13] Much the same is true of Harriss-White, currently an advocate of the 'disguised' wage labour argument.[14] Earlier she maintained that, as bonded labour was an obstacle to economic development, employers would supersede unfree working arrangements with free equivalents as capitalism spread throughout the Indian countryside.[15]

Now, however, Byres maintains both that '[f]or as long as the conditions for capitalist accumulation had not been established, domestic primitive accumulation would be necessary', and that primitive accumulation 'has been a necessary condition for successful capitalist transition and its accompanying structural transformation [and] has never been more than a preliminary to them.'[16] Similarly, Harriss-White, a geographer who writes about economic development, equates the increased use by capitalist producers in India of unfree production relations with primitive accumulation, a situation now described as 'a continuing characteristic of the on-going agrarian and non-agrarian capitalist transition.'[17] In other words, and like Byres, unfreedom remains for her decoupled from capitalism proper.

Unable any longer to deny that unfree workers are acceptable to commercial producers, both Byres and Harriss-White nevertheless still assert that unfree labour belongs to a pre- or non-capitalist (= 'primitive') stage.[18] For them, therefore, because primitive accumulation precedes an as-yet unrealized blossoming of the accumulation process

---

13 The capitalism-needs-a-proletariat argument is made (Byres, 2005: 87) with regard to rural Latin America, where 'communities are dispossessed by extra-economic means and there is clear proletarianisation'.

14 The influence on Harriss-White of the 'disguised' wage labour argument – on which see Chapter 4 – is evident from the claim (Harriss-White and Gooptu, 2000: 96, emphasis added) that 'small peasants and landless agricultural labourers [who] are obliged to work... by debt [and] by the coercive power of dominant landowners [are] effectively reduced to being *wage-workers in thin disguise* [*sic*]'.

15 For Harriss-White, therefore, the presence of debt bondage is attributed to the view that 'labour markets are only partially and imperfectly developed'. On how such 'market distortions' constitute obstacles to the formation of capitalist 'market perfection', see Harriss-White (1996: 255).

16 See Byres (2005: 85, 89).

17 See Harriss-White, Mishra and Upadhyay (2009: 512, 530, 535, 536), where it is noted that in Arunachal Pradesh 'long-term, tied labour contracts with [migrant] labour...seem to be the dominant mode of labour contract for many of the tribal landowners,' and further that '[c]ommercialization and market participation has created conditions for the new forms of bondage and unfreedom, hitherto unknown in the tribal context.'

18 That Byres has recently shifted his ground on this issue suggests that, perhaps, he has finally recognized the contradictory and untenable nature, not to say the

(= 'a fully functioning capitalism'), unfree relations consequently remain a prefiguring relational form as distinct from one compatible with capitalism 'proper'. A link between advanced capitalism and unfree labour is accordingly in effect denied.[19]

The same is true of Banaji, another exponent of the 'disguised' wage labour argument, but for different reasons. Primitive accumulation was associated by him initially with the colonial mode of production, a term he applied to a form of backward capitalism located in dependent nations, where it failed to develop into industrial capitalism proper.[20] At this point in the early 1970s, the dichotomies used by Banaji – nations were either a colony or imperial, with a labour regime that was either unfree or free – were in many respects indistinguishable from the core/periphery one that informed world systems theory.[21]

---

politically conservative implications, of his own earlier views. Over a decade ago, therefore, he stated unambiguously to this writer that free wage labour was 'crucial to a fully functioning capitalism' (letter from Byres to Brass, 11 September 1998). Now, however, he seems to accept that this may not actually be the case, and that 'a fully functioning capitalism' requires only a 'trend' away from unfree labour. Hence the more recent argument (Bernstein and Byres, 2001: 25, original emphasis) that '[a]n element of confusion may have entered the debate on bonded labour in India through conflation of various theoretical claims concerning the *tendencies* of peasant capitalism, with *trend* that may register a shift away from bonded and unfree labour in recent years....' The difficulty with the latter view is that any claim about relational trends depends in turn on being able to identify accurately the constituent elements concerned; unfortunately, Byres' inability to distinguish between free and unfree relations of production (see Chapter 3 above) negates any subsequent claim by him concerning the existence of a trend from one to the other. To paraphrase the famous criticism made by the Thorners (1962:187) half a century ago about the methodological shortcomings of the First Agricultural Labour Enquiry in India, if it is not clear to someone what constitutes unfree production relations, when that same person then says that there is a trend away from them, it carries no conviction.

[19] This is true also of some historiography, a case in point being the equation by Blackburn (1997: 572) of unfree labour with what he terms 'extended primitive accumulation'.

[20] According to Banaji (1973: 396, 397–8), therefore, '[w]e can thus define the colonial modes of production as the historical effects of a worldwide process of subordination of pre-capitalist modes of production to capitalism, that is of an epoch of primitive accumulation...phases of intensified primitive accumulation were followed by periods of relative stagnation and decline [when] a peasantry [was] crushed by the fiscal policies of primitive accumulation.'

[21] Noting the 'export of capital [by imperial nations] to the backward countries engaged in primitive accumulation,' Banaji (1973: 404–5) concludes: 'From this springs the basic dilemma of colonial capitalism – while dependent primitive accumulation by its very nature threatens the backward bourgeoisie with economic disintegration should the flow of capital cease abruptly and for a long period, perpetuation of its bonds of dependence offers no means of escape from the circle of primitive accumulation.' 'Backward capitalism', he continues (Banaji, 1973: 407), 'is the impossibility

His subsequent acceptance that there was in fact no such thing as a colonial mode appears to have resulted also in Banaji discarding primitive accumulation as a category

The absence of the latter is due additionally to another cause. Banaji currently regards unfree production relations as non-existent, preferring instead to interpret all historical working arrangements simply as 'disguised' wage labour (see Chapter 4). Since the corollary is that capitalism is now regarded by him as an ubiquitous and ever-present systemic form, his analytical framework consequently has no space for a stage that corresponds to primitive accumulation, any more than it has for one that corresponds to feudalism.[22]

Those who have recently accepted or currently recognize the existence of a link between advanced capitalism and unfree labour also take a seemingly different position. For world-systems theorists such as Wallerstein, therefore, unfree labour is acceptable to capital, but only on the periphery of the global economy where this relational form is encountered.[23] Primitive accumulation, it is similarly inferred, is a process also confined to the same kinds of location. In the core

of sustained capitalist development, of a successful bourgeois revolution which can accomplish the process of primitive accumulation…the impossibility of further development within the framework of the [capitalist core/colonial periphery] becomes the principal feature of colonial capitalism.' Not only was such a prognosis about the inherent economic backwardness of colonized nations spectacularly disproved by the case of India from the 1980s onwards, but the concept of primitive accumulation as used by Banaji locates its source of appropriation that exploits the indigenous peasantry simply as the foreign 'other'. In this, as in so much else, he departs substantially from the theory of Marx.

[22] The elimination by Banaji of a space for primitive accumulation as the 'prehistory' of capitalism is evident from his dismissive view of the way capitalist development features in historiography. 'That much of this history', he notes (Banaji, 2003b: 12), 'was seen as a "primitive accumulation" of capital stems of course from the almost universal orthodoxy that writes the history of capitalism as a genealogy of industrial capital. That is not necessarily the best perspective to adopt…'

[23] Hence the view (Wallerstein, 1979: 148) that associates a declining incidence of unfreedom with workers on the periphery, still attached to the land, and who are not paid: 'Over time, it has steadily become less profitable to use non-wage modes of remuneration. But they still continue to be used in part.' Wallerstein (1979: 149, original emphasis) is correct to note that 'it is the *combination* of free and "unfree" labor and land that characterizes the capitalist world-economy', but misses two crucial facts. First, that such a combination does not correspond to a dichotomy whereby core = free/periphery = unfree: the free/unfree combination can operate not only on the periphery but also within the capitalist core. And second, because unfreedom is confined to the periphery, epistemologically it is associated largely with tying labour to land: again, the fact that unfree relations are found also in the core economies means that unfree relations can just as easily apply to workers who are landless.

metropolitan capitalist countries the workforce is free, whilst unfree labour-power remains external to capitalism proper.[24]

On the basis of a dualistic modes of production framework, Miles comes to a similar conclusion: due to a combination of uneven capitalist expansion and the persistence of peasant smallholding in peripheral contexts, labour shortages there prevent the emergence of free wage labour on which capitalism depends.[25] In both cases, therefore, capitalism is said to require labour-power that free, and to draw on unfree equivalents solely whenever/wherever its preferred variant is unavailable.

Much current development theory that uses the concept 'primitive accumulation', therefore, tends to categorize the continuing employment of unfree workers as an instance of this process. Unfree labour is perceived as acceptable to, but not actually reproduced by, capitalism proper. This differs from the semi-feudal thesis in terms of emphasis only: advanced capitalism is not regarded as being in a fundamental sense incompatible with bonded labour, but accumulation does not actively seek out and reproduce a workforce that is unfree.

III

The recent and influential analyses by Harvey and Negri of what they term respectively the 'new' imperialism and 'empire' similarly categorize the global capitalist system as a form of primitive accumulation. The latter is for them both a continuing process, the main object of which is the separation of the direct producer from his/her means of production (= depeasantization). Each interprets dispossession linked

---

[24] Hence the following view (Wolf, 1982: 316): 'Yet the shift from slave labor to other forms of labor control within the British orbit must be understood not only in terms of internal British development but also in terms of the changing international system of which Britain formed a part. Under the rising hegemony of industrial capitalism, there was a growing preference for the use of free labor over slavery. It must be noted, however, that slavery continued in the United States, and it even intensified in Brazil and Cuba in the course of the nineteenth century... The end of slave trading and slave labor in one part of the world led to its continuation and even intensification in another part. One of the areas that continued to use slave labor was the American Cotton South, now the major producer of the strategic raw material for the expanding capitalism in Britain. The rise of industrial capitalism thus rested on the maintenance of slavery in another part of the world, even though that slavery was no longer dependent on the continuation of the slave trade.'

[25] See Miles (1987).

to *laissez faire* capitalism as a new form of enclosure aimed at the appropriation of 'the common', and the workforce that is reproduced in these circumstances is regarded by them both as a proletariat (= free). As in the case of the semi-feudal thesis and the 'disguised' wage labour argument, neither Harvey nor Negri perceive a transition to socialism as being currently on the political agenda.

Primitive Accumulation and/as 'New' Imperialism

Although he mentions all the forms of and processes involved in what he terms 'accumulation by dispossession', Harvey has next to nothing to say about how and why this affects the relations whereby labour-power is reproduced.[26] Whilst correct to note that '[a]ll features of primitive accumulation that Marx mentions have remained powerfully present within [capitalism] up until now', Harvey nevertheless equates coercion with proletarianization.[27] He regards the latter almost as the 'natural' outcome of development, not least because proletarianization is equated simply with separation from the means of production (='accumulation by dispossession').[28]

When he uses the term 'debt peonage', Harvey refers not to a production relation that is unfree but rather to high levels of personal borrowing by populations in metropolitan capitalist nations.[29] Even when using the term correctly elsewhere, he maintains that the continued presence of debt peonage amounts to 'a trace of pre-capitalist social relations in working class formation', and the labour regime of the 'new' imperialism is a 'new' proletariat'.[30] In short, Harvey is an exemplar of

---

[26] See Harvey (2003) which, although of interest, does not in theoretical terms go beyond earlier analyses of the capitalist system, not just by Bukharin (c. 1930) and Luxemburg (1951) during the first half of the twentieth century, but also by Amin (1974), Gunder Frank (1977, 1978), Wallerstein (1974, 1979), Fröbel, Heinrichs and Kreye (1980), Wolf (1982) and Mintz (1985) in the second half. What was then classified simply as imperialism that would necessarily extend the reach of a hitherto regional (Europe, North America) capitalism throughout the world is now doubly recategorized: as a process of 'globalization' that is 'new'.

[27] See Harvey (2003: 145–6), where he maintains that the 'process of proletarianization…entails a mix of coercions and of appropriations of pre-capitalist skills…on the part of those being proletarianized. Kinship structures, familial and household arrangements, gender and authority relations (including those exercised through religion and its institutions) all have their part to play.' The latter, he fails to note, are deployed in order to enforce production relations that are unfree, not free.

[28] See, for example, Harvey (2010b: 58 ff.).

[29] See Harvey (2004: 74).

[30] See Harvey (2003: 147, 164).

precisely the view being challenged here: that unfree labour is simply a pre-capitalist relation, and where encountered currently is wrongly labelled evidence for proletarianization. That is, the creation or reproduction by the 'new' imperialism of a worker that is free.

There is an irony here, in that Harvey fails to spot the space unfreedom might occupy in his theoretical framework. Why should unfree relations of production not be seen also as a case of 'accumulation by dispossession' (to use the term preferred by Harvey) where owners of labour-power are concerned? That is, literally 'dispossessing' workers ultimately of a capacity personally to commodify or recommodify their only commodity.[31] This, surely, is a logical final step in the class struggle waged by capital, one that would ensure that workers are deprived of the sole remaining weapon in their conflict with owners of the means of production: making or not making available their labour-power, according to the conditions stipulated by the market.

At the root of the difficulty is the way Harvey misinterprets Marxism. Because he is unaware of Marx's own categorization of unfree labour as an outcome of capitalist development – of the manner in which a 'fully functioning' capitalist system ultimately operates, in other words – Harvey identifies Marx's account of primitive accumulation as a break with the analysis by the latter of capitalism proper. However, no such break exists. The violence/coercion that Harvey argues is a characteristic Marx attributed simply to primitive accumulation is a characteristic that was perceived – not just by Marx but also by other Marxists (see above) – as central to the kind of capitalist development that followed on from its 'pre-history' – primitive accumulation.[32] Neither the occurrence nor the historicity of the latter stage is invalidated by this fact.

---

[31] Harvey could have extended the notion of dispossession to labour-power as a commodity, thereby covering the process of making a worker unfree, and thus separating a worker from the ownership of his/her own commodity, with the object of preventing him/her from personally selling it to an employer. But he does not do this. Instead, when talking about dispossession with regard to the labour process, what Harvey (2010a: 313) means is the loss by a worker of his/her job (= unemployment), not his/her recruitment/employment by capital as an unfree labourer.

[32] This is especially true of unfree labour. Its element of continuity, between primitive accumulation and capitalism proper, is identified by Marx (1976a: 899) thus: 'The silent compulsion of economic relations sets the seal on the domination of the capitalist over the worker. Direct extra-economic force is still of course used, but only in exceptional cases.' Although one might quibble over the current applicability of the qualification 'only in exceptional cases', this nevertheless describes rather well the

That in Harvey's case misinterpretation is empirical as well theoretical is clear from his erroneous claims about the role of gender. Criticizing Marx's account of primitive accumulation, Harvey maintains that 'there were important aspects to the dynamic that Marx ignores…the gender dimension is now recognized as being highly significant, since primitive accumulation frequently entailed a radical disempowerment of women, their reduction to the state of property and chattel and the re-enforcement of patriarchal social relations.'[33] About this two observations are in order.

First, and as noted above in Chapter 2, Marx was certainly aware of the important economic role of women in the workforce, to the extent that restructuring was linked by him to the employment of labour-power that was both age- and gender-specific. And second, it is Harvey, not Marx, who fails to note that the enforcement of production relations by means of patriarchy and kinship ideology results not in labour-power that is free (= proletarianization) but much rather in forms which are unfree (= deproletarianization). This, too, is a point noted above.

Production or Predation?

An important source of the problem – a failure to link unfree production relations to a process of deproletarianization – is that Harvey emphasizes the goal of capitalism as being predation and not production.[34] At times he implies that the 'new' imperialism entails a shift from capitalism as a system of production to one that is engaged simply in appropriating already existing assets, either in the public sector of core regions (= privatization), or more generally through hostile takeovers in order to break-up companies and resell the different parts (='financialization'). This is only partly the case, in that it overlooks the fact that a shift from free to unfree production relations is undertaken by capital in order to lower costs and increase profitability in the labour process it already owns or controls, or indeed acquires.

---

specific role of unfree labour in forcing down the wage levels received by workers that are free. In other words, neither the numerical smallness of workers who are unfree, nor the seeming infrequency of their deployment by employers is a true measure of their economic impact, which is felt throughout the rest of a workforce that is free.

[33] See Harvey (2010a: 304–5).

[34] Hence his view (Harvey, 2004: 64) that 'I also want to argue that an inability to accumulate through expanded reproduction on a sustained basis has been paralleled by a rise in attempts to accumulate by dispossession.'

In his most recent analysis, Harvey seems at times to want to dehistoricize primitive accumulation, if not banish it as a concept altogether.[35] At other points, by contrast, he appears to want to replace capitalism itself (= production) with a concept of primitive accumulation (= predation).[36] The notion of capitalism-as-predation rests on the idea that primitive accumulation corresponds mainly to a process of asset-stripping, or profitability that entails neither productivity nor investment. Capital takes over existing but under-valued commercial enterprises, breaks them up into their component parts and then sells them on to other companies, a process Harvey labels 'financialization'.[37] In this way, additional funds are generated so as to finance yet further take-overs. According to this procedure, therefore, a predatory form of capital engages in hostile take-overs, acquires thereby other corporations, becomes cash-rich, but has little or no effect on overall productivity.[38]

---

[35] According to Harvey (2010a: 310), therefore, '[w]e should not regard primitive accumulation…or accumulation by dispossession…as simply being about the prehistory of capitalism.' See also Harvey (2010b).

[36] The juxtaposition of these contrasting views is embodied not just in an earlier text (Harvey, 2004: 73 ff.) but also more recently. It is evident, for example, in the following two sentences (Harvey, 2010a: 305): 'But there is, in my view, a real problem with the idea that primitive accumulation occurred once upon a time, and that once over, it ceased to be of any real significance. In recent times, several commentators, including myself, have suggested that we need to take the continuity of primitive accumulation throughout the historical geography of capitalism seriously.' That Harvey wishes conceptually to substitute primitive accumulation for capitalism proper is suggested further by his stated intention to replace the latter with his notion 'accumulation by dispossession', a label synonymous with primitive accumulation. Having outlined the characteristics of present-day capitalism, he goes on to confess that (Harvey, 2010a: 309): 'Since it seems a bit odd to call them primitive or original, I prefer to call these processes accumulation by dispossession.'

[37] 'Financialization' is a crucial aspect of what Harvey terms 'accumulation by dispossession'. It is described by him (Harvey, 2003: 150) as 'the periodic creation of a stock of devalued, and in many instances undervalued, assets in some part of the world, which can be put to profitable use the capital surpluses that lack opportunities elsewhere.'

[38] The inference, strongly hinted at by Harvey, that this is somehow a 'new' aspect of capitalist development, and as such casts doubt on Marxist theory about the characteristics of a 'fully functioning' accumulation process, it itself open to challenge. Among the elements that are said to be specific to current forms of accumulation, therefore, are that it corresponds to a 'casino economy', based purely on gambling or 'gambling innovations' by banking and/or finance capital, one result of which is the ruin of small farmers, or 'accumulation by dispossession'. All these aspects were identified as undesirable characteristics of the internationalization of capitalism as it was occurring over a century ago, by Rühland (1896). Any claim that, where capitalism is concerned, the 'casino economy' and its effects are 'new' is accordingly mistaken.

Insofar as the focus is on the immediate act of acquisition/break-up/selling-on, the resulting accumulation pattern does indeed support the view of capitalism-as-predation. The difficulty with this is that it overlooks an important condition structuring the whole transaction: namely, that the profitability of asset-stripping itself depends on intensifying production, and thus enhancing the amount of surplus-value extracted from labour-power.[39] Hostile takeovers are invariably followed by cost-cutting: worker redundancies combined with higher productivity from those who remain employed. In the recent past, these kind of 'efficiency savings' have been accompanied by sacking higher-paid workers, downsizing and/or outsourcing employment. That is, restructuring the capitalist labour process, a procedure that – as has been argued above – frequently involves replacing more costly free workers with cheaper unfree equivalents.

Within a capitalism that is 'fully functioning', therefore, asset-stripping is a procedure that depends on increases in productivity and investment. It corresponds to a situation whereby most or all the advantages that have accrued to workers as a result of class struggle waged by them have been stripped away, including the all-important ability to sell their own labour-power to employers. Having become a proletariat (a class-in-itself), and acted consciously as such (a class-for-itself), even in the midst of a well-established accumulation process, to wrest better pay and conditions from capital.

Dehistoricizing Primitive Accumulation

If conceptually banishing primitive accumulation does not solve the theoretical problem Harvey faces, then neither does relabelling it or capitalism proper as a process of 'accumulation by dispossession'. It is necessary to ask, therefore, whether his approach includes the possibility of there ever having been either a process or a stage of primitive accumulation that corresponded to what Marx and other Marxists regarded as the pre-history of capitalism.

[39] Following the taxpayer bail-out of the banks after the sub-prime mortgage crisis on both sides of the Atlantic, it comes as no surprise to learn that 'America has seen national income rise by $200bn (£130bn), but profits have increased by $280bn while wages have fallen by $90bn. In Britain, where recovery has been slower, national income has grown by £27bn since the middle of [2009]; higher profits have accounted for £24bn of the rise. Wages have risen by £2bn.' See 'A few strikes don't make a spring of discontent', *The Guardian* (London), 29 March 2010.

This uncertainty generates additional problems, not least confusions about the pattern of historical transformation in particular contexts. Thus, for example, Harvey insists that before the 1950s and 1960s no characteristics associated with primitive accumulation occurred 'within the core regions of capitalism, particularly those with strong social-democratic state apparatuses.'[40] The inference is that, in some sense, the political system before that conjuncture made such practices (among them the employment of labour that was unfree) difficult, if not impossible, for employers to implement. Yet there is abundant evidence to the contrary: that even before 1950 commercial enterprises in the core regions of Europe and North America employed a workforce containing not just females and children but also unfree labour.

During the 1930s capitalist crisis, therefore, the replacement of free wage labour with unfree workers in Britain and Germany was designed both to lower wage costs by restructuring the capitalist labour process and simultaneously to weaken trade union organization and break down working class consciousness/solidarity.[41] Much the same is true of the United States during the 1940s.[42] Even in the core regions, therefore, where according to Harvey a particular characteristic he associates with primitive accumulation did not appear until around the last quarter of the twentieth century, substantial evidence underlines the extent to which it was already well established as part of the capitalist system in such contexts before then.

The political difficulties arising from such misinterpretations and confusions are not difficult to discern. Because his focus is on dispossession, an act he applies mainly to petty commodity producers but

[40] See Harvey (2010a: 310).

[41] The connection between low wages and unfree labour in 1930s Britain was made by Wal Hannington, of the Unemployed Workers' Movement, who rightly identified the role of residential 'training' camps in the Distressed Areas as an attempt by the state to unmake the working class (= 'outclassed', 'de-classing'), using the cheap unfree labour of the unemployed to undermine trade union opposition to wage cuts. This strategy, he noted (Hannington, 1937: 112–3, 114), 'is the sort of thing that tends to make the men feel that they are being outclassed; that they no longer belong to the wage-earning class... The mental effect of such a system is likely to produce a slave psychology... the tendency will be for them to regard themselves as fortunate if they can get an ordinary job at wages far below trade union rates... We must resist any scheme which has the effect of de-classing the unemployed. When work is available, whether it be for a private employer or for the Government, the unemployed should be entitled to receive proper payment for that work and so be restored to their normal position of wage-earners'. The same point was made with regard to 1930s Germany by many observers (see Chapter 6), including Kuczynski (1939).

[42] For details about the United States, see Chapter 6.

fails to extend to owners/sellers of labour-power (mistakenly described as a proletariat), Harvey's analysis licenses a form of anti-capitalist struggle no longer based on class.[43] Such movements, he accepts, are not merely not going in a socialist direction but in many instances are frequently hostile both to workers' movements and the end for which the latter struggle politically. The corollary, however, is not something he addresses.

Both historically and currently, agrarian mobilizations opposed to 'accumulation by dispossession' have been and are usually one of two kinds. Either those representing the interests of and/or led by rich peasants who – as tenants – fight a landlord class in order to acquire (or regain) private property rights over means of production (mostly land) they do not own. As such they become – if they are not already – capitalist producers, who proceed to employ bonded labourers.[44] Or they are movements of smallholders who wish similarly to acquire or regain the status of petty commodity producers who own the land they cultivate.[45]

Once they have secured property rights, those in each of these two categories strongly oppose any further attempts to socialize the means of production. Any further attempt at land reform, or redistribution of existing assets/property, is blocked as a result.[46] This is especially true

---

[43] 'Political struggles against accumulation by dispossession', Harvey (2010a: 313) notes, 'are just as important as more traditional proletarian movements.' However, he then accepts that such movements 'quite often take an antagonistic stance toward class-based workers'-movement politics...' In a similar vein, he (Harvey, 2010b: 257) states that '[t]o listen to the peasant leaders of the MST in Brazil or the leaders of the anti-corporate land grab movement in India is a privileged education. In this instance the task of the educated discontented is to magnify the subaltern voice so that attention can be paid to the circumstances of exploitation and repression and the answers that can be shaped into an anti-capitalist programme.' As has been noted elsewhere (Brass, 2000: Chapter 4), in many rural contexts the 'subaltern voice' is composed of utterances not just of landless labourers but also of small capitalist producers.

[44] For historical and current examples, from Latin America and India, of agrarian movements the better-off elements of which have themselves employed bonded labour, see Brass (1995; 1999; 2003).

[45] For a current example from Mexico, see Washbrook (2007).

[46] Observing that '[a]ffluent peasants fighting against land reform are not the same as landless peasants fighting for the right to subsist', Harvey (2004: 86, note 31) appears to recognize this problem, but nevertheless avoids its political implications. He continues: 'The left, embedded as it was (and still in many respects is) in the politics of expanded reproduction, was slow to recognize the significance of anti-IMF riots and other movements against dispossession... But it also seems right that we do a far more sophisticated analysis to determine which of the myriad movements against dispossession are regressive and anti-modernizing in any socialist sense and which can be progressive or at least be pulled in a progressive direction by alliance formation.'

of contexts where collectivization is linked to planning and price controls. Harvey also forgets that workers deprived of their jobs as a result of unemployment not merely do not have the same interests as peasants whose land is taken from them, but in some instances have interests that conflict with those of the latter.[47] This is particularly the case when, subsequently, they confront one another in the market as sellers and buyers of labour-power.

Primitive Accumulation and/as 'Empire'

A similar kind of confusion informs the equally influential analyses of capital by Negri, who – like Harvey – regards primitive accumulation simply as separating the direct producer from his/her means of labour, a modern characteristic (= 'capitalist primitive accumulation') associated with both fascism and socialism.[48] Dispossession effected in the course of primitive accumulation is equated by Negri with enclosure – a process roughly synonymous with privatization – of 'the common', a term he extends to cover all public sector activity in a capitalist economy.[49]

Enclosure of 'the common', insofar as it refers to privatization refers also to the prefiguring act of nationalization, and thus encompasses additionally a potential and subsequent act of renationalization. In theory, this cycle of expropriation/appropriation could go on

---

[47] Hence the problematic nature of the conclusion arrived at by Harvey (2010a: 313) when admitting that '[a]n opposition force made up of the "disempowered", no matter whether they are dispossessed in the labour process or dispossessed of their livelihoods, their assets or their rights, would require a re-envisioning of collective politics along rather different lines. I think Marx was in error in confining these forms of struggle to the prehistory of capitalism.'

[48] See Hardt and Negri (2001: 257–58, 300), who note: 'As we pass from modernity to postmodernity, the processes of primitive accumulation do indeed continue. Primitive accumulation is not a process that happens once and then is done with; rather, capitalist relations of production and social classes have to be reproduced….'

[49] See Negri (2008: 30), who maintains that such dispossession corresponds to the attempt by capital to impose the law of value on 'the common'. There is a rather obvious flaw in this view. Characterizing as primitive accumulation the imposition on the public sector by capital of the law of value infers that the public sector is not subject to the command of capital. Yet a central argument made by him over the years – see not just Negri (1980) but also his contributions to Red Notes (1979: 33–65, 93–117) – has been that the State-form was from the very start compromised by the drive to modernization, which suggests that the public sector economy under its control was anyway subject to the command of capital. What *was* different was the property relation, in that ownership of a resource belonging to the state was transferred to capital on privatization, but this kind of transformation does not seem to interest Negri.

indefinitely *within* capitalism. If enclosure of the common is equated with primitive accumulation, therefore, and with a supposed incompleteness of capitalist development, then such a process would *ipso facto* postpone for ever a transition to socialism.[50]

Although primitive accumulation is linked by Negri to the reproduction of slavery in the case of colonial countries, in current metropolitan capitalist nations the same process is said by him to generate a workforce that is free.[51] This confusion, which replicates the same duality as world systems theory (see above) stems from the analytical shift in his view about the subject of history and struggle, from the working class in all its forms to a more problematic notion of 'the multitude'. Now he talks merely of self-organization by a sociologically amorphous 'multitude' outside and against the capitalist State, the capture of which in his view is nevertheless unnecessary.[52]

---

[50] In a sense this is not so surprising, since where socialism is concerned, the dismissive attitude of Negri is evident from the way in which he resorts to the well-tried but erroneous formula (socialism = fascism) so beloved of cold warriors of old. Hence the assertion (Hardt and Negri, 2005: 255) that '...contemporary forms of right-wing populism and fascism are deformed offsprings [*sic*] of socialism – and such populist derivatives of socialism are another reason why we have to search for a postsocialist political alternative today, breaking with the worn-out socialist tradition. It is strange now to have to recall this amalgam of ideological perversions that grew out of the socialist concept of representation, but today we can finally preside over its funeral. The democratic hopes of socialist representation are over. And while we say our farewells we cannot but remember how many ideological by-products, more or less fascist, the great historical experiences of socialism were condemned to drag in their wake... There is no longer any possibility of going back to modern models of representation to create a democratic order.' The fact that what passed for socialism was nothing of the sort, and thus the root of the difficulty to which Negri alludes has more to do with the deployment of non- or anti-socialist ideas/arguments under the guise of socialism, is something which appears to escape his notice.

[51] See Hardt and Negri (2001: 120 ff.), and also the view (Negri, 2008: 5) that in 'the historical experience of certain colonial countries...primitive accumulation occurred with slavery'. Speaking of the workforce created by capital during the present epoch, however, Hardt and Negri (2001: 326) observe that 'in the processes of primitive accumulation, capital separates populations from specifically coded territories and sets them in motion. It clears the Estates and creates a "free" proletariat.'

[52] The object of initial critical analyses undertaken by Negri was the State, and specifically planned development controlled by capitalist and socialist alike. It was this that led to his regarding the State-form itself as inherently compromised, a system of power that amounted to command over the value-form. Hence the centrality to his theory of State-as-enterprise, State-as-Factory-Command-over-Living-Labour. Against this power of command, Negri posited the disruption of the cycle of accumulation, based on the process of class self-valorization – or autonomy – by the mass worker. Although as Negri (1980: 63) made clear this process of self-valorization was subject to a cyclical ebb-and-flow, and thus did not involve a process of recomposition signalling a once-and-for-all transition to consciousness of class, struggle was still

Neither does Negri say what sort of property relation – as regards both productive unit and labour-power – will emerge from this process. This is because he downplays the significance of property relations, the *sine qua non* of Marxist analysis, and opts instead for blaming the failure of socialism on workers, who are accused of not being able 'to construct democratic instruments of management and self-management'.[53] Accordingly, the distinction between labour-power that is free, and that which is unfree, plus the importance of this for the wider process of class struggle under capitalism (*not* primitive accumulation), eludes him.

'Multitude' versus 'Empire'?

A result of not recognizing the central importance to a 'fully functioning' capitalism of unfree production relations, therefore, is that Negri – like Harvey – also misinterprets the nature of the political struggle. Because in his view it is mainly smallholders who are the victims of current forms of primitive accumulation, Negri attempts to lever an economically undifferentiated the peasantry into his concept 'multitude', asserting incorrectly that Marxists generally regarded the peasantry as a class.[54]

The absence of class trapped between the exclusiveness of individual selfhood on the one hand, and the inclusiveness of being-in-the-world on the other, is evident from the observation by Negri that 'we are a multiplicity of singular forms of life and *at the same time* share a

informed by the latter identity. For this reason these earlier texts, written during the 1960s and 1970s, are important, not least because the element of Marxist theory continues to be present. Thus the process of struggle is guided by the need for worker unification – or class recomposition – in the face of the attempt by capital to decompose the proletariat. However, in his later texts, written during the new millennium in collaboration with Hardt, the element of class is replaced with the term 'multitude' (Hardt and Negri, 2005), and the analysis consequently ceases to be recognizably Marxist.

[53] Asked about the Left, Negri (2008: 27) replies: 'Faced by this order of questions and perspectives, the Left was completely unable to confront the problem. The Left was (and is) in a form of decline, hobbled by what they call the 'third way', a sort of New Labour post-Thatcherism… The complete insufficiency of this strategy has been demonstrated by a very simple fact: the problem isn't privatization or deregulation but the total incapacity to construct democratic instruments of management and self-management, in more or less articulated and sophisticated ways…' What he wrongly identifies as a failure of the Left – New Labour and advocates of the 'third way' – was much rather a form of conservatism, a last ditch attempt by populist enthusiasts of the market to 'rescue' capitalism.

[54] See Hardt and Negri (2005: 115–27).

common global existence'.[55] Consequently, his concept 'multitude' erases all economic and property relations linking the individual self to the world, thereby making the struggle against neo-liberalism so inclusive that it is difficult to conceive of any category of 'selfhood' not wholly signed up by Negri to the defeat of a correspondingly externalized global capitalism

At times it seems that, given the relentlessness of the continuing neoliberal onslaught, the mere fact of 'from below' rural agency is for Harvey and Negri in itself a sufficient cause for celebration.[56] Consequently, they are reluctant to question either the political objective or the direction of this grassroots agency, and whether in fact it possesses an agenda that amounts to a programme for change – let alone a viable one.

Their attention focusses instead on the supposedly novel (= postmodern) demand by smallholding peasants affected by primitive accumulation (= 'accumulation by dispossession') for a return to traditional culture and community authority, and with it the recuperation of an eternal identity emblematic of an authentic process of 'belonging' as embodied in indigenous autonomy. Henceforth cultivators are to be discussed in terms of non-economic agency, that of new social movements. This despite the fact that, where a 'fully functioning' capitalism

[55] See Hardt and Negri (2005: 127, original emphasis). For Negri, therefore, no distinction exists between a millionaire and an agricultural labourer, each of whom is simultaneously 'a singular form of life' and both of whom 'share a common global existence'. In other words, between the irreducibility of the self and the sameness of humanity at the global level there is nothing, and the space in which class relations are usually to be found is for Negri empty of socio-economic content. This is all of a part with their earlier framework based on the notion of 'Empire' (Hardt and Negri, 2000), the intellectual case for which have been effectively demolished by Petras (2002).

[56] This fact has been routinely overlooked by enthusiastic supporters of the Zapatistas in the Mexican state of Chiapas – among them Negri – who fail to question the extent to which the cultural empowerment sought by rural communities on the grounds of their traditions reproduces the historically entrenched forms of disempowerment (for example, that of indigenous women). Hence the following uncritical observation by Hardt and Negri (2005: 212–3) about the grassroots formation of an unproblematically uniform consciousness (= 'the common'): 'Revolts mobilize the common in two respects...the common antagonism and common wealth of the exploited are translated into common conduct, habits and performativity... These elements of style, however, are really only symptoms of the common dreams, common desires, common ways of life, and common potential that are mobilized in a movement...the EZLN in the Lacandon jungle in Chiapas mixes elements of national history...and forges them together with network relationships and democratic practices to create a new life that defines the movement.'

is concerned, such mobilizations do not resolve anything politically, nor can they.

IV

For a number of reasons, there are obvious difficulties with all these views. Where primitive accumulation is concerned, the theoretical problem lies in a frequent conflation of two distinct situations: between primitive accumulation as *creating the conditions* for capitalist accumulation proper, and its *actually being a form* of capital accumulation.[57] In earlier Marxist theory, primitive accumulation corresponded to the pre-history of capitalism. As used by many analyses of current development, by contrast, primitive accumulation is simply a form of 'savage capitalism' located within and emblematic of a neoliberal accumulation project.[58]

---

[57] Rightly eschewing the tendency of apologists for capitalism to separate 'domestic industry' from 'factory work', Hobsbawm (1964: 105 ff.) nevertheless associates outwork – a characteristic of primitive accumulation – with what he calls 'capitalist industrialization in its early phases'. Hence the following observation (Hobsbawm, 1964: 116, original emphasis): 'The almost universal argument of the optimists is that cottage-workers and outworkers before the industrial revolution were exploited as harshly as the factory proletariat, while their pay and material conditions were worse. But this is an artificial contrast. The early industrial period was not one which *replaced* domestic workers by factory workers, except in a very few trades… on the contrary: it multiplied them. That it later starved them to death, like the handloom weavers, or drove them elsewhere, is another matter, in itself relevant to the problem of social conditions under early capitalism; but the point is, that the handloom weavers and other who were starved out were not simply "survivals from the middle ages", but a class multiplied, and largely created *as part of capitalist industrialization in its early phases* just as factory workers were. The armies of seamstresses sewing cotton shirts in the garrets for 2s.6d. or 3s. 6d. a week belong to the history of the rise of the cotton industry just as much as the mule-spinners in the mills, or for that matter the Negro slaves who increased by leaps and bounds in the Southern States of America in response to the insatiable demand of Lancashire for raw cotton. It is as unrealistic to leave the non-factory workers of the early industrial period out of the picture, as it would be to confine the discussion of the social effects of the introduction of the typewriter to the wages and grading of workers in the mass-production engineering factories which make them, and leave out the typists.' His opinion, therefore, is that outwork must be considered as part of capitalism, but only in its initial stage. In mitigation of the latter qualification – which is clearly incorrect – it should be noted that Hobsbawm wrote this in 1958, before the outsourcing/downsizing of production that became a common aspect of 'fully functioning' capitalist development from the 1980s onwards.

[58] Yet others have used the term 'savage capitalism' to describe the violent struggle not between capital and labour but rather between rival commercial enterprises. Thus Andrade (1982: 179) uses the term to describe the way the Brazilian state became

Class Formation under Modern Capitalism

Where unfree labour is a characteristic not simply of 'the dawn of capitalism' – and is thus confined to primitive accumulation – but of capitalism *per se*, then this epistemology in effect concedes the point about the acceptability to capitalist enterprises of work arrangements that are not free.[59] It thereby deprivileges the cliché that a 'fully functioning' accumulation process ultimately depends on the generalized presence of labour-power that is free. If it is the case that primitive accumulation was long ago accomplished in Europe, as Marx himself insisted, how then is it possible to categorize the employment currently by gangmasters of unfree migrant workers in UK agriculture as an instance of primitive accumulation?[60]

Similarly, how can primitive accumulation come long after capitalist development established itself in specific national contexts outside Europe, such as Russia and China, to the degree that accumulation was said by Marxists there to be ripe for the socialism which supplanted it?[61] The fault lies not with Marx, who was clear about the fact that in every social formation primitive accumulation occurred at 'the dawn of capitalism', but with those who now apply this same concept in an a-historical manner, to contexts where capitalism is already established or has developed at an earlier conjuncture.

What Marx and other Marxists attributed to the process of primitive accumulation was a twofold transformation: separating the direct

---

'aloof' from competition among large capitalist enterprises for government favour during the 1968–73 era of the Brazilian 'miracle'.

[59] That unfree labour is not confined to 'the dawn of capitalism' is evident from the three case-studies – Germany, the United States, and the UK – outlined in Chapters 6 and 7.

[60] On the role of gangmasters in UK agriculture, plus the unfree nature of the labour regime involving the recruitment and control by them of migrant workers, see Chapter 7.

[61] That capitalism was already present in the Russian countryside towards the end of the nineteenth century was a central point made by Lenin (1964a) in his debate with populists, who maintained by contrast that villages were characterized not by capitalism but by peasant economy. As well as Latin America, post-socialist Russia and China are the two instances of neoliberal primitive accumulation cited by Byres (2005: 88–9). There is an irony in Byres' advocacy of primitive accumulation in the present-day rural Russia, since to do this he has in effect to align himself not with Lenin (for whom rural capitalism was present) but rather with the view of the countryside a century ago held by the populists (who maintained capitalism was absent). Hitherto, Byres has always insisted that populists were wrong and Lenin was right; it will be necessary for Byres to reverse this interpretation if he wishes to sustain his claim about primitive accumulation in Russia.

producer from the means of production – land – so as to make his/her labour-power available to capitalists engaged in accumulation. In certain respects, this view associating unfreedom with expropriation at 'the dawn of capitalism' (= 'primitive accumulation') is not so different from that of Henry George and Nieboer, whose argument is that unfreedom is necessary only as long as resources are open: that is to say land is available to those wishing to become smallholders.[62]

For both George and Nieboer, as also for Marxism, a producer has to compel labourers to work for him, by using coercion to prevent them becoming producers in their own right: namely, selling the product of labour rather than labour-power itself. Once all land has been acquired, however, and this economic resource is accordingly no longer available, then the owners of labour-power – no longer having an alternative – are forced to sell this for a living, and work for others. According to Nieboer, therefore, the end of open resources also marks the end of the need for employers to resort to unfree relations of production.

Although the kind of production relation that would result after the direct producer had been separated from his/her means of production and then offered his/her labour-power for sale to capital, was of interest, the central issue was dispossession (or 'de-peasantization').[63] Making workers available for the accumulation process was, in short, the main consideration, and in this not just Marxism but also non-Marxists such as Henry George and Nieboer, were right. The difficulty with this, however, is that whilst Nieboer and George explain the presence of unfreedom in a non-capitalist agriculture, neither of them can account for the continuation of such relations once capitalist development established itself. That is to say, once resources – land – have

[62] See George (1884: 142ff.) and Nieboer (1910). A version of this argument was invoked by Munro (1918) at the start of the twentieth century in order to account for the difference in plantation labour regimes between Guatemala, where debt peonage was endemic, and Nicaragua, where it was not. 'In Guatemala,' he observes (Munro, 1918: 95, note 1), 'the Indians depend upon the planters for a living, as they have little land of their own...whereas the Indians [of Nicaragua] have always secured at least a portion of their food by hunting... They have also great tracts of land of their own, of which, unlike the tribes in Guatemala, they have never been dispossessed.' That the profitability of agribusiness enterprises in Nicaragua at this conjuncture – no less than Guatemala – did indeed depend on a debt peonage system, the object of which was to keep down the wages paid to workers who were already landless, is evident from another account written at roughly the same time (de Nogales, 1928: 167–8).

[63] Since dispossession coincided with a transition from a feudal to a capitalist mode of production, the epistemological centrality of separation of the direct producer from the land s/he cultivated is in an important sense unsurprising.

become 'closed'. It is precisely the latter situation that is explained by Marxism: namely, the class struggle argument, based on deproletarianization of labour-power.

The assumption was, and remains still, that any subsequent working arrangement would be free in the double sense understood by Marx: a worker would be free both of the means of labour and of the control exercised by a particular employer. As such, dispossessed peasants were transformed into – and remained thereafter – a proletariat, in that they were henceforth able personally to sell their only commodity, labour-power. Marx was right, therefore, to identify as the object of dispossession – an object realized at the very moment of dispossession – the provision of the commodity labour-power to capital.[64] Again as is well known, this transformation corresponded to a process of class

[64] The importance of the moment of dispossession on those providing capital with their labour-power, and its impact on all that follows, can be illustrated with reference to 1990s Russia. As is well known, the end of the Soviet Union was characterized by three developments: the replacement of the centrally-planned economy by the market; the privatization of state-owned resources; and the distribution of shares to employees in state-owned companies. Less well known are the events leading to and licensing the subsequent consolidation of share ownership. Levy and Scott-Clark (2004: 14–26) set out to answer two interconnected questions: '[H]ow did [an oligarch] make so much money in such a short amount of time? How did one man come to control a reported £5.3bn stake in Sibneft, a state energy provider that only 10 years ago was bequeathed to Russia's citizens, predominantly the tens of thousands of Soviet oil workers and managers who built the industry?' Their conclusion is significant, revealing that – in a manner reminiscent of the truck system, where consumption is restricted to stores owned/operated by the employer – workers to whom the Russian government had issued shares in the oil company were compelled to part with them cheaply to the new owners, not least because the latter withheld their wages. Following the post-communist adoption of *laissez faire* policies, decontrolled prices led to mass impoverishment throughout Russia. This was compounded when oil companies stopped paying workers for months at a time ('our wages were held back', as one oil worker described it). However, oil companies then announced that they would purchase the shares that had been distributed to the workers. Company shops sprung up to facilitate this transaction, providing consumer items in exchange not for cash but for shares. Having no wages, oil workers were compelled to exchange the shares they had received, shares which enabled Russian oligarchs to acquire hugely valuable resources. This method of gaining control in order to extract surplus or appropriate resources was used by plantation and estate owners to force their workers into debt. It consists of holding back wages due, thereby compelling them to borrow and go into debt in order to survive. Owners of privatized oil companies did much the same thing to their workers: by holding back wages due the latter, workers were forced to part with their shares in the oilfields (which the owners then offered to 'buy'). The company store facilitated this procedure, offering workers consumer goods on condition they surrendered their shares.

formation, whereby buyers and sellers of a particular commodity – labour-power – faced one another in the market place.

Class Struggle under Modern Capitalism

At that particular moment, however, and following the initial process of class *formation*, the transaction between capital and labour gave rise to an additional process: class *struggle*.[65] The capacity of workers – once free – not just to combine and organize in furtherance of their class interests but also to withdraw their labour-power, either absolutely by going on strike, or relatively by selling their commodity to the highest bidder, posed a fundamental challenge to capitalist discipline and profitability.[66] It is hardly surprising, therefore, to find limiting or curbing the ability of workers to commodify/recommodify labour-power among the weapons deployed by capital in its struggle with a proletariat seeking to improve pay and conditions.[67]

Accordingly, it was this need to maintain or enhance profitability in the face of 'from below' class struggle that, dialectically, triggered an antithetical 'from above' response by employers interested in disciplining and cheapening the cost of their labour-power: either converting

---

[65] Among the Marxists who recognized that unfree labour could be an outcome of class struggle was Ernest Mandel. Having noted that in an advanced capitalist nation the object of unfreedom was 'to bring about a recovery in the rate of profit at the expense of the working class, which is deprived of its political and trade-union means of defence', he (Mandel, 1968: 537) then observed: 'In the extreme form which [the capitalist labour regime] assumed, above all in Germany, during the Second World war, fascism goes beyond the militarization of labour, to the abolition of free labour in the strict sense of the word, to a return to slave labour on an ever larger scale.'

[66] Lest one doubt the wish of capital to eliminate all obstacles to accumulation by any means necessary, the following view is a salutary reminder of a union-busting desire/intent. 'Frequently, new companies succeed because they are not burdened with out-of-date working practices that render the established players inefficient,' maintains a CEO of a private equity firm, adding that '[i]n the global 21st century economy, industry is simply too competitive for the destructive and unrealistic behaviour of the union dinosaurs...Non-union plants have been far more productive and successful... Militant confrontational unions are a throwback that the west can no longer afford.' See 'Unions are an obstacle to progress and change', *Financial Times* (London), 22 September 2010.

[67] This was what Lenin (1960a: 216) had in mind when observing that capitalist development may involve 'cruder, serf forms of exploitation...a situation where capital, not yet able to subjugate the worker, by the mere purchase of his labour-power at its value, enmeshes him in a veritable net of usurious extortion, binds him to itself by kulak methods, and as a result robs him not only of the surplus-value, but of an enormous part of his wages, too, and what is more, grinds him down by preventing him from changing his "master"'.

free workers into unfree equivalents, or replacing the former with the latter.[68] Hence the acceptability of unfree labour to capital: it is the process of class struggle subsequent to class formation which results in proletarianization giving rise to its opposite, deproletarianization.

As noted in previous chapters, this capacity on the part of capital currently to employ workers that are unfree is in turn facilitated by two conditions that are both currently a feature of neoliberal capitalism. The first is that in many contexts of the Third World, agricultural production is for export.[69] This means that one of the usual objections to employing unfree labour – that driving down the wages of a domestic workforce simultaneously deprives agrarian capitalists of consumers, thereby negating the economic advantages of using bonded labour – no longer holds.[70] And second, a consequence of seemingly limitless global migration patterns is that rural producers in many contexts – metropolitan capitalist nations no less that developing countries – now possess an ability to drawn upon a large industrial reserve army of labour.[71]

Since each of these conditions was either unmet or unrecognized at an earlier conjuncture, however, some Marxists questioned whether it was possible for capital to continue employing a workforce that

---

[68] Organized labour and its representatives have long recognized that, left to itself, capital would continue to employ labour-power that was unfree precisely to undermine any gains made by an existing proletariat. Because of this, workers' recognized the centrality to their own progress of the struggle against unfree production relations. Thus, for example, a Council Meeting of the First International held on 29 November 1864 sent a message drafted by Marx and addressed to the people of America, congratulating the latter on their opposition to slavery. In it European workers' representatives (Institute of Marxism-Leninism, 1964a: 52) declared themselves opposed to Southern planter ideology which 'maintained "slavery to be a beneficent institution," indeed, the old solution of the great problem of "the relation of capital to labour", and cynically proclaimed property in man "the corner-stone of the new edifice"'. It concluded by noting the far-reaching impact of that struggle, one in which 'for men of labour, with their hopes for the future, even their past conquests were at stake in that tremendous conflict on the other side of the Atlantic.'

[69] On this, see among others Murray (2003; 2006).

[70] This is examined in more detail elsewhere (Brass, 2007).

[71] Marx recognized that in the course of class struggle, employers who can draw on a seemingly limitless industrial reserve army soon cease to worry about living standards of their workers. Hence the view (Marx, 1985b: 145) that 'the length of the working day is also limited by ultimate, although very elastic boundaries. Its ultimate limit is given by the physical force of the labouring man. If the daily exhaustion of his vital forces exceeds a certain degree, it cannot be exerted anew, day by day. However, as I said, this limit is very elastic. A quick succession of unhealthy and short-lived generations will keep the labour market as well supplied as a series of vigorous and long-lived generations.'

was unfree.[72] For this reason, they persisted in regarding unfree labour simply as 'other', a relational anomaly somehow located within – but not actually part of, let alone actively reproduced by employers in – the wider capitalist system.[73] What they missed thereby was the way in which unfree labour currently fits into an employment matrix forming an optimal combination where agribusiness enterprises are concerned.

Where a worker employed by capital is also a migrant whose labour-power is unfree for the duration of the agricultural peak season, therefore, the wage payment remains low when labour costs are high. In such circumstances, a worker who is free would be able to sell his/her labour-power to the highest bidder, which a worker who is unfree cannot do. Such a combination (waged migrant who is unfree) is doubly advantageous: it permits an employer not only to pay less for labour-power than s/he would otherwise have to, but also to avoid the kind of costs associated historically with maintaining a permanent workforce – composed of chattel slaves or attached labour – during the off-peak season. In short, capital gets the best of all worlds: a workforce that has neither the cost disadvantages of being employed on a permanent basis, nor the ideological/organizational advantages of being a modern proletariat.

Conclusion

Each of the analytical frameworks examined in this chapter, for different reasons and in distinct ways, eliminates the possibility of a socialist transition as a result of misinterpreting unfree labour, externalizing capitalism and epistemologically relocating primitive accumulation. Adherents of the semi-feudal thesis and the 'disguised' wage labour position decouple unfree labour and capitalism, as do exponents of 'empire' and the 'new' imperialism. These attempts both to disconnect

---

[72] A case in point was Ernest Mandel, who confessed that he was uncomfortable with the view that unfree labour was acceptable to capital because this enabled employers in effect to do away with the idea of a subsistence minimum. 'The "payment" of labour is lowered so as not merely no longer to ensure survival in good health,' he observed (Mandel, 1968: 537, note), 'but even to imply certain death within a brief period of time.' Whilst it may have been inconceivable at that time, even to a Marxist of Mandel's intellectual calibre, the global expansion of the industrial reserve army of labour licensing a rapid use-up of the workforce are processes that no longer surprise.

[73] Among them Corrigan (1977), Miles (1987) and Cohen (1987).

unfree labour and capitalism and to dehistoricize primitive accumulation, not only break with Marxist theory but constitute a postponement/cancellation of a socialist transition.

In the semi-feudal thesis, unfree labour remains linked to primitive accumulation, but the latter is disconnected from a 'fully functioning' capitalism. Since it regards capitalism as an ever-present systemic form, the 'disguised' wage labour framework recognizes neither unfree labour nor primitive accumulation. World systems theory accepts the current existence of unfree labour, but only on the global periphery, where capitalism has yet to penetrate. By contrast, both 'empire' and the 'new' imperialism seek to relocate a predatory and violent primitive accumulation in the present, but insist on labelling its workforce as free.

It is argued here that that – insofar as it entails separating the direct producer from his/her means of production – primitive accumulation is indeed the pre-history of capitalism. That is to say, with regard to dislodging the widespread existence of petty commodity production (= depeasantization), a distinction between it and a 'fully functioning' capitalism does exist. Looked at in terms not of peasant economy but production relations determining the reproduction of the commodity labour-power, however, a connection between these capitalist stages is discernible.

Under primitive accumulation, debt is used principally to force peasants off the land, which is then acquired and consolidated by agrarian capitalist producers. Direct producers are thereby separated from the means of production. Under capitalism proper, however, the object of debt – as effected by means of debt bondage or debt peonage – is to acquire control over the labour-power of a worker, a process that results in a production relation that is not free but unfree. This entails separating a worker not from the ownership of his/her means of production (land, implements) but from the ownership of his/her labour-power, thereby preventing its subject from personally commodifying it.

Thus the unfreedom that in some instances characterizes employment in primitive accumulation, is a form of control which – because of the competitive intensity of struggle with their own workers and/or other producers – commercial enterprises in a 'fully functioning' capitalism also find very acceptable. The kind of workers and production relations considered specific to primitive accumulation as understood both by Negri (= Empire) and by Harvey (= accumulation by dispossession) not merely predated 1980s neoliberalism in the core regions but actually have a long history there, just as they do in peripheral ones.

Attaching a different label to primitive accumulation, and consequently renaming it 'accumulation by dispossession', is no more a theoretical solution than is attaching the same label to – and thus renaming – capitalism proper. Neither is required, since the original labels – found in the analyses of Marx himself and Marxism generally – serve adequately to identify the nature of both the theoretical problem (= capitalism) and its political solution (= socialism).

In contrast to those who regard primitive accumulation as a contemporary phenomenon, therefore, the case made here is somewhat different. Namely, that the social relations of production generally confined to a concept of primitive accumulation interpreted simply as the prehistory of capitalism are in fact present also in capitalism proper. As such, these kind of relations cannot be dismissed as historical anomalies, residual forms belonging to a mode of production long past, and thus merely awaiting replacement by what are thought to be the only relations characteristic of a 'fully functioning' capitalist system.

It is precisely this teleology that is questioned here, specifically with reference to the significance Marx and other Marxists have attached to the role of class struggle in reproducing social relations of production. In other words, what is being said is that it is unfree labour – not primitive accumulation *per se* – that is a contemporary phenomenon. This claim is tested empirically in the two chapters which follow, examining whether unfree labour in Germany in the period from the late nineteenth century to the mid-twentieth, the United States over the first half of the twentieth century, and Britain currently, is a characteristic simply of primitive accumulation, or is also present in a capitalism that is 'fully functioning'.

CHAPTER SIX

GERMANY AND THE UNITED STATES: 'PRIMITIVE' OR 'FULLY FUNCTIONING' ACCUMULATION?

That capitalists either strive to create, or actually require, a proletariat, while workers themselves resist such a transformation, is one of the more enduring myths informing the debate about systemic transition. The best test of this proposition is contexts such as Germany and the United States, where a capitalist transition had not only long since been achieved, but accumulation was itself a well-established process. That is to say, economies that had transcended what in historical terms might be categorized as 'primitive accumulation'.

About these two examples – Germany and the United States – one can ask three questions: in what kind of circumstances did this relational transformation occur; what kind of production relations were reproduced as a result; and why and at whose instigation did all this take place. Since it also posits whether or not a 'fully functioning' capitalism exists, and thus what kind of transition is on the political agenda, the debate about primitive accumulation also has implications for a socialist transition.[1]

[1] Even in the 1870s there was a fear among employers of rising levels of political consciousness amongst the workforce in Germany. According to an account written at the time (Leslie, 1968: 264), apart from war 'the capitalist of the Ruhr Basin sees but one other cloud in the horizon – in the attitude which labour is beginning to assume, and the power of organization over all Germany, of which already it displays no doubtful indications, although the trade union is a very recent growth. That a fundamental change in the relations between labour and capital throughout Europe is approaching seems beyond doubt...'. Fear of socialism was a constant refrain in writings about changes in the countryside. Among those who shared this view was Fiedler (1898: 3), who warned against the employment of workers who 'transplant false Social Democratic doctrines to the country.' That socialism and not capitalism was the object of struggle conducted by Junkers is clear from many things, not least the fact that among the committees operated by the Chamber of Agriculture was one concerned with day labour on farms, the task of which was to give employers 'advice in case of breach of contract' (United States Senate Commission, 1913: 371). In other words, an institutional form of employer collusion in rural areas, so as to police and enforce unfree labour relations in agriculture, thereby attempting to pre-empt the emergence of conditions favouring the development of a working class consciousness.

The first section of this chapter examines the development in Prussia of landlord capitalism, and the accompanying transformations in production relations on large estates. The way this was interpreted by Karl Kautsky and Max Weber, who from different political viewpoints expressed concerns about the impact of Polish immigration, is looked at in the second. A third section traces these changes in Germany to class struggle in what was now a 'fully functioning' capitalism. Sections four, five and six consider why the same kinds of transformations – from slavery to tenant, migrant and convict labour – occurred in the United States.

I

Rather obviously, debates about the nature of primitive accumulation, and where this is to be placed chronologically in the economic trajectory of any social formation, hinge on two considerations. First, when capitalist development emerged in such contexts; and second, when a 'fully-functioning' accumulation process established itself there. In the case of Germany, this debate concerns principally if – and when – the dominant class in Prussia, composed of large landlords (Junkers), can be said to have effected a transition to capitalism.

Prussian Junkers as Anti-Capitalist Class?

Where German history is concerned, much of the discussion about this transformation is influenced by the work of Alexander Gerschenkron.[2] He argued that, with the support of the peasantry, the Junkers contributed substantially both to the defeat of the Weimar Republic and thus to the rise of Hitler. Most controversially, however, Gerschenkron characterizes this as an attack on capitalism and democracy by pre-capitalist social forces, of which Junkers were a part. The political lesson drawn from this analysis is that it was bourgeois democracy which – together with an incipient capitalism – required defending from those on the far right in Germany.[3]

---

[2] The case about German history is made in an influential analysis by Gerschenkron (1943).

[3] For the centrality of economic backwardness to his ideas not just about Germany but also about Russia, see Gerschenkron (1955; 1962). The latter is classified by Renton (2001: 146 note 3) as one of the exponents of the *Sonderweg* thesis, and according to Fishlow (2003) 'Gerschenkron's analysis is conspicuously anti-Marxian'.

The dual inference is that the Junkers were in a fundamental way anti-capitalist, and thus a complete transition to capitalism had yet to be effected. Hence the political importance of asking whether, as Gerschenkron argues, German fascism was a result of a failed bourgeois revolution, and that a pre-/non-capitalist system in Prussia amounted at best to primitive accumulation based on production relations that were not free. Or, by contrast, unfree labour was a characteristic of a 'fully-functioning' capitalism, and consequently Junkers and the rise of fascism was not a feudal reaction against capitalism but much rather a capitalist reaction against the possibility of socialism.

The claim that Junkers were in any way anti-capitalist is controversial, and some analyses maintain that large landowners in Prussia took an active interest in agricultural production, and were already capitalist by or even before 1800.[4] Even if the latter conjuncture seems too early, it is clear from the United States Senate Commission appointed by President Wilson that on the eve of World War I the purpose of mortgage credit associations (*landschaften*) was to provide Prussian landowners with capital for agricultural improvements.[5] Large proprietors were accordingly able to borrow for agricultural investment 'at lower rates and under more favourable conditions than would otherwise be possible', and in 1912 some two thirds of estates larger than a hundred hectares had availed themselves of such loans. In purely economic terms, therefore, the existence of financial institutions specifically in order to provide Junkers with capital for agriculture, plus a 60% uptake of these credit facilities, is difficult to reconcile with the categorization of the Prussian landlord class as 'anti-capitalist'.

About this two things need to be said. First, that these same Junkers were in the forefront of the struggle against the Weimar Republic, and contributed to the rise of Hitler is evidence of their political opposition not to capitalism but to the possibility of socialism. And second, the characterization of Junkers as 'feudal' corresponds to the *Sonderweg* thesis, the central claim of which is that, because they were and remained an economically backward class, German fascism was an

---

[4] Tirrell (1951: 12, 16) places the development in Prussia of a capitalist agriculture at the very beginning of the nineteenth century, while others (Hagan, 1986: 75) note the presence there of efficient capitalist landlords in the half century before 1807, when Junkers adopted the techniques of the European agricultural revolution.

[5] On this and the following points, see the United States Senate Commission (1913: 267 ff., 381 ff.).

effect of bourgeois revolutions that failed.[6] The theoretical analysis of Gerschenkron means, therefore, that he ends up sharing the same assumptions as the 'semi-feudal' thesis about the inherently non-capitalist nature of the landlord class, and (consequently) the substitution of bourgeois democracy for socialism as the main political objective.

II

Following the Napoleonic wars, Prussia laid the foundations for German industrialization and capitalist development, a process consolidated economically from the mid-nineteenth century onwards and politically after unification in the 1870s.[7] Accordingly, the period before German unification amounted roughly to one of 'primitive accumulation' in the sense outlined above: that is to say, an era corresponding to the pre-history of capitalism. With the development of a 'fully-functioning' capitalism after that conjuncture, therefore, the assumption would be that workers employed by landowners, agribusiness enterprises, commercial farmers and rich peasants were no longer unfree.

---

[6] For a critique of the *Sonderweg* thesis see Renton (2001: 130, original emphasis), who argues that: 'Where it is accepted, *Sonderweg* theory changes our understanding of fascism. In blaming the *Junker* class for the success of Hitler in 1933, the suggestion appears to be that fascism was a *pre-capitalist reaction against capitalism*. The inference of the latter position is inescapable: such an argument breaks all links between capitalism as a system of production and fascism.' For a similar critique, see Eley and Blackbourn (1984), Eley (1989) and Evans (1987: 93 ff.), who maintain the 'bourgeois revolution that failed' thesis is inapplicable as an explanation of the rise fascism. Evans not only links the *Sonderweg* argument to claims about the feudal/semi-feudal aristocratic Junker class, but also points out that the thesis achieved prominence at the time the SDP came to power in Germany during 1966. This meant it became important to break the 'structural continuity' claim, whereby fascism was seen as an effect of capitalism, not feudalism, so as to 'dissociate the German past from the [capitalist] West German present' (Evans, 1987: 98). He continues: 'The catastrophe of 1933 was ascribed not to capitalism but to the survival of feudal or pre-capitalist élites. If industrialists supported Hitler it was not because they were industrialists but because they were "feudalized". Nazism succeeded because capitalism failed in Germany to produce its "normal" concomitants in the form of a liberal society and a parliamentary-democratic political system.'

[7] For standard accounts by economic historians about laying the foundations of Prussian industrialization during the first half of the nineteenth century, see Henderson (1961: Chapter III) and Clapham (1923: Chapter XI). This process was characterized by developments such as the customs union (*zollverein*), modernization of the transport and financial system, and coal and iron production.

This is indeed the claim advanced by exponents of the semi-feudal thesis: the employment by Prussian Junkers of foreign migrant workers from the 1870s onwards is regarded by them as evidence for the existence of free wage-labour, and thus also as confirmation of the fact that a transition to capitalism has been effected.[8] However, evidence suggests that the kind of workforce – consisting of labour-power that was unfree – was not merely favoured but actively sought out by commercial enterprises composing a 'fully functioning' capitalist agriculture in Germany.[9]

---

[8] On the semi-feudal thesis, see Chapter 3. An example of this kind of argument – whereby a transition to capitalism in Prussia means that labour-power there must automatically be free – is Byres. His argument (Byres, 1996: 123) is that, because workers wanted money-wages, a 'fully-formed rural proletariat, a free wage-labour force, was forced upon the Junkers…so it was, at last, that Prussian Junkers became thoroughly capitalist farmers [in 1871]'.

[9] For a history of agricultural labour in Germany from the nineteenth to the mid-twentieth century, see Wunderlich (1961). That Prussian landholders were loath to relax the control they exercised over their workers is evident from the following (Clapham, 1923: 205–6): 'From the first days of peasant emancipation, the squires of the east had been anxious not to lose control over their people. So they had secured… the ordinance of 1810 (*Gesinde-Ordnung*) regulating the relations of master and servant. Every agricultural labourer who could in any way be regarded as living with his employer came within its scope; and it remained the basis of the basis of the Prussian law of master and servant throughout the nineteenth century. Under this law, a contract once entered into could not be terminated prematurely from the workman's side; striking was a crime punishable with imprisonment; obedience was due to the point of absolute civility. Now the typical labour system of the east made these conditions applicable to most labourers, because the majority could be regarded as servants in the eye of the law…from 1875–80 [Prussian] landowners raised a long-drawn wail about rural depopulation, and imported all the cheap foreign labour they could get.' Nor was it the case that such producers could be regarded as operating large farms that were in any way economically backward or inefficient. The same source continues (Clapham, 1923: 206): 'Modern agricultural technique made things worse. The estates of the eastern plains were perfectly suited for its adoption: and there were few better farmers in Europe than the best of the Junkers in the later nineteenth century. After the decade 1840–50 Germany had little to learn from any country in agriculture and forestry. In agricultural chemistry she was unquestionably the leader. The network of railways, becoming denser each year, eased the transport of produce, machinery and fertilizers. As a result the best farmed eastern manors became models of their kind, especially after the hard work of their owners during the agricultural depression of the [eighteen-] eighties. But a model estate under modern conditions, especially in the climate of eastern Germany, requires a great deal of seasonal labour. Certain forms of agriculture, such as beet and potato growing, are particularly dependent on such labour. For both seasonal and permanent labour foreigners were drawn upon increasingly from about 1880.'

Kautsky and Weber on Rural Prussia

Just as Gerschenkron was influential in the characterization of the landowning class in Prussia, so perceptions of its rural workforce over the latter half of the nineteenth century have been guided mainly by the important analyses of Weber and Kautsky.[10] Each traces the changing patterns in the labour regime on large estates, a process corresponding to a fourfold transformation: in terms of access to land, duration of employment, forms of remuneration, and nationality. Thus permanent workers (*instleute*) who were sharecropping tenants with usufruct rights to smallholdings on the estate, were replaced by annual labour (*deputant*) and, finally, by seasonal and/or casual workers.[11] Over the period in question, payment in kind received by permanent workers gave way to a fixed yearly sum plus payments-in-kind made to annual labour, and seasonal/casual workers paid only wages.[12] This transformation coincided with the displacement of local workers

---

[10] See Weber (1979) and Kautsky (1988: 160 ff.), and also the useful commentaries on their interpretations by Bendix (1960) and Hussain and Tribe (1981). Accepting that his analysis of survey data conducted among Prussian landowners cannot but reflect the opinion of the latter, Weber (1979: 177) candidly agrees that, because of this focus, the resulting presentation is not so much on workers' employment conditions and wages, as on their role in national politics. Although the analysis is both informative and valuable, the bias alluded to nevertheless emerges periodically, not least in the form of Prussian landowners as victims of circumstances, as passive rather than active economic agents. Hence the view (Weber, 1979: 178, 179) about a diminution in the position of the Junker nobility because 'the [landlord] enterprises found themselves partly coerced by relations of exchange, which however were outside their control' is akin to the decline-of-aristocracy thesis advanced with regard to the landlord class in Britain (Cannadine, 1990).

[11] The kind of analytical confusion generated about these relational shifts is evident from the claims made by Byres (1996: 122–5) regarding the changes in the Prussian labour regime. Accepting that by 1860 the annual worker had become the main kind of production relation on Junker estates, he describes this relation as 'confined' rather than attached. The resulting transformation in the labour regime on Prussian estates is then categorized, equally unhelpfully, as marking a change from 'semi-feudal' to 'semi-capitalist' production relations. As has been noted in Chapter 3, the problem confronting Byres is his unwillingness to countenance the employment by agrarian capitalists of workers that are unfree. Hence the privileging by him (Byres, 1996: 122) of 'incentives', that is 'of relating reward to effort, a classic problem for the capitalist producer', an approach which underlines how close he remains to neoclassical economic theory. For the latter, as for Byres, capitalism is an economic system governed simply by consent/rewards (to entice workers who are free), not coercion (to compel workers who are unfree).

[12] According to McCulloch (1846: 552), tenants who were permanent workers on Prussian estates paid two forms of rent: not just in labour on the demesne holdings of the landowner, but also half of the crop grown on sharecropped land.

(permanent, annual) who were ethnic Germans by migrant labour (seasonal, casual) recruited from Poland.

Despite these multiple shifts in the labour regime, the different forms of employment shared one thing in common: all were unfree relations of production, as is clear from the analyses of Weber, Kautsky and others. Even after serf emancipation at the beginning of the nineteenth century, therefore, Prussian landholders deployed a variety of mechanisms to prevent their workers from personally commodifying (or recommodifying) their own labour-power: indebtedness to the company store, withholding wages, work permits (= pass laws) and contract labour.[13]

When the estate workforce was a permanent one, therefore, composed of tenants or sharecroppers, family members were compelled to work alongside the household head. Both the permanent worker himself and his kinsfolk were subject to Master and Servant regulations (*Gesindeordnung*), legislation which 'added to the restrictions on free movements the ability of the landlord to compel the return of any who left without permission.'[14] The same was true of attached labour employed on an annual basis, whose kinfolk also worked alongside him for the landowner, an arrangement described by Weber as one of 'bonded subjects.'[15]

Designated by Weber and Kautsky 'patriarchal' relations, these kinds of arrangements entailed the transmission of coercion onto the head of

---

[13] According to Tirrell (1951: 19), following the emancipation of the serfs 'a new class of landless agricultural worker' emerged from the peasantry by 1850. However, as the same source makes clear, its characteristics did not correspond to those of a proletariat: 'Though all former serfs were legally free, agricultural workers were usually brought under the classification of servants by the eastern landlords, and thus came under the jurisdiction of the Servants' Ordinance of 1810, the terms of which placed the agricultural worker in a status of semi-bondage to his master.'

[14] See Weber (1979: 181), and also Fiedler (1898: 3) who notes that '[d]isadvantageous for the permanent labourer is his great dependence… [i]f he quits his position on one farm, he has to sign on for work in the next one under similar conditions.'

[15] See Weber (1979: 185–6), who elaborates on the economic advantages such access to the labour-power not of an individual but of a whole kin group confers on the cost base of a commercial landlord enterprise. 'The labourer's family thus becomes indispensable for the reproduction of the labour force, and the family community becomes in this way useful to the landlord…as an association of producers', the result being that 'it permits the reduction of the costs of maintenance and reproduction of the labour-force to a minimum, presenting a better outcome for the landlord….' Also writing in the late 1890s, Fiedler (1898: 2) confirms this view when he observes that the 'station of the permanent labourer constitutes a contract with the labourer's entire family'.

the tenant household, and resulted in the subordination of labour-power belonging to this kinship unit. Among the sanctions exercise by a landowner was the threat of eviction from a tenant dwelling in cases where family members (wife, children) refused to work only on the estate.[16] The same kind of coercion was also used by landowners against the kin of a worker in order to secure support for policy initiatives that reflected the economic interests of their own class.[17]

That smallholding tenancies are a source of unfree, and thus cheap, labour-power was of course central to the agrarian question as interpreted by Kautsky, who maintained that because of this such units are never wholly displaced by large commercial enterprises.[18] It was this, and not economic efficiency, that determined the survival of 'peasant economy'. Employers continued to prefer the system of wages-in-kind linked to smallholding, even into the 1920s, since – as socialist trade unions pointed out – this enabled them to reproduce and reinforce unfree production relations (and with them low wages) in German agriculture.[19]

---

[16] It is clear that this kind of sanction – reminiscent of the 'tied' cottage in British agriculture at the same conjuncture (see Chapter 7) – continued to be exercised in 1920s Germany. According to Wunderlich (1961: 98–100), therefore, '[s]ome collective agreements obliged the labourer's family to work only on the estate of the employer and forced the labourer's children over [fourteen] years of age who did not work on the estate to leave their father's dwelling; otherwise the parents might be evicted. The organized workers were opposed to the wife's obligation to be at the employer's disposal all year round and to the restrictions on his children's mobility. Where bona fide trade unions bargained, they frequently succeeded in abolishing the compulsion of wives and children to work. Even when the agreement did not explicitly require the labourer's wife to work on the estate, it was nevertheless expected of her.'

[17] See Baranowski (1995: 140–1, 156), who reports both that – again, even in the Weimar period – 'estate owners warned of job forfeiture if they did not secure the expected cooperation, and their employees understood completely the consequences of refusing...', that 'administrators of the vast Putbus estates twisted the arms of estates' employees [although] absolute proof had been hard to come by...because the workers had been too frightened to testify', and that 'employers bore down on their female employees sufficiently to induce tears.'

[18] For details of Kautsky's views about this, see Chapter 2. 'The small peasants not only flog themselves into this drudgery,' observes Kautsky (1988: 110–1), but 'their families are not spared either. Since the running of the household and the farm are intimately linked together in agriculture, children – the most submissive of all labour – are always at hand!... Opportunities for the more intensive use of child-labour also work in the same direction [= intensification of labour, lengthening of the working day].' Subsequently he notes (Kautsky, 1988: 226) that '[n]ew smallholdings are created which are rented out by the landowner in return for the obligation to perform certain labour services.'

[19] See Wunderlich (1961: 112), who reports the opposition of trade unions to this method of remuneration, since 'wages in kind were a cloak for low wages and created

The Road to Auschwitz

The uniformity of their approach to the changes in Prussian agriculture notwithstanding, Kautsky and Weber – responsible for the two most important commentaries on its labour regime – drew politically different conclusions from their analyses. For Kautsky, a Marxist, the concern was on how changes in agrarian relations contributed to or detracted from what for him was the main objective: class struggle facilitating a transition to socialism. The latter outcome, regarded by Kautsky as desirable, was by contrast what Weber, a non-Marxist, most feared.

Hence the concern of Weber lest the intrusion into Prussian agriculture of capitalism, in the form of economic competition from abroad, undermined the traditional socio-economic ties between German worker and German landowner, a link regarded by him as economically stable and politically desirable. An inevitable consequence of the increasing reliance placed by capitalist landowners on immigrant labour was for him a process of class struggle and cultural erosion, which raised in turn a problem of nationalism.[20]

Weber understood the potency of pitting workers of different ethnicities against one other, arguing that a necessary result of economic rationalization, itself the equally necessary outcome of international competition, was that rural labour would remain fragmented.[21] In other words, the employment by Prussian landowners of cheap, unfree migrants was a weapon in the class struggle, to be used against locals who were free and growing in political consciousness.[22]

---

such a degree of dependence on the part of the worker as almost to cost him his freedom of…mobility'.

[20] Weber attributes the subordination exhibited by migrants not to the effectiveness of coercive relations imposed and reproduced by landowners, contractors and the Prussian State, but simply to an innate form of cultural backwardness when compared to German workers, a difference he ascribes to their ethnic 'otherness'. 'For these people,' he says (Weber, 1927: 106) of Polish migrants, 'it was not necessary either to build dwellings or to allot land; they allowed themselves to be herded together in barracks and were satisfied with a style of living which any German labouring man would have rejected.'

[21] It was the opinion Weber (1979: 200) that the 'contemporary estate owner', having expropriated the surrounding peasantry, had depopulated the villages, and thus lost the source of local workers on which landlord production depended. Hence the reliance on Polish migrants, a situation which in Weber's view 'threatens us all with a Slavic invasion…which could mean a cultural regression of major proportions.'

[22] Hence the observation (Weber, 1979: 199) that '[t]he introduction of Poles is here a weapon in the anticipated class struggle, which is directed against the growing

Where German agriculture was concerned, Kautsky shared an important aspect of this view. When he talks of 'economic backwardness', therefore, he is referring as much as anything to the impact of unfree labour on the capitalist workforce.[23] For Kautsky, as for Weber, the effects of such relations on its subjects was – and could only ever be – deleterious: for the members of a rural household the result of what populists misrepresented as 'self-exploitation' Kautsky defined as overwork and underconsumption imposed by the landowner. It amounted to what he called memorably 'the peasant art of starving'.[24]

At the end of the nineteenth century, therefore, Weber and Kautsky saw working class unity in Prussia (and elsewhere in Germany) as desirable, but for different reasons: the former saw it as contributing to and strengthening national unity, whereas the latter perceived it as furthering a transition to socialism.[25] Where these divergent paths led politically and historically is not difficult to discern. Warning against opportunistic attempts by German Social Democracy to construct an electoral base among peasant smallholders, Kautsky maintained that

---

consciousness of the workers, and it is obvious that in this connection it is a very effective weapon.' In a similar vein, Wunderlich (1961: 24, 29) notes, 'organized labour complained that the employment of prisoners of war [during 1918] kept wages of German workers down. … [a] vicious circle had arisen: the employment of foreigners prevented improvement of working conditions and methods.'

[23] From the point of view of rural labourers, economic backwardness is of course an effect of the downward pressure on wages and conditions of work resulting from intensification in capitalist competition. From the point of view of capital, however, the plight of its workers is of little consequence as long as employers can draw on an industrial reserve army of labour, such as that composed of Polish migrants recruited for Prussian agriculture. This distinction – what is economically backward for workers is not necessarily so for capitalism – can be linked in turn to the issue raised in Chapter 1: the rapid use-up of labour-power in contexts where its conditions of work are not regulated and its supply is either plentiful or not limited.

[24] On the 'peasant art of starving', see Kautsky (1988: 110, 112–16), where he argues that the 'economic superiority' of the poor peasant – the household of which in Prussia was the source of unfree labour – is due not to an internally-generated process of 'self-exploitation' but rather to the high levels of externally-generated surplus appropriation. It was the latter that necessitated overwork and cutting back on consumption on the part of the rural household.

[25] 'In this,' states Weber (1979: 200) of the changing labour regime on East Elbian estates, 'can be seen the helplessness of the struggle for both parties. The class struggle in eastern agriculture is a vain and hopeless combat in which both property and labour will suffer. This is all the more certain on the part of labour, since even after the abolition of proscriptions on unionization it will of necessity remain unorganized… Even after the present ongoing process of proletarianization has reduced them [locals and migrants] to equality, there is no possibility of a general union on the basis of common interests of the widely separated groups.'

rural support must be sought instead from among agricultural workers.[26]

By contrast, Weber's fears lest Polish immigration not only fuel class struggle but also erode Prussian village life, German culture and national identity found an echo subsequently in the colonization pattern (*Generalplan Ost*) that followed the Nazi annexation of Poland. The aim of the latter, argued its main advocate, Konrad Meyer, was 'the revival of national community' to replace 'a society disrupted by class strife', an object that entailed the resettlement of a conquered 'the German East' with peasant farms cultivated by German families.[27]

Arguing that the growth of peasant economy refuted Marxist theory about land concentration and depeasantization, Meyer made it clear that one of the reasons he wished to reverse the interrelated process of rural exodus and the resulting decline of smallholdings was the role of the latter in providing large farms with 'peasant servants, maids and farm hands.'[28] In line with the latter, his intention was that economic growth in the 'German East' would involve the employment of unfree labour in both industry and agriculture.[29] That is to say, a process not of 'primitive accumulation' but rather of a 'fully functioning' capitalist development.

To some degree, this policy bears out the concerns of John Stuart Mill, who maintained that if it was possible to obtain such kind of workers, then there was no reason why – in purely utilitarian terms – unfree labourers could not be 'worked to death.'[30] The approach of

---

[26] See Salvadori (1979: 43 ff., 55) who reports that during 1894–5, Kautsky 'was no longer thinking in terms of a somewhat independent political mobilization of the peasants alongside the proletariat in the fight against reaction, but rather of a direct linkage of the agricultural proletariat of the great farms of the East and West to the struggle of Social Democracy.'

[27] The centrality of peasant economy to his project was outlined by Konrad Meyer (1939: 56–68), an agronomist and *Obersturmbannführer* in the SS, in the course of a presentation to the 1938 Conference of Agricultural Economists. What he termed 'a healthy peasant culture' that embodied German 'racial values' was necessary, argued Meyer (1939: 62), 'owing to the economic preponderance of the industrial-urban development, rural folk were to a great extent won over to an urban mentality, so that its own specific life-pattern and life-values could no longer assert themselves. The social contrast between town and country, which stands out through the whole century, is ultimately one of the causes of the growth of class feeling which, originating in the cities, was a typical feature of the bourgeois world.' For the role of Meyer in planning the resettlement of territory annexed from Poland (= the 'German East'), see van Pelt and Dwork (1996: 138 ff.) and Aly and Heim (2002: 252 ff.).

[28] On this see Meyer (1939: 60).

[29] See van Pelt and Dwork (1996: 308).

[30] For the views of Mill on this subject, see Chapter 1.

Meyer to this issue underlines the extent to which the object of concentration camp was indeed to 'work to death' in the course of capitalist production what he and his fellow planners regarded as a 'surplus population' inhabiting the eastern territories in Poland and Russia conquered by the German armies during the early 1940s.[31]

III

The case of German agriculture, both in the latter part of the nineteenth in the first half of the twentieth century, underlines in a rather stark fashion the kinds of difficulty faced by exponents of the semi-feudal thesis. Perhaps no other context at no other period refutes so comprehensively the epistemologically interrelated claim that after 1870 a capitalist transition was complete because unfree relations were non-existent, that free labour was consequently ubiquitous and proletarianization irreversible.

Polish Migrants and German Capitalism

The effects of German industrialization on urban wage levels were dramatic: real earnings increased by 35% between 1871 and 1913, and as wages were two or three times higher in towns than in agriculture, rural workers who were able to do so left the latter for the former.[32] In the period 1878–1908 the cultivated area in Germany increased by one million hectares, agriculture became what one source has described as 'industrialized', and the most profitable crop of all was sugar beet, grown mainly in Prussia.[33] Sugar beet work was seasonal, lasting from March to November or December, and also hard, which is why it was done both by women and also by foreign labour, composed for the most part of migrants from Poland.[34]

---

[31] On the policy of 'working to death' the unfree labour generated by German conquests in the east, see especially Aly and Heim (2002).

[32] See Rabinovitch (1932a: 216) and Knauerhase (1972: 15). According to Rabinovitch (1932a: 217), '[t]he special needs of the sugar-beet industry were at first met by the migration of workers from the Eastern provinces of Prussia. Very soon, however, as a result of the attraction of Rhenish-Westphalian industry...the volume of this internal migration decreased, and German agriculture was obliged to have recourse to foreign labour. There was no need to go far afield to find this labour; on its eastern frontiers Germany could find a vast rural proletariat in search of employment and ready...'.

[33] Rabinovitch (1932a: 216).

[34] For the gender-specific nature of employment on sugar beet harvesting, together with the pay and conditions, see Rabinovitch (1932a: 220; 1932b: 347, 355 note 1).

The element of coercion exercised by landowners over migrants was linked by Weber to the power of Junkers in the local class structure, providing them with a form of 'control over the Poles [that] is limitless.'[35] If migrant workers asked for higher wages, better working conditions or a shorter working day, and began to organize so as to withdraw their labour in furtherance of these objectives, a landowner possessed the political capacity quickly to arrange for their deportation. During the 1914–18 war farm workers in Germany were forbidden by the State from seeking alternative employment during the harvest season as long as a landowner withheld his permission for them to do this.[36]

That these Polish migrant workers employed on a seasonal basis in German agriculture were deproletarianized is clear from the trajectory of their employment history. In Poland, therefore, such workers – who were either landless or poor peasants – were initially a proletariat, in that they offered their labour-power for sale.[37] Once they had migrated to Germany, however, such workers were no longer permitted to offer their labour-power for sale to the highest bidder, and in fact, were specifically prevented from doing so: in a word, they had been deproletarianized.[38]

Not only were agricultural labourers prevented from leaving large estates because of debts owed to the company store, but the wages they themselves were owed were for the same reason frequently withheld by employers or labour contractors.[39] Recruited by the latter

---

[35] Weber (1979: 199) makes the following point: 'It is not those workers with the higher living conditions that are favoured, but those with the lowest. This situation is not solely produced by the purely economic interests of the estate owners, but is bound up indirectly with their local authority. The control over the Poles is limitless: one nod, and the local administrator – who is also an estate owner – sends them back to Poland.'

[36] On this point see Wunderlich (1961: 29–30), who notes that 'the mobility of farm labor [was restricted] by [a] ruling that the latter were not to leave their jobs before the end of the harvest without consent of the employer', and, further, that 'persons engaged in agriculture were prohibited from passing on to non-agricultural employment without written local police authorization.'

[37] Most seasonal migrants employed in Prussian agriculture were in Poland either landless labourers or poor peasants owning/operating less than 5 hectares. In Poland during the 1920s, there were a million and a half agricultural labourers, 75% of whom were landless 'and formed the rural proletariat', while some 65% of all rural holdings at the same conjuncture were under 5 hectares (Rabinovitch, 1932a: 218; 1932b: 340). 'Most of the emigrants or would-be emigrants', the same source emphasizes (Rabinovitch, 1932b: 345–6), 'are proletarian or semi-proletarian workers who are forced to emigrate [to Germany] because [in Poland] they own no land or not enough to live on'.

[38] Although neither of them use the term, it is clear from what Herbert (1990; 1993; 1997) and Roth (1997) write that they are both in effect describing just such a process.

who managed gangs of workers, Polish migrants became indebted to labour contractors as a result of receiving cash advances.[40] Moreover, state enforced labour contracts were introduced in the 1890s, and breach of contract became a criminal offence; in order to prevent breach of contract, foreign migrants were controlled by means of work permits issued by the state, which remained in the possession of employers and without which it was impossible to seek alternative jobs.[41]

Until the 1890s, foreign workers were recruited by means of labour contractors.[42] From then on, the recruitment/placing/control of foreign workers was undertaken by the *Deutsche Arbeiterzentrale*, an employers' association, and in 1907 all foreign workers employed in Prussia were subject to compulsory registration.[43] The object of the latter was 'mainly to prevent breach of contract by foreign workers. To this end the regulations provided that no foreign worker could obtain work...without producing an identity card certifying him to be a seasonal worker. This card was issued only if he could prove that he had concluded an agreement with a German employer'.[44]

That the registration/identity card system for foreign workers employed in agriculture continued into the 1920s, underlined the unfree nature of the production relation. Workers were not allowed to leave employment without the agreement of employer, nor were they permitted to seek industrial jobs.[45] As one contemporary observer of

---

[39] Together with 'a comprehensive governmental system of monitoring and control, which would restrict freedom of movement for foreign workers and make breach of contract a criminal offence', mechanisms such as indebtedness to the company store and the withholding of wages were just two of the many ways in which '[n]umerous employers tried...to hamper the freedom of movement enjoyed by migrant workers' (Herbert, 1990: 32, 38–9). Debts owed by workers to the company store were also used to control the economic mobility of indigenous German migrants (Herbert, 1990: 270, note 60).

[40] See Fiedler (1898: 4).

[41] The foreign migrant 'was obliged to work for [a particular] employer for the duration of the season. The work permit had to be handed over to the employer when the worker began his period of employment: a job arrangement could be changed only with the agreement of the employer...*In this way, foreign Polish agricultural workers were deprived of [an ability] to sell their labour as free ...workers in the labour market*' (Herbert, 1990:36, emphasis added).

[42] About this arrangement Rabinovitch (1932a: 220) observes: 'The commercial agents profited in every way, charging exorbitant fees, exploiting the credulity and ignorance of the workers, fraudulently altering contracts, etc. They were entirely unscrupulous in their search for profit'.

[43] On this, see Rabinovitch (1932a: 220 ff.).

[44] See Rabinovitch (1932a: 224).

early 1930s Germany noted, '[t]he purpose of the whole procedure is obviously to control the movements of foreign labour and to prevent foreign workers from being engaged by employers who are not authorized to do so.'[46] The employment of convicts as unfree agricultural labour also increased during the late 1930s, when under the supervision of guards some 15,000 prisoners were allocated to tasks such as harvesting.[47]

The reason for the resort to foreign labour is not difficult to discern: the problem was not a shortage of workers *per se*, therefore, because the high unemployment level prevailing at this conjuncture ensured that German workers were indeed available.[48] Much rather, it was because, in the context of the 1930s economic crisis, capitalist producers in German agriculture themselves wanted a tractable, more easily controllable, and thus a cheaper workforce than that available locally.[49]

---

[45] According to Rabinovitch (1932a: 232), therefore, '[a] foreign worker who wishes to change his employment must first have his registration card signed by his last employer, stating that there has been no breach of contract, and must produce a certificate from the employment exchange showing that there is no reason why he should not accept fresh employment. In the case of agricultural workers, only further employment in agriculture can be considered'. There are numerous parallels between the kind of restrictions placed on foreign workers employed in German agriculture during the late nineteenth and early twentieth centuries, and those preventing the emergence of a proletariat in colonial contexts. Thus the registration/identity card system for foreign workers employed in German agriculture was no different from, on the one hand the logic of the Pacific Island Labour Acts of the 1890s, the object of which was to prevent Melanesian migrant workers employed in the Queensland sugar industry from seeking employment outside agriculture (Graves, 1993; Brass, 1994b), and on the other a similar prohibition operating under the South African apartheid system which prevented black workers employed in agriculture from seeking jobs in towns.

[46] See Rabinovitch (1932a: 232). On the restrictions of freedom of movement by workers in agriculture during the mid-1930s, with the object of preventing them migrating to cities in search of better-paid jobs, see Wunderlich (1961: 294).

[47] See Wunderlich (1961: 324).

[48] On this point, see Rabinovitch (1932a: 216). Legislation during the late 1930s permitted the withholding of wages (Wunderlich, 1961: 232), the object being to 'tie the worker by allowing the employer to withhold a large part of his wage until the end of the contract. The worker who broke his contract forfeited the withheld amount.'

[49] As Rabinovitch (1932a 215–6) notes: 'These workers, the majority of whom are Polish, are indispensable to German agriculture…because, in the opinion of agricultural employers themselves, the economic situation of German agriculture at the moment [the capitalist crisis of the early 1930s] is such that it would cease to pay its way if it had to meet the more exacting demands of German workers.' For a similar verdict, see Grunberger (1974: 208).

Foreign Labour and Class Struggle in Germany

Even prior to the emergence of Nazism, therefore, foreign workers employed in Prussian agriculture on a seasonal basis were unfree. The latter took multiple forms: identity cards, plus a registration system designed to prevent workers from changing jobs within agriculture itself without the permission of their employer, and also from seeking jobs outside agriculture. Such 'from above' responses by landholders to 'from below' attempts to commodify labour-power served to 'protect agriculture from wage competition with industry', and it was only half a century later, after the 1918/19 German revolution, that agricultural labour became free.[50]

As Roth shows, the freedom secured by foreign migrants at the end of the first world war was itself short-lived; rather than the usual practice of linking the re-emergence of unfree labour to the beginning of the Nazi dictatorship in 1933, he places its recurrence in the period 1930/31. Between the latter date and the mid-1940s, unfree labour in Germany increased from virtually nothing to around 43 percent of the workforce.[51]

In an argument that not only underlines the compatibility between capitalism and unfree labour but also vindicates the deproletarianization thesis, Roth demonstrates that fascism represented the culmination of and continuity with the more general process of capitalist response to the economic crisis of the 1930s: an important reason for the deployment of unfree labour (low-paid foreign workers, concentration camp prisoners) was to undermine working class resistance to restrictions in mass consumption, thereby permitting capital investment in rearmament. By decommodifying labour-power in a context where full employment might otherwise generate pay increases, capital was able to hold wages down to the level of the 1930s Depression.

What emerges from all this is clear: it is simply impossible to confine the concept of an unfree labour regime to the era of primitive accumulation, understood as part of the pre-history of German capitalism.[52]

---

[50] On these points see Herbert (1990: 16, 44).

[51] See Roth (1997). As van Pelt and Dwork (1996: 59) point out, the location of what became Auschwitz concentration camp during the 1939–45 war had for a long time occupied a pivotal role in the transfer of unfree labour from the east. It was, for example, a place where in the years before the 1914–18 war the Galician government built a migrant worker barracks and dormitories for some 12,000 seasonal labourers.

[52] Nor was it the case that unfree labour was restricted to agriculture. As many studies (Homze, 1967; Hayes, 1987; Bellon, 1990; Herbert, 1997: 205 ff.; Gregor, 1998;

Those who do so, and continue to regard unfree labour as pre-capitalist, or as a characteristic only of 'primitive accumulation', and consequently equate a 'fully functioning' capitalism only with free labour are faced with the following rather obvious dilemma. Either to accept that Germany in the years 1930–45 was capitalist, but to deny that foreign workers and concentration camp inmates were unfree; or to accept that the latter were indeed unfree, but to deny that Germany at this period was capitalist.[53]

IV

In the United States the reproduction of three kinds of unfree worker – chattel slaves, foreign migrants and convict labour – spanning different historical conjunctures was determined in each instance by a familiar struggle: that between capital and labour. Over the latter part of the nineteenth century, it provides many instances of labour cost reduction by means of displacing free workers with unfree equivalents or converting the former into the latter. Evidence confirming the importance to a 'fully functioning' capitalism of production relations that are not free can be sought from the most advanced form of capitalism: the United States during the nineteenth and twentieth centuries.

Slaves, Tenants and American Capitalism

Thus a divide-and-rule strategy operated in the antebellum American south, where one of the economic objectives behind the employment of unfree labour was to undermine the bargaining power of and thus keep down the wage levels for workers who were free.[54] Such views

---

Black, 2001) confirm, large-scale, 'fully-functioning' capitalist industrial processes, such as business machines (IBM), automobiles (Daimler-Benz, Volkswagen), steel (Krupp), and chemicals (IG Farben), also employed labour that was unfree.

[53] Significantly, perhaps, a variation on the former view – that foreign workers were free labour – was advanced by the German state when challenged as to the nature of its labour regime, at home or abroad. This, for example, was the defence of unfreedom in German East Africa over the 1885–1918 period advanced by its last colonial governor, Heinrich Schnee (1926: Chapter VI – The Question of Slavery and Forced Labour). The continuation of what he described as a 'voluntary' system of 'mild peonage' based on a 'subsistence guarantee' was justified by him in terms (Schnee, 1926: 130, 132) of a 'reasonable consideration for the ancient customs and existing economic needs of the natives…the serfs themselves manifested no general desire for formal emancipation.'

[54] During the 1850s, therefore, Frederick Law Olmsted (1953: 90) noted that 'white labour cannot live in competition with slave-labour. In other words, the holder of

were confirmed by Frederick Douglass, an ex-slave who regarded poor whites as victims of slavery; he attributed the racism he experienced to the fact that free workers were forced to compete with unfree labour, and thus found it difficult to secure improvements in wages and conditions of employment.[55] Despite the presence of unemployed free workers, therefore, cotton planters refused to hire them because they feared it would contribute to a developing consciousness of class.[56]

That the object of restructuring was to replace more expensive free labour with workers who, because they were unfree, were also cheaper to employ, was a point conceded even by supporters of the slave labour regime as it existed on the Southern plantation. According to one such – Ulrich Bonnell Phillips – this kind of workforce recomposition was driven mainly by considerations of cost and control. Unfree labour-power was preferred because a capacity of free workers to go on strike at harvest time amounted to 'an overindulgence by the labourers in the privileges of liberty [that] might bring ruin to the employers'.[57] The perceived economic inefficiency of unfree labour-power was accordingly offset by its cheapness and governability.

An example from the antebellum American South is the Tredegar Iron Works of Virginia, which attempted to offset a competitive

---

slave-labour controls the local market for labour', while Harriet Beecher Stowe (1853: 427) observed similarly that 'the filling up of all branches of mechanics and agriculture with slave-labour necessarily depresses free labour'.

[55] See Douglass (1845).

[56] Noting that in the 1840s there was something akin to 'mass unemployment of white labour', Russel (1923: 53) nevertheless goes on to observe that '[t]oo many slaveholders, however, opposed manufactures on the very ground that they would aid in developing a class consciousness among white labour, which would be hostile to slavery. In fact, it was already evident that such a class consciousness was developing, particularly in the cities and towns.'

[57] Writing about the labour regime on antebellum Southern plantations, Ulrich Bonnell Phillips – a prominent defender of slavery – used the following example to illustrate why employers opted for a workforce that was unfree: 'Free workingmen in general, whether farmers, artisans or unskilled wage earners, merely filled the interstices in and about the slave plantations,' he noted (Phillips, 1918: 337), and proceeded to explain why. 'One year in the eighteen-forties a planter near New Orleans, attempting to dispense with slave labour, assembled a force of about a hundred Irish and German immigrants for his crop routine. Things went smoothly until the midst of the grinding season, when with one accord the gang struck for double pay. Rejecting the demand the planter was unable to proceed with his harvest and lost some ten thousand dollars worth of his crop. The generality of the planters realized, without such a demonstration, that each year must bring its crop crisis during which an overindulgence by the labourers in the privileges of liberty might bring ruin to the employers. To secure immunity from this they were more fully reconciled to the limitations of their peculiar labour supply.'

disadvantage with Northern and British manufactures by replacing free labour with slaves, thereby lowering the overall cost of labour-power by 12 percent between 1844 and 1850.[58] The employment of unfree labour in this particular instance was due not to the lack of labour as such but much rather to struggles by members of the existing workforce composed of free labour against attempts by employers to reduce wages cut costs by wage reduction.[59]

Following the abolition of chattel slavery, the labour regime on southern cotton plantations increasingly took the form of tenants paying rent. During the 1930s a study of landlord/tenant relations found that 58 percent of the plantation workforce in the south consisted of impoverished sharecroppers.[60] Despite its somewhat idealized depiction of these relations, the study revealed the presence of a familiar mechanism: cash advances and debt incurred by a tenant family as a result of purchases from the company store were repaid in the form of the harvested crop – the basis of the truck system.[61] In a context where it was 'a misdemeanour to quit the contract while in debt', this transaction enabled a planter to fix the price for the crop at a low level, and to retain control over the labour-power of tenant kin.

Convict Leasing and American Capitalism

That unfree production relations are not restricted to the 'pre-history' of capitalist development in the United States is also evident from the continuing importance economically of prison labour.[62] During the

---

[58] On this point see Dew (1966: 30).

[59] 'Until the 1840s,' observes Stampp (1964:71), 'the famed Tredegar Iron Company in Richmond used free labour almost exclusively. But in 1842, Joseph R. Anderson, the commercial agent of the company, proposed to employ slaves as a means of cutting labour costs. The board of directors approved his plan, and within two years Anderson was satisfied with "the practicability of the scheme". In 1847, the increasing use of slaves caused the remaining free labourers to go on strike, until they were threatened with prosecution for forming an illegal combination. After this protest failed, Anderson vowed that he would show his workers that they could not dictate his labour policies: he refused to re-employ any of the strikers. Thereafter, as Anderson noted, Tredegar used "almost exclusively slave labour except as Boss men. This enables me, of course, to compete with other manufacturers"'.

[60] See Woofter (1936).

[61] Woofter (1936: 1936: xxviii, 31, 203 Table 13) draws attention to the continued link between compulsory purchases from the plantation store and sharecropper debt, an arrangement which he admits constitutes 'an added profit-maker for the landlord'.

[62] The most rigorous theoretical analysis of prison labour in the United States remains that by Lichtenstein (1996). Although the leasing of prison labour in the United States was referred to briefly in the 1950s United Nations and International

late 1860s convict leasing in Mississippi was advocated not by an economically backward (= 'feudal') landowning class that had been defeated in the Civil war but rather by an economically dynamic capitalist class composed of commercial farmers, rich industrialists and businessmen, all of whom wanted to see black prisoners 'serve their sentences in the coal mines, sawmills, railroad camps, and cotton fields of the emerging New South'.[63]

That the employment preference of those owning means of production was for workers who were unfree and not free ones is underlined by the fact that in the mid-1870s the number of offences carrying a prison sentence was extended by the state, precisely in order to increase the number of unfree workers made available to capital through the convict lease system.[64] Capitalist firms in the post-bellum South either employed prisoners directly, on their own cotton plantations, coal mines and textile mills, or else leased them to other employers, such as railroad construction companies, who hired unfree labour thus obtained in preference to the free workers (migrants from Europe) already available for hire.[65]

Convicts deployed in this manner were used in the production of cheap iron, lumber, turpentine, sugar, and tobacco, among other commodities.[66] The reasons for the employment of this kind of unfree labour are evident from a recent account of the Tennessee coalfields

---

Labour Office report on forced labour, its presence was dismissed as unimportant. Hence the irony of the view expressed (United Nations and International Labour Office, 1953: 121) that, in the case of the United States, there was 'no evidence to indicate that [convict labour] plays a significant part in the economy of the country, and for this reason the Committee [on Forced Labour] considers that this allegation is not relevant to its terms of reference'.

[63] See Oshinsky (1997: 35–6).

[64] See Oshinsky (1997: 40–1), who comments: 'As the legislature increased the penalties for minor property crimes, the local courts moved to weaken the protections only recently afforded black defendants'.

[65] Hence the view (Oshinsky, 1997: 58) that, in the aftermath of the Civil war '[t]he advantages of convict labour were quickly perceived. When the Cincinnati Southern Railroad decided to run a trunk line over the Cumberland mountains to Chattanooga, it first hired gangs of Irish, Italian, and black workers at wages ranging from $1.25 to $3.50 a day. But free labour proved hard to manage, on and off the job…so the railroad turned to convicts. Four hundred of them were leased…at the daily rate of $1 per man… The convicts worked 16 hour shifts with a short break for meals. Completed in a single year, the Cumberland line came in well under budget, and the high quality of the work led some to call it the "best railroad built in the United States"'.

[66] According to Oshinsky (1997: 44), in Mississippi the employment of unfree labour was indeed profitable, not least because it does '30 percent more work than free labourers'.

during the late nineteenth century, where the 'public rhetoric of mine managers…masked their most important motivation in seeking the use of convict labourers. Attracting free workers to Tennessee's mines may have been a worry in their early years of operation; but as both blacks and whites flocked to and helped build coal towns in the 1880s and the early 1890s, problems of labor supply dissipated…These industrialists viewed the convict lease first and foremost as a means of cutting labor costs, both directly and by dampening the activity of mining unions'.[67]

V

In order to understand why the United States agribusiness enterprise restructured its capitalist labour process in the years after the 1939–45 war, and also why – long after the abolition of slavery – this involved a process of deproletarianization that took the form of the displacement of better-paid (free) locals by cheaper (unfree) foreign workers who were seasonal migrants, it is necessary to contextualize this both economically and politically. That is, in terms of the balance of forces in the class struggle at that particular conjuncture.[68]

Class Struggle and Foreign Labour in America

The deployment of peonage as a weapon in the struggle between capital and labour was confined neither to the South nor to agriculture. During the Chicago railroad strike of 1894, for example, the Pullman Company used debt as a way of coercing workers engaged in the withdrawal of labour-power.[69] After a long period of retreat, rural labour in the United

---

[67] See Shapiro (1998: 51).

[68] Historically, commercial producers in the southern states have always attempted to prevent 'their' workers from leaving, a problem that became particularly acute during the 1914–18 war (Scott, 1920). When in 1916–17 some 400,000 black workers from the southern states migrated northwards, where wages were higher and conditions better, southern farmers and businessmen attempted to stop this. Not only was 'anti-enticement' legislation enacted, but police arrested migrants waiting at train stations, and north-bound trains themselves were stopped and searched.

[69] For details, see United States Strike Commission (1895). In an era of capitalist depression, in order to maintain profitability the Pullman company reduced wages by 25%. Members of the American Railway Union Workers went on strike, not just over a reduction in wages, but also because rents for company housing were 20–25% higher than elsewhere. In the rural south, of course, unfreedom connected to debt endured long after the ending of slavery.

States during the immediate post-war years was in the ascendant, mainly as a result of wartime labour scarcities: this turnaround in the class struggle, in the form of an enhanced bargaining power on the part of rural labour, was itself reflected in the improved wage levels for rural workers.

Following the steep decline in rural wage levels throughout the United States over the period 1910–40, a decline that was unsurprisingly particularly marked during the capitalist crisis of the 1930s, farm wages as a percentage of factory wage levels rose during wartime, but began to decline once again towards the end of the 1940s.[70] How was the upward wage trend reversed, and why – despite this – did farmers continue to complain about labour shortages, indicating a context where wages might be expected not decline but rather to rise?

The answer to these questions contained in The President's Commission is unequivocal.[71] Noting the anomaly in terms of the economics

---

[70] For these data, see in particular The President's Commission on Migratory Labor (1951: 131–2, Chart X). During the depression era, farm wages declined to one quarter of those paid to factory workers; in the war years, however, farm wages as a ratio of factory wages rose to 44%, but declined subsequently, reaching 37% in 1950 (The President's Commission on Migratory Labor, 1951: 17). As a number of different sources (McWilliams, 1945; Weiner, 1978) all show, unfree migrants were also used in the capitalist agriculture of the US (mainly in California) during the 1930s in order to maintain or restore profitability by forcing down wages and preventing rural labour from organizing to prevent this. Comparing what was happening in America and Germany during that decade, McWilliams (1945: 205–6) observed presciently: 'Today we are witnessing the beginnings of a process which, if permitted to proceed unchecked, is likely to break down the free labour market in this country. Every worker in Germany must carry a Work Book; today it is being suggested that we adopt the same procedure. Employment is monopolized in Germany by the employment service; the same suggestion has been made repeatedly in this country. It is also suggested that all migrant labour be fingerprinted and registered as a means of controlling its movement. It is suggested that we adopt a system of universal registration and a system of domestic passports as a means of controlling migration. ... As production tends to become monopolized, a free labour market becomes anachronistic. It must be controlled and integrated as production is controlled and integrated. The major objection, therefore, to migration in a society such as ours is that it leads, sooner or later, to the elimination of the free labour market... Freedom to move is perhaps the most basic of human liberties. It is the very antithesis of bondage and slavery'.

[71] Lest it be thought that the political stance taken by The President's Commission on Migratory Labor (1951) was pro-labour, not to say socialist, in the concern it expressed for the plight of foreign migrants employed on farms in America, it should be noted that the real object of its anxiety was not workers – either foreign or domestic – but rather the future well-being of the peasant family farm, the central emplacement of both the agrarian and the foundation myth in the US. As The President's Commission on Migratory Labor (1951: 23) makes clear, its principal concern was that the employment by agribusiness enterprises of cheap foreign migrants in preference to local workers would deprive peasant family farms which supplied this

governing the demand for and supply of labour, the report observes that in a situation where farmers complained about a shortage of workers, wages should go up and not down. That wages did not rise, in a situation where the expectation was that they should, is then attributed by The President's Commission to a combination of two factors.[72] Not just to an increased supply in foreign migrants that the United States government made available for American farmers, therefore, but also – and more importantly – to the fact that this external workforce was, unlike its local counterpart, employed on a seasonal basis, low paid, without access to the social wage, and, as will be seen below, unfree.[73]

The reason why this seemingly paradoxical combination – of on the one hand a poorly paid, over worked labour force composed of

---

labour of the off-farm wages necessary to their survival as family farmers. Hence the tenor of the following observation: 'We have long wavered and compromised on the issue of migratory labor in agriculture. We have failed to adopt policies designed to insure an adequate supply of such labor at decent standards of employment. Actually, we have done worse than that. We have used the institutions of government to procure [foreign] labor willing to work under obsolete and backward conditions and thus to perpetuate those very conditions. This not only entrenches a bad system, it expands it. We have not only undermined the standards of employment for migratory farm workers, we have impaired the economic and social position of the family farm operator'.

[72] On this question, The President's Commission on Migratory Labor (1951: 17) observes: 'It may be noted that while the drop in comparative wages during the depression was caused by oversupply – through unemployed industrial workers returning to farms – the present decline comes at a time when farm employers complain of labor shortage. Normally, if there were a labor shortage, wages would rise. Since on the contrary they have declined, it seems reasonable to infer that the supply of illegal [foreign] labor, plus the contract labor the Government has admitted or imported, has helped to depress farm wages relative to factory wages'. 'It appears to us significant', continues The President's Commission on Migratory Labor (1951: 133) subsequently, 'that the regions in which farm wages are well below the national average and have been so for 40 years are those regions containing the States in which the major portion of the post-war foreign labor contracting has centered. Florida has been the principal user of British West Indian contract labor and Texas has been the principal user of Mexican contract labor. Both States have wage rates much below the national average. We cannot, therefore, escape the conclusion that the demand for foreign labor in these States is in part, at least, due to the desire to keep low wages from rising'.

[73] Unlike locals, foreign migrants suffered from bad housing, poor sanitation, lack of medical facilities, and absence of schooling for their children (The President's Commission on Migratory Labor, 1951: 17–8). In addition to being paid less than locals, foreign migrants also had no job security, nor did they have the social protections usually extended to industrial workers in the US (unemployment insurance, minimum wage, pension rights, disability insurance, and workmen's accident insurance). The same report continued (The President's Commission on Migratory Labor, 1951: 16): '[Foreign migrants] are expected to work under conditions no longer typical or characteristic of the American standard of life. In a period of rapidly advancing job and employment standards, we expect them to work at employment which, for all practical purposes, has no job standards'.

temporarily employed migrant workers, and on the other the fact that such labour was subordinated by unfree production relations – was not just acceptable to but actively sought out by agribusiness capital, is not difficult to discern. American agribusiness capital preferred temporary foreign migrants who were unfree because such workers met the three conditions most desired by an employer, then no less than now: because they were unfree, therefore, foreign migrants were available when and for as long as required, more easily controlled while in the labour process, and also more easily dismissed once they were no longer needed, all of which resulted in a relatively less risky production schedule yielding lower cost output and thus higher profits.

During the 1940s, wartime manpower shortages occurred in the United States, as agricultural workers went into armed services and war industries, and wage levels rose. Throughout the following decade, agribusiness turned increasingly to cheaper migrant workers an attempt to force wage levels down one again. That this was successful is clear from the contrast between states which obtained large amounts of contract labour, and those which did not. For example, in 1949 only eight percent of Mexican contract workers went to California, which was accordingly compelled to raise wages paid to agricultural labour by 15 percent; Texas, however, was able to lower its wages by eleven per cent, since it received no less than 46 percent of Mexican contract workers.[74]

Ready to Work, Ready to Go

Mechanization and improved farming techniques contributed to the increasing productivity of agricultural labour: thus, for example,

---

[74] See President's Commission on Migratory Labor (1951: 58). The same source goes on to make the following point: 'The association between wage changes and foreign labor supply as here indicated is consistent with the national picture for all farm wages.... Farm wages have declined in comparative terms and in purchasing power. When we find that there was little change in the Nation-wide average of farm wages, and ...that wages by States were inversely related to the supply of [foreign] labor, it would seem that foreign labor has detrimentally affected the wages of domestic labor. It is our conclusion that the evidence demonstrates that the agencies of Government responsible for importing and contracting foreign labor have not been successful in protecting domestic farm labor from detrimental effects of imported contract [...] labor. We find [the latter] has depressed farm wages and, therefore, has been detrimental to domestic labor' (President's Commission on Migratory Labor, 1951: 58–9).

in 1949 some 27 percent more was produced on farms that in 1940, but with five percent less workers.[75] Contrary to the theoretical views examined above, therefore, unfree migrant labour was not only efficient economically but could also be deployed in the context of a mechanized agriculture. As noted by The President's Commission, the large capitalist farms which used most migrant labour had two basic requirements of their workers: 'To be ready to go to work when needed; to be gone when not needed'.[76] Of these two desirable attributes, it was the capacity to dismiss workers that was the easiest to effect: to retain them in a situation where other employers were offering premium rates (in agriculture, or in manufacturing), however, was more difficult.

A farmer who offered only low wages and bad conditions could not expect to retain a workforce composed of free labour in such circumstances, since a competitive labour market would deliver them to the highest-paying employer; by contrast, capitalist producers unwilling to provide competitive pay rates and conditions necessary to retain workers could indeed expect to do so when they were unfree foreign migrants. The presence of the latter in the agrarian labour process also prevented or pre-empted unionization, since unfree migrants were not only unable to bargain with capital over pay and conditions (by threatening to withdraw their labour-power) but could also be deployed in order to break strikes.[77]

In order to ensure that the first requirement – 'to be ready to go to work when needed' – was met, therefore, agribusiness capitalists in

[75] See The President's Commission on Migratory Labor (1951: 8). As a result of employing foreign migrants, in the form of contract labour from the British West Indies, the productivity of sugarcane cultivated in Florida increased by some thirty per cent over the period 1963–73 (DeWind, Seidl and Shenk, 1979: 392).

[76] See The President's Commission on Migratory Labor (1951: 16), which notes in this connection: 'The basic dilemma faced by farm employers, particularly those with farm operations requiring seasonal hands in large numbers is this: They want a labor supply which, on the one hand, is ready and willing to meet the short-term work requirements and which, on the other hand, will not impose social and economic problems on them or their community when the work is finished. This is what is expected of migratory workers. The demand for migratory workers is thus essentially twofold: to be ready to go to work when needed; to be gone when not needed'.

[77] On this point, see US House of Representatives Special Subcommittee on Labor (1969) and DeWind, Seidl and Shenk (1979). As the latter text makes abundantly clear, foreign migrants who went on strike over pay and conditions were immediately repatriated.

America at this conjuncture required labour-power the owners of which were unable to recommodify this in response to the offer of higher wages and/or better conditions elsewhere, as long as they (the agribusiness capitalists who had acquired it) wanted the use of it. By employing foreign migrants that were unfree – by deproletarianizing them, in other words – agribusiness capital denied others access to them, thereby ensuring that such workers remained within its own labour process under conditions and for payment of its own choosing.[78] For the duration of the harvest period, therefore, these migrants no longer had the capacity to sell their only commodity, labour-power, and were thus not a proletariat in the sense understood by political economy. When the harvest was complete, however, such workers could be dismissed, a procedure which generally coincided with a return to their country of origin.

This combination of attributes – 'to be ready to go to work when needed; to be gone when not needed' is in many respects the ideal employment situation from the point of view of agrarian capital. However, it is also one that far too many commentators – neo-classical economists and exponents of the semi-feudal thesis among them – have thought would hinge on the employment of free wage labour, the proletariat of classical political economy.

As has been seen above, this is due to a mistaken belief that the employment of labour-power that is unfree is incompatible with economic efficiency, with advanced productive forces, with profitability, and thus with capitalism itself. The historical and contemporary existence of deproletarianization challenges this belief. It is not capitalist profitability which gives rise to the employment of free labour in preference to unfree equivalents, therefore, but rather the opposite: namely, the capacity to replace an existing workforce composed of free labour with unfree equivalents is what gives rise to or enhances capitalist profitability.

---

[78] As one producer in the State of Colorado explained in 1950 (The President's Commission on Migratory Labor, 1951: 20): '...I am convinced ...that any nation is very fortunate if that nation can, from sources near at hand, obtain the services on beck and call of labor, adult male labor, on condition that when the job is completed the labor will return to his home. That is exactly the situation of this area'. Not the least interesting aspects of this observation are the following: first, the invocation by the farmer concerned of the term 'nation', equating capital with the national interest; and second, the use of the term 'beck and call' to describe his preferred relation with the workforce, a term applied by the Thorners (1962) to delineate the unfree character of bonded labour in India.

VI

Where the history and present structure of the free/unfree dialectic are concerned, the United States – no less than Germany – illustrates the problematic nature of two things. First, of confining unfree labour simply to the 'pre-history' of capitalism. And second, of invoking the current existence of such production relations as a reason why a more contemporary notion of primitive accumulation should replace a concept of 'fully functioning' capitalism.

Unfree Migrants, 'Fully Functioning' Capitalism

That foreign migrants employed by agribusiness capital in the US at this conjuncture were unfree is beyond doubt. Coercion took a number of different forms, including the familiar ones of tied housing, the requirement on the part of the migrant to provide additional unpaid labour of kinsfolk (particularly children), the deposit system, and debt bondage, all of which were enforced by the threat of deportation, employer collusion, and physical threats. Migrants working in Florida and Oregon at this conjuncture confirmed that residence in housing provided by a farmer precluded the capacity to recommodify their labour-power whilst in his employ, as did the practices of debt to the farmer's store and/or the withholding of wages due (the 'deposit system') in order to prevent the departure or secure the return of the worker concerned, while employers and contractors specified the requirement to provide child labour.[79]

On the existence of coercion, therefore, even The President's Commission compared the situation of foreign migrants during the early 1950s to that of peonage, and concluded that '[f]or the migratory farm worker the contractor system has all the evils of the sweatshop

[79] On all these points, see The President's Commission on Migratory Labor (1951: 77 ff., 142, 162–3). About the role of tied housing in immobilizing the labour-power of migrants the same source observed: 'A worker so housed has less freedom to use his idle time by working for other employers than he would if his housing were free of employer restrictions. Such restrictions on the movements of workers are disadvantageous to him and also to the community at large because less effective use is made of the labor supply. When the provision of housing by employers is used to restrict either wage adjustments or freedom of movement by workers, both the individual interest of the worker and the interest of the community in effectively using its labor supply are obstructed'.

system that disappeared long ago from American industry'.[80] Farmers left the task of control to labour contractors, who exercised coercion over their particular work gang in order to guarantee maximum output at the cheapest cost, and also to ensure that its members worked for the employer concerned and no other.[81] The fact that migrants were refused employment by farmers whom they approached directly, and instructed to seek this under the aegis of a contractor, undermines the oft-heard view that employers resort to contractors only in contexts where workers are otherwise unavailable: it suggests that the real reason is connected with control, exercised indirectly by the farmer via the labour contractor.

Rural employers do not willingly improve the socio-economic circumstances of their workforce, either in terms of pay and conditions or of production relations. Given the choice, in other words, capital – industrial and agrarian – actively seeks out cheaper, more easily

---

[80] For the comparisons with the sweatshop system and peonage, see The President's Commission on Migratory Labor (1951: 5, 19). On the question of peonage, the observation is as follows: 'Under constant threat of apprehension and deportation, [the Mexican foreign worker's] life is one of furtive insecurity. In the hands of employers inclined to make use of the wetback's [illegality], the result is virtually peonage'. The link between the illegal status of the foreign migrant and his vulnerability to employer and/or contractor coercion is equally clear (The President's Commission on Migratory Labor, 1951: 130), since such kinds of worker have 'even less bargaining power than the domestic migrant, for if he [the foreign worker] does not like the wages or working conditions that are set for him, and protests, he is subjected to...possible deportation'. Very much the same kind of observation was made about the way in which Mexican migrants were controlled by employers and contractors during the 1930s (McWilliams, 1945: 142): 'The threat of turning recalcitrant workers over to the immigration officials is, also, an effective method by which Mexicans are held to the strict fulfillment of their contracts of employment. Through the use of such methods, "deserters" soon discover that they are not free agents. Since Mexicans are always in debt – to the contractor or to the company commissary – they have not been able to move freely from one employment opportunity to another. There is an abundance of evidence verifying the widespread use of such methods to enforce a state of virtual peonage'.

[81] Hence the observation (The President's Commission on Migratory Labor, 1951: 18) that '[w]orkers testifying in California told us that it was difficult and often impossible to obtain a job directly from the farmer: instead, they were referred to labor contractors'. For the kinds of control exercised by the contractor over the members of his crew, see the same source (The President's Commission on Migratory Labor, 1951: 77–8), which describes not just how migrants are 'sold' from smuggler to labour agent, and from the latter to the employer, but also the mechanics of induced indebtedness, occasioned by the 'deposit' system of withholding wages and advances redeemable only at the equivalent of the company store ('[t]o assure that he will stay until his services are no longer needed, his pay, or some portion thereof, frequently is held back. Sometimes, he is deliberately kept indebted to the farmer's store or commissary until the end of the season, at which time he may be given enough to buy shoes or clothing and encouraged to return the following season').

controlled and unfree forms of labour-power. This goes against the myth, perpetuated by neo-classical economists and exponents of the semi-feudal thesis alike, that where capital is profitable, it will automatically seek out workers who are free, and rely on the market (= competitive conditions) to deliver them to its labour process.

The situation is altogether different: it is the capacity of the workers engaged in class struggle against employers, and a corresponding ability to exercise pressure on capital (via the state) as much as anything which determines whether or not pay and conditions improve, and whether or not unfree production relations continue. This element of class struggle, and not an employer's capacity either to install more advanced productive forces or to pay higher wages, is the deciding factor in the issue of wages, conditions and unfree relations of production.

In the United States during the 1920s, therefore, manufacturing, construction and other non-agricultural industries all attempted – unsuccessfully – to secure access to resources of foreign migrant labour, citing as a reason the unavailability/unsuitability of local workers.[82] Unlike agribusiness, however, they had 'to develop working conditions and job standards compatible with the expectations of American workers'.[83] By contrast, those rural employers in 1950s America who used foreign migrants 'continue[d] to offer jobs and working conditions that [were] no better and in many respects [were] worse than those offered three and four decades [previously]'. As subsequent reports confirm, this situation not merely extended into the 1960s and beyond but has now become far more common.[84]

Incarcerated Workers, 'Fully Functioning' Capitalism

Convict labour is in one important sense a misnomer: used in a general sense, the term conveys the ostensibly neutral activity of work

[82] The President's Commission on Migratory Labor (1951: 19,21–2) makes the telling point that 1950s employer discourse utilized by agribusiness enterprises was exactly the same as that deployed in the 1920s by industrial capitalists. Both justified their requests for an immigrant workforce on the spurious grounds that local workers were scarce, inadequate or unreliable. As the same report confirms (The President's Commission on Migratory Labor 1951: 80–2), local workers were not scarce, inadequate or unreliable.

[83] On this point, see The President's Commission on Migratory Labor (1951: 21–2).

[84] For the reliance of American agribusiness enterprises on cheap, unfree labour provided by foreign migrants throughout the entire period from the 1960s to the 1990s, see among others Galarza (1964), Friedland and Nelkin (1971), History Task Force (1979), and Mann (2001).

carried out by inmates, a perception that translates easily into the concept of prison work as a form of occupational therapy. The role discharged by incarceration in contexts such as the New South (and South Africa), however, possessed a different logic: it was not a case of an already existing inmate population being put to work, therefore, as of a free workforce being turned into a prison population with the object of converting its subjects into labour that was no longer free. This commercial leasing of prison labour has continued to fuel the 'fully functioning' accumulation process in the United States.

A consequence of the expansion in the numbers of inmates and the privatization of prison operations is that incarcerated subjects in the United States are perceived nowadays by industrial capitalist enterprises as a reliable and cheap source of labour-power. Contrary to the view of Adam Smith and others that the work they produced was of poor quality, and that consequently they were less profitable and more costly to employ, and in economic terms generally less efficient, therefore, unfree labourers in the United States completed the tasks to which they were allocated by capital not only more cheaply, more profitably, and quicker than free labour, but the work itself was also of a higher quality.[85] This is even more so the case today.

According to a recent account, in the United States 'the number of privately-operated prisons has jumped from five to 100 in the past decade alone, and is still growing...the private use of prison labour is legal in 37 states and has been enthusiastically embraced by dozens of household-name firms, including IBM, Boeing, Microsoft and AT&T.'[86] The same account continues: '[T]he scale of US prison labour makes it a first-choice source of reliable, pliant workers who can be paid less than the minimum wage and cannot strike. That's deemed unfair on the prisoners but more so on local non-prison workers, because it drives down wages and conditions. Prisoners are increasingly taking on the kind of low-skilled farmwork done until recently by immigrant labour. There are also reports in the US press of "maquiladora" operations – US firms that exploit cheap labour in Mexico – shifting factories back north of the border to take advantage of US prisoners.'

---

[85] Not only did coal production in Alabama increase from 67,000 to 8.4 million tons over the 1875–1900 period, therefore, but 'convict leasing was essential to this growth' (Oshinsky, 1997: 76).

[86] See 'Free markets, unfree labour', *MoneyWeek*, 15 April, 2008.

In contrast to the argument that, from the point of view of a prospective capitalist employer, a major problem with using workers who are unfree is the non-assured or unreliable nature of the supply, in contexts where such production relations have been – and are – reproduced institutionally in the form of workers leased from prison (not just in the United States but also in South Africa under the apartheid system), they constitute an assured and dependable source of labour-power precisely because its subjects are not free.[87]

Conclusion

Over a century and a half the rural labour regime in Germany metamorphosed from a permanent workforce of tenants and/or sharecroppers to one composed of attached labour employed on a yearly contract, and subsequently to casual/seasonal migrants recruited from Poland on a temporary basis. These transformations coincided with the development in Germany of what can only be described as a 'fully functioning' capitalism. During the same period, there was an analogous shift in the United States labour regime, from chattel slavery to tenancy, foreign migrants and convict workers.

That unfree labour was actively sought out by what were among the most advanced forms of capitalism in Europe and the Americas during the twentieth century, therefore, suggests that such production

[87] 'From a business standpoint,' notes Oshinsky (1997: 44), 'the subleasing (of convict labour in Mississippi during the latter half of the nineteenth century) was ideal. It plugged the major weakness of the old system: the high fixed cost of labour. Under the sublease, an employer was not stuck with a set number of prisoners over a long period of time. He did not have to feed, clothe, and guard them when there was little work to be done. He could now lease convicts according to his specific, or seasonal needs.' For the regular and dependable nature of the supply of unfree black labour to commercial farmers in South Africa during the apartheid era, see Ainslie (1977) and Cook (1982). As the report into forced labour by United Nations and International Labour Office (1953: 77) confirms, in South Africa 'prison labour is hired out to railways, harbours local authorities, certain gold mines, farmers and other private persons.' The same source (United Nations and International Labour Office, 1953: 78) noted further that commercial farmers themselves formed associations to secure such unfree workers from the state, noting that '[t]he districts where these prisons are situated include the country's highest food-producing centres, where labour is extremely short.' On the dependability of the supply of prison labour in the United States, see Oshinsky (1997: 80–1), who notes: 'Convicts did not skip work for picnics, holidays, funerals, and excursions. Nor did they…leave town in search of better wages, or go out on strike. "Convict labour is desirable by firms or corporations for the reason that it can be depended on – always ready for work," boasted one prison official. "Contracts for the output can be made with the knowledge that the goods can be delivered."'

relations cannot be interpreted simply as systemic residues, encountered if at all only during the early stage of 'primitive accumulation'. The presence of workers who are unfree in Germany and the United States – both of which are instances of a 'fully functioning' capitalism – serves to confirm that it is wrong to categorize this kind of labour regime as in some sense prefiguring the onset of capitalism proper.

In both these advanced social formations, unfreedom was a production relation used by capital neither to displace smallholders from land (= depeasantization) nor to affix them to land (= repeasantization). Rather, its object was to prevent workers from selling their labour-power to the highest bidder; that is, personally commodifying or recommodifying their own labour-power (= deproletarianization). The aim of unfreedom was, in short, connected not with the economic dissolution or reproduction of peasant economy, but with the conditions in which labour-power was reproduced.

The continuation of unfree labour long after the ending both of southern slavery in the United States and of Prussian serfdom/servanthood in Germany undermines a number of arguments considered in previous chapters. The first of these is the decoupling of unfree labour and a capitalism that is 'fully functioning'. The second is that such workers are merely 'disguised wage labourers' who are 'free'. And the third is that, even where they are acknowledged to co-exist alongside what is undeniably capitalism – such production relations indicate the presence of nothing more than primitive accumulation.

Accordingly, the presence and role of unfree migrant/local workers in the advanced capitalist labour processes of Germany and the United States over the nineteenth and twentieth centuries is not explained as – and cannot be confined epistemologically to – the 'pre-history' of capitalism. Nor can it be dismissed in terms of an analogous claim that such production relations are not – and cannot be considered to be – a central feature of a 'fully functioning' accumulation process. Foreign migrants and incarcerated workers – the concentration camp in Germany and the commercial leasing of prison labour in the United States – were (and in some instances are still) centrally a feature of 'fully functioning' capitalism in both these national contexts.

CHAPTER SEVEN

'MEDIEVAL WORKING PRACTICES'? BRITISH AGRICULTURE AND THE RETURN OF THE GANGMASTER

Consider the following description of the methods of recruitment and control by labour contractors of casual labour employed in agriculture. Poorly-paid foreign migrants who work for long hours at low wages and live in overcrowded, barrack-style accommodation (in this case, containers or 'chicken-shacks'), are subjected by labour contractors to a culture of fear and intimidation. The latter includes deductions by contractors from what are already below-minimum wages, the withholding of wages, and threats of physical beatings if workers complain.

Migrant casual labourers are not only fined by the contractor if they do not work hard or fast enough, therefore, but have no freedom of movement, are required to borrow from contractors at high ('exorbitant') interest rates, and to repay what are considerable recruitment costs if they wish to cease employment. Regulation by the State of such agricultural labour is non-existent, not least because government neither knows nor appears interested in knowing how many migrants there are or what their employment involves: legislation covering pay for and conditions of work are either unenforced or routinely disregarded.

The twofold response to this description on the part of most of those reading it would be unambiguous. First, that it was an account of a situation long past. And second, that – if it was about an extant situation – it could only refer to agricultural workers in South Africa or an historically backward rural area of a so-called Third World country (perhaps the northeast of Brazil or India). It is, however, the description accepted by a revealing and important Report from the Environment, Food and Rural Affairs (EFRA) Committee of the House of Commons of the way in which recruitment and control of part-time workers are effected currently in the most advanced agriculture of a metropolitan capitalist country – Britain.[1]

[1] Citation used in this Chapter follows the twofold referencing method adopted by the EFRA Committee document. First, to the section that is the Report itself (EFRA, 2003: 1–33). And second, to the section containing Evidence (EFRA, 2003: Ev 1–109).

To insist on a connection in Britain between the intensification of the accumulation process and the employment of labour that is not free nevertheless remains a controversial proposition. For this reason, the first part of the chapter examines the general theoretical questions raised by the link between capitalism and labour contracting, the way the gangmaster system operated in nineteenth century British agriculture, together with the reasons for its existence. The second part considers these issues in relation to the resurgent gangmaster system of the late twentieth century. The third looks at the some of the analytical difficulties structuring the otherwise excellent EFRA Committee Report, and also how the discourse concerning the role, the control and desirability of rural labour contracting – both for and against – has changed very little over the nineteenth and twentieth centuries. It is argued that the contemporary gangmaster system offers an insight into the way a 'fully functioning' agribusiness capitalism operates at the start of the twenty-first century.

I

As is well known, historically the process of labour contracting has played an important role in the *development* of a capitalist agriculture in many different global contexts. In this sense, it can be seen as corresponding to the 'pre-history' of capitalism (= a process of 'primitive accumulation'). Contractors are necessary in the initial stages of accumulation, it is claimed, in order both to coax reluctant peasants off the land to work elsewhere, and to ensure the supply of the resulting migrant labour to those commercial farms and plantations that need it. Once the migration flow has been established, so the argument goes, these contractors are no longer needed, as the pattern of migration is regularized and reproduced over time and space.[2]

Labour Contracting as Primitive Accumulation?

According to this view, the contractor makes an important socio-economic contribution to the process of rural labour market formation

The latter consists both of written materials submitted to the Committee and the cross-examination by its members of the witnesses themselves.

[2] An example of this view, applied to coal mining, is Taylor (1960: 234), who argues that '[s]ub-contracting, in short, both from a narrowly economic and from a managerial point of view, was a form of organization peculiar to the adolescence of industrial society and destined to disappear as the British economy grew to maturity'.

during the early stages of agrarian capitalism (its 'pre-history'), fulfilling a benign role as facilitator of the migration process and as mentor of the migrant worker him/herself. The development of a 'fully functioning' capitalist agriculture marks the completion of this important function, and the labour contractor then simply vanishes from the historical stage for good.

The view that labour contracting is simply an arrangement that is necessary only during the course of early capitalist development licenses another claim: that the relation between the worker and the labour contractor is basically harmonious and non-coercive.[3]

[3] The most robust defence of this position comes, unsurprisingly, from conservative historians. Its most succinct expression is that of Hayek (1954: 9–10), who protests that: 'There is, however, one supreme myth which more than any other has served to discredit the economic system to which we owe our present-day civilization… It is the legend of the deterioration of the position of the working classes in consequence of the rise of "capitalism" (or of the "manufacturing" or the "industrial system"). Who has not heard of the "horrors of early capitalism" and gained the impression that the advent of this system brought untold suffering to large classes…. The widespread emotional aversion to "capitalism" is closely connected with this belief that the undeniable growth of wealth which the competitive order has produced was purchased at the price of depressing the standard of life of the weakest elements of society'. It was, perhaps, this kind of view that the author had in mind when, in the following fictional account, Buckman (1891: 42–4) satirized both the way rural life in nineteenth century England was idealized, and in particular the manner in which the work regime of the agricultural labourer was depicted. 'We have mentioned previously that the Arcadian plebeians work for the chiefs. That's what they will tell you if you inquire. Their methods of working are, however, thoroughly Arcadian. For instance, having been to the homestead in the morning, the son of toil receives his orders and starts to his work. He has not proceeded far before he meets another Arcadian of like attern to himself. The two Arcadians stop when they are alongside of one another, and give a half turn round. Then they commence the important ceremony known as passing the time of day. Each one makes some topical observation to the other. …. The son of toil at last reaches his field, after going through the same ceremony with other Arcadians whom he may meet, and perhaps he does a full fifteen minutes' work – really honest toil. Then he leans on his implement with a smile of satisfaction and contemplates the view. Possibly he descries in the roadway some Arcadian acquaintance, and he forthwith commences conversation. It matters not how far it be from the road, or wherever it is that the other Arcadian is situate. Even if there be a matter of thirty chains between them, the conversation will be just as spiced and just as confidential as if they were within a yard of each other. Fifteen to thirty minutes will be consumed in this ceremony, and then there will be some more work done. It is not etiquette in Arcadia for any one to pass down the road without holding a conversation of at least five minutes in the case of a mere casual acquaintance to thirty or forty minutes in the case of better known personages. Besides these ceremonies is the homage to be paid to the bottle. Worship at this shrine is performed as devoutly as any religious ceremony in the world, and the worship must be repeated a number of times in the day. Furthermore, there are certain specified times for the consumption of "nuncheon" and the necessary dinner-hour of an hour and a half. What with all the ceremonies and observances, and the labours performed, a more industrious man than an Arcadian plebeian is not easy to meet with.'

One exponent of this idealised view warns that, where nineteenth century British agriculture is concerned, '[i]t is easy to become over-preoccupied with the gang…public opinion was more sensitive to the hardships and moral changes to which women and children were exposed when they appeared in concentrated form…it would be misleading to infer from evidence of this kind that there was increased reliance on child and female field labour at the expense of the livelihood of adult male workers'.[4]

Because they ignore the real reason why contractors are used, however, adherents of this highly romanticized view cannot account for the reason why this kind of recruitment process continues beyond the early stage of agrarian capitalism, and is found also in contexts where accumulation is well established, as is currently the case in India, California, and Brazil.[5] In short, labour contracting such as the gangmaster system has less to do with labour market formation during the early stages of accumulation and more to do with the need of rural producers engaged in commercial agriculture at *any* stage of capitalism to

---

[4] This view is found in a recent and highly problematic history by Armstrong (1988: 97) of agricultural workers in Britain. Ironically, Armstrong counterposes his own approach to the issue of rural labour with what he terms 'a new style of social history… dominated by a conviction of the explanatory value of the concept of "class"', which, he maintains (Armstrong, 1988: 13), is 'not to the taste of all historians'. The irony derives from the fact that, where the analysis of gangmasters is concerned, the approach of the 'new social history' closely identified by him with the *History Workshop Journal* is in some important respects no different from his own. Thus, for example, in her account of the gender-specific aspects of participation in gang labour by women workers, Kitteringham (1975: 98ff.) comes dangerously close to dismissing criticisms of the exploitation by gangmasters of child and female labour as 'Victorian bourgeois moralizing', and consequently of recategorizing exploitative relations of production as their 'other' – evidence for working class (and especially women's) empowerment. This difficulty stems from a laudable but problematic objective informing much 'new social history' associated with the *History Workshop Journal*: namely, the desirability of identifying all 'from below' forms of agency as empowering, or – as Thompson (1963: 12) put it, memorably – to rescue 'those below' from 'the enormous condescension of posterity'. The same approach also informs earlier historiographical accounts of the rural labourer, such as that by Fussell (1949), a celebratory text that is almost a plebeian variant of *Country Life*; its highly romanticized account of rural habitations should be contrasted with that contained in Dodd (1976: 56–7) and Heath (1989: 28ff). Both the 'new social history' and its precursors suffer from the same kinds of shortcoming. First, the privileging of locality over the wider context, and with it the downgrading of an over-arching political economy. And second, taken to its logical conclusion, the 'new social history' approach necessarily leads ultimately to a denial that *any* 'from below' activity in which rural workers participate can ever be disempowering – which is precisely what the more conservative historiography of Armstrong also does.

[5] For coercive recruitment/control by labour contractors in these different national contexts, see respectively Singh and Iyer (1984), Krissman (1997) and Martins (2002).

maintain or improve control over (and thereby cheapen the cost of) their workers by means of coercion.[6]

This idealized view of rural labour contracting in Britain contrasts markedly with earlier accounts. The latter emphasize both the coerciveness and the harshness of together with the exploitation inherent in the gangmaster labour regime, an aspect depicted graphically not just in mid-nineteenth century Government Commissions (and in particular the Sixth Report of the 1862 Children's Employment Commission, published in 1867) but also outlined in the classic analyses – by Marx, Hasbach and Green – of the workforce employed in British agriculture.[7] These earlier accounts indicated both that control exercised by the gangmaster was based on violence and coercion, and that where the

[6] As such, recruitment/control/coercion by a gangmaster corresponds to workforce decomposition/recomposition involving the replacement of free labourers with unfree equivalents, a form of capitalist restructuring that amounts to a process not of proletarianization as much as deproletarianization. Because proletarianization is equated invariably with the cessation only of ownership of means of production (= land), and not also with the capacity of a worker personally to commodify his/her own labour-power, the cessation of the latter as a result of coercive control exercised by an employer or contractor does not prevent rural labourers being categorized – incorrectly – as a proletariat. Thus, for example, Howkins (1985: 9) wrongly equates the casualization by the gangmaster system of the agrarian workforce in late nineteenth and early twentieth century Norfolk with the emergence of a rural proletarian 'with nothing to sell but his labour power in a free market which was overstocked, and which valued him at naught'. Others to whom this same criticism applies include Hobsbawm and Rudé (1969) and Morgan (1982).

[7] Classic accounts of the nineteenth century rural gangmaster system in Britain are found not just in the Children's Employment Commission (1867) and Marx (1976a: 850–3) but also in Heath (1989: 148 ff.), Hasbach (1908: 193–204) and Green (1920). They are absent from the equally classic history by the Hammonds (1920) of rural labour only because their account deals with the period before the gang system rose to prominence and became a focus of concern. Marx himself regarded official publications issued periodically by the British State as an invaluable source of information. His views merit quoting at length (Marx, 1976a: 91): 'The social statistics of Germany and the rest of Continental Western Europe are, in comparison with those of England, quite wretched. But they raise the veil just enough to let us catch a glimpse of the Medusa's head behind it. We should be appalled at our own circumstances if, as in England, our governments and parliaments periodically appointed commissions of inquiry into economic conditions; if these commissions were armed with the same plenary powers to get at the truth; if it were possible to find for this purpose men as competent, as free from partisanship and respect of persons as are England's factory inspectors, her medical reporters on health, her commissioners of inquiry into the exploitation of women and children, into conditions of housing and so on.' It comes as no surprise, therefore, that the findings contained in nineteenth century commissions of enquiry have been challenged periodically by conservative historiography. Thus for, example, Hutt (1954) insists that child labour employed in British factories was well-paid, 'wholesome' and light in nature, that child labourers were 'free agents' (= 'choice-making' subjects), and that factory owners were 'men of humanity'.

gang system operated adult male workers were increasingly replaced with child labour.[8]

That the main concern of the 1867 Report was the 'moral well-being' of children and girls employed in gangs is in an important sense irrelevant. It was precisely the relay-in-statement – from 'child-as-victim' to 'child-as-*worker*', permitted (and perhaps even encouraged) by the 1867 Report – that enabled in turn not just Marx but also Hasbach and Green to indict the capitalist system and its effects. The conclusion of Hasbach is that the condition of the agricultural labourer 'can hardly be described as one of complete personal freedom', while Green underlines the link between the challenge to the gangmaster system and the rise of trade unionism.[9]

That unfree production relations applied not just to mine workers but also to both permanent and temporary agricultural labour employed in nineteenth century Britain is a matter of well-established record.[10] All the accepted characteristics of unfreedom are

---

[8] Hasbach (1908: 199, 203, 272) indicates that where the gang system flourished, as it did in the Fenland area, the labour-power of men was increasingly replaced by that of women and children, the reason being that the latter not only worked as hard as men but were also easier to control and less costly to employ. In such circumstances, he emphasizes (Hasbach, 1908: 200, 201), control exercised over the workforce by the gang overseer was based on coercion.

[9] See Hasbach (1908: 362) and also Green (1920: 77), who observes: 'The pinch of poverty was increased, too, by the falling off in family earnings. It was chiefly through the action of the trade unions that the degrading gang system of employing married women, young girls and boys on field work under a ganger who exploited their labour…had largely disappeared.' Some official accounts offer a different reason for the decline of the gangmaster system towards the end of the nineteenth century. Hence the report by Board of Agriculture and Fisheries (1906) about the decrease in the rural labouring population maintained that it was the Elementary Education Act of 1870 that put a break on gangmaster recruitment,. This it did by restricting the employment of children, thereby depriving gangmasters of this source of easily-controlled and cheap labour. Hence the claim (Board of Agriculture and Fisheries, 1906: 10) that: 'These changes paved the way for the agitation of the early [1870s], when for a time capital and labour on the farm organized their forces and came into the open, and in some districts bitter, conflict. From this period dates a change in the relationship of masters and men. Agricultural labour attained economic freedom, [even] if it did not acquire at once the same degree of mobility as industrial labour….' The National Union of Agricultural Workers was founded in 1872, but dissolved in 1896. It was reconstituted in 1906 as the Eastern Counties Agricultural labourers and Smallholders' Union, becoming the National Agricultural Labourers' and Rural Workers Union in 1912 and the National Union of Agricultural Workers in 1920 (for the history of which see Groves 1949). It eventually became part of the much larger Transport and General Workers Union.

[10] For the unfree nature of mine labour, see Anonymous (1899: 121 ff.) and Page Arnot (1955: 5–6, 9–10). In an attempt to exculpate capitalism, the conservative

encountered: for example, immobilizing legislation, tied cottages, the truck system, child labour, coercion, agricultural workers not permitted to seek alternative employment without the agreement of their existing employer.[11]

Truck made it possible for employers and/or gangmasters either to deduct 'fines' from a worker's wage, or to restrict the spending of the latter to shops or a company store controlled/owned by the employer/gangmaster, thus enabling them to charge high prices which resulted in worker indebtedness.[12] Although the 1887 Truck Act made this illegal, domestic servants and agricultural labourers were excluded from its

---

historian Ashton (1954: 37) argues that in Britain unfree labour was found not in towns but in villages, the sub-text being that industry – which was capitalist – employed only free labour, whilst agriculture – which according to him was still in a pre-capitalist stage – did not. This view (unfree labour = pre-capitalist relation, free labour = capitalist relation) is one shared, unsurprisingly, by neo-classical economic historiography that in the mid-1970s attempted to revise the meaning of antebellum plantation slavery, and, more surprisingly, by the supposedly Marxist interpretations of rural India advanced at that same conjuncture by exponents of the semi-feudal thesis.

[11] Under the Master and Servants Act of 1824, any agricultural labourer attempting to leave his existing work and seek an alternative job without first obtaining the permission of his current employer was liable to imprisonment for breach of contract. It was finally repealed in 1867. Other, more subtle, forms of control – based on employer collusion – were also practised. Hence the relationship between labourer and farmer in early nineteenth century Britain, described by Howitt (1838: 176,178) in the following terms: 'They hire for the year, under very severe punishment in the case of misbehaviour, or quitting service; they cannot have fresh service, without a *character* from the *last master*, and also from the *minister of the parish!*...The farmer takes the man, just at the season to get the sweat out of him; and if he dies, he dies when the main work is done. The labourer is wholly at the mercy of the master, who, if he will not keep him beyond the year, can totally ruin him, by refusing him a character' (original emphasis). The same source (Howitt, 1838: 182) continues: 'but the fact, that these poor people must bring a character from the last master before they can be employed again, is one which may seem at first sight a reasonable demand, but is in fact the binding link of a most subtle and consummate slavery. I have seen the effect of this system in the Derbyshire and collieries. There, amongst the master colliers a combination was entered into... This rule, that no man should be employed except he brought a character from his last master was adopted; and what was the consequence? That every man was the bounden slave of him in whose employment he was'.

[12] The operation of the truck system in the early 1840s is described (Dodd, 1976: 43, 53) in the following manner: 'It is a common practice in these counties [Kent, Surrey, Sussex] to pay the wages, both of men and women, by a check drawn upon the miller of the village, who is generally related to the farmer, the laborer getting part of his wages in flour and part in money; or it may be, that the miller again hands him over to the grocer; and thus the poor man in general pays from 25 to 30 per cent more for his victuals than in justice and honesty he should... [T]he truck-trading oppression of the gangmaster, who not only screws down his [worker's] wages to the lowest cent, but supplies him with inferior articles at the highest price; while it subjects [the worker] to greater personal toil...'.

provisions.[13] There is accordingly plenty of evidence, anecdotal and otherwise, confirming that much agricultural labour in England also remained unfree throughout the first half of the twentieth century – long after a capitalist transition had taken place.[14]

Trade Unions and Tied Cottages

Prior to World War I, permanent workers were farm servants employed for the whole year, during the course of which they were forbidden legally from seeking an alternative job. It is clear, moreover, that such an arrangement was perceived by permanent workers themselves as one in which they became in effect the property of the farmer who had

---

[13] The generally oppressive and exploitative conditions faced by rural labour in Britain are outlined by Howkins (1990: 113): 'Since at least the middle of the nineteenth century the farm worker has been among the worst paid and worst treated of all male English manual workers. At virtually no point since 1850 have agricultural wages exceeded 50% of the national wage; until the Second World War farm workers were excluded from the provisions of the National Insurance Act and the Bank Holidays legislation; employment by the day remained common until the 1920s while the hours worked were long and irregular. For women who worked the land conditions were worse.'

[14] Over the late nineteenth and early twentieth century concern about the coercive power exercised by commercial farmers over their agricultural workers was expressed by liberals and socialists alike. Thus, for example, the following comments by an investigative journalist (The Special Commissioner of The 'Daily News', 1891: 110–1) with Liberal party affiliations: 'Nobody would say Lord Wantage was a man to exercise any improper influence on his people; but he is a strong Tory, has been a member of the Tory Government, his agents are Tories, and he owns all the land and all the houses, and can give or take away employment. I could not find anybody who knew of a political meeting having been held in these places. I heard it rumoured that there was one man who dared to avow himself a Liberal, but I couldn't find him. "Oh, yes sir," said a woman in the place, "they all votes Lord Wantage's way, of course. It wouldn't do for 'em to go agin 'im." I am assured that the admirable little public house in Ardington is to a great extent a failure, because the men find that they are not free to talk there, and that whatever they say is liable to be carried by the birds to the agent's or bailiff's ears. The people are managed and governed and controlled without the least voice in their public and collective affairs, and, though they undoubtedly have strong opinions on certain matters, they dare not give expression to them.' A Fabian Society pamphlet (Pedder, 1904: 11–3) published at the beginning of the twentieth century indicates how the tied cottage system operated to the advantage of the farmer, enabling him to exercise what amounted to extra-economic control over an agricultural labouring family: 'If [the worker] goes into the cottage provided, the trap falls. He will be had up before the magistrates if he refuses to fulfill his agreement of service, in writing or verbal'. The twin issues of rural employer collusion to hold down agricultural wages and the use of tied housing to prevent workers joining unions or voting for political candidates not approved by the farmer also emerged at a Conference held at Ruskin College, Oxford, during 1916, where trade unionists discussed the policy they wanted to see implemented after the 1914–18 war (Orwin, 1917: 82, 95–6).

acquired their labour-power.[15] Debt was used also to coerce smallholders in England, and prevent them from organizing in producer cooperatives, as is evident from evidence presented to the 1913 United States Senate Commission.[16]

Investigations conducted by the Board of Agriculture and Fisheries into rural wages and employment conditions at the end of the 1914–18 war revealed that permanent farm workers were bound contractually for a year, an arrangement enforced in a court of law.[17] Employers withheld the bulk of payment due until the end of the contract period, a method of bonding labour practised in India.[18] Such contracts frequently stipulated that the worker must 'fill up his time at anything he may be required to do, and continue working in haymaking and harvest as long as he may be required.'[19] Although at that conjuncture women labourers disliked 'the long hours and constant tie' of agricultural tasks, nevertheless it was reported that 'only the fact that they are bound by an undertaking…keeps them at work.'[20]

Why forms of unfree labour continued to be sought out by commercial farmers in Britain immediately after the 1914–18 war is clear. With labour in short supply, agricultural workers who remained available demanded higher wages and better conditions, joining trade unions to

---

[15] 'Hiring-fairs are about done away with nowadays', noted one observer (Kitchen, 1940: 99–100, 101), who had himself been an agricultural labourer, 'no farm servant being compelled to stay at his place twelvemonth. But at the time of which I am writing, when a hired servant had taken his "fastening-penny" he was bound by statute to live in and sleep on the premises from 1st December to the following 24th November; to become, in fact, the property of his master… So that is how we carried on before the Great War [pre-1914]. Then the Agricultural wages Act came into force, and altered the custom of hired servants being tied for twelvemonth. To me it always seemed a wretched business, especially for a lad of thirteen or fourteen, to be taken like a sheep or calf to market and sold to the highest bidder'.

[16] Having addressed a nearly empty meeting in Sussex about the economic advantages of small farmers joining together in producer cooperatives (United States Senate Commission, 1913: 841), the Secretary of the Agricultural Organization Society of England noted that the 'secret of the failure of the meeting, as I afterwards learned, was the fact that the last man who entered the room was the local dealer, and he had gone around that district a week before and visited every farmer, saying: "If you attend that meeting for cooperation, remember you are on my books up to a certain amount and you will have to pay within 48 hours."'

[17] See Board of Agriculture and Fisheries (1919: 82–3), which notes that such a contract was 'sealed by the acceptance [by the labourer] of the "fastening penny"', a term that accurately depicts its binding nature.

[18] See Board of Agriculture and Fisheries (1919: 87). On the connection between withholding wages and debt bondage, see Brass (1999).

[19] See Board of Agriculture and Fisheries (1919: 84).

[20] See Board of Agriculture and Fisheries (1919: 89).

press for these improvements.[21] For their part, rural employers were unwilling to pay their workers more than they had done in the pre-war era.[22] However, pressure on them to do so increased, a process fuelled by rapid unionization.[23] Where they were able to do so, therefore, commercial producers resorted to immobilizing mechanisms such as withholding wages and the tied cottage.

This situation persisted well into the twentieth century, thereby undermining the oft-heard attempt to label such unfree working arrangements as 'residual' or 'anomalous' relational forms unconnected with accumulation. In Britain, labour camps or 'training centres' opened in 1925, and were extended to the 'Distressed Areas' in 1927. Throughout the 1930s, attendance by unemployed males at these 'training centres' was compulsory, the work long and arduous, and payment for the latter either non-existent or well below the going rate.[24]

---

[21] According to the Board of Agriculture and Fisheries (1919: 164), dissatisfaction on the part of rural labour stemmed from a desire for 'shorter hours, free time, higher wages and general improved conditions of living obtained by workers in other industries.'

[22] On this the normally pro-farmer discourse informing the report by the Board of Agriculture and Fisheries became more critical. Hence the observation (Board of Agriculture and Fisheries, 1919: 176) that: 'Before the war the time wages of workers on the land were on a very low scale relatively to those in most other great industries... For most of the workers it has always been a severe struggle to bring up a family of children, so long as they are below earning age, and it has usually been very difficult for them to save up any money against unemployment or old age. Farmers, as a rule, admit all this, and attribute it to the impossibility of paying higher wages during the long period [1873–96] of agricultural depression. They had to compete against the importation of cheaply produced foreign food-stuffs, and had a bare margin, if any, of profit on which to live and carry on. It must be observed, however, that wages were no better, and probably worse, in relation to the cost of living, in the preceding period, when farming profits and landowners' rents were high. Agricultural workers [have never unionized effectively to secure] a fair share in the profits of the industry. This seems to be the sole reason why they did not get a larger share in the good times during the thirty years before 1880. As it was they worked then and afterwards during the next thirty years of depression, for very long hours at very low wages.'

[23] Hence the following comment (Board of Agriculture and Fisheries, 1919: 173): 'Trade union organization among agricultural labourers has been, before [the 1914–18] war, notoriously deficient. There were many reasons for this... As the reports show, each man's position as to work, wages or allowances is very largely an individual matter. Further, the whole conditions of agriculture, with the rather feudal position of the squire, were against unions of labour... Nevertheless, since the war a rapid development in Trade Unionism among agricultural labourers has taken place... The labourers' unions are therefore becoming strong...In some counties already the majority of labourers belong.'

[24] For accounts of these labour camps, which existed in Britain from 1927 until 1939, see Hannington (1937:Chapter VII), Colledge (1989), and Colledge and Field

As in the case of Germany at the same conjuncture (see previous Chapter), lowpaid/unpaid workers in these camps provided agriculture generally and local farmers in particular not only with labour-power that was relationally unfree and economically cheap, but also did work which had previously been carried out by free workers remunerated at trade union rates.[25] Because such camps were used to provide a cheap workforce to undercut organized labour, a process of restructuring which involved replacing free workers with unfree equivalents, the Trade Unions Congress refused to cooperate with the government.[26]

Much evidence suggests that the institution of the tied cottage was indeed deployed coercively by rural employers in order to deter their workers from joining trade unions or seeking higher wages. Even a pro-farmer report by the Board of Agriculture and Fisheries after the 1914–18 war accepted that the 'objection taken to the tied cottage is that the occupant sacrifices his independence…in short, he is too much in the power of the farmer.'[27] It concludes that 'the farmer who owns his labourer's cottage has more power over him than he would have if the man held his cottage of some other person.'[28]

Agricultural labourers who complained about under-payment of wages, or protested at an employer requiring domestic kin to work

(1983). The work done by those sent to such 'training camps' consisted of forest clearing, road-making, drainage, excavating, and quarrying.

[25] See Hannington (1937: 100, 102–3,107), who reports one labour camp inmate as saying that 'many of the trainees…soon find themselves used to cut down the wages of the workers in the south [of the UK]'. Another, based in Scotland during the mid-1930s, observed similarly that '[i]t was meant to be public work that we were doing, but in fact the big landlords were paying the government and we were working on their estates for four bob a week' ('Jobless "hardened" in labour camps', *The Guardian*, London, 12 August, 1998).

[26] See Hannington (1937: 105). Opposition to this process of workforce restructuring was behind the TUC General Council decision that 'no support should be given to training …schemes which have for their object the supply of semi-skilled labour in competition with skilled workers, or for the training of men and women to take their place in industries in which there is already considerable unemployment'.

[27] See the Board of Agriculture and Fisheries (1919: 136).

[28] Comparing its own findings with those of an earlier report into housing for agricultural labour, published in the 1890s, the Board of Agriculture and Fisheries (1919: 134) concludes: 'Nearly a quarter of a century has elapsed since this report was published – It cannot be said that the result of the present investigation shows that any improvement has taken place in the housing of the labourer, or that there has been any successful effort to deal with the shortcomings disclosed by those who reported on the condition of things in the early "nineties"'.

unpaid, were evicted.[29] Observing that 'the notorious "tied" cottage system still flourishes,' and noting further (and correctly) that this 'servile system is a tremendous engine in the hands of capitalism for maintaining its class power', an account by the CPGB of the early 1930s class structure in the British countryside describes it somewhat contradictorily as 'simply a relic of feudalism [which] stinks of serfdom.'[30]

Even after the end of the 1939–45 war, tied housing continued to be regarded by some in a positive light – as a 'hidden subsidy' to rural labour, rather than as a method of controlling/coercing workers.[31] The surplus extracted from agricultural labourers as a result of long hours they worked for low pay, plus the deterrence effect where joining trade unions was concerned – all the result of coercive mechanisms such as

[29] See the case-studies cited by Hutt (1933: 220–1), whose account drew on files containing unpublished evidence presented to the National Union of Agricultural Workers by its members.

[30] See Hutt (1933: 219). 'Taken as a whole,' noted the Labour Research Department (1944: 12), 'housing conditions for farm workers are, without exaggeration, appalling... Nearly half of our farm workers live in tied, or service, cottages, many of which are without any sort of amenity, in disrepair, insanitary, damp, and isolated. The tied cottage is a constant source of irritation to workers and of complaints to union officials. The tied cottage [system] interferes with their freedom and independence, for their liberty of speech and action is curtailed because of the knowledge that it might deprive them of their homes.'

[31] For the 'hidden subsidy' argument, see for example Butler (1946: 140) and Newby (1980: 137–8). A more persuasive argument (Newby, Bell, Rose and Saunders, 1978: 159) is that the tied cottage is a factor which helps 'explain why the earnings of agricultural workers are amongst the lowest in Britain and why, since the Second World War, the average hourly earnings of agricultural workers have deteriorated markedly *vis-à-vis* those of industrial workers.' Standard accounts of the tied cottage in post-war rural England are also found in Newby (1977: 178 ff.; 1980: 136–9), who notes that between 1948 and 1976 the number of farm workers living in tied cottages increased from 34 to 53 per cent. A detailed account of the more recent political struggle to abolish tied housing is contained in Danziger (1988: 164–85). The latter text underlines the centrality of tied housing to struggles between farmers and agricultural workers: 'Although it may appear to an outsider to be uncontroversial, the agricultural tied cottage system represents far more than simply a means of accommodating 50 per cent of the country's farm labour force: it can be found at the heart of many of the most bitter and intense conflicts in the history of agricultural labour relations. The attitudes held by farmers and farmworkers to the tied cottage system are in some cases diametrically opposed...The importance of the tied cottage issue to each side is attributable to its close bearing upon the objective economic interests of agricultural employers and workers as defined by the capitalist economy in which they interact. For the employer, the tied cottage is a valuable instrument for ensuring adequate supervision of valuable livestock, as well as being a means of controlling labour supply. Conversely, for the worker, the tied cottage represents a tool for depressing agricultural wages, restricting labour mobility to other industries, and sharpening the worker's sense of insecurity and isolation' (Danziger, 1988: 156).

tied housing – more than compensated economically for any supposed 'wage subsidy' from which workers were alleged to benefit.[32]

Women, Children, Control and Coercion

What is of particular significance is that as permanent farm servants were increasingly replaced by temporary workers, so the element of unfreedom shifted from the former to the latter, and the gangmaster system was central to this process. Composed for the most part of young (and sometimes very young) children supervised by adult males, nineteenth century gangs were deployed only on large commercial farms.[33] Although commercial farmers insisted they used child labour only because adult male workers were unavailable, it is clear that the gangmaster system operated because of the cost to the producer of adult workers, and not their availability.[34] Supervision/control by the

[32] According to one account (Labour Research Department, 1944: 12–3), '[u]nder this system [the tied cottage], victimization for trade union activity is still sharp and widespread...this fear of losing homes is, more than anything else, the cause of continued illegal under-payment of farm workers. This is especially true of overtime payments, and it is no exaggeration to say that immediately before the [1939–45] war thousands of farm workers were being illegally underpaid...the loss sustained from 1925 to 1937 amounted to £6,344,000, 20% of farm workers were being underpaid...'

[33] This raises the important issue of the connection between kinship and coercion. For example, in the case of tied housing, compulsion might be exercised on a young agricultural labourer (to work in a gang and/or accept a lower wage, etc.) by members of his family resident in such accommodation. Rather than being simply 'kinship coercion', however, such pressure is more accurately identified as originating from the employer, being transmitted via the family of the labourer concerned. The extent of the pressure to which parents were subjected in order to send their young children to work in gangs is evident from an observation in the 1867 Sixth Report, that they would welcome legislation compelling the attendance of their children at school. In other words, only by invoking an alternative source of power – the State – would it be possible for agricultural labouring families to resist the coercive power of the local rural establishment (farmer and clergy). On this point, the Children's Employment Commission (1867: xx) concluded: '[T]here is much evidence that shows that the parents of the children would in many instances be glad to be aided by the requirements of a legal obligation [for their children to attend school] to resist the pressure...to which they are often subject. They are liable to be urged at times by the parish officers, at times by employers, under threats of being themselves discharged, to allow their children to be taken to work at an age when it would manifestly be to their greater advantage that the school attendance should not be broken in upon, or entirely discontinued; and it is plain that many naturally well-disposed parents would welcome a regulation...'

[34] Hence the observation by witnesses (Children's Employment Commission, 1867: 36, 38) both that '[f]armers complain of not being able to get labourers when there are labourers in the town wanting work', and that child workers were 'treated harshly' and

gangmaster ensured that women and children worked as hard as but were paid less than the men whom they supplanted.[35]

Central to the efficiency of this labour regime was the control/coercion exercised over women and children by the adult male gangmaster, who – because his pay was linked to the completion on schedule of piece-work – drove his gang hard.[36] Issues such as the difficulty of the agricultural tasks undertaken by child labour, their frequent

---

taken from schools because gangs were a response by the farmer to the '*expense* of adult labour' (emphasis added).

[35] The parallel between the gang system in the north of England during the early nineteenth century and slave gangs in the West Indies was lost neither on observers writing at that time, nor on gang members themselves. Hence the following comments by Howitt (1838: 165–6): 'A person from the south or midland counties of England journeying northward, is struck when he enters Durham, or Northumberland, with the sight of bands of women working in the fields under the surveillance of one man. One or two such bands, of from half a dozen to a dozen women, generally young, might be passed over; but when they recur again and again, and you observe them wherever you go, they become a marked feature of the agricultural system of the country, and you naturally inquire how it is, that such regular bands of female labourers prevail there. The answer, in the provincial tongue, is – "O they are the Bone-ditches," i.e. Bondages. Bondages! That is an odd sound, you think, in England. What have we bondage, a rural serfdom, still existing in free and fair England? Even so. The thing is astounding enough, but it is a fact. As I cast my eyes for the first time on these female bands in the fields working under their drivers, I was, before making any inquiry respecting them, irresistibly reminded of the slave gangs of the West Indies: turnip-hoeing, somehow, associated itself strangely in my brain with sugar-cane dressing; but when I heard these women called Bondages, the association became tenfold strong.' That such a view was shared by 'those below' is confirmed by a woman who worked as a gang labourer in the 1860s. 'On that day I was eight years of age', she recalls (Groves, 1949: 30), 'I left school, and began to work fourteen hours a day in the fields, with from forty to fifty other children, of whom, even at that early age, I was the eldest. We were followed all day long by an old man carrying a long whip in his hand which he did not forget to use. A great many of the children were only five years of age...For four years, summer and winter, I worked in these gangs – no holidays of any sort, with the exception of very wet days and Sundays – and at the end of that time it felt like heaven to me when I was taken to the town of Leeds and put to work in the factory. Talk about the white slaves, the fen districts at that time was the place to look for them.' This was confirmed by others writing in the 1870s (Heath, 1989: 152): 'And even supposing that by strict and careful supervision the grosser forms of evil are kept down, the private gang system does not afford any alleviation in the labour-slavery which has been the lot of these poor fen women and children for two generations.'

[36] Of children working in gangs, one witness (Children's Employment Commission, 1867: 39) observed: 'If idle or careless, they are excited to greater care and diligence with oaths and curses, an occasional kick, and if these fail, are beaten with a stick'. According to another witness (Children's Employment Commission, 1867: 35) who also worked in a gang when young: 'The first gang I was in was composed of 20 to 30 boys...The ganger was a man well known for his cruelty. I saw him beat one boy till his wounds had to be dressed. He kept us in the wheat when it was above our waists the whole of a wet day, so that we were working in drenched clothes, and any attempt to leave was met by a beating'.

illnesses as a result for having to work in inclement weather, and the intensity of the work regime under the gangmaster, all emerge clearly from testimony made to the 1867 Report.[37] The resulting cheapness of the labour provided meant the gang system was profitable for landlord and commercial farmer, in the process impoverishing rural labouring households.[38] As adult day labourers were increasingly replaced by child workers, income levels for poor rural households declined accordingly. This in turn led to rural households having to send yet more children out to work in gangs, thereby further accentuating the spiral descent into poverty.[39]

---

[37] Gangs sometimes worked throughout the night, and as a local official noted (Children's Employment Commission, 1867: 35–6, 37), '[f]requently sicknesses arise from little girls going to work in the wet and cold weather, and being thinly clad…' One 14 year-old female worker complained (Children's Employment Commission, 1867: 36): 'Digging carrots is very hard work. The gangers takes the work, and makes the children work so hard. We always know when he has taken the work. We have to work so much harder'. Similarly, another labourer observed (Children's Employment Commission, 1867: 37): 'Many of the children have to stay at home from having got bad from wet'. A 78 year-old ex-gangmaster himself admitted (Children's Employment Commission, 1867: 38) that 'I have hold on heavy land… It was a very nasty job for girls when the corn was wet… It is very bad work for girls'. This was confirmed by a bookseller who ran a Sunday school (Children's Employment Commission, 1867: 35), who pointed out that 'on Sunday children attending my Sunday school show a state of exhaustion which is painful to witness'. The Children's Employment Commission (1867: xii) concludes that 'the interest of the gangmaster leads him to keep the whole of his gang at full stretch while at their work, with the shortest possible intervals of interruption'.

[38] This was also true of workers in the 'butty' gangs deployed in coal mining where, as even conservative historians such as Taylor (1960: 217, 218) accept, labour 'was difficult to obtain [,] and a premium, therefore, was placed upon efficient and forceful management'. The same source concludes both that 'it is no cause for wonder that the small mine owner should have found in the system of sub-contracting not only the most feasible but also the most desirable solution to his managerial and labour problems', and that '[t]he butty, raised in a harder if no more exacting school, responded only to the stimulus of profit, and was encouraged to drive his men to the utmost in its pursuit'. As with the gangmaster system in agriculture, the 'butty' gang was strongly opposed by the miners and trade unionists (Taylor, 1960: 219, 231).

[39] This downwards economic spiral is described by Dobb (1946: 165) in the following manner: 'It is often the poverty of male wage-earners which compels the women members of the family to go out and seek employment, and so enables the "sweated trades" to thrive on the supply of cheap labour thereby created; and once the price of labour falls substantially, its supply-price is likely to be reduced, so that worse terms of employment are readily accepted in the future'. This very point is confirmed by the 1867 Sixth Report itself (Children's Employment Commission, 1867: xx): 'It is averred that under the present system, by which the labour of children and women is so largely employed, the price of many kinds of work which is ordinarily done by adult male labourers is much reduced, and such labourers are kept out of employment for several weeks, or even months, while their wives and children are doing the work'.

The processes driving the search by commercial farmers for cheaper forms of labour-power, and a corresponding need on their part to restructure capital by means of decomposing/recomposing the rural workforce, are not difficult to discern.[40] To begin with, throughout the nineteenth century industrialization and urbanization drew off at least some of the workers on which commercial farming depended for its labour, a situation reflected in the frequently voiced concerns about rural depopulation.[41]

It is necessary, however, to qualify claims about 'labour scarcity' so often appended to discourse lamenting rural exodus. As always, such concerns failed to differentiate between the presence of agricultural workers generally, and the acceptability/availability to commercial farmers of gender/age-specific forms of labour-power. Where/when it occurred, therefore, rural outmigration was the effect not just of mechanization together with poor working conditions and pay levels (the most frequently cited reasons), but also of agrarian restructuring (adult male labour being replaced by that of women and children).

Gangmasters and Capitalist Competition

This restructuring was in turn linked to the pattern of nineteenth century capitalist development in the agriculture not just of Britain but also of Europe and North America.[42] Partly through the enclosure of village commons and the expropriation of smallholders (who were transformed into landless labourers), landlords and rich farmers in Britain both consolidated/extended their own holdings and improved

---

[40] This element of workforce restructuring escapes Armstrong (1988: 98, 99), who notes in Panglossian terms: 'There is no reason to suppose that the gains of migrant workers, whether drawn from English towns, from Ireland, or from other agricultural districts, were at the expense of local people…the inference must be that male workers were more regularly employed as the demand for and supply of labour more nearly approached equilibrium, due to downward migration and to the progress made by agriculture in raising production and creating opportunities for employment'. His conclusion is couched in similarly idealized terms: 'To sum up, the case for inferring an improvement in the farm worker's position rests less on demonstrable improvements in real wages than on better opportunities to earn those wages'.

[41] Concerns about rural depopulation were voiced by almost all those writing the about rural issues in late nineteenth century Britain – see, for example, The Special Commissioner of the 'Daily News' (1891), Millin (1903), Pedder (1904), Board of Agriculture and Fisheries (1906), Collings (1906: 376ff.) and Levy (1911).

[42] See Tribe (1981: 35ff.) for an account of the 'English Model' of agrarian capitalist transformation.

production.[43] Higher corn prices during the Napoleonic wars generated more land reclamation by these better-off proprietors, but no additional housing for rural labour working this land. Commercial farmers complained that, in the absence of tied accommodation, 'we have no hold' over labourers, who as a consequence 'come and go'.[44]

Given this inability to restrict the economic mobility of casual workers to the extent needed, farmers unsurprisingly delegated this role to labour contractors, who exercised it on their behalf over child labour deployed in gangs.[45] Significantly, when the Gang Act of 1867 made the employment of female and child labour more problematic, farmers resorted to another bonding mechanism: they constructed more tied cottages, the importance of which increased over the latter part of the nineteenth century.[46]

---

[43] Both the reasons for and the result of enclosures carried out in nineteenth century Britain are of course a matter of debate (Wells, 1979, 1981; Charlesworth, 1980; Reed, 1986; Mills, 1988; Mills and Short, 1983; Donajgrodzki, 1989). Among the issues raised are whether or not a peasantry can be said to exist, what dynamic structured its economic reproduction (depeasantization or repeasantization), and what was the object of agency undertaken in rural areas.

[44] For this complaint by farmers about labour mobility, see the Children's Employment Commission (1867: vii).

[45] That the alleged incompatibility between unfree labour and more advanced productive forces – a claim made by exponents of the semi-feudal thesis, among others – is wrong emerges clearly from the strong link between them as set out in the 1867 Sixth Report. The latter indicates that the gangmaster system emerged only when better technology had made possible the draining of fenland, the rich soil being ideal for the cultivation of wheat (Children's Employment Commission, 1867: vii, 14). Both the clearing of the land and the harvesting of the crop were tasks undertaken by child labour organized by and under the control of gangmasters. In the early 1890s, Heath (1989: 151) described the resulting situation in the reclaimed fenlands as follows: 'These enormous tracts of land require constant labour to keep them well cultivated. The soil is so prolific that the weeds would soon choke everything else if they were not vigorously kept in check. The farms are generally very large, and run a long way into the fen. As a rule, there are no cottages upon them, and they therefore depend almost entirely for their labour on the native supply in the various villages...The want of house-room naturally prevents any influx from other parts of the country, and the consequence is, that for about eight months of the year, every available woman and child is pressed into service.'

[46] On this point see Newby (1987: 85–6), who states: 'The Act introduced a licensing system and restricted the employment of females and minors, thereby eliminating many of the economic advantages of employing a semi-permanent "casual" labour force. Farmers...then sought to secure their supply of labour by building cottages near their own farms...Tied cottages could be held only for the duration of employment on the farm; if the worker ceased employment for any reason he could be required to seek housing elsewhere. In the final quarter of the nineteenth century the significance of tied housing was to grow [thereby increasing] the degree of dependence upon farming employers and [rendering] farm workers even more vulnerable to petty harassment and oppressive threats'. Elsewhere the same writer (Newby, 1977: 41) notes that the

More importantly, competition from rural producers in rival capitalist nations (North America, Germany) had intensified, to the degree that the 1870s marked the beginning of a long period of economic depression in Britain which, with the exception of 1881 and 1889, lasted from 1873 until 1896.[47] It is because they stop short of asking about this wider international context, and how it influenced the pay and conditions of agricultural workers in Britain, that many texts are unable to pose questions about the restructuring by capital of the agrarian labour process.

An effect of on the one hand the repeal of Corn Laws in 1846, and on the other increasing competition between agrarian capitalist producers internationally, was that the cheaper corn grown in the United States entered the domestic English market and forced indigenous commercial farmers to cut the costs of their workforce, which they did by restructuring.[48] It was the latter objective – whereby more costly and

---

origins of the post-1860s tied cottage 'lay in the desire by farmers to control the supply of their labour force and to restrict its mobility'.

[47] Calls for protection exposed the well-known economic contradiction between farmers and manufacturers. Farmers wanted higher food prices, which in turn required tariffs to exclude cheaper food imports from abroad. By contrast, manufacturers wanted low food prices, so that the bundle of wage goods consumed by their workers remained low, and with it the wage costs of industry. Crosby (1977) attributes the development of not just conservative ideology but a nationalist political consciousness amongst English farmers during the first half of the nineteenth century to the fear of foreign competition, and in particular cheaper grain imports. From the 1850s to the early 1870s, this fear diminished, as infrastructural improvements contributed to a 25 per cent increase in farming profits. From the 1870s onwards, however, the fear of foreign competition increased once again, and with it calls for protectionism, a pattern that was repeated during the 1930s.

[48] The constant downward pressure on agricultural wages and living standards of the rural poor generated much debate about causes of and solutions to 'distress' in the countryside. Hence the following combination of acute observation and resignation (Anonymous, 1840: 21–2): 'The situation of the labourers, and of the whole class of agricultural poor, has attracted, for a considerable time, the attention of the country… As the complaints of distress are very general in all branches of industry, the agricultural poor appear to be suffering in common with those other portions of the community, whose subsistence does not depend upon a settled income. But the labourer suffers in a greater proportion: his gains in the most favourable periods do not much exceed the amount of the sum required to purchase the bare necessaries of life; he has no superfluities; and whenever a reduction of his profits takes place, no economy can supply the deficiency. The means are withdrawn by which his health and strength, his sole property, can be preserved, and the term poverty is not a metaphor applied to him, as it often is when used with respect to higher classes, whom a change of cicumstances only makes poor by comparison with that which they possessed before… if there be any laws resulting from the institutions that establish property in land which necessarily limit, in a country fully peopled, the share of the labourer to a portion

less easily controlled forms of labour-power were replaced by less costly and more easily controlled equivalents – which the gangmaster system was designed to achieve.[49]

II

A form of recruitment and control which has its roots in agricultural production during the nineteenth century, the gangmaster system as it now exists in British agriculture involves labour contractors who are 'providers of temporary labour' to agribusiness enterprises. The latter consist of commercial farming and food processing companies, which in Britain currently employ some 72,000 seasonal workers, half of whom are supplied by between two and three thousand gangmasters.[50]

This seasonal workforce is heterogeneous in its composition. Some are the urban unemployed, transported to rural areas where they work as casual agricultural labour, while others are either students recruited from other European countries for seasonal work, or foreign migrants (usually from Eastern Europe) working illegally on the large commercial farms of East Anglia. The two obvious questions to ask here are: why gangmasters, and why now? If, as some argue, labour contracting is a benign relation facilitating the migration of free workers only where agriculture is in the early stages of capitalist development, then its resurgence in 1980s Britain is seemingly inexplicable.

---

which can only procure for himself and family a bare subsistence, it is vain to seek any considerable improvement of his condition, and the government can do no more than protect him in the enjoyment of the part allotted to him… History does not deal much in the records of the poor'.

[49] The same appears to have been true of the 'butty' system in coal mining where, in the context of increasing competition, sub-contracting permitted employers to cut costs yet simultaneously intensify control over their workers (Taylor, 1960: 227 ff.). Even on farms that attempted to combine economic efficiency with 'social' objectives, such as that carried out in the northeastern country of Cumberland during the 1860s, more expensive permanent workers were replaced with cheaper temporary variants (Lawson, Hunter, et al., 1874: 319 ff.). Although the State introduced regulation following the recommendations of the 1867 Sixth Report, legislation was in many cases ignored, and gangs continued to flourish. Thus, for example, Heath (1989: 151–2) reported hearing the following admission from a large farmer in the 1870s: 'The result of legislation for public gangs will be great evasion of the Act under the form of private gangs, which will require dealing with just as much'.

[50] See EFRA (2003: Ev 2, 36, 37).

Gangmasters and Deproletarianization

Commercial farmers insist that the gangmaster system is necessary because they are unable to obtain sufficient labour to harvest, pack and process crops.[51] This labour shortage is attributed in turn to the presence in East Anglia of other, better-paid remuneration. The accusation that, where the recruitment and control of workers is concerned, the cheapest option is the illegal option is denied by agribusiness. According to gangmasters themselves, however, 'farmers on the whole look at the price before checking the quality', while supermarkets 'have created a situation where it is uneconomic for directly employed labour to exist in the horticultural/food sector'. Because on the one hand farmers 'are dependent on casual workers, but do not wish to pay legal rates of pay', and on the other labour contracting and subcontracting means that neither producers nor supermarkets are legally liable for the pay/conditions of agricultural workers, agribusiness denies that it is responsible for any exploitation that might occur.

Such protestation is rightly dismissed as 'passing the buck' by one EFRA Committee member, who observes that: 'it must be agreed that the [supermarkets] by constantly screwing down the price they pay for produce to sell in order to screw up their own profits are basically the cause of the problem...by constantly screwing down prices it makes a mean system in which it pays to behave in this [exploitative] fashion'.[52] In other words, the role of the gangmaster is a systemic one, reproduced by capitalism itself – or, as another Committee member put it, 'the increasing use of gangmaster labour [in agriculture is] a direct function of greater price pressure which producers are experiencing currently'.[53]

From the viewpoint of agribusiness capital, therefore, each category of worker (foreign, indigenous) discharges the classic function of an industrial reserve army of labour: lacking the capacity to bargain with gangmasters over pay and conditions, they are all forms of cheap temporary worker, and as such depress the price of labour employed in agriculture generally, casual and permanent alike. As noted by a

---

[51] For the details of the information in this paragraph, see EFRA (2003: Ev 3, 4–5, 6, 9, 10, 14, 25).

[52] See EFRA (2003: Ev 7). The Committee member was Austin Mitchell, a leftish 'old' Labour Member of Parliament, who not only asked consistently searching questions but – as importantly – also showed a commendable disinclination to accept evasive or incorrect answers from witnesses appearing on behalf of (or sympathetic to) government, agribusiness and gangmasters.

[53] For this and the following points, see EFRA (2003: 22, Ev 25, 30, 46).

member of the Committee, the essence of the gangmaster problem is cheap labour: those workers who are able to do so 'are not prepared to accept [low] wages [and] the refusal of farmers and supermarkets and the whole [food] industry to pay people adequate pay for a hard job'.

The profits made by gangmasters from the supply to farmers of labour are high, while the risks of prosecution by the State are negligible.[54] Both the latter either stem from or license what is the crux of the gangmaster system: the recruitment and coercion of labour that is unfree.[55] Intimidation and physical beatings as a method of control are frequent occurrences, illegal deductions from wages are a common feature, and the employment of female and child labour is widespread.[56]

Some of the methods currently used by labour contractors to curtail the economic mobility of the workforce (to decommodify labour-power, in other words) would have been very familiar to their nineteenth century counterparts. Thus, for example, workers employed by gangmasters are not only paid very low wages, live in poor quality but high-cost tied accommodation, have large deductions made from their wages (in one case rent of £80 being deducted from pay of £83.85), but

---

[54] According to one witness, the turnover of a single gangmaster increased from £3 million to £10 million in a relatively short period, between 1992 and 1996 (EFRA, 2003: Ev 50 note 8, Ev 52). Despite widespread fraud and evasion of tax and labour legislation, only 13 gangmasters were prosecuted in the eighteen months prior to the EFRA Committee hearings (EFRA, 2003: Ev 36). Those prosecuted by the State (Home Office, Inland Revenue, Customs and Excise) are workers who are either illegal immigrants or drawing unemployment benefit, not gangmasters (EFRA, 2003: Ev 39, 46), an anomaly to which Austin Mitchell draws attention. In the 1,800 'removals' only 170 were failed asylum seekers (EFRA, 2003: Ev 40).

[55] That the object of the gangmaster system is capitalist restructuring, or the replacement of free labour by unfree – and thus cheaper and more easily controlled – workers so as to enhance profitability, is finally being recognized. Hence the following: 'Ensuring the influx of foreign labour is not used to undercut the wages of domestic employees is another key challenge. The Low Pay Commission's last annual report expressed concerns that the growing use of migrant workers was being used by unscrupulous employers to circumvent the minimum wage'. See 'Immigration drives an economic revival', *The Guardian* (London), 21 March 2007. Even the normally conservative members of the Bank of England monetary policy committee now accept that resort by employers to such low wage unfree workers is 'limiting the bargaining power of labour' in other sectors of the economy – see 'wage claims kept low by fear of foreign workers, says MPC member', *The Guardian* (London), 31 May 2007 – which is precisely what capitalist restructuring is designed to do.

[56] See EFRA (2003: Ev 26–7, 28–9, 31, 40). It is clear that, just as in the nineteenth century, the element of worker indebtedness is both inbuilt into the relationship between a gangmaster and his labourers, and licenses the control/coercion exercised by him over them. Not only were the workers – mostly young people – housed on farms in portacabins supplied by the gangmaster, therefore, but their wages were subject to multiple deductions – again by the gangmaster – as a result of which they went into debt (EFRA, 2003: Ev 54 note 15).

are also compelled to repay substantial recruitment 'costs' if they leave their present job.[57]

It is clear, moreover, that the element of tied housing, a method of control applicable only to permanent agricultural labour in the nineteenth and early twentieth centuries, has now become an additional weapon in the armoury of the labour contractor, and as such a reinforcing mechanism in the already extensive coercive power exercised by gangmasters over their casual workers. One trade union organizer pointed out that the problem was not simply due to lack of knowledge about wage rates, employment law, and more broadly workers' legal rights, since the 'real fear of people was firstly coming forward and then secondly being able to act on the information that we were able to give them'.[58]

It is not knowledge but rather coercion, of one kind or another, that is at the root of gangmaster control, and thus central to the gangmaster problem as addressed by the Select Committee.[59] The Report concludes, rightly, 'that Operation Gangmaster [= State regulation of labour contracting] remains a woefully inadequate response to the complex enforcement arising from the illegal activities of gangmasters'.[60]

Gangmasters and the Moral Order

Although the EFRA Report is a very welcome addition to the sparse literature about labour contracting and agribusiness, it nevertheless

---

[57] See EFRA (2003: Ev 91). These (and other) cases were supplied by the Citizens Advice Bureaux (EFRA, 2003: Ev 90–5) located in the Eastern region of the country, where the large commercial farms are located. Together with the trade unions, the Citizens Advice Bureaux provided the Committee with both the most powerful evidence of coercion/control exercised by gangmasters and the most radical criticisms of their labour regime. Among the many instances of employer coercion was one in which a gangmaster agency 'brought along their own security people'. Generally speaking, '[m]ost workers who have sought advice …are experiencing exploitative employment contracts, which commonly have closely interlinked employment and housing issues, with one being reliant on the other. Long hours and poor working and accommodation conditions seem to be common. Poor employment practices include infringements of the National Minimum Wage, rights to paid holidays and statutory sick pay, notice rights and protections from illegal deductions from wages'.

[58] See EFRA (2003: Ev 29).

[59] Hence the view (EFRA, 2003: Ev 94) that: 'Fear of retribution, combined with the assumption that they may be working illegally, and fear of loss of job and home means not only that such workers fear to seek advice but they are also highly unlikely to complain or use the Employment Tribunal System. Employers and agencies are able to take advantage of this'.

[60] See EFRA (2003: 17).

fails to address a number of crucial issues. To begin with, the main input to the Report about the gangmaster system itself adopts a standpoint of 'neutrality', being as a result more interested in the workings of the supermarkets' 'business models' and whether or not these are economically rational/efficient than in whether or not (and why) the workers themselves were being exploited.[61] Also missing from this Select Committee report on the gangmaster problem in Britain are three significant contextualizing elements.

First, the international dimension, or the wider economic background to which recruitment/control/coercion by the labour contractor in a specific national situation is itself a response. Second, those developments at the national level itself – deregulation, union busting, deindustrialization, and high levels of unemployment – which have facilitated this response. And third, the voice of the workers themselves, or those who are employed by gangmasters. To some extent, therefore, the EFRA Report adheres to a familiar historical approach which locates opposition to the gangmaster system in Britain within a moral discourse.

That views about a moral order structured the positive/negative epistemology informing the free/unfree contrast structuring liberal political economy in nineteenth century Britain was delineated most clearly in the 1824 Committee on Labourers' Wages chaired by

[61] See EFRA (2003: Ev 49–57). In what at times comes close to being supermarket-centric testimony that is also sympathetic to gangmasters, the witness who supplied this input to the EFRA Committee had a difficult time disguising this sympathy (despite trying 'to take a balanced view'). Among the claims made by this witness (EFRA, 2003: Ev 59–61) was that the idea of corporate responsibility was 'a difficult question', that there was no solution to the gangmaster problem, and that 80 percent of workers interviewed 'expressed satisfaction with their employer'. Maintaining that no difference existed between gangmasters and labour agencies, the witness confessed that 'I cannot sit here and truly believe that they [gangmasters] set out to abuse people' (EFRA, 2003: Ev 61–2). This particular witness was accused by Austin Mitchell of 'extolling gangmasters' and of rushing to form 'the National Association for the Rehabilitation of Gangmasters'; when asked by him whether the gangmaster himself was 'standing around when 80% expressed satisfaction', the witness replied 'I have no idea' (EFRA, 2003: Ev 61). It is somewhat disconcerting, to put it mildly, to come across the following kind of contradictory evidence: on the one hand, the admission that the gangmaster system corresponds to 'a kind of slavery', yet the simultaneous insistence that 'all I can say is that I have been in the hostels, I have eaten the food, I have slept in the hostels. There are people trying to give good jobs to people who want to do them and I feel that to just come at this totally from that area [i.e., gangmaster system = slavery], although I know the Committee has said that there are good gangmasters and so on, is not on' (EFRA, 2003: Ev 63).

Earl Russell.[62] The central theme of this dichotomy is not so much economic as moral, based as it is on a set of virtues attached simply and only to a worker who is free, not the least important of which is an acceptance of subordination to the employer. Such a worker is perceived mistakenly to be non-threatening politically, a species of *homo economicus* interested only in adapting to or ascending up the existing capitalist hierarchy. The attributes of a worker who is unfree, by contrast, are perceived as wholly negative: resentful, idle, and politically threatening.

Over the latter part of the twentieth century and currently, however, it could be argued that the free/unfree distinction as envisaged in early nineteenth century discourse has been reversed. Although still a dichotomy, it is now based on the opposite kind of images when compared to those advanced nearly two hundred years ago. Because s/he is able to organize and thus challenge employers from a position of strength, it is the free not the unfree worker who constitutes a challenge (actual or potential) to the capitalist hierarchy. Correspondingly, because s/he lacks precisely these attributes, and thus presents to the employer a position of relative weakness, it is the unfree not the free worker who constitutes the lesser threat, both economically and politically.

III

This reversal helps explain why deproletarianization is no longer the anomaly that non-Marxist political economy perceived it to be. As all Marxists know, intense capitalist competition leads to systemic crisis, as manifested in overproduction, and the consequent need on the part of agribusiness enterprises to restructure the agrarian labour process in order to maintain or enhance profitability. Too often this is taken to involve simply economic efficiency generated by new technology, whereas as crucial are ever-cheaper sources and forms of labour-power.

---

[62] It states (Brassey, 1879: 212): 'There are but two motives by which men are induced to work: the one, the hope of improving the conditions of themselves and their families; the other the fear of punishment. The one is the principle of free labour, the other the principle of slave labour. The one produces industry, frugality, sobriety, family affection, and puts the labouring class in a friendly relation with the rest of the community; the other causes, as certainly, idleness, imprudence, vice, dissension, and places the master and the labour in a perpetual state of jealousy and mistrust.'

What agrarian capital seeks to do, therefore, is to unite more advanced productive forces with social relations of production that permit a greater degree of surplus extraction.

The latter it achieves frequently and, as this Select Committee report confirms, increasingly by utilizing the kind of recruitment/control/coercion that the gangmaster system can and does deliver. Like the strategy of relocation currently pursued by capitalist firms generally, whereby corporations seek out cheaper workers elsewhere, so the labour contractor enables agribusiness enterprises necessarily rooted in a particular location to 'outsource' their employment costs/practices/conditions. This in turn is made possible by a combination of national and international political developments.

The Return of the Gangmaster

Broadly speaking, it is difficult to sustain the argument that either permanent or temporary workers employed in British agriculture were free historically. Whilst the presence of such relational forms during the era of feudalism is theoretically unproblematic, however, the same cannot be said where agrarian capitalists seemingly thrived on the employment of unfree workers, as was increasingly the case during the nineteenth century. That their counterparts are also using these same relational forms at the start of the twenty-first century, and thriving thereby, appears to offend against the logic proclaimed by much – mostly non-Marxist – political economy.[63]

Yet according to the 2002–03 EFRA Committee Report this is precisely what has been happening in the fields of East Anglia, where a resurgent gangmaster system has been in operation from the 1980s onwards. The return to British agriculture of the gangmaster, the Report makes clear, has been and is an effect of the desire for cheap labour on the part of agribusiness enterprises producing food for supermarkets. The resulting combination of low wages, poor safety practices, and gangmaster violence as a method of labour control – a situation found in manufacturing industry as well as agriculture – has been described by government sources as corresponding to one of 'medieval working practices'.[64] The gangmaster system,

[63] For details of these views, see Chapters 1 and 3.

[64] As the Report makes clear, the kind of recruitment/control/coercion associated with the gangmaster system is currently found also in some areas of British

however, is a characteristic not of a medieval but of a capitalist agriculture.[65]

The re-emergence in British agriculture during the 1980s of the gangmaster system was entirely consistent with the supply side economic policies implemented by what was the most reactionary post-war government, the objective being to increase capitalist profitability by reducing the wages/conditions of its workforce in both industry and agriculture.[66] At the national level, therefore, most of the gains made by labour since the Second World War were stripped away by Thatcherism, while the demise of actually-existing socialism at the end of that decade increased the size of the industrial reserve army of labour on which British (and European) capital could draw. Hence the necessity of addressing the problem at a systemic level rather than at a national one.

Instead of a systemic difficulty, and one addressed from the viewpoint of the workers (whose unmediated voice is absent from this report), the approach informing this Report tends to be the point of view of consumers (getting a better deal) or the State (lost tax revenue).

---

manufacturing industry, particularly where 1980s deregulation of employment pay and conditions has given rise to subcontracted economic activity (= sweatshops), albeit disguised conceptually by terms such as 'outsourcing', 'self-employment' and 'the informal economy'.

[65] The government view of it as a 'pre-capitalist' form coincides with the interpretation advanced by exponents of the 'semi-feudal' thesis (see Chapter 3). The government intention, announced at the end of the 1990s, to eradicate this form of labour contracting, was due to a concern not for workers' rights so much as for revenue lost as a result of tax evasion.

[66] These are the conditions to which English politicians, capitalists and central bankers refer when they aver proudly that migrant workers keep wages and interest rates low, thereby increasing the profitability of British manufacturing industry. See, for example, 'Migrants hold down inflation, says governor', *The Guardian* (London), 14 June 2005; and 'Migrants have lifted the economy, says study', *The Guardian* (London), 27 February 2007. According other accounts – 'The PR tycoon, a private dinner and PM's meeting with Euro lobby group', *The Observer* (London), 17 September 2006, and 'Shortage of pickers may hit strawberry crop', *The Guardian* (London), 28 May 2007 – businessmen and the National Farmers' Union are lobbying for open access by East European workers to UK markets, thereby providing capitalist producers with an expanding industrial reserve army of labour. Invoking *laissez faire* principles, the house journal of UK capitalism makes no secret of the fact that the object of expanding the reserve army of labour composed of (unfree) workers who are cheap is to enhance profits by depressing wages: '...it must be remembered that the case for free immigration is primarily one of liberty. Employers should be free to hire whom they want... [i]f a government doesn't respect these basic liberties, isn't it likely to violate investors' freedoms too?...[s]o it's clear that free immigration is a good thing for the economy and the stock market... Lower wages mean lower prices and lower interest rates...', etc., etc., *Investors Chronicle*, 27 April to 3 May, 2007.

The problem is accordingly framed rather too simplistically, in terms of illegality both of the contractor and his/her workforce. Where workers are foreign, this licences in turn a slide into a discourse that is xenophobic and reactionary, and not progressive: that is, the problem shifts from being one about capitalist exploitation and workers' rights to being one about contractor legality and keeping out illegal migrants.[67]

Hence the view of the agribusiness enterprises and the gangmasters themselves that the problem centres on the question of forged/genuine documents, and the way in which the 'abuses of the asylum and immigration system are perpetuated'.[68] It goes without saying that such an approach is one that plays well with conservatives, a point underlined by the way in which one member of the Committee continually focused on the issue that those involved in the gangmaster system – workers and contractors alike – were foreign.[69] By contrast, in its evidence to the Committee, representatives of the Transport and General Workers Union maintained, rightly, that 'the gangmaster issue is not just an issue about illegal immigrant labour, the majority of gangworkers are UK workers and, therefore, it is a problem for UK workers as well as illegal workers'.[70]

One of the striking things to emerge from this report is the degree to which the oppositions structuring the debate about labour contracting, its role and desirability, are still the same. Thus an account of rural England during the early nineteenth century published in its third edition an addendum to its chapter on unfree labour in the northern counties presenting (and also rebutting) the defence of the gang system by 'an active magistrate, an eminent agriculturist and a promoter of the interests of the agricultural class'.[71] Admitting that it was

---

67 See EFRA (2003: 21–3).

68 See EFRA (2003: 13, 20, Ev 3).

69 See EFRA (2003: Ev 3–4, 10, 18, 34, 41). It should be emphasized that the Committee member concerned was not racist, merely protecting the interests as she saw them of workers in her constituency. The same cannot be said of groups on the political right, for whom the element of ethnicity/nationality would be paramount.

70 See EFRA (2003: Ev 26).

71 Details of this defence are contained in Howitt (1862: 132–8), who comments as follows: 'This account of the Bondage System in the first edition excited, as was to be expected, a strong feeling in the public mind, both in the north and the south. In the south great surprise, for it was a system totally unknown to nine-tenths of readers; in the north great indignation on the part of the supporters of the system. I have received many conflicting statements from the Bondage district, – some thanking me for having made public so accurate a description of an objectionable system; others vindicating the system, and applauding.'

'the sunny side of the picture', this defence consisted of claims that living and working conditions of bonded labour amounted to 'a scene of comfort and contentment'.[72] However, the author of the original account pointed out that, 'despite their bounteous and Arcadian lot', in 1836 these same unfree labourers were 'found by us…in a most discontented state [and] described their situation as wretched.'[73]

In the case of the 1867 Sixth Report, farmers, overseers and gangmasters generally perceived little harm in the gang system, and most of them saw no reason why it should not continue as before.[74] By contrast, child workers, their parents (also workers), male agricultural labourers, and women workers (sometimes married to agricultural labourers) were all highly critical of the gangmaster system.[75] Whereas the objections of (bourgeois/petty-bourgeois) rural clergymen invariably focussed on the 'moral evil' of agricultural gangs, those advanced by witnesses from the rural working class emphasized that for them and

---

[72] According to Howitt (1862: 133) this defence of gang labour was advanced by 'a native of Northumberland…thoroughly persuaded of the excellence of its agricultural system.' Notwithstanding the claim by the latter that unfree workers employed in gangs enjoyed above-average habitations and living conditions, a local doctor familiar with the rural situation is reported as saying (Howitt, 1862: 137) in 1838 that cottages inhabited by estate workers constituted 'a disgrace to Northumberland…The miserable tenements of numbers of this class are less carefully constructed than the stables of their horses'.

[73] See Howitt (1862: 135), who adds that these labourers had 'turned out in great numbers, [unsuccessfully] calling upon their employers to abolish the system.'

[74] Hence the view (Children's Employment Commission, 1867: xxi) that '[s]ome of the largest occupiers also and others maintain that, within their own experience, no physical hardships not common to all agricultural labour are inflicted upon the young or upon females who have worked for them in a public gang; that some public gangs are well conducted, and are therefore unobjectionable…'. Similarly, in his testimony (Children's Employment Commission, 1867: xxii) the Earl of Leicester maintained that the gangmaster system was 'as beneficial to the labourer as it is profitable to the employer'. These claims, made by commercial farmers and landlords to justify the gangmaster system they used, were dismissed by the Children's Employment Commission (1867: xxi) in the following terse manner: 'We do not think that these views are likely to prevail against the great mass of testimony of a contrary description throughout the evidence…We cannot think that the perusal of the evidence will leave room to doubt that the public gang system is one which, – whether the mode in which it is carried on be looked to, or the circumstances out of which it had its origin, – can deservedly excite any reluctance to place it under salutary regulations.'

[75] On this point, the conclusion in the Sixth Report of the Children's Employment Commission (1867: xxi) is unambiguous: 'Should, however, the gradual abandonment of the public gang system be the result of the legislative interference proposed, the entire evidence proves that such a result would be in accordance with the best interests of the labouring agricultural population now subject to it.'

their children the agricultural gangs meant ill-treatment, overwork, illnesses, underpayment, and the denial of a basic education.[76]

Gangmasters, Class and Class Struggle

Not only do class divisions in the British countryside yesterday and today – agribusiness capitalists and employers versus agricultural workers and trade unions – remain roughly the same, therefore, but the politics/ideology – even the very language itself – justifying or opposing the existence of this kind of recruitment/control process have scarcely changed. This is *not* to say that capitalism has not changed: it is to say, however, that in terms of employment practices there is little evidence that employers are currently any more 'progressive' in outlook than their nineteenth century counterparts. As in the case of the latter, modern agribusiness enterprises are hardly ever willing to suggest improvements in working conditions, let alone pay for them or implement social legislation introduced by the State aimed at achieving these ends.[77]

---

[76] That the incompatibility of child labour with education was a central part of the class struggle was a fact recognized by both parties to this conflict – rural working class families and employers. That the latter perceived this to be so is clear from Hannington (1940: 9–10), who makes the following observation about the British capitalist class during the early nineteenth century: 'Their attitude on education was clearly expressed by one of their spokesmen, Mr. D. Giddy, President of the Royal Society and a Member of Parliament. In a speech in 1807, opposing elementary education for working-class children, he said: "However specious in theory the project might be, of giving education to the labouring classes of the poor, it would in effect be found to be prejudicial to their morals and happiness; it would teach them to despise their lot in life, instead of making them good servants on agriculture and other laborious employments to which their rank in society had destined them; instead of teaching them subordination, it would render them factious and refractory, as was evident in the manufacturing counties; it would enable them to read seditious pamphlets, vicious books and publications against Christianity; it would render them insolent to their superiors; and in a few years the result would be that the legislature would find it necessary to direct the strong arm of power towards them, and to furnish the executive magistrate with much more vigorous laws than were now in force".'

[77] This was rather obviously true of most, if not all, capitalists at that conjuncture. In the last decade of the nineteenth century, for example, an anti-socialist text included a lengthy argument supportive of the urban sweatshop system (Howell, 1892: 109ff.) and opposing State legislation/regulation, described as contrary to the interests of the working class. For holders of such views, therefore, the slogan 'liberty for labour' meant freedom not from capitalist control/coercion but rather from State intervention. The argument consisted essentially of the assertion that, as nothing could be done about the urban sweatshop, there was no point even in trying. The oppression inherent in it was blamed not on capitalism but rather on 'feckless' working class families ('The head of the family, the responsible bread-winner, has been the chief promoter of sweating').

During the first part of the nineteenth century, pro-farmer ideology stressed both that the gangmaster system was uneconomic, and that it amounted to no more than a method of lifting the cost to the public purse of the 'burden' of maintaining the rural poor.[78] The self-serving inference was that benign (not to say soft-hearted) commercial farmers in Britain utilized labour gangs only reluctantly, as a way of providing the idle (= unworthy) poor with work.[79] At that same conjuncture, the defence by landlords and their representatives of slavery on West Indian plantations followed the same line of argument, claiming that planters did not maltreat, coerce, exploit or overwork their labourers, who as a consequence were happy with and benefited from their unfreedom.[80]

---

[78] Hence the claim by a farmer (Children's Employment Commission, 1867: 38) that the 'employment of child labour seems cheap but it is not really cheap, because the work is not done well...' In a thinly disguised piece of propaganda that sought to justify existing inequalities and production relations by putting strong arguments into the mouth of a farmer ('Stubbs') and weak ones into that of his labourer ('John Hopkins') and the latter's spouse ('the wife'), the following exchange is found (Anonymous, 1833: 114–5): '...so you see', [said Stubbs], 'that this humane regulation of the magistrates encourages idleness just as much as it encourages early marriages, and a superabundance of children'. 'But worst of all,' said the [labourer's] wife, 'is, that it teaches them to be idle, discontented, and riotous, and madly burn the very ricks of corn that might have made them bread... my uncle said that the labourers now-adays were quite different from what they used to be. Their characters quite changed within his memory; not but there may be some among them right-minded still, but, take the general run, they are a bad set. There was one of them so impudent as to say to his employer, – 'If you don't give me better wages, I will marry to-morrow, and then you must maintain me at double cost'. For the fellow was sharp enough to know, that, though the magistrates paid the difference, it came out of the farmer's pocket in the shape of the poor's rate.' 'But when the parish maintains them, the parish ought to make them work,' said John. 'So they do, as far as they can [said Stubbs]: they send them round to the farmers in gangs, and when the farmer can find them work, they pay the wages to the parish....' Significantly, the anonymous writer of this pro-farmer propaganda was Jane Marcet (1769–1858), born into a wealthy Swiss banking family and an influential populariser of arguments about political economy in the early nineteenth century.

[79] This was in keeping with farmer ideology generally, the patronizing (and indeed class) attitude of which towards agricultural workers is epitomized by the following (Anonymous, 1834: 120): 'As to the obstinacy of labourers, it has a very obvious, and a very justifiable source... A kind word may do something; reason and a draught of ale more;... Encouragement, of this substantial kind, is the surest way to secure good servants; but it should be sparingly administered, and never except for extra exertion. Ignorant people are too apt to regard spontaneous favours as rather due to their own merits than to the generosity of their master, and if not thus frequently indulged, they become discontented and sulky. The full performance of their regular duties should, therefore, be rigidly exacted for the stipulated remuneration; but occasion may be found to show them little acts of kindness, without increasing their sense of self-importance;....'

[80] An abstract of the Report of the Lords' Committees on the Condition and Treatment of the Colonial Slaves (London Society for the Abolition of Slavery,

Where the coerciveness of the regime could not be refuted, however, a different kind of defence was mounted. This involved the denial of either responsibility for or knowledge of what were dismissed by employers as a-typical and infrequent 'abuses' inflicted on their workers.[81] As evidence from plantations in India a century later suggests, in a politically sensitive context where pay, conditions and the production relation itself are (or have recently been) the object of official scrutiny, the use of contractors to recruit/control labour enables planters, farmers and owners of urban enterprises to disclaim any responsibility for workers recruited and managed not by them but by intermediaries.[82] In a similar vein, at the same conjuncture Mexican *hacendados*

1833: 477 ff.) outlines evidence taken by them on that subject during 1832. Among the many pro-slavery witnesses interviewed, the Duke of Manchester testified that '[t]he treatment of the slaves was excellent; their food and clothing abundant (though he cannot specify quantities); and their dwellings remarkably good in general…[t]he only idea, he conceived the slaves had of emancipation was having nothing to do'. He accepted that slave insurrections in Jamaica during 1824 'were to be traced to the [slave's] desire to emancipate himself,' but maintained that these 'disturbances' had nothing to do with and 'certainly did not arise…from ill usage'. His concluding words were that on estates 'the Duke always found old slaves comfortably provided for, he supposed by their own families'. Another pro-slavery witness, a lawyer from Jamaica, insisted that 'want, as to food or clothing, was unknown among them [plantation slaves]…and, as far as he knew, their treatment was good and kind. The same witness continued that floggings were not severe, and the 'treatment of the slaves was, he also believed, lenient; and the leaning of jurors, on trials, in their favour: but he could not recollect particular instances. Indeed he had never seen a slave trial. The judges were almost all planters'. These kind of views about the well-being and easy life of their unfree plantation labour have an almost universal existence where agribusiness capitalists are concerned, and similar claims can be found in almost any account by them of the nature of the labour regime on their rural properties.

[81] During the early 1840s, therefore, the gangmaster system enabled a farmer to disclaim knowledge of and responsibility for his workers. Dodd (1976: 53) makes this clear: 'There is a complete disseverment between the farmer and the laborer; the former has no interest either in the character or condition of the latter; the whole power, as well as responsibility, is delegated to a…grasping gangsman, whose tyranny is the more oppressive…'.

[82] In the course of taking evidence for the 1931 Royal Commission investigating the working conditions of industrial and plantation labour in British India, an Indian representative was strongly discouraged by the Chairman from pursuing a line of questioning about the extent to which carpet-making factories owned by British capital were responsible for the coercive practices utilized by master weavers against unfree child labour employed indirectly by the former and directly by the latter. What had happened was that, when challenged that he himself was responsible for the employment of low-paid unfree labour in carpet-making, the representative of the British factory denied culpability by claiming that, although as far as he personally was concerned child labour was free to come and go as it wished, he was unable to guarantee that this was how the master weaver – the direct employer of such workers – perceived the situation. That is to say, any shortcomings in the pay, working conditions and

accepted the existence and harshness of debt peonage, but always insisted that it was a relation found on neighbouring rural estates, never on their own.[83]

Like their early nineteenth century counterparts, witnesses appearing in front of the 2002–03 EFRA Committee who were representatives of agribusiness insisted time after time either that they did not know what was happening on the ground, or that if 'abuses' indeed occurred there, it was not their fault but that of the gangmaster who was responsible for the workers.[84] For their part, gangmasters dismissed the generally 'very bad reputation' they had by claiming this was the fault of 'one or two undesirable gangmasters'.[85] Again like their early nineteenth counterparts, gangmasters said they did not know who was or was not 'legal', a view presented also by the National Farmers Union.[86]

---

treatment of these workers were nothing to do with him. For these exchanges, see Royal Commission on Labour in India (1931: 98–9, 277, paragraphs B-1279 to B-1280 and B-1277[a] to B-1277[g]).

[83] Following the extensive documentation of widespread coercion and violence practiced against debt peons employed on sisal producing capitalist estates in Yucatan, landlords accepted that this had occurred, but always on estates other than their own. On this point, Gruening (1928: 138) makes the following laconic observation: 'In 1923 I travelled through those regions. Even the Yucatan *hacendados* denied little, although at the time with a militantly revolutionary governor, Felipe Carrillo Puerto, in the saddle, recollections of that nature were painful. It was on the other fellow's hacienda that those things happened. "We treated our peons very much better than the rest." The *hacendados* were unanimous on that point.'

[84] This ideological defence is by no means confined to agribusiness, and is deployed also by urban industrial capitalists relying on the gangmaster system. When confronted with the long hours worked and low pay received by migrants employed in his factory, the English managing director of a Korean-owned multinational blamed the gangmaster, saying the latter 'was entirely responsible for the Chinese workers, who were technically employed by [the gangmaster's] agency, not by the company... [the gangmaster] submits a claim. We pay him direct, the minimum wage per worker plus a management fee. He houses the workers and feeds them. We provide space at the factory for his Chinese cook. What he pays the workers is up to him' ('Tragic death that uncovered the shadowy world of Britain's hidden Chinese workers', *The Guardian* [London], 13 January 2004). Perhaps the least surprising thing about this case is that, when this same multinational corporation first based its subsidiary in Northeastern England, the local Member of Parliament – one of the chief architects of 'New' Labour – praised the company effusively, insisting '[s]ome have the impression that the success of the tiger economies is based on sweatshop labour...[t]his is a false picture'.

[85] See EFRA (2003: 52), where in an entirely predictable form of blame avoidance, one gangmaster eschewed the very label itself, insisting that 'we're an employment agency now...so we are not gangmasters; although we came from gangmaster stock shall we say'.

[86] See EFRA (2003: 13, Ev 14).

Equally unsurprising was the fact that supermarkets were unwilling to take action about gangmasters: thus, for example, The Fresh Produce Consortium, a trade association (retailers, wholesalers, importers and packers), blamed gangmasters but nevertheless opposed state regulation, and argued for a 'voluntary' code of practice.[87] The existence of what are termed 'abuses' was attributed by agribusiness and its representatives to a lack of transport, an argument that mimics that advanced in the nineteenth century by gangmasters and commercial farmers. Similarly, the claim by agribusiness enterprises about who benefits nowadays is also familiar one: those in the food chain who make the profits are not them (nor nowadays the supermarkets), they protest, but labour contractors. Again like their nineteenth century counterparts, farmers themselves now claim that workers are not only not exploited but do well economically from the existing system ('a great many of the gang workers that are employed are actually employed on a piece-work basis where in fact there are substantial rewards for people who work very hard').[88] *Plus ça change....*

Conclusion

Both the fact of and the dynamics structuring the return to British agriculture of the gangmaster system are outlined in a 2002–03 EFRA Report, the findings of which have been examined here. Wrongly described by some observers as an aspect of a developing capitalism, by conservative historiography as benign/non-coercive, and by the 'New Labour' government as the resurgence of 'medieval working practices', this highly exploitative form of labour contracting was condemned earlier, by the 1867 Children's Employment Commission. Then, as now, it involved the recruitment/control of casual workers, and is currently based on much the same kinds of coercive mechanisms as its nineteenth century counterpart. Rather than being a pre- or non-capitalist relic, however, the gangmaster system corresponds to the restructuring of the rural labour process by cost-cutting agribusiness enterprises and commercial farmers. As such, it is argued here, it represents not 'primitive accumulation' but the authentic face of a twenty-first century 'fully functioning' capitalist agriculture.

---

87 See EFRA (2003: Ev 1, 2).

88 See EFRA (2003: Ev 18, 23). In an important sense, this claim about the improving conditions of the rural labourer has always been a central component of farmer ideology, as Howkins (1990: 14) makes clear.

What emerges clearly from this EFRA Committee Report is the degree to which forms of labour recruitment/control/coercion long associated either with a developing capitalism in the nineteenth century, or with backward agriculture in so-called Third World countries during the twentieth, are in fact a characteristic of current agribusiness in metropolitan capitalist contexts. In this regard, the Report merely confirms the presence of a global trend in the relational forms and employment practices utilized by capital, but a trend that has not always been recognized.

Where rural labour relations are concerned, therefore, most observers – including a number of Marxists (especially those who subscribed to the 'semi-feudal' thesis) – have espoused what can only be termed a Whig interpretation of history. They claimed that in the course of agrarian transformation, and indeed a characteristic of the latter, the pay/conditions of rural workers would get better and better, as capital replaced more oppressive relational forms (= pre-capitalist/unfree) with less oppressive ones (= capitalist/free).

However, a few Marxists (including this writer) have argued strongly against this view, pointing out that the opposite was the case, and that frequently the competitive edge enjoyed by agribusiness capital in whatever national/regional/historical context derived precisely from its willingness/capacity to introduce or reintroduce unfree production relations wrongly deemed to be 'pre-capitalist', 'non-capitalist' or 'semi-feudal'.

Far from being an example of 'medieval working practices', therefore, which is what the government imagines the gangmaster system currently operating in British agriculture to be, this form of labour recruitment/control/coercion is much rather the epitome of agrarian capitalist relations. The value of this EFRA Committee Report lies in the fact that, like its mid-nineteenth century counterpart dealing with the gangmaster system, it succeeds in providing a snapshot – however imperfect, and for whatever reason – of the way in which agrarian capitalism operates at a particular historical moment.

Just as the 1867 Sixth Report of the 1862 Children's Employment Commission concerned mainly with exposing the 'moral evils' of the gangmaster system also showed – accidentally, perhaps – the connection between capitalist exploitation and child labour, so the 2002–03 EFRA Committee Report enables one to see (literally) how similar kinds of exploitation are still central to a 'fully functional' accumulation process over one hundred and thirty years later. This excellent

Report is in many ways a worthy successor to the Government Commissions (revealing as they did the ugliness – 'the Medusa's head' – underlying respectable bourgeois British society) which Marx (and others) found so useful in the late nineteenth century.

In an important sense, given the increasing global competition between agribusiness enterprises, the gangmaster system in Britain is not merely not an historical anomaly (='medieval working practices'), nor even a necessary aspect of the accumulation process, but a *sine qua non* of capitalist reproduction in rural areas. The similarity between the two conjunctures giving rise to the gangmaster system is striking. Like the era following the repeal of the Corn Laws, the 1980s was a period characterized by increasing economic competition on a global basis. At each conjuncture, therefore, the gangmaster represented for its respective commercial agrarian enterprise a specifically *capitalist* method of keeping labour costs low and simultaneously maintaining control over the workforce.

CHAPTER EIGHT

CITIZENSHIP AND HUMAN RIGHTS – OR SOCIALISM?

Apart from adherents both of the semi-feudal thesis, who believe that capitalists will voluntarily dispense with unfree labour for economic reasons to do with cost and efficiency, and of the 'disguised' wage labour argument, for whom a free/unfree distinction is epistemologically non-existent, those who recognize that this will not happen maintain such production relations will vanish as a result of political action taken by the state. The latter category, however, divides into two distinct approaches.

On the one hand, therefore, are non-Marxists who insist that eradication is possible within the existing legal framework of capitalism itself. Based on a moral/ethical discourse devoid of material content, such a process involves the promotion of human rights through the agency of non-government organizations lobbying to secure an end to unfree relations. The resulting implementation of an abolition policy and its enforcement by a benign state means that an unfree worker accordingly becomes free, and attains thereby citizenship, an empowering status henceforth guaranteed by the exercise of democracy, or – where this is lacking – pressing for redemocratization.

On the other, it is argued here against such a view, on the grounds that there has been an historical shift in the perception by the capitalist state of the economic role of unfree labour. From being seen as an obstacle to growth, unfree labour is now regarded as making a contribution to the accumulation process. For this reason, neither commercial enterprises nor the bourgeois state are interested any longer in eradicating this form of production relation. Consequently, the abolition of unfree labour will be achieved not by NGO or ILO agency but only through class struggle, with the object of transcending capitalism as an economic system, and replacing it with socialism.

This chapter is divided into three sections, the first of which examines why changes in the economic role of unfree labour mean that abolition can only be accomplished by putting socialism on the political agenda. Considered in the second are approaches (by the ILO and NGOs) which seek to bring about the eradication of unfree labour within the capitalist system, by means of human rights legislation. The third looks critically at the desired method and outcome of such an attempt, to establish citizenship and civil society as a result of redemocratization.

I

It is crucial to understand that a distinction between peasant-as-debt-bonded and worker-as-debt-bonded is significant also in another way. Thus the characterization of unfree labour as acceptable or unacceptable to capitalism affects in turn what kind of systemic transition is on the political agenda. Historically, the concern expressed by British colonial administrators in India about the parasitic role of debt and moneylending derived from its negative impact on agricultural production, and thus also on land revenue.[1] Currently, however, it could be argued that a noticeable shift has taken place in the way the economic role of debt is perceived.

Hence the difference between historical and existing forms of bonded labour in India. In terms of categories of worker affected (permanent/non-permanent), their usufruct rights (access to or separation from property), and other crucial dimensions of the bonded labour relation (duration, heritability, coercion and enforcement), current unfree relations of production do indeed differ from past variants. Contrary to recent claims it is precisely this difference that is addressed by and embodied in the concept deproletarianization.[2]

Peasants or Workers?

Not only has attachment shifted from permanent to casual and/or migrant labour, and the debt bondage relation involve what are increasingly landless agricultural labourers, therefore, but the latter are no

---

[1] As numerous historical studies underline, the connection between peasant indebtedness and agricultural productivity in India was a constant theme informing the work of colonial administrators. The main concern of, for example, Darling (1925, 1930, 1934) and Trevaskis (1928, 1931–2), was to break the hold moneylenders had traditionally exercised over the rural economy, particularly in the agriculturally important region of Punjab.

[2] See Brass (2008) for an examination of what purport to be critiques of theory about deproletarianization, 'critiques' which are not merely wrong but also ironically and unwittingly reproduce many of the arguments and positions associated with this approach.

longer unfree throughout the whole agricultural cycle or on an inter-generational basis.[3] Furthermore, such workers may under specific conditions (and only with the consent of their creditor) transfer their labour-power and indebtedness to another employer.[4] Both the nature of coercion and the enforcement of debt-servicing labour obligations have also undergone change.[5] All these points have been and are central to the case about deproletarianization.

A further distinction concerns both the political effect of deproletarianization, and the implications of this for the way in which systemic (not relational) transition is interpreted. Rather obviously, this issue is not one considered by exponents of the semi-feudal thesis or neo-classical economics, and those who confuse such views with Marxism. Within some Marxist theory, however, unfree labour has been interpreted specifically with regard to cultivators and smallholders: that is to say, coercion designed to affix producers to land on a permanent basis.[6]

---

[3] These shifts have to some degree eroded the usual epistemological distinctions cited by Marxism as separating free labour from slavery. Among the more significant is the conceptualization of the free worker as someone whose labour 'must confront capital as *pure use value*, which is offered as a commodity by its owner himself' (Marx, 1986: 218, original emphasis). The labour of debt bonded workers who are either migrants employed on a seasonal basis or locals hired as casuals, and in receipt of wages, do indeed confront agrarian capitalists as 'pure use value'. Once acquired by the employer, however, labour-power 'offered as a commodity by its owner himself' is then prevented from being recommodified, and as such ceases to be relationally free.

[4] This phenomenon, known as 'changing masters', is examined by me elsewhere (Brass, 1999: 23), when it was argued that the transfer of debts between masters 'constitutes a precise relocation of unfreedom in terms of the rural labour process. This transformation corresponds to a shift in the immobilizing function of debt from a continuous and inter-generational basis to a more period- and context-specific basis. Its operationalization is as a result confined to the months of peak demand in the agricultural cycle, when sellers of labour-power would otherwise command high prices for their commodity. Whereas the traditional form of bondage is unprofitable (requiring payment for time when labour-power is not engaged in productive activity), the modern form is not (and is akin to the kind of control exercised by a plantation over the seasonal labour-power of poor peasant households that reproduce their own subsistence during the off-peak in villages on its periphery.'

[5] Coercion to enforce debt-servicing labour obligations is exercised not 'from above', by a landlord, but rather 'from below', by fellow caste members and/or members of the worker's family/kin group.

[6] Even Marx (1986: 184) himself took this view ('the gradual transformation of... the hereditary, half-tributary and often unfree tenant into the modern farmer, and the serf and villein tied to the soil and subjected to labour-services' etc.), although at the time he was writing the object of unfreedom as a means of affixing producers to land was more common than it is now. Hence the perception (Marx, 1986: 413, original emphasis) that in 'the relation of slavery and serfdom there is no such separation;

Although still important in some places, this objective is not – or is no longer – central to the process of deproletarianization. The latter concept has extended the debate about unfreedom in two ways: first, to those who are no longer cultivators, but who rely on the sale of labour-power for their livelihood; and second, to categories of worker (migrants, seasonal and temporary) that are not permanent or local. This it has done by focussing both on the conditions impeding the commodification of labour-power by its owner, and by highlighting that unfree relations are reproduced as the result of class struggle waged 'from above'. These were all considerations that Marx and a number of other Marxists regarded as central to an understanding of capitalism and the relational forms acceptable to it.[7]

Where agricultural workers, who earlier have personally commodified their own labour-power, subsequently become unfree (their labour-power either ceasing to be a commodity, or being recommodified by someone other than themselves), what has occurred currently in a neo-liberal capitalist context is a relational transformation that corresponds to *de*proletarianization.[8] Such workers are still landless; they still work for someone else on a permanent, seasonal or casual basis; they can still be employed in conjunction with advanced productive forces; they still receive cash wages; they may be migrants or work locally; and (under the control of a contractor, or in the form of changing masters) their labour-power can still circulate in the labour market; *but* – and this is the crux of the matter – they are no longer able personally to sell their own labour-power.

In short, because they do not meet the second of the two criteria laid down by Marxist political economy as necessary for the existence of free labour – freedom from the means of labour and also freedom personally to sell their own labour-power – they are now unfree

---

rather, one part of society is treated by another as the mere *inorganic and natural* condition of its own reproduction. The slave stands in no relation whatsoever to the objective conditions of his labour; rather, *labour* itself, both in the form of the slave and of the serf, is placed along with the other natural beings such as cattle *as an inorganic condition* of production, as an appendage of the soil.' The same is true of Kautsky (1988: 226, 233): the reason why he tended to label unfree relations used by agrarian capitalists as a process of 're-emerging' feudal forms (*not* feudalism or 'semi-feudalism) is that they applied to household of poor peasants to whom landowners leased plots specifically in order to secure labour-power of resident kinsfolk.

[7] See Chapters 2 and 5.

[8] This would include the rebonding of workers who, having previously been unfree, then managed to emancipate themselves, only to re-enter bondage subsequently, a process widely reported throughout India. On this point see Brass (1999).

workers who have been deproletarianized. Unsurprisingly, the difference between the latter and historical forms of bonded labour in India has economic and political implications. Not just for the role of bonded labour in the accumulation process, but also for the nature both of class struggle in the countryside and – consequently – of systemic transition itself.[9]

Capitalism or Socialism?

Debt bondage in rural India was seen historically as a relation affecting mainly smallholding peasant farmers, not as sellers of labour-power but rather in their capacity as cultivators. In the colonial era, therefore, unfreedom occasioned by indebtedness was viewed as a problem that threatened the economic independence of the peasant cultivator in rural India, where in the words of an influential observer there was a 'perennial shortness and extreme expensiveness of working capital so as to get the best result in production from the land.'[10] Even those opposed to British colonialism held this view.[11]

[9] Where the element of transition is concerned, the conservatism of the semi-feudal thesis is due in part to its adherents being trapped in a particular epistemological circularity. Since for them a 'fully functioning' capitalism is synonymous with labour-power that is free, any accumulation process where debt bondage is present cannot *ipso facto* be defined as 'fully functioning' capitalism. A transition to the latter – and thus also to socialism – is postponed indefinitely, notwithstanding the fact that current evidence from many different global contexts where capitalism is 'fully functioning' confirms that accumulation thrives on the employment of unfree labour.

[10] See Mann (1929: 73–4). An untypical view about moneylending in agriculture was that of Jack (1916: 109): 'To western eyes it may seem utopian to expect Shylock to forgo his pound of flesh; but in India it is no uncommon experience. During our investigations my officers and I have often arranged terms of composition and induced moneylenders to accept far less than their nominal dues.' Others were more critical. 'The Marwāris,' observed Crooke (1907: 111), 'have an evil repute as usurers and skinflints. They are found in all the great trading cities, and much of the economic difficulties of the peasantry may be laid to their charge.' Earlier the same writer (Crooke, 1906: 5) noted similarly that the 'hope of improvement in agriculture depends on such a rise in the condition of the farmer that...he can select his own seed grain, instead of taking any rubbish the money-lender chooses to give him.' Writing about the Deccan in Western India at the beginning of the twentieth century, Keatinge (1912: 57–8) argued that 'when a cultivator is so heavily indebted that all the produce of his land, excepting a bare subsistence, must inevitably go to the *saukar* (money-lender), his incentive to strenuous work naturally decreases. He sees little prospect of extracting himself from debt...[in] numerous cases the results of such conditions may be seen in badly cultivated and undeveloped fields.' At that conjuncture the same point was made about debt as an obstacle to the economic efficiency of peasant agriculture in Eastern India (Brackenbury, 1915: 91): 'If land were only mortgaged to raise loans for agricultural improvements there would be nothing unsound in ryots' [= peasants']

Borrowing from landlords or village moneylenders involved high-interest repayment on loans, which prevented peasant farmers from investing in – and thus improving – their own agrarian labour process. The resulting appropriation of surplus from indebted smallholders was regarded by the colonial authorities as an obstacle to their productive capacity.[12] The assumption was that by legislating against debt

indebtedness. It is unproductive debt and borrowings necessitated by caste and social customs to which exception must be taken inasmuch as they constitute a burden on the land which the land should not be called upon to bear. It is this aspect of the ryot's indebtedness that renders his position so precarious, as a succession of bad seasons, the immediate effect of which he has no means of avoiding, except by further borrowing, quickly strains his resources to the breaking point.' Just before the second world war, Blunt (1938: 108–9) noted: 'Neither in India nor in any other country can a farmer avoid incurring debt... indebtedness, often amounting to insolvency, is the normal condition of a majority of Indian farmers. The difference between them and farmers of other countries lies chiefly in this – that the latter seldom borrow except for productive purposes, whilst a considerable part of the borrowings of Indian farmers are for unproductive purposes... In such circumstances, the moneylender must demand high rates of interest...he is often guilty of usury and other serious malpractices. Smaller cultivators become his bondsmen....It is not strange that he [the peasant debtor] has little incentive to experiment with improvements, or to work any harder than he does already.' Mann was an agronomist, and Jack, Crooke, Keatinge, Brackenbury and Blunt all belonged to the Indian Civil Service. Much the same point was made subsequently by a member of the 1927 Linlithgow Commission on Indian agriculture (Gangulee, 1935: 21): 'The outstanding fact of the whole village was the heavy indebtedness usually incurred, not for productive purposes, but in order to meet their ordinary requirements. This unproductive debt had naturally placed the villagers not only in the grip of the *Mahajan* [moneylender], but had also left them in the midst of a vicious circle out of which it was difficult to extricate them.'

[11] During the colonial era analyses of rural India condemning debt and moneylending as an impediment to the efficiency and thus wellbeing of peasant economy were the norm, critiques of imperialism not excepted. For instances of the latter see Macdonald (1910: 140 ff.), Hyndman (1919: 221 ff.), Huque (1939: 150 ff.), Roy (1990: 103) and the report of the India League (1932: 346–7). In a similar vein, Sapre (1926: 166) observes that 'the strength of a chain depends upon its weakest link. We must, therefore inquire into other causes of the inefficiency of Indian agriculture and one is to be found in the indebtedness of the cultivator. It is nothing less than his fragmentation. He is not able to order his economic life as he would: he is not able to retain for himself the fruit of his labour, which he has to share in various diminishing proportions with his moneylender. No evil has perhaps attracted greater attention of [colonial] Government than that of indebtedness.'

[12] The impact on agricultural production of peasant indebtedness to moneylenders was considered at length in Voelcker (1897: 84 ff., 236 ff., 290–2) and the 1927 Royal Commission on Indian Agriculture. Lamenting the plight of the peasantry in India, an ICS member posted to the United Provinces over the period 1910–34 makes the following observation in his memoirs (Macleod, 1938: 205–7, original emphasis): 'The next problem is the indebtedness of the peasants...Unfortunately, the peasant's very poverty tends to make him poorer. For he is too poor to build a barn, or even if he could do that, to wait for payment for his crops, so he has to sell the produce to the *banya* [moneylender] at harvest-time when the market is glutted and prices are at their

bondage, smallholding peasants who no longer had to repay high interest loans to village moneylenders would as a result possess sufficient funds for improving cultivation. This would then generate increases in economic growth on holdings operated by petty commodity producers.[13]

Significantly, on the issue of moneylending as an economic obstacle to a flourishing peasant economy there was little difference between the colonial authorities and those opposed to colonialism.[14] Among the latter group were the Indian National Congress and also

---

lowest. And the loan which poverty compels him to take from the *banya* itself seals his doom finally: for he will have to pay interest at the rate of 2 or 3 per cent a *month*, or even higher, and liquidation of the debt is almost hopeless. As a matter of fact the *banya* usually makes no attempt at first to exact full payment by any drastic measure such as the sale of the debtor's property, but finds it more profitable to treat his victim as his slave, squeezing out of him continuously all his earnings beyond what he needs to keep body and soul together.' The focus of another account at that same conjuncture, this time by a journalist (Brown, 1927: 190–1, original emphasis), is on the coercive measures adopted to enforce debt repayment: 'These moneylenders are Kabulis…[a]ll of them stand six feet or thereabouts in height, and they carry sticks nearly as high as themselves…The first of the following month sees the Kabuli waiting outside the office or mill wherein his victim is employed. With him is another of his tribe, for these men usually hunt in couples…The debtor is duly buttonholed on emerging from his work, and the instalment due demanded then and there…Woe betide the borrower who defaults, for the big sticks are not carried merely as ornaments; more than once a wretched defaulter has been beaten to death, and his assailants have escaped scot-free.'

[13] Hence the kind of tenure that, as a result of eliminating debt bondage relations, either would be reproduced or came into being was *individual* peasant proprietorship, against which virtually all Marxists have argued (for many different reasons: political, economic, ideological).

[14] It is important note that during the colonial era opposition to moneylending also stemmed from those economists who saw debt generally as an undesirable burden on the finances of empire, and through this an obstacle to economic growth throughout British imperial domains. Hence the following observation by one such, Wilson (1909: 9): 'My contention has always been a simple one, that debt is a cancerous disease and morally deadly in the course of time alike for the nation and the individual; and inasmuch as the age we live in is distinguished above all that have gone before it as the age of credit, which means debt, it follows that our peril is the greatest ever seen, and it grows in intensity – the peril to our civilization and liberties. Few people have any conception of the extent to which our civilization has been created by and is buoyed upon debt. In lightness of heart, with hardly a thought for the morrow, we have gone to the credit manufacturer for the means to gratify every whim, passion and aspiration. By help of credit we have carried on our wars, created our iron highways, cleansed and beautified our cities, and enlarged our dominions; and now credit is called in to assist us in keeping our unemployed from dying of starvation.' Not only would such views have fed into discourse about peasant debt in the empire, but its concerns with the impact of deficit financing on economic development also prefigured the post-Keynesian economic theory that rose to prominence once again during the 1980s.

pro-Moscow elements and agrarian organizations.[15] Given its bourgeois social composition, Congress was unsurprisingly ambivalent on the subject of the rural moneylender: accepting that smallholder indebtedness and the intergenerational bondage to which it gave rise were economically undesirable, Congress nevertheless blamed this on colonialism, arguing for a return to pre-British 'friendly relations' between moneylender and cultivator.[16]

Much the same kind of approach informed pro-Moscow discourse at that conjuncture, when indebted smallholding cultivators (= peasant-as-debt-bonded) were seen as evidence of feudal/semi-feudal relations in an Indian agriculture from which capitalism was as-yet absent. Writing about the inter-war period, for example, the influential theorist R. Palme Dutt attributed the slow advance of industrialization to the impoverishment of the peasantry and stagnant agriculture to 'the increasing indebtedness of the cultivators still in possession of their holdings'.[17] As he saw it, in India the agrarian problem which stemmed from 'the maintenance of landlordism and feudal and semi-feudal institutions' ranged 'against the masses' could be solved by a 'people's democracy'.[18]

---

[15] On the historical policies and programmes of peasant organizations following the Moscow line, such as the All-Indian Kisan Sabha, see Rasul (1974).

[16] The juxtaposition in Indian nationalist discourse of an idealized image of pre-colonial moneylender as 'benign' with the negative image of moneylender-as-vampire unleashed by colonialism is evident in a mid-1930s analysis of rural indebtedness by Malani (1935). On this subject he writes (Malani, 1935: 3–4, 5, 9–10): 'The ancestral debt which is handed down from father to son, generation after generation, is another important cause of the present indebtedness...The moneylender, or the *Sahukar* as he is generally called, has existed in India since times immemorial and has performed a very useful function; but with the advent of British rule he has deteriorated very sharply...In the pre-British regime when the *panchayat* functioned as an active institution...the relations between the *sahukar* and the *ryot* were friendly and mutually helpful. It is the maladjustment in the organization of the village life brought about by the centralized policy of the present [British colonial] government which is at the root of the trouble between the *sahukar* and the *ryot*; and in our opinion the solution of the problem lies not in breaking the moneylender but in restoring the old, friendly relations between them through the agency of an actively functioning *panchayat*.' For a similarly idealized depiction of village moneylending, see Singh (1933: 36–9, 58–60, 75).

[17] See Dutt (1955: 34ff., 90ff.). On the subject of smallholder pauperization as a result of debt bondage he writes as follows (Dutt, 1955: 85–6): 'Descending still further in the scale...we reach the dark realms of serfdom, forced labour and debt slavery...In many parts these agricultural serfs and debt slaves are representatives of the aboriginal races. But the position of the former free peasant, who has lost his land and become virtually enslaved to his creditor through debt, or has been reduced to the bondage of sharecropping, is not far removed from legal serfdom.'

[18] See Dutt (1955: 94–5, 215). Much the same kind of focus on indebted smallholding agriculture as an indicator of peasant economic stagnation under feudalism

In other words, both colonial authorities and those opposed to colonialism regarded indebted poor peasants essentially as sellers not of labour-power but of the product of their labour. That is, producers who – in the absence of high interest repayment necessitated by borrowing – would be able to increase output on their holdings.[19] For colonialism, opposition to smallholder debt stemmed from concerns about agricultural production: a desire to increase output of foodgrains for domestic consumption, and simultaneously to ensure the payment of land revenue.[20] The problem was accordingly one of

informed the views expressed by Soviet studies of rural India at this conjuncture (Komarov, 1960; Kotovsky, 1960). In answer to his own question, 'What is the essence of the Feudal Survivals?', Kuusinen (1961: 476) states: 'The survival of feudal economic relations take various forms, of which the main and most typical are...the system of compulsory labour on the landlord's land...[t]his makes the peasants virtually the serfs performing corvée labour for the feudal lord...a dense web of debts entangling most of the peasants, making them insolvent and increasing their dependence on landlords and usurers. The results of all these survivals of feudalism are...extreme technical backwardness of agriculture', etc.

[19] In the course of a BBC radio interview just before Indian independence, Sir Malcom Darling, a member of the Indian Civil Service from 1904 to 1943, reiterated the centrality of economically efficient peasant family farming to the future of Indian agriculture. Replying to an observation by his interviewer, that 'there are only two things the peasants want – more land and fewer taxes', Darling stated (Steed, 1944: 4): 'There's no doubt he wants more land, nowhere more so than in India. There the peasant would rather lose his life than his land. Never is he more eloquent than when he asks for land. "Why does Government not give me land?" once pleaded a peasant to me. "Our work is farming. What else can we do? Where else can we go? We *must* have land. I have committed no fault. I have not stolen. I have done no crime. I have a wife and two children, and only three acres." A typical cry, and a typical case. There are millions of peasants who have less than five acres. The hunger for more is extreme...The real remedy is increased production all round' (original emphasis).

[20] Apart from colonial administrators and Marxists, opposition to peasant debt came from two additional sources. One was composed of anthropologists (e.g., Hutton, 1941: 422–3) who were concerned about the negative impact of moneylenders on tribal culture and society. This was a concern that merged with discourse about imperial 'trusteeship' advanced by colonial authorities; see, for example, the depiction of moneylenders in the fictional account of the Santal uprising by Carstairs (1935: 58). The other was composed of liberals who objected to State intervention, a case in point being A.J. Wilson, an economist who wrote for the *Investors' Review*. His indictment of British imperial financial policy in general and the land revenue in particular (Wilson, 1909: 21 ff., 62 ff., 87 ff.) was as savage as any made by Indian nationalists or, indeed, Marxists. Thus, for example, the following observation (Wilson, 1909: 70): 'India has always been a poor country. You must put out of your mind altogether the idea of a country shimmering and bustling with wealth, of a population living in affluence and comfort. The long series of harrowing famines which have swept over one region or another of the peninsula since we first knew it ought to have disabused our minds long ago of that fancy picture. India as a country is excessively poor, and one result of the strain put upon the humble people by the burden of the alien overlordship has been a steady increase in the sales of real estate, forced upon small landowners and peasant cultivators by their inability to meet the land rent and other charges levied by the

economic efficiency, and debt bondage was characterized as an obstacle to the transformation of these smallholders into commercially viable producers.[21]

Unfreedom and Systemic Transition

The theoretical focus and political effect of a case based on the concept deproletarianization is somewhat different. It is no longer concerned simply with the unfreedom of smallholders *qua* cultivators, or about the desirability of establishing – or reproducing – an efficient peasant economy.[22] Rather, it is about class struggle involving labour and capital, and thus a transition not to capitalism but to socialism. As interpreted by deproletarianization, therefore, unfreedom linked to the rising incidence of rural indebtedness in India (and elsewhere) concerns the viability of the subject as landless (or land poor) *worker*, not cultivator.

The political implications of this epistemological shift are twofold. First, it is no longer the case, as argued by semi-feudalism, that still on the political agenda are nationalism, bourgeois democracy, and electoral alliances with a 'progressive' bourgeoisie: the latter become, much rather, the target of class struggle. And second, debt bondage – which enhances control by rural employers over their workers – is now seen by the capitalist state not as an obstacle but much rather as a contribution to the economic efficiency of agriculture. Since it facilitates

---

supreme Government. So bad did this alienation become in the Punjab that a law had to be passed to put a stop to it, and to limit the tyranny of the local usurer, a harpy largely of our breeding.'

[21] Significantly, perhaps, much of the discourse advanced by colonial officials is still encountered today, but now in the defence of Indian peasant agriculture mounted by adherents of the semi-feudal thesis. Couched in a barely disguised nationalist idiom, where struggle is not between classes within countries but rather one between nations (advanced versus ex-colonial), therefore, the focus of the current semi-feudal approach of Patnaik (2007) is on 'livelihoods' and 'food security'. It comes as no surprise that, in place of class struggle, her argument (Patnaik, 2007: 9) is that '[w]e are today on the threshold of a major revival of peasant resistance to the iniquitous process of globalization [and] the grabbing of peasant land and forest resources, the undermining and pauperization of the peasantry'. That in her view peasant economy should be resuscitated is evident from the conclusion (Patnaik, 2007: 231): 'The small producer in this country [= India] is one of the lowest cost producers in the world, and there is a good prospect of small production stabilizing and facing international competition...'

[22] In current debate about development, the desirability of reproducing peasant economy is a view espoused not just by exponents of the semi-feudal thesis (see previous note) but also by present-day agrarian populists such as Bernstein (on which see Brass 2007: 117–25).

accumulation by lowering the cost of labour-power and also disciplining it, unfreedom can no longer be regarded as having a negative impact on agricultural production.

Because of this, the form taken by opposition to the existence of debt bondage has shifted, also in two distinct ways. Those who are not socialists can only invoke a moral/ethical discourse, one about the infringement of human rights.[23] In a neoliberal global capitalist system this kind of opposition is fruitless, and destined to fail precisely because unfree labour is now such a crucial part of the accumulation process. By contrast, those who are socialists locate bonded labour within the wider dynamic of present-day class struggle, and argue that it is a relation that will – like the accumulation process itself – cease only with the transcendence of capitalism as a system of production. Accordingly, opposition to debt bondage – in India and elsewhere – necessarily entails opposition to capitalism itself, apart from which it has no – and now cannot have – meaning.

Like a City Built in the Crater of a Volcano

That opposition to unfree labour might extend ultimately to include capitalism itself was not lost on those who objected to these kinds of work relation on ethical/moral grounds. The latter position on occasion possesses a different subtext, as is evident from fears expressed by Sir James Kay-Shuttleworth in a late nineteenth century variant.[24] Having accurately noted that, in the interests of economic efficiency, it is indeed possible to work a slave to death, he then argued that such a course was undesirable, because it was incompatible with the teachings of Christian ethics.[25] However, the reason why such a course was

---

[23] Epitomized in the mid-nineteenth century account written by Charles Dickens (1842: 249–84), there is of course a long history of specifically moral opposition to slavery in British popular culture.

[24] Sir James Kay-Shuttleworth was an influential advocate of educational reform, a result of investigations conducted in the working class areas of Manchester (Kay, 1969). Throughout the nineteenth century the formation and consolidation of an urban industrial working class in Britain was accompanied by a fear on the part of capitalist producers lest this process lead to the emergence of a socialist consciousness. For this reason, employers unsurprisingly concerned themselves with the political content of any education – formal or informal – on offer to or received by their manual labourers. Calls for the reform of public education at this conjuncture rarely failed to mention its potential role as a way of counter-acting the spread of socialist ideas.

[25] 'Economically, therefore, the driving of men like helots enslaved by…rude, tyrannous middle-men, may occasion the ruin of a colliery,' argued Kay-Shuttleworth

deemed by him as inadvisable is then revealed: it would generate social unrest on the part of those oppressed in this fashion, which in turn might lead to a socialist revolution and a threat to property.[26] This was an underlying fear acknowledged also by John Stuart Mill.[27]

(1973: 326–7), before considering what if ruin was not the outcome: 'But suppose this catastrophe avoided. Suppose that the colliery master has not ultimately drowned his own conscioence in punch, or hardened it by greed. Suppose that any one approach him in the solemn hour when, with a lightning glance of retrospection, we all review our lives, and pour into his ear the story of ruined health, debauched lives, profligate families, fever, misery, and death which have been the real wages of his rule as a master. Can his wealth repay him for that pang of conscience? Are his riches so lasting an inheritance that they provide him with an eternal paradise of satisfaction apart from his victims? If he have been economically successful, have the gains which he has wrung from the blood and souls of his dependants not encountered the Nemesis of the *higher Law* which requires, as second only to the love of God, that we should love our neighbours as ourselves? .... *The co-ordination of moral and physical forces in the constitution of man and society is, therefore, such that the purely economic laws governing the production of wealth are necessarily subject to higher laws of moral obligation*' (original emphasis).

[26] In the words of Kay-Shuttleworth (1973: 324): 'Moreover, a slave State is like a city built in the crater of a volcano; the fire of a servile revolution destructive of every trace of civilization smoulders below...There is, therefore, no ultimate security, either for property or civil institutions, in such a State.' Such concerns arose from the fear of 'the mob in the streets', or as one influential educational reformer (Kay, 1969: 42–3) put it, 'a turbulent population, which, rendered reckless by dissipation and want, misled by the secret intrigues, and excited by the inflammatory harangues of demagogues' would engage in 'frantic violence of an ignorant and deluded rabble'. Warning against allowing associations of workmen from focusing their discontents on capital, he (Kay, 1969: 111) goes on to state that the 'radical remedy for these evils [trade unions, strikes] is such an education as shall teach the people in what consists their true happiness, and how their interests may be best promoted.' Some four decades later, his warnings have become even stronger (Kay-Shuttleworth, 1973: 24–5): 'These unions exert a domination over their members like that of any army, and are capable of sustained action... Regarded as political and social phenomena, such results may be a most potent means of attaining any object which the manual labour class may have a strong conviction would be for their common interests.'

[27] In a 1844 letter addressed to Henry S. Chapman, Mill (1963: 640–1) writes that '[t]here is a prodigious current setting in every day more strongly, of superficial philanthropy. English benevolence can no longer be accused of confining itself to niggers [= plantation slaves] and other distant folks; on the contrary everybody is all agog to do something for the poor. A great many things have conduced to this, some good, some bad. The anti-poor-law cry; the state of the houses of the poor, their sanitary condition, as made known by Chadwick's official investigations; the conditions of large masses of people as shown by the enquiries of Commissions about factories, mines, etc., then in another way the speculations of Carlyle, the Puseyites, and others, about the impossibility of any social stability or security if there is not a habitual bond of good offices and sympathy between the ruling classes and the ruled, especially the poor – which speculations would have had no effect whatever if there were no chartism and socialism to frighten the rich. One sees plainly that while the noise is made up by a few sincere people, the bulk of the following has for its motive the desire of preventing revolution...'

Such a rapid use-up of workers is possible only as long as replacements are and remain cheap and available, which – as has been argued in previous chapters – is a process realized increasingly in the context of the global spread of capitalism.[28] One effect of this is the rundown of welfare provision in metropolitan capitalist nations, now that other forms of labour-power elsewhere – including unfree production relations – are less costly to employ in terms of direct and indirect remuneration. With the relocation of jobs to low-wage to countries in the so-called Third World, where such provision is minimal or lacking, it is no longer necessary for the metropolitan capitalist State to ensure the well-being of its own (free) workforce.

The direction taken by restructuring/recomposition undertaken by a 'fully-functioning' capitalism seeking less costly and more easily controlled forms of labour is now clear for all to see. Thus, for example, an environmentalist campaigner whose views have been taken up by some on the left in the UK, and are said to be influential in the anti-globalization movement, can now openly celebrate the relocation of already poorly-paid jobs from the UK to India, where they are done by yet cheaper labour, as on the one hand a just punishment for British imperialism in general and for the UK workforce in particular, and on the other an empowering development for Indian workers.[29]

---

[28] This was a process identified by Sidney and Beatrice Webb (1923: 89–90) as contributing to the decay of capitalist civilization: 'But if the instrument of production is not a machine, but a living organism, the problem becomes sentimentally complicated at once. If the savage, instead of spending a day to make an implement, has to spend ten days catching a wild horse and breaking it in, and he proceeds to over-work, ill-treat and starve the horse to death before it has repaid the ten days' work with something to boot, then clearly he will share the horse's fate presently. Like the employer with the machine, he has to ascertain how long he should let the horse live in order to make the utmost profit out of him. A slave-owner has to make the same calculation as to his slaves. Such calculations are made quite cold-bloodedly as a matter of capitalistic business. Before slavery was abolished in the southern States of North America it had become accepted on certain plantations that the most profitable system was to wear out the negroes in eight years...Obviously the substitution of hired white labour for enslaved black labour...does not change the nature of the calculation. When the Lancashire factory owners were reproached with using up nine generations of men in one generation, their reply, when they were imprudent enough to reply frankly, was that the calculation worked out that way whether they liked it or not, and that business is business.'

[29] For the elaboration of this view, see George Monbiot, 'The flight to India', *The Guardian* (London), 21 October 2003, p. 25. Significantly, perhaps, the same kind of argument can now be heard from journalists giving voice to the interests of the capitalist class. When opposing suggestions for raising trade barriers against cheap textile imports, therefore, spokespersons for European capitalists invoke the plight of

This endorsing approach to the transfer of jobs, away from workers in one national context to those in another, is not a position any socialist would hold, particularly when it involves the replacement of free workers with ones that are unfree. Nor should any movement that considers itself progressive – let alone socialist – allow itself to be associated with such a view. The result of this kind of capitalist restructuring that entails relocation of the labour process is – and can only ever be – economically disempowering for workers in both contexts. Those who lose their jobs become impoverished, while their counterparts in India now have these same jobs but without the relatively better pay and conditions enjoyed by those who had them previously.[30]

In terms of political outcome, the result of this economic relocation is equally clear. Not only is a 'fully-functioning' capital the sole

---

impoverished peasants in China, arguing that it is they who will suffer most from protectionist measures. See Will Hutton, 'China's poorest will suffer', *The Observer* (London), 28 August 2005, p. 24 (also – and more generally – Brittain 2005: 73). Such crocodile tears shed by capital on behalf of the rural poor demonstrate the degree to which behind an ostensible 'concern' for the Third World rural 'other' lurks the desire of employers to justify restructuring using ever cheaper sources/forms of labour-power. This, too, has a long history, as an anarchist (Rocker, 1937: 261) writing seven decades ago reminds us: 'The love of his own nation has never yet prevented the entrepreneur from using foreign labour if it was cheaper and made more profit for him. Whether his own people are thereby injured does not concern him in the least; the personal profit is the deciding factor in such a case, and so-called national interests are only considered when they are not in conflict with personal ones. When there is such a conflict all patriotic enthusiasm vanishes.' Much the same concern was expressed even earlier in the course of a General Council Meeting of the First International during January 1870 (Institute of Marxism-Leninism, 1964b: 203): 'But why do non-producers desire Free Trade? If not in order to make a profit out of other people's labour? To bring things from abroad because they are cheaper than they can be made at home is only done because they yield a larger profit, it is filching.'

[30] Both the reasons for and the dynamic of what in the 1980s became known as the new international division of labour were to some degree anticipated by Trotsky (1934: 906) in the following words: 'The backward country does not follow in the tracks of the advanced, keeping the same distance. In an epoch of world-wide economy the backward nations, becoming involved under pressure from the advanced in the general chain of development, skip over a whole series of intermediate stages. Moreover, the absence of firmly established social forms and traditions makes the backward country – at least within certain limits – extremely hospitable to the last word in international technique.' Although written about Russia, this description could just as well apply to the rise of the Asian 'Tiger' economies in the so-called Third world over the last two decades of the twentieth century. As is well documented, the dynamic informing this was restructuring of the capitalist labour process, with the object of shifting production from contexts where workers were unionized and well-paid to one where labour was non-unionized and cheap. This workforce decomposition/recomposition amounted to segmentation, an object achieved by means of decentralization/relocation.

benefactor of this restructuring, but labour – in the UK and in India – is as a result encouraged to see the relocation through nationalist lens. Rather than capital exploiting workers in India to the detriment of their counterparts in the UK, therefore, this discourse projects difference in terms of capital and labour in a specific national context 'exploiting' capital and labour in another. The conflict arising from this kind of 'difference' is similarly national in its identity; unsurprisingly, the corresponding rise of nationalism has generated grassroots support for the political right. Socialists, by contrast, would see the difference as being one of class, the struggle international and not national, and consequently between labour, of whatever national/ethnic origin, and global capital.[31]

II

Also opposed to the continued existence of unfree labour is non-Marxist theory, which advocates a very different solution to the problem. Instead of linking bonded labour to the accumulation process, and arguing that both must be eradicated simultaneously, such an approach insists that unfree labour can be eliminated by non-revolutionary agency effected within the capitalist system itself. This emancipatory agency will be undertaken by the ILO and NGOs, and realized by

---

[31] There ought to be no mystery about this, as the following analysis makes clear: 'National economics are not, or at any rate were not until recently, water-tight compartments. The wages of any one country influence wages in any other country, and so do all other conditions of work. .... In order to be effective, the competition between labour groups with different standards of living need not take place in one country only. Labour at a low rate of wages is dangerous to well-paid labour not only when the lower paid workers are immigrants. It is just as dangerous when those labourers are set to work abroad, and give their employers an advantage in their competition with industries burdened with a higher wage rate... From this realization the transition is easy to the conclusion: it is in the interest of labour that wages should rise and working conditions improve everywhere. The strongest labour movements, and labour in the countries with the highest standard of living, must help the more backward sections of labour to rise.' This argument was advanced not by someone writing about the new international division of labour in the 1980s, but rather forty years earlier, by the socialist Franz Borkenau (1942: 11–2). His point was that, even then – he was writing during World War II about the struggle between national and socialist politics – capital was engaged in a global search for cheaper forms of labour-power. Unless worker solidarity was international and based on class, he maintained, plebeian agency designed to protect existing living standards when capital eventually found these less costly forms elsewhere would of necessity be nationalist and/or ethnically based.

utilising against capitalism both its own legal framework and its state apparatus.

Human Rights as (Capitalist) Emancipation?

Based as it is on natural rights philosophy, the concept of human rights relies for its implementation on an additional notion: a capitalist state that is benign and, where this involves conflict between capital and labour, politically neutral. Yet, as has been shown above, the perception of unfree labour on the part of the capitalist state has changed from one in which unfreedom is seen as an obstacle to economic growth to the opposite position, whereby unfreedom is now seen as contributory factor to this same process. If this is so, then a concept of human rights dependent for its enforcement on a benign capitalist state is going to be realized either with great difficulty or not at all.

This problem – the shift in the perception by the state of the economic role of unfree labour – is one that faces all those who continue to place their faith in human rights legislation as a disinterested guarantor of worker protection under the present capitalist system. Much of the opposition to neo-liberalism is currently undertaken by single-issue NGOs, the object of which is advocacy of pro-poor/anti-poverty policies such as 'decent workplaces', worker security, ethnic group empowerment, the realization of which is in all instances to be achieved by 'a-political' moral pressure.[32] Although in themselves laudable ends,

[32] For a useful critique of NGO activity in Latin America, see Petras (1997); for similarly useful critiques of NGO activity in Africa, see Maren (1997) and Polman (2010). Because advocates of the moral/ethical approach to unfree labour eschew an engagement with capitalism, they remain unclear about how to formulate a political economy of unfree labour, never mind put into practice effective opposition to its reproduction. This much is evident from a recent and somewhat confused attempt by one advocate of the ethical/moral viewpoint (Ferguson, 2010) to push forward the debate about the political economy of unfreedom simply by using an a-systemic concept of social reproduction. 'In order to contextualize this discussion,' argues Ferguson (2010: 5), 'I want to make clear exactly what I mean by unfree labour. I am not referring predominantly to the work from a Marxist tradition…this paper is not attempting to engage with Marxist debates in this area. More specifically, I want to explore recent work [which] explores issues such as bonded and forced labour. This work engages with Marxist debates but overall presents a heterodox approach, and as such is distinct from debates around unfree labour within exclusively Marxist analyses. This contemporary debate over unfree labour also has an activist counterpart through the campaigns of organizations such as Anti-Slavery International'. Such a view is based on a number of mistaken assumptions. To begin with, the issues it then addresses – the role of kinship and gender in reproducing unfree labour – are precisely those that have been raised in the recent past by Marxist analysis. Rather than seeing

such objectives are destined to fail, since they eschew politics generally, let alone those connected to class and class struggle.

Opposition to unfree labour by NGOs accordingly takes the form of mistakenly categorizing it in human rights discourse as socially marginal 'abuses'. Such an a-political approach, which avoids wider systemic causes, licenses piecemeal solutions based simply on an appeal to a moral order. Instances of unfree labour are accordingly perceived as 'anomalies', to be eliminated as such, rather than what they actually are; relational forms central to the economic reproduction of capital. In this moral discourse, 'abuses' of human rights are to be rectified by declaring that henceforth workers are free. At the same time citizenship is conferred on its subject, a status delivered by a benign state enabling the erstwhile bonded labourer to enter the market and become part of a wider civil society from which hitherto s/he has been excluded.

A partial exception in this regard is the International Labour Organization (ILO), which in theory ought to be able to play a progressive role both in formulating and ensuring adherence to global standards for work conditions and payment. That it has not been able to do so can be attributed to the rise from the 1980s onwards of *laissez-faire* economic theory which not so much opposed state regulation on behalf of labour as advocated state regulation of labour on behalf of capital.[33]

This shift in emphasis was in keeping with the changed perception by the capitalist state of the economic role of unfree labour.

---

the reproduction of unfree relations as part of the class struggle, however, the moral/ethical approach simply reconstitutes them as an epiphenomenon of gender subordination. This, too, overlooks the centrality of gender- and age-specific labour-power to Marx's own analysis of unfree production relations, a point outlined above in Chapter 2. Equally problematic is the inference that Marxism does not have an agency capable of effectively opposing/eradicating unfreedom, which of course it has, in the shape of class struggle. Alternatives to the latter are not evaluated, since agency based on moral/ethical opposition on the part of NGOs is incorrectly perceived as being sufficiently efficacious.

[33] The main critic of current ILO programmes and policies is Standing (2008), who underlines the point made here about the impact of the sea-change in the way governments view labour legislation since the rise of neo-liberalism. He notes (New Unionism, 2009: 2) that '[t]he roots of the ILO's current problems began in the 1970s with the rise of economic philosophies that tended to view any kind of regulation as a "market distortion". It was not long before the ILO was seen as a symbol of an antiquated way of thinking', adding that '[t]he trouble was that the ILO did not wish to offend the Americans, the World Bank or other institutions and governments supporting neo-liberalism.'

The economic acceptability of relations such as debt bondage and peonage were transformed: from being seen negatively as an obstacle to economic growth, and thus institutional forms that had to be eliminated, to being regarded positively as a contribution to the accumulation process. In short, the reproduction of which the state should no longer oppose but much rather encourage.

Because of this shift, the eradication of bonded labour is now for governments no longer an option, a problem that can be solved materially without too much difficulty.[34] In truth, this merely reinforces what has in fact been a long-standing policy of the state on this issue, which is that governments have shown a marked reluctance to do anything concrete about bonded labour.[35] What does happen is that slavery and other forms of unfreedom are *pronounced* illegal, and the problem deemed 'solved' thereby.

Emancipation by (Capitalist) Legislation?

The stock response by governments faced with accusations by human rights organizations that unfree labour continues within their jurisdiction has been – and remains – one of denial. When confronted with evidence of its continued presence, the answer given by a representative of the State challenged in this manner is that as such relations are illegal, they could not possibly exist.[36] Declared abolished simply as a

---

[34] Hence the erroneous view (Lerche, 2007: 7) that this 'cocooning of the forced labour issue makes it relatively safe for governments and organizations to deal with.'

[35] The reason for this is simple. To do so would entail challenging the economic interests of rural capitalist producers – rich peasants, commercial farmers and agribusiness enterprises – whose increasing political power in post-1947 India is a matter of record (Chattopadhyay, Sharma and Ray, 1987; Brass, 1995).

[36] Typical, perhaps, was the official response by the Indian government when asked in the mid-1960s by the UN Special Rapporteur on Slavery (Awad, 1966: 166) if 'slavery or any institution or practice similar to slavery, as defined above (including bonded labour) exist in the country?' The Indian Constitution, he was informed (Awad, 1966: 169–70), 'prohibits all forms of slavery including forced labour and consequently the existence of slavery or any institution does not arise.' The official reply noted that 'a practice in the form of "bonded labour" had been in existence in some parts of India,' adding both that '[a]nyway this practice is dying out,' and that '[t]he State Governments concerned have taken recourse to legislative executive measures to abolish the system [of unfree labour] wherever in existence.' This was also the government response to detailed submissions on *Modern Unfree Labour in India* (1983), on *Modern Unfree Labour in India and Peru* (1984), and on *Modern Bonded Labour in India* (1987) – all drafted by me – presented by the Anti-Slavery Society for the Protection of Human Rights (now Anti-Slavery International) to the 36th, 37th and 40th Sessions of the UN Special Commission on Human Rights. The similarity of the official response over a

result of being outlawed, bonded labour in effect vanishes from the political agenda. Not only is there no reason for any further action on this issue, but those who attempt to enforce such legislation themselves become the target of State action.[37]

If bonded labour is disappearing because agrarian capitalists seek to replace unfree relations with ones that are free, as neoclassical economists and advocates of the semi-feudal thesis claim, then in an important sense this relational form is indeed 'on the way out' and as such 'not worth bothering about'. According to this prognosis, bonded labour will vanish of its own accord as economic development takes place, and intervention by the ILO is effectively redundant.

However, if the opposite is the case and – as has been argued here – bonded labour is in particular circumstances for rural capital the preferred relational form, then it will increase as economic development occurs. According to *this* prognosis, bonded labour is *ipso facto* part of the problem of capitalism. Unfree relations have therefore to be addressed politically as an aspect of the way in which the capitalist system functions and reproduces itself.[38] To do so is not a distraction from but rather part of the wider struggle against the accumulation process and its labour regime.[39]

---

twenty year period underlines the extent to which nothing much had changed in this regard. No such relations exist any longer, it was – and is – asserted, because law proscribes them. By virtue of being illegal, therefore, unfree labour is said not to occur by governments who are challenged on this issue.

[37] Because it now affects producers who are capitalists, legislation outlawing bonded labour is either not passed, or – if passed – not implemented. For evidence of this see Das (1979) who outlines how, following the mid-1970s emergency, in Bihar government officials attempting to put into practice the 20-point programme abolishing debt bondage relations met with strong opposition, and were soon transferred elsewhere.

[38] In this respect, the issue of bonded labour is similar to that of the agrarian question. The inability or unwillingness of capital to solve the agrarian question in terms of production relations (not surplus generation and transfer) stems from the fact that to do so would adversely affect its own economic interests as much as those of feudal (or semi-feudal) landowners. Because of this, therefore, an agrarian bourgeoisie (or more accurately a bourgeoisie with agrarian property rights and interests) does not and will not sweep away unfree labour, a task which as Trotsky inferred only the proletariat will accomplish.

[39] This was the position taken by Marx (1985: 189), who commented as follows during the course of the Geneva Congress of the First International in 1866: '...the more enlightened part of the working class fully understands that the future of its class, and, therefore, of mankind, altogether depends upon the formation of the rising working generation. They know that, before everything else, the children and juvenile workers must be saved from the crushing effects of the present system. This can only be effected by converting social reason into social force, and, under given circumstances, there exists no other method of doing so, than through general laws, enforced by the power

Rather less plausible in terms of criticism is the accusation that, by focussing on unfree production relations, the ILO lets capitalism off the hook, since it diverts attention from the issue of free labour.[40] Because it overlooks the impact eliminating bonded labour would have both on free labour and on capitalism, such a view is misplaced. Similarly incorrect is another claim levelled at the ILO, that what it has done is to 'ghettoize' the issue of unfree labour, thereby forcing debate about labour standards into a cul-de-sac.

However, the situation is much rather the opposite: the ILO has helped to bring this work relation out of ghetto, and thus to underline the extent to which exploitative relations many of those in the development debate said would vanish, are still with us. Not the least valuable contribution of the ILO to the discussion is to indicate the extent to which hired workers in agriculture are also unfree.[41]

The Problem of Indigenous 'Otherness'

Although currently making a positive contribution to the debate about unfree labour, simply by recognizing the fact of its presence, the ILO approach is indeed hamstrung, but by another – less obvious – aspect of its own discourse. Because the ILO has in the past reified the category of the indigenous 'other', therefore, it still tends to confine the operation of certain institutional forms – among them bonded labour – to

---

of the state. In enforcing such laws, the working class do not fortify governmental power. On the contrary, they transform that power, now used against them, into their own agency.' This kind of mobilization, undertaken by workers as a class, has to be distinguished from contemporary forms of non-class agency, directed by bourgeois NGOs designed to mobilize 'the poor' along ethnic, gender or national lines.

[40] Objections are levelled specifically at two recent reports published by the ILO (International Labour Organization, 2001, 2005).

[41] One reason why bonded labour has not been asked about is methodological: a belief widely held among those conducting research that such relations no longer existed, and there was thus no need to enquire as to their presence. Because they were invariably hidden, whether or not labour was bonded by debt was either not asked about (by the researcher) or not revealed (by the informant). Either way, the point is that during fieldwork investigations conducted by researchers coercion *should* be asked about, and insofar as these days this is done more often than it has been in the past, as illustrated by the ILO research project, this object has to some degree been met. A problem does exist with regard to past forms of unfreedom, where the subject of an agrarian relation is no longer around to be asked what his/her views about this were. In these situations, it is necessary to rely on descriptions of what the relation entailed. What does remain lost to the historical record, however, is what the subjects themselves though about these relations, or the very dimension (= perception) that is privileged by interpretations which claim that 'patronage' has changed.

the presence of peasant or tribal populations.[42] Unfreedom comes to be seen as not merely connected to but in some instances part of grass-roots culture, a perception that simultaneously rests upon and seemingly reinforces a twofold impression.

First, that along with the rest of indigenous tradition and custom, the dynamic generating or reproducing these production relations is encountered only in contexts where the organization of work follows a pre- or non-capitalist pattern.[43] And second, that in some cases unfree working arrangements are part of a local cultural matrix, and thus form an important component of indigenous society itself.[44] In the present

---

[42] In the past, the ILO certainly has been aware of the problems involved in attempting to attach the label of indigenous 'otherness' to specific groups. Hence the following admission (ILO, 1953: 3): 'The notions with reference to which such groups are classified ['indigenous'] are so flexible and varied that there are often discrepancies in statistical data or estimates within a single country, and useful comparisons between one country and another are impossible. Different and often contradictory criteria tend to be used by administrators, lawyers and sociologists as a basis for their definitions, such as the colour of the skin, language, customs, tribal conditions and living standards.' In another passage a little further on, the ILO (1953: 5) accepts that '[h]istorically speaking the ['indigenous' populations] in these countries were those sections of the original inhabitants or autochthons which were not subjugated by or assimilated with the subsequent settlers and maintained, in most cases, by moving to forests, mountains or inaccessible areas, a distinct culture and way of life. Subsequently, however, under the growing pressure of the social and economic system of the main body of the population, the social and cultural isolation of the ['indigenous' populations] has gradually but definitely altered.' Later admissions in the same survey add to this undermining of the specificity of indigenous 'otherness', noting that indigenous people do the same kind of jobs, and just as well, as the non-indigenous inhabitants in the vicinity. Hence the following (ILO, 1953: 205, 442): 'Official statistics do not give a clear picture of the situation since, apart from some cases in which the definition of "indigenous" is based on purely racial considerations, indigenous workers...have assimilated the customs... and economic life of the nation and have broken away from the communities from which they came...with the result that those who enter industry rapidly lose the characteristics of language and tribal organization which distinguish them from the rest of the population, and are gradually absorbed into the working class as a whole. [...] In fact, where indigenous peoples who have had some association with the dominant communities around them have been recruited with the usual preliminary instruction for work in mines, for handling machines, or for driving motor vehicles, etc., they have as a rule shown themselves to be as capable and efficient in their jobs as anyone.'

[43] Hence the frequent references in an ILO survey conducted during the early 1950s to the fact of 'personal services' – a term that encompassed a variety of working arrangements that were not free – as evidence for the presence in such contexts of a 'feudal' or 'semi-feudal' agriculture (ILO, 1953: 202, 344, 357, 367 ff., 380–2, 388, 390, 470).

[44] Hence the view of the ILO (1953: 367) that the continued existence in India and Latin America of 'personal services', its term for unfree labour, 'is due in many cases to the survival of immemorial customs and usages...may be regarded as a form of servitude, made possible by the condition of social and economic inferiority of the [indigenous people] themselves.'

intellectual climate, dominated as it is by the 'new' populist postmodernism, these institutional arrangements are in effect declared untouchable, since they are perceived as being a part of an authentic indigenous cultural 'otherness' that must be protected from an encroaching capitalism, and thus unconnected with capitalism itself.[45]

That there was a problem with the category of ethnic 'otherness' was recognized, albeit reluctantly, by the ILO in the course of conducting a global survey of indigenous people during the early 1950s.[46] It became increasingly apparent that the category was merely a synonym for those who were poor/exploited. What marked out the distinctiveness of such people across many contexts in Asia and Latin America was not so much an innate ethnic or cultural 'difference', reproduced unchangingly 'from below', as their common economic subordination reproduced 'from above'. Nevertheless, at that conjuncture the ILO insisted on the continued heuristic utility of cultural/ethnic identity, thereby reifying indigenous 'otherness'.

To some degree, the 1960s 'development decade' signalled the possibility of a change in emphasis, as the need to assert 'otherness' was challenged by – and analytically switched to – the view that it should be transcended in the name of modernity. In keeping with this, the definition of identity was shaped as much by the economic as by the hitherto overriding importance given to notions of cultural-'difference'-as-tradition, and the role of unfreedom now came to be seen as an obstacle to social and economic progress.

With the academic rise to prominence of the 'new' postmodern populism in the 1980s, however, the emphasis was once again reversed. Concepts such as 'class', 'development' and 'progress' were declared 'foundational', and as such inappropriate Eurocentric impositions on

---

[45] On the privileging of ethnic otherness by the 'new' populist postmodernism, and its political effects, see Brass (2000).

[46] Even in the early 1950s the ILO recognized both the importance of tenure and agrarian reform, and also the link between the latter and the continued presence of forced labour. It accepted that, to change fundamentally, it was insufficient to oppose per se the labour performed by indigenous tenants on large rural estates. That is to say, simply to target the bad working and living conditions arising from tenancy, but leave the relation itself intact. This situation, argued the ILO (1953: 389) would end only as a result of 'eliminating anachronistic systems of land tenure and employment which not only keep the Indians in a socially and economically inferior position in relation to the rest of the population but arrest the economic and social development of the country as a whole.' The link with forced labour was made at the same conjuncture in another report (United Nations and International Labour Office, 1953).

the pristine culture of ethnic 'otherness'. Whether its subjects liked it or not, therefore, henceforth their subordination was defined yet again in terms not so much of worker/employer relations but rather of a minority identity based on a tribal/ethnic affiliation.[47] As such, their subordination was affixed once more to an 'old' and non-class form of belonging: namely, an ancient and more 'authentic' nationhood prefiguring but now located within a larger and historically more recent nation state.[48]

Not the least of the many ironies accompanying this idealization of indigenous 'otherness' as an appropriate and empowering identity was that the very same epistemology, which underwrote the unfree labour system of apartheid, was shortly to end in South Africa as a result of an enduring struggle waged 'from below'.[49] In other words, precisely those

---

[47] Reviewing a case study by Novo (2006), Jackson (2009: 202) cites the example of migrant Mixtecs from Oaxaca 'who were working as day labourers for a transnational agribusiness in Baja California [and how they were constituted in the eyes] of the non-indigenous people involved: federal and regional government agents, NGO employees, merchants, ranchers, and social scientists.' This context was characterized by 'the development of a perverse multiculturalism in which government actors interested in attracting global capital in effect colluded with the company to control costs. The substandard benefits and lower wages that migrants received were justified, according to the company, because, as *indios*, they did not need anything better. Minimal medical services were sufficient, for indios preferred their own traditional medicine. Child labourers? Not a problem – it was part of native culture. Indios were used to living in huts with dirt floors and no running water... Of course, virtually all colonial labour-extraction projects offer such convenient rationalizations. What is newsworthy here is that the neoliberal state worked to fashion indigenous identities suitable for insertion into transnational business in order to create a flexible workforce entitled to far fewer protections...The migrants in question themselves rejected indigenous identity.'

[48] The difficulties generated by characterizing a particular ethnic group as constituting the 'original inhabitants' in a given social formation – as encountered in many seemingly progressive legislative ordinances identified by the ILO (1953: 3, 293) – have a long history, and are (or should be) well known. Not the least problematic outcome is that, once conceded, such a principle can be deployed by parties and/or groups on the far right in support of exclusionary policies. A case in point is the BNP, which currently maintains that the 'white English' correspond to just such an oppressed minority within a nation that was once their own, but – due to immigration – no longer is.

[49] The endorsement by the ILO during the early 1950s of indigenous 'otherness' finds an echo in the justification of the South African apartheid system at that same conjuncture by the Minister of Native Affairs, Dr H.F. Verwoerd. His view (United Nations, 1953: 54) was as follows: 'One of the most striking phenomena of the world in which we live is the diversity of human races. They were created separate. This separation must be maintained even when economic or other circumstances have brought about a certain mingling of racial groups...each race stands separated by characteristics which are permanent because they are hereditary. A race can only "fulfil itself" if it remains faithful to its inner law. This is especially true of the Bantu who have languages and their own distinct customs, rites and institutions.'

who were supposed to be empowered by the identity in question rejected it. The latter notwithstanding, insofar as the ILO continues to endorse the view that capital 'de-authenticates' indigenous 'otherness', resistance must necessarily be based on ethnic/ecological/peasant essentialisms. The political difficulty with this is clear.

In this discourse an unfree worker is seen by the ILO as a 'natural' smallholder, a component of peasant society, and not as a worker who has been deprived of an ability personally to commodify/recommodify his/her own labour-power. Its discourse privileging indigenous 'otherness' means in effect that the ILO ends up sharing many of the same assumptions as bourgeois nationalists, pro-Moscow elements and the colonial authorities regarding the identity of the subject.[50] That is, the identity of an unfree labourer is primarily that of a cultivator and not a worker, a view licensing the desirability of establishing or re-establishing an efficient peasant economy in the context of village community.[51] The significance of this is that, together with human rights legislation,

---

[50] For these assumptions, see above. Not the least of the many ironies is the fact that this ahistorical view – held by the ILO, bourgeois nationalism, pro-Moscow elements and colonialism – of the indigenous subject as a 'natural' smallholding peasant was shared also by anarchists. This is evident from the anti-urban/pro-rural critique of socialism advanced by Tolstoy (1900: 50), who states: 'According to their theories, the workers will all join unions and associations and cultivate solidarity among themselves by unions, strikes, and participation in Parliament, till they obtain possession of all the means of production, as well as the land; and then they will be so well fed, so well dressed, and enjoy such amusements on holidays, that they will prefer life in town, amid brick buildings and smoking chimneys, to free village life amid plants and domestic animals; and monotonous, bell-regulated machine work to varied, healthy, and free agricultural labour.'

[51] This desire to re-establish peasant economy is part of a much older discourse, one about the fear of cultural erosion that results when smallholders migrate to cities, a disquiet that (for different reasons) is shared also by anthropologists and landowners. The latter have been concerned that such a process would undermine the political hold that this class has exercised historically over cultivating tenants. Because they have tended to idealize the village community they study as eternal, unchanging and composed of 'natural' peasants, anthropologists have similarly regarded rural outmigration as a destabilizing process. The methodological and theoretical biases to which this gave rise were recognized by one anthropologist (Mangin, 1970: xvi) writing just after the development decade: 'The neglect of cities has been encouraged further by our preferences for theories of dynamic equivalence, dating from Pareto, Henderson, Parsons, Malinowski, Radcliffe-Brown, and others. These theories present rather static models and make it difficult to account for change even when things are changing before one's eyes. The avoidance of national political issues has many of the same roots as the avoidance of cities, as well as the problem of sponsorship, both local and in the investigator's own country. The study of isolated villages have been less sensitive politically than those of displaced peasant migrants, city slum dwellers, political decision-making, and so on.'

findings contained in ILO surveys are often invoked by those engaged in NGO agency.

III

The concept 'citizenship', like human rights, is rooted epistemologically in notions of bourgeois democracy, which is itself a political gift accompanying the spread of the market. Hence citizenship is perceived as a virtuous effect following on from the eradication of unfreedom, an identity proclaiming the presence of capitalism which, it is inferred, led to the cessation of bonded labour and its replacement with production relations that are free. Ontologically, the dichotomy is familiar: a result of having displaced unfree work arrangements, a victorious combination of the market, capitalism and democracy confer freedom on labour-power, a newly-acquired status that is equated with citizenship. In this matrix, unfree labour is seen stereotypically as a non- or pre-capitalist relation, of no interest or use to the accumulation process.

From Unfree Labourer to (Capitalist) Citizen?

Terms such as 'civil society' and 'citizenship' form part of a broad conceptual matrix at the centre of which lie rival political interpretations about the nature and scale of 'community'.[52] In social formations other than socialism, 'civil society' operates at different levels: it can be applied to the nation as a whole, or be equated simply with a village 'community'.[53] The term 'citizenship' – and by inference 'civil society' – can for most Marxists have no real meaning in a capitalist system where there are still class differences.[54] For this reason, it is a political identity

[52] For different political interpretations structuring the general term 'community', see Gusfield (1975), Kamenka (1982a), Mosse (1982), and Etzioni (2001). An attempt has been made by Anheier (2004) to construct an index revealing the extent to which particular contexts can be said to constitute a 'civil society'.

[53] For examples of the current application of 'community' to virtually all/every kind(s) of global social identity, see Spellman (2002) and the contributions to the volume edited by Herbrechter and Higgins (2006). As an earlier commentator (Marshall, 1950: 21) on 'citizenship' pointed out, '[t]he original source of social rights was membership of local communities…'.

[54] An obvious exception is Gramsci, who – as in the case of many non-Marxist theorists – not only perceived 'civil society' as being present in social formations other than socialism but also adopted the familiar 'civil society'/State dichotomy. In his

that Marxism associates neither with smallscale rural community in a wider capitalist system nor with an all-embracing form of 'belonging' under capitalism itself. Much rather, and insofar as some Marxists use this term, 'citizenship' is a form of 'belonging' that comes into being only with the advent of socialism.[55]

Among non-Marxists, by contrast, the issue of 'citizenship' has oscillated between attempts to define it with and without reference to class. During the *laissez faire* era of the late nineteenth century, therefore, liberal bourgeois theory about 'citizenship' avoided the issue of economic inequality by confining this identity to the realm of culture. This amounted to the view that in England at that conjuncture 'the inequality of the social class system may be acceptable provided the equality of citizenship is recognized'.[56] By the mid-twentieth century – an era of

opinion (Gramsci, 1971: 12), therefore, 'we can…fix two major superstructural "levels": the one that can be called "civil society", that is the ensemble of organisms commonly called "private", and that of "political society" or "the State". These two levels correspond on the one hand to the function of "hegemony" which the dominant group exercises throughout society and on the other hand to that of "direct domination" or command exercised through the State and "juridical" government.' Although he subsequently downplays the extent of the distinctiveness between 'civil society' and the State, Gramsci (1971: 262–3) nevertheless infers that – as a result of the exercise of 'hegemony' by subaltern intellectuals – the State is in some sense absorbed by 'civil society'. Unsurprisingly, this reformist interpretation – whereby the bourgeois system is persuaded democratically by a gradual and non-antagonistic process of cultural incorporation (= 'hegemony') – is one that currently informs not Marxist but 'new' populist postmodern approaches to the State.

55 That Trotsky (1972: 45, original emphasis) associated the realization of 'citizenship' only with the process of permanent revolution – a transition to socialism, in other words – is evident from the following: 'The expression "*permanent revolution*" is an expression of Marx which he applied to the revolution of 1848. In Marxist, naturally not in revisionist but in revolutionary Marxist literature, this term has always had citizenship rights. Franz Mehring employed it for the revolution of 1905–1907. The permanent revolution, in an exact translation, is the continuous revolution, the uninterrupted revolution…[that] does not come to an end after this or that political conquest, after this or that social reform, but that continues to develop further and its only boundary is the socialist society.' Much the same is true of Rosa Luxemburg. In her 1899 critique of the reformism of Eduard Bernstein, she (Luxemburg, 1937: 50, emphasis added) makes the following comment: '…as it is used by [Eduard] Bernstein, the word "bourgeois" itself is not a class expression but a general social notion. Logical to the end he has exchanged, together with his science, politics, morals and mode of thinking, the historic language of the proletariat for that of the bourgeoisie. When he uses, *without distinction*, the term "citizen" in reference to the bourgeois as well as to the proletarian, intending, thereby, to refer to man in general, he identifies man in general with the bourgeois, and human society with bourgeois society.'

56 This is the description by T.H. Marshall (1950: 8) of the view about 'citizenship' held by the influential liberal economist Alfred Marshall (1842–1924). For the latter, therefore, 'the claim of all to enjoy these conditions [= culture] is a claim to be

planning and State intervention – bourgeois social theory advocated an ideologically and politically egalitarian programme of 'citizenship' whilst at the same time leaving an economically inegalitarian class structure intact.[57]

Part of the problem is historical, in that one sociologically influential formulation of 'citizenship'– by T.H. Marshall – was undertaken just after the 1939–45 war.[58] It was conceptualized during a period when pro-market economic theory appeared to be on the retreat in the face of State intervention, as embodied in nationalization, progressive taxation, central planning, and income redistribution.[59] At that conjuncture, therefore, the struggle to eradicate unfree working arrangements was regarded as already having been accomplished. Consequently, the ending of unfreedom in the previous century signalled the achievement of civil rights, the first and least problematic step on the gradual path to 'citizenship'.[60]

Once achieved, so this argument went, the resulting emancipation of a worker employed in the capitalist labour process was guaranteed by bourgeois democracy.[61] Henceforth free relations of production could

---

admitted to a share of the social heritage, which in turn means a claim to be accepted as full members of society, that is, as citizens.'

[57] At this conjuncture the central questions were (Marshall, 1950: 9): 'Is it still true that basic equality, when enriched in substance and embodied in the formal rights of citizenship, is consistent with the inequalities of social class?...Is it still true that the basic equality can be created and preserved without invading the freedom of the competitive market? Obviously it is not true.' Subsequently, however, he appears to contradict this when insisting (Marshall, 1963: 118, 120, 122) that 'citizenship' does not negates the continuation of capitalism and its class system. Addressing the market/ 'citizenship' link, therefore, Marshall (1963: 115) states: 'I said earlier that in the twentieth century citizenship and the capitalist class system have been at war...it is quite clear that the former has imposed modifications on the latter... But are these principles [defining 'citizenship'] quite foreign to the practice of the market today, or are they there already...I think it is clear that they are.'

[58] The formulation of 'citizenship' was undertaken by T. H. Marshall (1963: 67–127) in the course of the Marshall Lectures given at Cambridge during 1949.

[59] For the different components of the Welfare State in Britain at this conjuncture – legal aid, the national health service, comprehensive education, social insurance, council housing – regarded as having contributed to the egalitarian concept of 'citizenship' he is formulating, see Marshall (1963: 101–7). This was a period when Keynesian economic policies based on State intervention were applied in the UK, with the object of eradicating what Beveridge (1943; 1944; 1945) labelled the five giant evils (want, disease, ignorance, squalor and idleness) generated by mass unemployment during the 1930s. Significantly, even this reformist programme was attacked by champions of *laissez faire* theory, such as de Jouvenel (1947).

[60] See Marshall (1963: 88, 90).

[61] Because of his wholehearted endorsement of bourgeois democracy as the guarantor of 'citizenship', Marshall was just as strongly opposed to any notion of

not – and would not – be reversed. Because he confined the historical process of 'becoming citizens' to incremental legislation gifted 'from above', however, Marshall overlooked both the reason for and the extent to which such gains might be eroded.[62] Just as social rights linked to citizenship were obtained largely as a result of class struggle waged 'from below', so they can be rolled back in the course of class struggle waged subsequently 'from above'.[63]

This is precisely what happened from the 1980s onwards, as *laissez faire* policies replaced Keynesian demand management throughout the global capitalist system. It was a process characterized by taking back into private ownership property that had been nationalized by the State, withdrawing or diluting rights/concessions made earlier to the working class and its organizations, and outsourcing production to cheap labour areas of the so-called Third World. Reproducing, introducing or reintroducing into the capitalist labour process production relations that are unfree is no more than one aspect of this broader economic restructuring.

Any attempt to reconcile 'citizenship' with capitalism, therefore, necessarily fails to recognize this development as part of the *continuing* class struggle. As long as the bourgeoisie avoid expropriation, therefore, and the class structure accordingly stays intact, those who still retain ownership/control over economic resources retain also the weapons of the class struggle. Where profitability and/or competitiveness

---

revolutionary agency aimed at transcending capitalism. Hence the view (Marshall, 1963: 97) that 'vast changes could be brought about by the peaceful use of political power, without a violent and bloody revolution', coupled as it is with fear both about collective action by workers and by trade union empowerment (Marshall, 1963: 97, 116–7).

[62] Hence the observation (Marshall, 1963: 88): 'The impact of citizenship on such a system [= capitalism] was bound to be profoundly disturbing, and even destructive. The rights with which the general status of citizenship was invested were extracted from the hierarchical status system of social class, robbing it of its essential substance. The equality implicit in the concept of citizenship, even though limited in content, undermined the inequality of the class system..'

[63] This tendency to over-optimism where challenges to and a rolling back of 'citizenship' are concerned is evident from two issues. First, the view (Marshall, 1963: 93) that 'class monopoly in politics, unlike class monopoly in law, has definitely been overthrown', which overlooks middle class dominance of government and Parliament, and also the co-option of the working-class representatives elected to State office. And second, the assertion that those with wealth were no longer able to influence the outcome of elections (Marshall, 1963: 93). The difficulties envisaged were historical ones – bribery, corruption – and it is understandable that Marshall was at that conjuncture unable to anticipate the fact that elections are nowadays influenced by the ownership/control exercised by the wealthy over the electronic and print media.

require it, therefore, commercial producers in a 'fully functioning' accumulation process can and will resort to employment arrangements that are unfree. In these circumstances, labour regime change cannot but involve the reversal of gains which theory about 'citizenship' regards as immutable.

Citizenship as Cultural Empowerment?

In an important sense, the presence or absence of 'civil society' in a context where unfree labour exists, and the difficulties this raises for any positive interpretation of the former, is highlighted by the way in which it featured in the longstanding debate about plantation slavery in the Americas and the Caribbean.[64] In the case of the latter contexts, the notion of a local grassroots 'civil society' among the slave population has been invoked – ironically, by both left and right – either to indict or to play down the oppressiveness of the unfree labour regime.

Those on the political left and centre who wrote about plantation slavery from the mid-twentieth century onwards – such as Frank Tannenbaum, C.L.R. James, and Herbert Gutman – found themselves trapped in a 'culturalist' framework which was easily absorbed into the discourse of their opponents.[65] In order to attack the plantation labour

---

[64] In the case of the Caribbean, the equation of slave society with a form of local grassroots 'civil society' has a long history. Noting the importance for slave loyalty of small plots of land cultivated on the plantation system in the West Indies, the Bishop of London (Porteus, 1812: 196, original emphasis) went on to stress the significance of what is clearly a form of 'civil society' as this operated within slave society in 1784: 'But it is of still more importance to give them a *property* in their own families; to attach their wives and children to one and the same plantation, and not allow them to be torn asunder from each other, as they too often are, and disposed of into different and distant estates, and even different islands. By putting a stop to this cruel and unnatural kind of divorce, and allowing them to entertain the soothing idea of being inseparably united to the plantations, and to each other, their social affections will be strengthened and improved; they will have something to be careful and anxious about; and begin to taste the comforts and pleasure of domestic life; will feel themselves rising into importance, and becoming as it were members of the civil community in which they live.'

[65] For many on the political left and centre, the rescue of the plantation slave from what Thompson (1963: 12) famously called 'the enormous condescension of posterity' was effected principally by highlighting the resilience of slave culture and society. This took many forms. During the 1930s, for example, C.L.R. James (1938) showed how at the end of the eighteenth century and the start of the nineteenth Caribbean slaves led by Toussaint L'Ouverture defeated the armies of most powerful European nations. In the following decade Tannenbaum (1992) maintained with regard Latin America that, because of the benign influence of church and monarch in the colonizing nation, the rights of planters over their slaves were not absolute, leaving intact the space in which a slave culture might fruitfully develop. This theme was explored further

regime, therefore, the critique from the centre and political left emphasized the humanity of slaves, arguing that – like their masters – they, too, possessed all the characteristics associated historically with the existence of 'the private domain': a family life, kinship links, religious belief and practice cultural institutions, a moral code, and a strong sense of community. In short, the main critique of unfreedom took the form of the argument that slaves, no less than their owners, had what was akin to a local 'civil society' within the plantation system.

This in turn created a space for revisionist interpretations of unfree labour made by neo-classical economic historiography. The argument that a form of slave culture (= 'civil society') flourished despite the oppressiveness of the plantation labour regime was accordingly seized upon during the mid-1970s by cliometricians such as Fogel and Engerman.[66] These neoclassical economic historians argued that, because slave culture was not crushed, the plantation system itself could not have been as exploitative and tyrannical as usually depicted. In this redrawn picture, slaves are able to do pretty much as they liked, including establishing themselves as peasant farmers.[67] Indeed, this empowering capacity of slaves to reproduce themselves within such agrarian units not just as smallholders but also as a *de facto* 'civil society' underwrote the revisionist attempt by cliometricians generally to portray the

during the 1970s and 1980s, when the family life, music, religion and folklore of plantation slaves were the subject of analyses by Blassinghame (1972), Gutman (1976) and Stuckey (1987).

[66] In what amounted to a defence of plantation slavery, Fogel and Engerman (1974) maintained that the slave family did well not just in economic terms (income, food, clothing, medical care and housing), but also in social terms. The latter, in their view, meant that planters neither broke up the slave family through sale of its individual members nor used it as a breeding unit. In short, the *de facto* boundary around this form of 'civil society' within the plantation system was respected by its owner. This internal social space is contrasted by Fogel and Engerman to the power of the State, suggesting that they do indeed regard it as a form of 'civil society'. Hence the view (Fogel and Engerman 1974: 129) that for 'most slaves it was the law of the plantation, not of the state, that was relevant…Their daily lives were governed by plantation law. Consequently, the emphasis put on the sanctity of the slave family by many planters, and the legal status given to the slave family under plantation law, cannot be lightly dismissed.'

[67] This is the view advanced by another neoclassical economic historian (Schwartz, 1992), where it is argued that resistance by slaves in Brazil more or less undermined this relational form, which as consequence could not have been as horrific as depicted. In this redrawn picture, slaves are able to do pretty much as they liked including establishing themselves as peasant farmers. Much the same point is made with regard to the antebellum plantation by Fogel and Engerman (1974: 127): 'By permitting families to have de facto ownership of houses, furniture, clothing, garden plots, and small livestock, planters created an economic stake for slaves in the system.'

plantation system as a 'benign' institution, and its labour regime as being based not so much on coercion as on 'consent'.[68]

If neo-classical economic historiography has encountered theoretical problems where unfree labour is concerned, therefore, then the same issue has also generated difficulties for those who have been – and are now (wrongly) – perceived as belonging to the political left.[69] This applies with particular force to 'new' postmodern populists currently engaged in recasting indigenous grassroots institutions in a positive light, as prefiguring 'civil society' and thus harbingers of an 'authentic' process of 'redemocratization'.

To Civil Society via Redemocratization?

In the case of rural Third World contexts, therefore, the notion 'civil society' is said by them to extend to traditional institutions that have always been 'outside' capitalism and successfully resisted penetration by it.[70] Now, as in the past, these constitute 'authentic' grassroots organizations and/or arrangements that not only spearhead resistance to capitalism but also form the embryonic 'civil society' on which to build the process of 'redemocratization'.[71] The latter will be accomplished in Latin America and elsewhere by 'new' social movements composed, it is claimed, of an undifferentiated peasantry that is also ethnically homogenous.

The difficulty with this is that evidence from rural contexts in Latin America suggests that traditional indigenous institutions frequently mask what are in fact production relations between capital and labour. In the case of Peru during the mid-1970s, for example, exchange labour groups based on notionally reciprocal *mink'a* and *ayni* work arrangements involved capitalist rich peasants cultivating the profitable coffee

---

[68] According to Fogel (1989: 392), his own confidence in the view of slavery as oppressive was undermined by the research of cultural historians, who 'found more scope for…culture than convention dictated. Mistreatment was not excluded from the new histories of slave culture, but its role was considerably diminished'. Focussing on the empowering role of slave culture and downgrading the element of coercion cannot but generate a perception of the plantation as a labour regime based on 'consent', notwithstanding the fact that democracy – one of the constitutive elements of 'civil society' – was rather obviously missing from this agrarian system.

[69] Emancipation from unfree working arrangements has always been central to liberal bourgeois concepts of 'civil society' and 'citizenship'. Hence the observation by Marshall (1950: 18) that: 'In the towns [of seventeenth century England] the terms "freedom" and "citizenship" were interchangeable. When freedom became universal, freedom grew from a local to a national institution.'

[70] For an example of this view, see Elena Garcia (2005).

[71] See, for example, the text by Knight, Chigudu and Tandon (2002).

crop for export markets. What they swapped with one another in these 'traditional' institutional forms was not their own personal labour-power but that of their kin, neighbouring poor peasants, or seasonal migrants, all of whom were their unfree workers.[72] Yet it is these same kinds of 'traditional' institutional forms that indigenous movements such as CONAIE in Ecuador are struggling to preserve.[73] Very clearly, a contradiction exists between liberal bourgeois notions of 'civil society' and the wish on the part of those at the rural grassroots to retain such 'traditional' institutional forms.

Current exponents of 'redemocratization' fail to spell out what – if anything – this would solve, other than provide a symbolic element of political accountability. At the centre of the discourse advocating a process of 'redemocratization' as a solution to the political and economic problems generated by capitalism is an inescapable contradiction: the attempt to combine *laissez faire* with a social programme the moral basis of which the market does not (and cannot) recognize. What the call for 'redemocratization' overlooks, therefore, is the systemic logic of capitalism: the latter cannot but extend the market at the expense of the State. Neoliberalism and globalization are in a very real sense the outcome of the accumulation process, and not the 'anomalies' that many advocates of 'redemocratization' maintain.

That politically non-specific notions such as 'civil society', human rights and 'redemocratization' disempower workers is evident from the acceptability to capitalists and their political representatives of its main institutional form – the NGO – and the reason for this. To begin with, agribusiness enterprises involved food production see the endorsement by NGOs campaigning for ethical trade or labour practices as good publicity, a form of approval that enables them to compete with rival corporations lacking this.[74] Because of this, many agribusiness and other enterprises actively seek to obtain such recognition, only to

---

[72] Details about this are outlined in Brass (1999: Chapter 2).

[73] Hence the observation by an indigenous leader (Lucas, 2000: 105) that '[f]or the indigenous world, power, *ushay*, means perfecting living conditions, it is a collective concept. It is the capacity to develop collectively, with each making his or her own distinct contribution, as happens in the *minga*, in which children, women and old people have a role.' In keeping with this view, the ethnic consciousness that has emerged among Aymara and Quechua peasants in Peru and Bolivia over the latter part of the twentieth century is categorized endorsingly by Rivera-Cusicanqui (1994) as a specifically postmodern development, one that she also equates with the realization of an authentic form of 'citizenship'/'civil society' at the Andean rural grassroots.

[74] One learns without surprise, therefore, that a supermarket chain in England the vegetables for which are picked and packed by migrant workers exploited by a

break the conditions subsequently.[75] For their part, corporations favour NGO 'solutions' precisely because these are non-threatening and also in an important sense validating, in that these give the impression of a solution being achieved. Accordingly, NGOs provide the agency prefigured by the 'new' populist postmodernism, the most common form of which is grassroots 'resistance' aimed at 'redemocratization'.

In this connection it is important to note the presence of an obvious danger, and the political responses to this by two seemingly distinct variants of 'redemocratization', the first of which concerns socialists. If those on the left do not link unfree labour to capitalism and its form of class struggle, and – like exponents of the semi-feudal thesis – continue to regard such relations as systemic anomalies that capital will dispense with, then into this policy vacuum will step those on the political right. The latter have, historically, *ethnicized* discourse opposing foreign migrant workers on the grounds of 'cultural otherness'. Currently, however, the views of, for example, the British National Party emphasize much rather the *economic* role of foreign migrants as competitors with locals in the same labour market.[76] Socialists ignore this ideological development at their peril.[77]

---

gangmaster who recruited/controlled them is one that has signed up to the Ethical Trading Initiative. According to this report, 'the [Bulgarian] workers said they had lived "like pigs on scraps", scavenging vegetables from fields when their Latvian gangmaster withheld their pay for 34 days, and each had to pay £50 a week to be housed in overcrowded caravans.' See 'Scraps to eat and £3 a day: misery at the bottom end of the supermarket supply chain', *The Guardian* (London), 15 August 2007.

[75] One press report outlined how Peruvian workers picking coffee marketed under the Fairtrade label, and sold at a corresponding higher price to 'ethically concerned consumers', were being paid less than the minimum wage. See '"Ethical-coffee" workers paid below legal minimum', and 'Bitter cost of "fair trade" coffee', *Financial Times* (London), 9 September 2006. Another notes that 'while supermarkets are launching new schemes to prove their ethical credentials to UK shoppers, they are locking suppliers – particularly women – into "appallingly" low pay and dangerous conditions abroad.' See '6p a T-shirt. 30p an hour for shelling cashews. Supermarkets accused of exploiting women', *The Guardian* (London), 23 April, 2007. Yet another investigation reveals the employment of child labour by a multinational corporation committed publicly to 'ethical and socially responsible manufacturing' practices. See 'Child sweatshop shame threatens Gap's ethical image', *The Observer* (London), 28 October, 2007. And so it goes on.

[76] This discursive shift does not, of course, mean that the political right has abandoned racism. There is still a racist sub-text but – and this cannot be emphasized too strongly – it is now one that plays on specifically *economic* fears concerning loss of jobs to foreign migrant workers who are cheaper to employ.

[77] Even where a workforce is unionized, therefore, a defensive response to the introduction by capital of cheap unfree migrant labour can take a politically reactionary

The second political response is that currently taken by advocates of 'redemocratization' who subscribe to a human rights discourse based on ethical/moral arguments. In the case of Britain, a variant of this position maintains that adherence to the free/unfree distinction should be discarded, since it serves to divide migrants from one another and also from non-migrants, thus hindering them from making common cause.[78] What this overlooks, however, is that no attempt to unite migrants who are unfree with workers who are free is going to succeed as long as the main obstacle to such unity remains in place. Namely, the ability of an employer and/or contractor using the debt mechanism to control migrants and – by paying them less and stopping them from doing anything about this – to undercut wages received by local workers (who are free).[79]

There is no – and cannot be a – kind of capitalism that remains 'benign' in the steady-state 'caring' fashion desired. To bring about the kind of society exponents of 'redemocratization' appear to want, it is necessary not merely to address the issue of property relations but also to accept the fact that these have to be transformed. In the absence of a political willingness to do this, any talk of 'redemocratization' is meaningless, and any attempt to put it into effect is pointless. Sooner or later, therefore, capital will break the fetters imposed on its accumulation project by State regulation and then proceed to strip away any legislation that protects the workforce.

Conclusion

The continuing global spread of capitalism, and the consequent international extension of the market, has led unsurprisingly to the intensification of class struggle. This in turn has generated changes in

---

turn. This, for example was how the seeds of fascism were sown in Austria at the end of the nineteenth century, when German workers attempted to protect themselves from economic competition in the labour market by Czech migrants (Whiteside, 1962).

[78] An example of this view is Davidson (2010), whose suggested alternative to the free/unfree distinction in effect privileges migrant identity. Not only is this a thinly disguised variation of the privileging by postmodernism of ethnic/national identity at the expense of class, but – more worryingly – it is a view that unwittingly plays into the hands of the political right (migrant as foreign 'other').

[79] Preventing indebted migrants from being able to sell their labour-power elsewhere, to negotiate about pay levels, or to join ranks with locals they have been recruited to undercut, are all effects of this kind of control exercised by contractor or employer.

discourse supportive of and opposed to unfree labour. Not only has the economic role of unfree labour and the kind of subject it affects been transformed, therefore, but so too has the efficacy of the object and form taken by political opposition to such production relations. The implications of all this for current debate about the link between unfreedom, capitalist development and systemic transition, are obvious.

Based as it is on an ethical/moral discourse ('human rights', 'citizenship', 'civil society', 'redemocratization'), opposition to unfree labour by NGOs and the ILO corresponds to the reformist route to abolition, one that leaves unchallenged either the capitalist system or its State. What such an approach overlooks, however, is that the capitalist state has shifted its position regarding the economic role of unfree labour; from being seen as an obstacle to productivity and accumulation, this relation is perceived as making a contribution to the profitability of such processes. Because neither the capitalist state nor commercial enterprises are for this reason interested any longer in eradicating unfree labour, opposition based simply on a moral/ethical discourse is destined to fail.

Not only is moral/ethical opposition to unfree labour the form taken by current objections on the part of NGOs, but – because of this economic shift – it is the reason why abolition of this production relation (other than in a purely legislative form) will not be achieved as long as the global economy remains a capitalist one. As the case with all single issue movements and organizations, therefore, the NGO is destined to fail for two reasons in particular.

First, and rather obviously, small lobbying institutions whose sole authority is moral ('this ought not to happen', etc.) lack power. And second, a smallscale organization or movement the focus of which is on a single issue fails to address processes/structures beyond its particular remit, despite the fact that these contribute substantially to the existence and reproduction of the latter. Thus, for example, NGOs opposed to the issue of poverty cannot do much about this beyond recommending more aid, not least because refuse to accept that the issue is incapable of eradication without systemic change.

By contrast, linking the issue of unfree labour to class struggle ties its reproduction not only to an economic cause (= capitalism as a *system*) but also to the political complicity of the state apparatus with that dynamic (fostering conditions favourable to accumulation). In short, the approach outlined here takes the problem of unfree labour out of the realm of human rights (= a moral disgruntlement that capitalism ought really to be much 'nicer' than it is) and reinserts it in a framework that is Marxist, which is where it more properly belongs.

In many so-called Third World countries the role of unfree labour is currently no different from the one it has discharged in the UK, Germany and the United States, where a capitalist transition had not only long since been achieved, but accumulation was itself a well-established process. In all these contexts, deproletarianization was effected in economies that had transcended what in historical terms might be categorized as 'primitive accumulation'. Commercial enterprises deployed unfree labour so as to pre-empt the formation/consolidation of a consciousness of class, by undermining free workers whose livelihood stemmed from the sale of labour-power, not the product of labour.

However, as represented historically in the discourse of bourgeois nationalists, colonial authorities and pro-Moscow elements, and currently in the discourse of the ILO and NGOs, these subjects are either actually or potentially a viable smallholding peasantry. According to this view, the emancipation of the debt bonded subject would result in him/her reverting to or being reconstituted as an independent proprietor. That is to say, the outcome of emancipation was a peasant who was no longer debt bonded.

Despite performing a useful advocacy role by highlighting the presence and continuing importance of the free/unfree distinction, the ILO and NGOs remain hamstrung by a moral/ethical discourse that fails to address all these shifts. In keeping with an historical and continuing privileging of indigenous 'otherness', this non-Marxist approach to unfreedom envisages the outcome of emancipation as being a reconstituted peasantry in the context of a more benign capitalism.

In keeping with the theory of Adam Smith, Hegel and Marx considered in previous chapters, unfreedom is regarded here as part of specific ontological progression. Labour is identified first as the source of value, then as labour-power which is the property of its subject, and finally as a commodity which its owner is able to sell on a time-specific basis to a capitalist producer. Such an interpretation permits the loss of this capacity to be conceptualized as deproletarianization. The latter also recognizes that the object of unfreedom in a 'fully functioning' capitalism is no longer to affix a smallholder to land or simply to separate the latter from his/her means of production, but rather to deprive the subject of owning/controlling his/her own labour-power.

For this reason, the outcome of emancipation is different: the subject is reconstituted not as a peasant in a benign capitalism but rather as a worker engaged in struggle to transcend this. Of the two main approaches seeking to eradicate unfree labour, therefore, the moral/ethical advocates an intra-systemic one while Marxism links abolition to systemic transcendence. Emancipation from unfreedom premissed on the identity of the subject as a worker points to a socialist transition, whereas any eradication of unfreedom based on peasant identity still puts a 'fully-functioning' capitalism on the political agenda.

CONCLUSION

Labour-power is neither always and everywhere free, nor is it always and everywhere unfree. What has to be understood is that historically there is a dynamic interaction between labour-power that is free and forms which are unfree, a dialectic informed by class struggle. Hence the latter process cannot but structure the prevalence in the trend of each form, the kind of social relation dominant at a given conjuncture being determined by the respective power – economic, political and ideological – exercised by those who either own or are separated from the means of production.

In non-Marxist political economy which eschews class struggle – that of Smith, Malthus, Mill, Bright and Weber – the idea that unfree labour might be acceptable to capitalists was dismissed on the grounds that such workers would necessarily be inefficient, unskilled, costly, and scarce. Because it was an obstacle both to market formation and expansion, and to the installation of advanced productive forces, these non-Marxists argued, unfree labour-power was incompatible with a dynamic process of accumulation within particular national contexts. This interpretation currently informs the theoretical approach not just of neo-classical political economy but also the semi-feudal thesis, notwithstanding the fact that in the present global capitalist system none of these objections continue to hold.

Those who insist that free labour is the *sine qua non* of a 'fully functioning' capitalism, and invoke Marx in support of this position, are confounded by the fact that Marx's views about the historical centrality of class struggle to the shaping of the accumulation process lead to the opposite conclusion. The same is true of many of the major Marxists – among them not just Engels, Kautsky, Lenin and Trotsky but also Hilferding, Mandel, Dobb, Kuczynski and Guérin – all of whom accepted that unfree production relations are indeed compatible with a 'fully functioning' capitalist system.

Labour-power is unfree not because capitalism is at its beginning – that is to say, where accumulation is in its early or 'primitive' stage – but much rather because it is mature, is accordingly an interpretation consistent with Marxist theory. Where accumulation has a global reach, as it does currently, it could be argued capital now has the confidence and the power to dispense with the compromise with labour it has had to make in the past. Put bluntly, because they can draw upon what is now a global industrial reserve army of labour, employers no longer have to accommodate the wishes and interests of their workers.

Attempts to confine unfree production relations to the 'pre-history' of capitalism, either by denying the acceptability to the latter of anything other than free workers, or by labelling such relations as evidence for 'primitive accumulation', are signalled by phrases such as 'slavery and the rise of capitalism' and 'slavery: capitalism's savage birth'. Similarly, those who concede the presence of bonded labour in the midst of capitalism, and consequently accept that violence/coercion is part of the current labour regime, nevertheless equate these production relations with proletarianization. In one way or another, therefore, exponents of each variant of modern Marxism – semi-feudalism, 'disguised' wage labour, 'empire' and the 'new' imperialism – decouple unfree labour and capitalism.

Dehistoricizing primitive accumulation, both the 'empire' and the 'new' imperialism framework seek to relocate its predatory and violent aspects in the present, but insist on labelling the workforce as free. Against this, it is argued that unfree social relations of production generally confined to the pre-history of capitalism are in fact present also in a 'fully functioning' capitalism. Unlike either Negri (= Empire) or Harvey (= accumulation by dispossession), therefore, who regard primitive accumulation itself as a contemporary phenomenon, the case made here is that it is unfree labour – not primitive accumulation *per se* – that is a contemporary phenomenon.

Since it regards capitalism as an eternal systemic form, the 'disguised' wage labour variant of Marxism recognizes neither unfree labour nor primitive accumulation. By abolishing the free/unfree distinction, and maintaining instead that all rural workers – in late antiquity no less than in present-day capitalism – are simply hired labourers who are contractually free, this view breaks with Marxism and is indistinguishable from neo-classical economic historiography. Locating capitalism in ancient society also reproduces the claim made by cliometricians that capital and labour are ever-present, historically non-specific and thus 'natural' economic categories that cannot be transcended.

Claims about the acceptability to capitalist producers of bonded labour – an unfree production relation that is prevalent in the agrarian sector of many countries, not just those in the so-called Third World – are grounded in Marxist theory, an insistence to the contrary notwithstanding. This concerns in particular Marxist views about the interrelationship between the separation of the direct producer from his/her means of labour, the reproduction of the industrial reserve army, the process of workforce restructuring, and – most importantly – the conflict between labour and capital.

Marxist theory about the connection between on the one hand capitalism and class struggle, and on the other the process of deproletarianization and the consequent acceptability to employers of unfree production relations, can be traced back to an epistemological metamorphosis of labour-as-value and labour-as-property into labour-power-as-commodity. In the political economy of Adam Smith, therefore, the link is made between labour and value. Hegel took this a step further, and maintained that a concept of freedom required that labour-power be seen as owned by its subject, otherwise there was no way of differentiating a bondsman from an individual who was free.

Combining both these positions in an important synthesis, Marx took the next step and argued that since labour-power is both a source of value and the property of its subject, the latter is in a capitalist system free to sell it to (or, indeed, withhold it from) any given employer. In cases where a worker is prevented from exercising this freedom personally to commodify or recommodify his/her own labour-power, the production relation cannot be regarded as free. Marx added to the significance of this free/unfree dichotomy by locating it a dynamic context: class struggle generated by capitalism.

It is precisely this ownership, exercised by workers over their labour-power, that an employer has to deprive them of so as to exert in turn full control over a modern production process. Deproletarianization captures this fact, by underlining the extent to which it is necessary for capital to close off even this limited economic autonomy. It recognizes conceptually that what has happened to workers is that, finally, they have become what Marx said they would: men and women of no property. Capital has in short taken from them their sole remaining property, the ownership by workers of their own labour-power. It signals the completeness both of the subordination of the worker to the employer, and thus also of the *class* inequality between capital and labour.

Although Marx shared with Hegel a common perception of history as a process of 'becoming' consistent with the attainment of freedom, they saw this in terms of different agents, objectives and means. Thus agency of the subject-in-general in Hegel's analysis became in Marxist theory that by subjects-of-a-particular-class. Whereas Hegelian teleology culminated in a metaphysical outcome (= the attainment of the Absolute Idea), Marxism envisaged a materialist one: class formation and class struggle leading towards socialism. The free/unfree dichotomy plays a crucial role in this trajectory.

Allocating a central role in this process of 'becoming' to the achievement by workers of a consciousness of class, Marx nevertheless accepted that its realization – and thus progress towards socialism – faced serious political obstacles. Among them was the capacity of employers to use unfree production relations, either by imposing them on free workers or by replacing the latter with bonded labour. The replacement of free wage labour with unfree workers in the advanced capitalist economies of Germany, the United States and Britain was designed both to lower wage costs by restructuring the capitalist labour process and simultaneously to weaken trade union organization and break down working class consciousness/solidarity. One result of the latter process is ideological individualization imposed on workers by employers, a political strategy adopted by capital in its struggle with labour.

Only in the undialectical framework used both by neoclassical economists and by exponents of the semi-feudal thesis is there a failure to recognize such a dynamic. Thus adherents of the semi-feudal thesis share with neoclassical economists a touching faith in the emergence and continued reproduction of a benign (= 'kind', 'caring') form of capitalism, one that will voluntarily do away with oppressive and exploitative relations such as unfree labour. Only then will there be a 'fully functioning' accumulation process, under the benevolent eye of selfless capitalists who are gentle, sweet and good. Not only was this never going to happen, but the developments in the world economy from the 1980s onwards, when capitalism went global and competition and class struggle became correspondingly more acute and international in scope, have effectively rebutted this conservative interpretation.

An indicator of the theoretical contradiction generated by this seemingly incompatible process – capitalist development on the basis of unfree production relations – is the argument made by neoclassical economists defending the employment of unfree labour by agribusiness enterprises. Gangmasters and unfree migrants, we are told, are necessary because they supply a need by filling jobs no indigenous worker wants to do. What is not said by these neoclassical economists are two things.

First, that such a defence in effect negates one of the central tenets advanced by *laissez faire* theory: namely, that where workers are scarce and/or not available in the desired quantities, wages should rise until this need is met, thereby establishing the equilibrium structuring the marginalist analytical framework. As Marxists have long argued, the operation of the market depends ultimately on the intervention of the state – the very institution and the very activity (= intervention) which neoliberalism wishes to ban from the economic sphere – both to regulate the supply of labour and to strip away legislative protections secured by workers in the course of the class struggle.

And second, implicit in this defence is the view that the role of the migrant 'other' is to fill undesirable jobs, working long hours under bad conditions for less pay than their local counterparts. Not only is the assumption that there is nothing wrong with such employment remaining undesirable and ill-paid, therefore, but this argument is akin to that advanced during the nineteenth century by opponents of abolition. Namely, that plantation work was fit only for black slaves, a role in keeping with (and justified by) their subordinate position as unfree labour.

Where the acceptability of unfree labour to capitalism is finally conceded, the argument frequently takes the form of maintaining that this kind of link is an historical once-off, and as such amounts to no more than the coercion/violence signalling primitive accumulation, understood as the 'pre-history' of capitalism proper. The inference is that once the latter establishes itself, commercial employers will replace unfree relations with free equivalents. This view was until recently advanced by the semi-feudal thesis, enabling its adherents to switch tack and argue currently that the presence of unfree production relations within a capitalist context are no more than evidence for a continuing pre-capitalist stage of 'primitive accumulation'.

Relations of production sought out by capital historically show this inference to be doubly mistaken. Not only were unfree workers perfectly acceptable to commercial enterprises, therefore, but landlords and agribusiness enterprises continued to prefer such forms of employment long after a stage corresponding to the 'pre-history' of capital had passed. In the case Germany, the United States, and Britain, unfree production relations (peonage, debt bondage, convict leasing, gangmasters) not merely endured well beyond abolition (of serfdom, slavery) but consolidated as a 'fully functioning' capitalist agriculture developed.

As instances of capitalist restructuring involving outsourcing/downsizing confirm, these unfree production relations surfaced where migrants displaced locals, permanent workers were replaced by casual/seasonal/temporary ones, and the relocation of jobs overseas. In other words, the multiple shift in employment patterns – from permanent to casual, local to migrant, and to other locations – in a number of instances corresponded also to a shift from a workforce that was free to one that was unfree. All these shifts have in common the search by capitalist producers for cheaper sources of labour-power.

Far from being systemically peripheral, economically marginal or indicative of primitive accumulation, therefore, unfree workers are central to a pattern of labour regime change that characterizes a 'fully functional' twenty-first century capitalism. It has become increasingly evident that epistemologically this is a break with non-Marxist analyses which questioned the utility of unfree labour to capitalist producers on grounds of cost and efficiency.

The same narrow focus on questions of economic efficiency and the transitory nature of what were (wrongly) deemed to be non-capitalist social relations of production informed the concern of the semi-feudal thesis – influential in theoretical frameworks brought to bear on the study of agrarian transformation in Asia and Latin America – with obstacles to the development of a capitalist agriculture. It became increasingly evident that such a teleology was misplaced, and that institutional forms hitherto characterized as incompatible with profitability, advanced technology and accumulation were in many instances the social relations of choice where agrarian capital was concerned.

A difference in interpretation about the capitalism/unfreedom link has implications for debates surrounding both the desirability and the nature of systemic transformation. Not the least important aspect in this regard is the changed perception by the capitalist state of the economic role of unfree labour: from being seen negatively as an obstacle to economic growth, and thus institutional forms that had to be eliminated, to being viewed positively as a contribution to the accumulation process. This *volte face* in turn undermines moral/ethical discourse which maintains that the post-emancipation identity of the subject is that of a smallholding peasant.

Where primitive accumulation is concerned, therefore, the object of debt is to force peasants off the land. In a 'fully functioning' capitalism, by contrast, the object of debt is to acquire control over the labour-power of a worker, a process that results in a production relation that is not free but unfree. Not only has the economic role of unfree labour and the kind of subject it affects been transformed, therefore, but so too has the efficacy of the object and form taken by political opposition to such production relations.

Most crucially, the capitalist state has shifted its position regarding the economic role of unfree labour. From being seen as an obstacle to productivity and accumulation, this relation is perceived as making a contribution to the profitability of such processes. This shift has wrong footed all those whose opposition to unfree labour is informed by an ethical/moral discourse about 'human rights', 'citizenship', 'civil society', and 'redemocratization'. Among them are NGOs and the ILO which advocate a reformist route to abolition, one that leaves unchallenged either the capitalist system or its State. In their discourse, subjects of unfree relations are either actually or potentially a viable smallholding peasantry. For the ILO and NGOs, therefore, the outcome of emancipation was – and remains – a peasant who was/is no longer debt bonded.

Marxist theory, unlike adherents of an ethical/moral discourse, links the issue of unfree labour to class struggle waged by capital. For this reason, Marxism ties the reproduction of such relations not only to an economic cause (= capitalism as a *system*) but also to the political complicity of the state apparatus with that dynamic (fostering conditions favourable to accumulation). It is an approach that takes the problem of unfree labour out of an ethical/moral realm about human rights and reinserts it in a class struggle framework.

Because of this, the outcome of emancipation is different: the subject is reconstituted not as a peasant in a benign capitalism but rather as a worker engaged in struggle to transcend this. Of the two main approaches seeking to eradicate unfree labour, therefore, the moral/ethical advocates an intra-systemic one while Marxism links abolition to systemic transcendence. Emancipation from unfreedom premissed on the identity of the subject as a worker points to a socialist transition, whereas any eradication of unfreedom based on peasant identity still puts a 'fully-functioning' capitalism on the political agenda.

This is borne out by the current and recent object of unfreedom in Britain, the United States and Germany. Unconnected with smallholding per se, unfreedom is and has been neither repeasantization nor depeasantization, but deproletarianization. The object of unfreedom in these contexts was not to keep peasants on the land (= repeasantization), or to eject them from this (= depeasantization), but rather to prevent workers – not peasants – from personally commodifying or recommodifying their labour-power, by selling it to the highest bidder. This explains why convict labour has been a feature of capitalist development in Germany and the United States, most notoriously in the form of concentration camp in Germany and the leasing of prisoners in the United States.

Many of those on the left, who subscribed to a unilinear epistemology, thought that – once implemented – a socialist programme was irreversible. Because it ignores the fact and the impact of class struggle, however, such a view is mistaken, in that it counts without the capacity of those whose property has been expropriated to continue to campaign for its return (= class struggle 'from above'). Hence the current attempts on the part of families whose holdings were confiscated by revolutionary governments (for example, Russia in 1917) to secure either a return of the same, or compensation payments from the state following the end of actually existing socialism in 1989.

For this reason, class struggle waged 'from above' does not end with expropriation; it merely continues in a different form (legal agitation for restitution or compensation). Unless an equivalent form of class struggle is also waged 'from below', ceaselessly defending gains made – however modest, and however limited in scope – in the course of implementing a socialist programme, the latter will therefore be overturned in what is an unending process of socio-economic conflict. This applies as much to property rights exercised by workers over their sole commodity, labour-power, as it does to property rights enjoyed by owners of means of production (land and other resources).

Analysing a twenty-first century capitalism though the lens of class struggle therefore undermines the hitherto prevalent approach to ways of conceptualizing the labour regime. Today unfree workers are more profitable to employ but no less efficient than their counterparts who are free. Moreover, deskilling combined with a reserve army that is global in scope makes it possible for capitalist producers to use many different kinds of worker, many of whom are unfree. Instead of the linearity which structures the semi-feudal thesis, whereby capitalist producers automatically replace unfree labour with free equivalents, the concept of deproletarianization includes the possibility of historical reversals, understood not in a chronological but rather in an emancipatory sense.

Because it is informed by the dynamic of class struggle, deproletarianization accepts that such a process (conflict) is waged 'from above' as well as 'from below'. Consequently, just as unfree relations can be – and have been – eliminated by 'from below' class agency, so they can be – and on occasion are – reinstated or introduced by 'from above' class agency. This is the dynamic that is missing from those who interpret history as an unproblematic and irreversible progression from unfree labour that is unpaid and employed on a permanent basis to free labour in receipt of a wage and hired on a daily, seasonal or casual basis.

Unlike the semi-feudal thesis and neoclassical economics, most Marxist theory accepts that gains made in the course of class struggle can just as easily be reversed, the 'from below' relational emancipation (plus the advantages this confers) unravelling as a consequence of class struggle waged 'from above'. This is especially true of the way global capitalist regimes have been transformed over the past quarter of a century, a period dominated by *laissez faire* development policies. In such circumstances, economic and ideological benefits secured by workers and poor peasants in the course of conflict with employers and the capitalist state can be – and have been – watered down or cancelled by the reintroduction of unfreedom.

In short, proletarianization can be – and on occasion has been – displaced by its 'other', deproletarianization. An inability to recognize this, however, has led to frequent claims about the requirement or non-completion of a capitalist transition, which have as a result tended to conflate systemic change (which has been effected) with relational transformation (which is not always necessary). There is – or ought to be – no mystery about this apparent contradiction (the employment of unfree workers in a 'fully functioning' accumulation process), not least given current opposition by capital everywhere to a reduction in labour market 'flexibility', to improving legislative protection, pay and conditions.

All the latter are characterized by employers as unwarranted attempts to undermine competitiveness. Capital is able to sustain this opposition to improvements in the pay/conditions of its workforce by drawing on a seemingly inexhaustible supply of labour-power. Following the Green Revolution, and particularly in the era of neoliberal policies, the industrial reserve army of labour has expanded to the degree that that imposing (or re-imposing) unfreedom is an economic option now available to and used by commercial producers.

To return to the question posed in the introduction, about whether or not the distinction between free and unfree labour-power matters any longer. A focus on unfree production relations does not deflect attention from capitalist exploitation of workers that are free, much rather the opposite. Criticism of bonded labour leading to its elimination would in effect knock away the bottom rungs of the ladder that is a significant part of a twenty-first century labour regime.

This it would do by making costlier to employ the reserve army of labour on which agrarian capitalist profitability and competitiveness depends, as unfree workers were converted (or reconverted) into free equivalents. Once this relational and price differential was eliminated, it would be easier for workers of different ethnic/regional/national identities to unite, organize and fight *as a proletariat* in the Marxist sense of the term. As is well established historically, this is the kind of outcome which capital everywhere has always feared.

BIBLIOGRAPHY

Abdel-Fadil, Mahmoud, 1975, *Development, Income Distribution and Social Change in Rural Egypt (1952–1970): A Study in the Political Economy of Agrarian Transition*, London: Cambridge University Press.

Ainslie, Rosalynde, 1977, *Masters and Serfs: Farm Labour in South Africa*, London: IDAF.

Ajay, 2008, 'Post-Green Revolution Production Relations in the Agrarian Society of Haryana', paper presented at the Conference on *The Character and Trajectory of the Indian Economic Formation in an Era of Globalization*, held in New Delhi during 26–28 November.

Althusser, Louis, 1971, *Lenin and Philosophy and Other Essays*, London: New Left Books.

Althusser, Louis, and Etienne Balibar, 1970, *Reading Capital*, London: New Left Books.

Aly, Götz, and Susanne Heim, 2002, *Architects of Annihilation: Auschwitz and the Logic of Destruction*, London: Weidenfeld & Nicolson.

Amin, Samir, 1974, *Accumulation on a World Scale: A Critique of the Theory of Underdevelopment* (Vols. 1 and 2), London and New York: Monthly Review Press.

Andrade, Regis de Castro, 1982, 'Brazil: The Economics of Savage Capitalism', in Manfred Bienefeld and Martin Godfrey (eds.), *The Struggle for Development: National Strategies in an International Context*, Chichester and New York: John Wiley & Sons Limited.

Andreano, Ralph L., 1970, *The New Economic History*, New York: John Wiley & Sons, Inc.

Anheier, Helmut K., 2004, *Civil Society: Measurement, Evaluation, Policy*, London: Earthscan.

Anonymous [Sir Arthur Helps], 1851, *Friends in Council: A Series of Readings and Discourse Thereon* (Volume II), London: William Pickering.

Anonymous, 1833, *John Hopkins's Notions on Political Economy*, Boston: Allen and Tickenor.

Anonymous, 1834, *British Husbandry; Exhibiting the Farming Practice in Various Parts of the United Kingdom*, Vol. I, London: Baldwin and Cradock.

Anonymous, 1840, *Husbandry; Reports of Select Farms*, Vol. III, London: Baldwin and Cradock.

Anonymous, 1899, 'Slavery in Modern Scotland', *The Edinburgh Review*, Vol. CLXXXIX.

Anti-Slavery and Aborigines Protection Society, 1913, *Portuguese Slavery: Debate in the House of Lords, Wednesday, 23rd July, 1913*, London: Anti-Slavery and Aborigines Protection Society.

Arlacchi, Pino, 1986, *Mafia Business: The Mafia Ethic and the Spirit of Capitalism*, London: Verso.

Armstrong, Alan, 1988, *Farmworkers: A Social and Economic History, 1770–1980*, London: B.T. Batsford, Ltd.

Ashton, T.S., 1954, 'The Treatment of Capitalism by Historians', in F.A. Hayek (ed.) [1954].

Assies, Willem, 2003, 'From Rubber Estate to Simple Commodity Production: Agrarian Struggles in the Northern Bolivian Amazon', in Tom Brass (ed.), *Latin American Peasants*, London and Portland, OR: Frank Cass Publishers.

Austin, M.M., and P. Vidal-Naquet, 1977, *Economic and Social History of Ancient Greece*, London: B.T. Batsford, Ltd.

Awad, Mohamed, 1966, *Report on Slavery*, New York: United Nations.

Baer, Werner, and Isaac Kerstenetzky (eds.), 1964, *Inflation and Growth in Latin America*, Homewood, IL: Richard D. Irwin, Inc.

Bagehot, Walter, 1911 [1883], *Economic Studies*, London: Longman's Green and Co.

Balogh, Thomas, 1963, *Unequal Partners - Volume Two*, Oxford: Basil Blackwell.

Balogh, Thomas, 1966, *The Economics of Poverty*, London: Weidenfeld & Nicolson.

Banaji, Jairus, 1970a, 'Hierarchy and Power: Reflections of a Blind Materialist', *Journal of the Anthropological Society of Oxford*, Vol. I, No. 1.

Banaji, Jairus, 1970b, 'The Crisis of British Social Anthropology', *New Left Review*, No. 64.

Banaji, Jairus, 1972, 'For a Theory of Colonial Modes of Production', *Economic and Political Weekly*, Vol. 7, No. 52.

Banaji, Jairus, 1973, 'Backward Capitalism, Primitive Accumulation and Modes of Production', *Journal of Contemporary Asia*, Vol. 3, No. 4.

Banaji, Jairus, 1977, 'Modes of Production in a Materialist Conception of History', *Capital & Class*, No. 3.

Banaji, Jairus, 1978, 'Capitalist Domination and the Small Peasantry: Deccan Districts in the Late Nineteenth Century', in Ashok Rudra et al. [1978].

Banaji, Jairus, 1980a, 'Gunder Frank in Retreat?', *The Journal of Peasant Studies*, Vol. 7, No. 4.

Banaji, Jairus, 1980a, 'The Comintern and Indian Nationalism', in K.N. Panikkar (ed.), *National and Left Movements in India*, New Delhi: Vikas Publishing House.

Banaji, Jairus, 1999, 'Agrarian History and the Labour Organization of Byzantine Large Estates', in Alan K. Bowman and Eugene Rogan (eds.), *Agriculture in Egypt: From Pharaonic to Modern Times*, Oxford: Oxford University Press.

Banaji, Jairus, 2001, *Agrarian Change in Late Antiquity: Gold, Labour, and Aristocratic Dominance*, Oxford: Oxford University Press.

Banaji, Jairus, 2003a, 'The Fictions of Free Labour, Contract, Coercion, and So-Called Unfree Labour', *Historical Materialism*, Vol. 11, No. 3.

Banaji, Jairus, 2003b, 'Islam, the Mediterranean and the Rise of Capitalism', paper presented at the Conference on *Theory as History: Ernest Mandel's Historical Analysis of World Capitalism*, held in Amsterdam during 10–11 November.

Baranowski, Shelley, 1995, *The Sanctity of Rural Life: Nobility, Protestantism and Nazism in Weimar Prussia*, New York: Oxford University Press.

Bardhan, Pranab, 1984, *Land, Labour and Rural Poverty*, Delhi: Oxford University Press.

Barraclough, Solon (ed.), 1973, *Agrarian Structure in Latin America*, Lexington, MA: D.C. Heath and Co.

Bateson, F.W. (ed.), 1946, *Towards a Socialist Agriculture*, London: Victor Gollancz Ltd.

Bauder, Harald, 2008, 'Foreign Farm Workers in Ontario (Canada): Exclusionary Discourse in the Newsprint Media', *The Journal of Peasant Studies*, Vol. 35, No. 1.

Beals, Carleton, 1932, *Porfirio Díaz*, Philadelphia and London: J.B. Lippincott and Company.

Bedoya Garland, Eduardo, and Alvaro Bedoya Silva-Santisteban, 2005a, *Enganche y Servidumbre por Deudas en Bolivia*, Geneva: International Labour Organization.

Bedoya Garland, Eduardo, and Alvaro Bedoya Silva-Santisteban, 2005b, *Trabajo Forsozo en la Extracción de la Madera en la Amazonia Peruana*, Geneva: International Labour Organization.

Beer, M., 1948, *A History of British Socialism*, London: George Allen & Unwin.

Belloc, Hilaire, 1924, *Economics for Helen*, New York: G.P. Putnam's Sons.

Bellon, Bernard P., 1990, *Mercedes in Peace and War: German Automobile Workers, 1903–1945*, New York: Columbia University Press.

Bendix, Reinhard, 1960, *Max Weber: An Intellectual Portrait*, London: Heinemann.

Bernstein, Henry, and Terence J. Byres, 2001, 'From Peasant Studies to Agrarian Change', *Journal of Agrarian Change*, Vol. 1, No. 1.

Beveridge, Sir William, 1943, *The Pillars of Security*, London: George Allen & Unwin.

Beveridge, Sir William, 1944, *Full Employment in a Free Society*, London: George Allen & Unwin.

Beveridge, Sir William, 1945, *Why I am a Liberal*, London: George Allen & Unwin.

Beynon, Huw, 1973, *Working for Ford*, London: Allen Lane.

Bhaduri, Amit, 1973, 'A Study in Agricultural Backwardness under Semi-Feudalism', *The Economic Journal*, Vol. 83, No. 329.

Black, Edwin, 2001, *IBM and the Holocaust*, London: Little, Brown and Company.

Blackburn, Robin, 1997, *The Making of New World Slavery: From the Baroque to the Modern, 1492–1800*, London: Verso.

Blassinghame, John W., 1972, *The Slave Community: Plantation Life in the Antebellum South*, New York: Oxford University Press.

Blok, Anton, 1974, *The Mafia of a Sicilian Village 1860–1960: A Study of Violent Peasant Entrepreneurs*, New York: Harper and Row.

Blunt, Sir Edward, 1938, *Social Service in India: An Introduction to Some Social and Economic Problems of the Indian People*, London: His Majesty's Stationery Office.

Board of Agriculture and Fisheries (England), 1919, *Wages and Conditions of Employment in Agriculture: Volume I – General Report*, London: HMSO.

Board of Agriculture and Fisheries, 1906, *Report on the Decline in the Agricultural Population of Great Britain, 1881–1906*, London: HMSO.

Bonnet, Michel, 2000, 'Child Labour in the Light of Bonded Labour', in Bernard Schlemmer (ed.), *The Exploited Child*, London and Paris: Zed Books and l'Institut de Recherche pour le Développement.

Borkenau, Franz, 1942, *Socialism, National or International?*, London: George Routledge & Sons, Ltd.

Bouhdiba, Abdelwahab, 1982, *Exploitation of Child Labour*, New York: United Nations.

Bowker, Gordon, and John Carrier (eds.), 1976, *Race and Ethnic Relations*, London: Hutchinson & Co (Publishers) Ltd.

Bowman, Shearer Davis, 1993 *Masters and Lords: Mid-19th-Century US Planters and Prussian Junkers*, New York: Oxford University Press.

Brackenbury, C.F., 1915, *Madras District Gazetteers: Cuddapah*, Madras: Government Press.

Brass, Tom (ed.), 1995, *New Farmers Movements in India*, London: Frank Cass Publishers.

Brass, Tom (ed.), 2003, *Latin American Peasants*, London: Frank Cass Publishers.

Brass, Tom, 1994, 'Contextualizing Sugar Production in Nineteenth Century Queensland', *Slavery and Abolition*, Vol.15, No.1.

Brass, Tom, 1999, *Towards a Comparative Political Economy of Unfree Labour: Case Studies and Debates*, London: Frank Cass Publishers.

Brass, Tom, 2000, *Peasants, Populism and Postmodernism: The Return of the Agrarian Myth*, London and Portland, OR: Frank Cass Publishers.

Brass, Tom, 2002, 'Rural Labour in Agrarian Transitions: The Semi-Feudal Thesis Revisited', *Journal of Contemporary Asia*, Vol. 32, No. 4.

Brass, Tom, 2003, 'Why Unfree Labour is Not "So-Called": The Fictions of Jairus Banaji', *The Journal of Peasant Studies*, Vol. 31, No. 1.

Brass, Tom, 2007, 'Weapons of the Week, Weakness of the Weapons: Shifts and Stasis in Development Theory', *The Journal of Peasant Studies*, Vol. 34, No. 1.

Brass, Tom, 2008, 'Capitalism and Bonded Labour in India: Reinterpreting Recent (Re-) Interpretations', *The Journal of Peasant Studies*, Vol. 35, No. 2.

Brass, Tom, 2009, 'Capitalist Unfree Labour: A Contradiction?, *Critical Sociology*, Vol. 35, No. 6.

Brass, Tom, 2010, 'Capitalism, Primitive Accumulation and Unfree Labour', in H. Veltmeyer (ed.), *Imperialism, Crisis and Class Struggle: The Enduring Verities of Capitalism*, Leiden: Brill.

Brass, Tom, 2011a, 'Primitive Accumulation, Capitalist Development and Socialist Transition: Still Waiting for Godot?', *Journal of Contemporary Asia*, Vol. 40, No. 1.

Brass, Tom, 2011b, 'Unfree Labour as *Primitive* Accumulation?', *Capital & Class*, Vol. 35, No. 1.

Brass, Tom, and Marcel van der Linden (eds.), 1997, *Free and Unfree Labour: The Debate Continues*, Bern: Peter Lang, AG.

Brassey, Thomas, 1872, *Work and Wages*, London: Bell & Daldy.

Brassey, Thomas, 1879, *Foreign Work and English Wages*, London: Longmans, Green and Co.

Braverman, Harry, 1974, *Labour and Monopoly Capital: The Degradation of Work in the Twentieth Century*, New York: Monthly Review Press.

Breman, Jan, 2010, *Outcast Labour in Asia: Circulation and Informalization of the Workforce at the Bottom of the Economy*, New Delhi: Oxford University Press.

Bright, John, 1865, *Speeches of John Bright, M.P., on the American Question*, Boston: Little, Brown, and Company.

Brittain, Samuel, 2005, *Against the Flow: Reflections of an Individualist*, London: Atlantic Books.

Brown, A. Claude, 1927, *The Ordinary Man's India*, London: Cecil Palmer.

Brunt, P. A., 1971, *Italian Manpower, 225 B.C. – A.D. 14*, Oxford: The Clarendon Press.

Bücher, Carl, 1901 [1907], *Industrial Evolution* (translated by S. Morley Wickett), New York: Henry Holt and Company.

Buckman, S.S., 1891, *Arcadian Life*, London: Chapman & Hall Limited.

Bukharin, Nicolai, 1927, *The Economic Theory of the Leisure Class*, New York: International Publishers.

Bukharin, Nikolai, c. 1930, *Imperialism and World Economy*, London: Martin Lawrence Limited.

Butler, J.B., 1946, 'The Farm-Worker', in F.W. Bateson (ed.), *Towards a Socialist Agriculture: Studies by a Group of Fabians*, London: Victor Gollancz, Ltd.

Byres, Terence J., 1972, 'The Dialectic of India's Green Revolution', *South Asian Review*, Vol.5, No.2.

Byres, Terence J., 1974, 'Land Reform, Industrialization and the Marketed Surplus in India: An Essay on the Power of Rural Bias', in A.D. Lehmann (ed.), *Agrarian Reform and Agrarian Reformism*, London: Faber and Faber Limited.

Byres, Terence J., 1977, 'Agrarian Transition and the Agrarian Question', *The Journal of Peasant Studies*, Vol. 4, No.3.

Byres, Terence J., 1982a, 'The Political Economy of Technological Innovation in Indian Agriculture' in R.S.Anderson, et al., eds., *Science, Politics and the Agricultural Revolution in Asia*, Boulder: Westview Press.

Byres, Terence J., 1982b, 'India: Capitalist Industrialization or Structural Stasis?', in Manfred Bienefeld and Martin Godfrey (eds.), *The Struggle for Development: National Strategies in an International Context*, Chichester: John Wiley and Sons, Ltd.

Byres, Terence J., 1987, 'Sukhamoy Chakravarty on Marxist Economics and Contemporary Developing Economies: Some Comments', *Cambridge Journal of Economics*, Vol. 11, No. 2.

Byres, Terence J., 1991, 'The Agrarian Question and Differing forms of Capitalist Agrarian Transition: An Essay with Reference to Asia', in Jan Breman and Sudipto Mundle (eds.), *Rural Transformation in Asia*, Delhi: Oxford University Press.

Byres, Terence J., 1992, Review of Patnaik, *Agrarian Relations and Accumulation* [1990], *The Journal of Peasant Studies*, Vol.19, No.2.

Byres, Terence J., 1994, 'State, Class and Development Planning in India', in Terence J. Byres (ed.), *The State and Development Planning in India*, Delhi: Oxford University Press.

Byres, Terence J., 1995, 'Political Economy, the Agrarian Question and the Comparative Method', *The Journal of Peasant Studies*, Vol. 22, No. 4.

Byres, Terence J., 1996, *Capitalism from Above and Capitalism from Below: An Essay in Comparative Political Economy*, London: Macmillan Press.

Byres, Terence J., 1999, 'Rural Labour Relations in India: Persistent Themes, Common Processes and Differential Outcomes', *The Journal of Peasant Studies*, Vol. 26, Nos. 2 & 3.

Byres, Terence J., 2000, 'Pre-capitalist Economic Formations and Differential Agricultural Productivity: A Tentative Hypothesis', in K.N. Panikkar, Terence J. Byres, and Utsa Patnaik (eds.), *The Making of History: Essays presented to Irfan Habib*, New Delhi: Tulika.

Byres, Terence J., 2003, 'Paths of Capitalist Agrarian Transition in the Past and the Contemporary World', in V.K. Ramachandran and Madhura Swaminathan (eds.), *Agrarian Studies: Essays on Agrarian Relations in Less Developed Countries*, London: Zed Books.

Byres, Terence J., 2005, 'Neoliberalism and Primitive Accumulation in Less Developed Countries', in Alfredo Saad-Filho and Deborah Johnston (eds.), *Neoliberalism*, London: Pluto Press.

Cadbury, William A., 1909, *Labour in Portuguese West Africa*, London: George Routledge and Sons, Ltd.

Cameron, Averil, 1993, *The Later Roman Empire: AD 284–430*, London: Fontana Press.

Cannadine, David, 1990, *The Decline and Fall of the British Aristocracy*, London and New Haven, CT: Yale University Press.

Carr, E.H., 1961, *What is History?*, London: Macmillan & Co., Ltd.

Carstairs, Robert, 1935, *Harmak Village: A Novel of Santal Life*, Pokhuria, Manbhum: The Santal Mission Press.

Chakravarty, Sukhamoy, 1987, 'Marxist Economics and Contemporary Developing Economies', *Cambridge Journal of Economics*, Vol. 11, No. 1.

Charlesworth, Andrew, 1980, 'The Development of the English Rural Proletariat and Social Protest, 1700–1850: A Comment', *The Journal of Peasant Studies*, Vol. 8, No. 1.

Chattopadhyay, B., S.C. Sharma and A.K.Ray, 1987, 'Rural/Urban Terms of Trade, Primary Accumulation and the Increasing Strength of the Indian Farm Lobby', in B. Chattopadhyay and P. Spitz (eds.), *Food Systems and Society in Eastern India*, Geneva: UNRISD.

Chattopadhyay, Paresh, 1978a, 'On the Question of the Mode of Production in Indian Agriculture', in Ashok Rudra et al. [1978].

Chattopadhyay, Paresh, 1978b, 'Mode of Production in Indian Agriculture: An Anti-Kritik', in Ashok Rudra et al. [1978].

Children's Employment Commission (1862), 1867, *Sixth Report of the Commissioners (on Organized Agricultural Gangs, Commonly called "Public Gangs", in some of the Eastern Counties), with Appendix*, London: HMSO.

Chonchol, Jacques, 1965, 'Land Tenure and Development in Latin America', in Claudio Veliz (ed.), *Obstacles to Change in Latin America*, London: Oxford University Press.

Chowdhry, Prem, 1993, 'High Participation, Low Evaluation: Women and Work in Rural Haryana', *Economic and Political Weekly*, Vol. 28, No. 52.

Clapham, J.H., 1923, *The Economic Development of France and Germany, 1815–1914*, London: Cambridge University Press.

Coats, A.W., and Ross M. Robertson (eds.), 1969, *Essays in American Economic History*, London: Edward Arnold (Publishers) Ltd.

Cohen, Robin, 1987, *The New Helots: Migrants in the New International Division of Labour*, Aldershot: Gower Publishing.

Colledge, Dave, 1989, *Labour Camps: The British Experience*, Sheffield: Sheffield Popular Publishing.

Colledge, Dave, and John Field, 1983, '"To Recondition Human Material...": An Account of a British Labour Camp in the 1930s', *History Workshop Journal*, No. 14.

Colletti, Lucio, 1973, *Marxism and Hegel*, London: NLB.

Collings, Jesse, 1906, *Land Reform: Occupying Ownership, Peasant Proprietary, and Rural Education*, London, New York and Bombay: Longmans, Green, and Co.

Conan Doyle, Arthur, 1929, *Sherlock Holmes: The Complete Long Stories (A Study in Scarlet, The Sign of Four, The Hound of the Baskervilles, The Valley of Fear)*, London: John Murray, Albermarle Street, W.

Conrad, Alfred H., and John R. Meyer, 1965, *Studies in Economic History*, London: Chapman & Hall, Ltd.

Cook, Allen, 1982, *Akin to Slavery: Prison Labour in South Africa*, London: IDAF.

Corrigan, Philip, 1977, 'Feudal Relics or Capitalist Monuments? Notes on the Sociology of Unfree Labour', *Sociology*, Vol. 11, No. 3.

Cotlear, Daniel, 1979, *El sistema de Enganche a Principios del Siglo XX: Una Versión Diferente*, Lima: Universidad Católica.

Crooke, William, 1906, *Things Indian: Being Discursive Notes on Various Subjects connected with India*, London: John Murray, Albemarle Street.

Crooke, William, 1907, *Natives of Northern India*, London: Archibald Constable and Company, Ltd.

Crosby, Travis L., 1977, *English Farmers and the Politics of Protection 1815–52*, Hassocks, Sussex: The Harvester Press.

da Corta, Lucia, and Davaluri Venkateshwarlu, 1999, 'Unfree Relations and the Feminization of Agricultural Labour in Andhra Pradesh, 1970–95', *The Journal of Peasant Studies*, Vol. 26, Nos. 2 & 3.

Dandamaev, M.A., 1986, *Slavery in Babylonia*, De Kald, IL: Northern Illinois University Press.

Dange, S.A., 1949, *India from Primitive Communism to Slavery*, Bombay: People's Publishing House Ltd.

Danziger, Renée, 1988, *Political Powerlessness: Agricultural workers in post-war England*, Manchester: Manchester University Press.

Darling, Malcom Lyall, 1925, *The Punjab Peasant in Prosperity and Debt*, London and Bombay: Oxford University Press.

Darling, Malcom Lyall, 1930, *Rusticus Loquitur, or the Old Light and the New in the Punjab Village*, London: Oxford University Press.

Darling, Malcom Lyall, 1934, *Wisdom and Waste in the Punjab Village*, London: Oxford University Press.

Das, A.N., 1979, *Does Bihar Show the Way?*, Calcutta: Research India Publications.

Day, Richard B., 1973, *Leon Trotsky and the Politics of Economic Isolation*, London: Cambridge University Press.

de Nogales, Rafael, 1928, *The Looting of Nicaragua*, London: Wright & Brown.

de Ste. Croix, G.E.M., 1957, 'Slavery', *The Classical Review* (new series), Vol. 7, No. 1.

de Ste. Croix, G.E.M., 1981, *The Class Struggle in the Ancient Greek World: From the Archaic Age to the Arab Conquests*, London: Duckworth.

de Ste. Croix, G.E.M., 1984, 'Class in Marx's Conception of History, Ancient and Modern', *New Left Review*, No. 146.

de Ste. Croix, G.E.M., 1988, 'Slavery and Other Forms of Unfree Labour', in Léonie J. Archer (ed.), *Slavery and Other Forms of Unfree Labour*, London: Routledge.

Degler, Carl N., 1959, 'Starr on Slavery', *The Journal of Economic History*, Vol. XIX, No. 2.

Degler, Carl N., 1976, 'The Irony of American Negro Slavery', in H.P. Owens (ed.), *Perspectives and Irony in American Negro Slavery*, Jackson, MS: University of Mississipi Press.

Desai, A.R., 1984, *India's Path of Development: A Marxist Approach*, Bombay: Popular Prakashan

Deutscher, Isaac, 1954, *The Prophet Armed: Trotsky 1879–1921*, London: Oxford University Press.

Deutscher, Isaac, 1959, *The Prophet Unarmed: Trotsky 1921–1929*, London: Oxford University Press.

Deutscher, Isaac, 1963, *The Prophet Outcast: Trotsky 1929–1940*, London: Oxford University Press.

Dew, Charles B., 1966, *Ironmaker to the Confederacy: Joseph R. Anderson and the Tredegar Iron Works*, New Haven, CT: Yale University Press.

DeWind, Josh, Tom Seidl, and Janet Shenk, 1979, 'Contract Labor in U.S. Agriculture: The West Indian Cane Cutters in Florida', in Robin Cohen, Peter C.W. Gutkind, and Phyllis Brazier (eds.), *Peasants and Proletarians: The Struggles of Third World Workers*, London: Hutchinson & Co. (Publishers) Ltd.

Dickens, Charles, 1842, 'Slavery', in *American Notes for General Circulation*, Vol. II, London: Chapman and Hall, 186, Strand.

Dilke, Sir Charles W., 1968 [1885], *Industrial Remuneration Conference: The Report of the Proceedings and Papers* (Reprints of Economic Classics), New York: Augustus M. Kelley Publishers.

Dobb, Maurice, 1940, *Political Economy and Capitalism*, London: Routledge & Kegan Paul.

Dobb, Maurice, 1946a, *Wages*, Cambridge: Cambridge University Press.

Dobb, Maurice, 1946b, *Studies in the Development of Capitalism*, London: George Routledge & Sons Ltd.

Dobb, Maurice, 1963, *Economic Growth and Underdeveloped Countries*, London: Lawrence and Wishart.

Dobb, Maurice, 1967, *Papers on Capitalism, Development and Planning*, London: Routledge & Kegan Paul.

Dodd, William, 1976/[1848], *The Laboring Classes of England, especially those concerned in Agriculture and Manufactures*, Fairfield, NJ: Augustus M. Kelley.

Donajgrodzki, A.P., 1989, 'Twentieth Century Rural England: A Case for "Peasant Studies"?', *The Journal of Peasant Studies*, Vol. 16, No. 3.

Douglass, Frederick, 1845, *Narrative of the Life of Frederick Douglass*, Boston, MA: Anti-Slavery Office.

Drèze, Jean, and Anindita Mukherjee, 1987, *Labour Contracts in Rural India: Theories and Evidence*, London: LSE Development Research Programme.

Dubois, Pierre, 1976, *Sabotage in Industry*, Harmondsworth: Penguin Books.

Dutt, R. Palme, 1955, *India Today and Tomorrow*, London: Lawrence and Wishart.

Edmonds, Thomas Rowe, 1832, *An Enquiry into the Principles of Population exhibiting a System of Regulations for the Poor*, London: James Duncan, Paternoster Row.

Edmunds, Cyrus R. (ed.), 1873, *Cicero's Three Books of Offices, or Moral Duties*, London: Bell & Daldy, York Street, Covent Garden.

Elena Garcia, Maria, 2005, *Making Indigenous Citizens: Identities, Education, and Multicultural Development in Peru*, Stanford, CA: Stanford University Press.

Eley, Geoff, 1989, 'What Produces Fascism: Preindustrial Traditions or a Crisis of the Capitalist State?' in Michael N. Dobkowski and Isidor Walliman (eds.), *Radical Perspectives on the Rise of Fascism in Germany, 1919–1945*, New York: Monthly Review Press.

Eley, Geoff, and David Blackbourn, 1984, *The Peculiarities of German History; Bourgeois Society and Politics in Nineteenth-century Germany*, Oxford: Oxford University Press.

Engels, Frederick, 1985a [1868], 'Review of Volume One of *Capital* for *The Fortnightly Review*', *Marx/Engels Collected Works*, Vol. 20, Moscow: Progress Publishers.

Engels, Frederick, 1985b [1868], 'Synopsis of Volume One of *Capital* by Karl Marx', *Marx/Engels Collected Works*, Vol. 20, Moscow: Progress Publishers.

Engerman, Stanley L., 1973 [1967], 'The Effects of Slavery Upon the Southern Economy: A Review of the Recent Debate', in Peter Temin (ed.).

Engerman, Stanley L., and Eugene D. Genovese (eds.), 1975, *Race and Slavery in the Western Hemisphere: Quantitative Studies*, Princeton, NJ: Princeton University Press.

Ercelawn, A., and M. Nauman, 2004, 'Unfree Labour in South Asia: Debt Bondage at Brick Kilns in Pakistan', *Economic and Political Weekly*, Vol. XXXIX, No. 22.

Etzioni, Amitai, 2001, *The Monochrome Society*, Princeton, NJ: Princeton University Press.

Evans, Richard J., 1987, *Rethinking German History: Nineteenth-Century Germany and the Origins of the Third Reich*, London: Allen and Unwin.

Farnam, Henry W., 1938, *Chapters in the History of Social Legislation in the United States to 1860*, Washington, DC: Carnegie Institute.

Ferguson, Lucy, 2010, 'Social Reproduction and Unfree Labour in Global Political Economy', paper presented at SGIR 7th Pan-European International Relations Conference, Stockholm, 9–11 September.

Fiedler, Ernst, 1898, 'The Workers Question in the Country and Suggestions for Reforming the Character of Rural Workers' (Leipzig), in *German History in Documents and Images – Volume 4, Forging an Empire: Bismarckian Germany, 1866–90* (Categories of Rural Workers in the Late Nineteenth Century).

Finley, M.I., 1983a, *Ancient Slavery and Modern Ideology*, Harmondsworth: Penguin Books.

Finley, M.I., 1983b, *Economy and Society in Ancient Greece*, London: Pelican Books.

Fishlow, Albert, 2003, 'Review of Alexander Gerschenkron's *Economic Backwardness in Historical Perspective*', http://eh.net/bookreviews/library/fishlow.shtml.

Flynn, Elizabeth Gurley, 1916, *Sabotage: The Conscious Withdrawal of the Workers' Industrial Efficiency*, Cleveland, OH: IWW.

Fogel, Robert William, 1975, 'Preface', in Stanley L. Engerman and Eugene D. Genovese (eds.).

Fogel, Robert William, 1989, *Without Consent or Contract: The Rise and Fall of American Slavery*, New York: W.W.Norton.

Fogel, Robert William, and Stanley W. Engerman, 1974, *Time on the Cross: Volume I - The Economics of American Negro Slavery*, London: Wildwood House.

Fossier, Robert (ed.), 1989, *The Cambridge Illustrated History of the Middle Ages: Vol. I 350–950*, Cambridge: Cambridge University Press.

Frank, Andre Gunder 1967, *Capitalism and Underdevelopment in Latin America*, New York: Monthly Review Press.

Frank, Andre Gunder, 1977, 'On So-Called Primitive Accumulation', *Dialectical Anthropology*, Vol. 2, No. 2.

Frank, Andre Gunder, 1978, *Dependent Accumulation and Underdevelopment*, London: Macmillan Press.

Friedland, W.H., and D. Nelkin, 1971, *Migrant Agricultural Workers in America's Northeast*, New York: Holt, Rinehart & Winson.

Fröbel, Folker, Jürgen Heinrichs, and Otto Kreye, 1980, *The New International Division of Labour: Structural Unemployment in Industrialized Countries and Industrialization in Developing Countries*, Cambridge: Cambridge University Press.

Fussell, G.E., 1949, *The English Rural Labourer: His Home, Furniture, Clothing and Food, from Tudor to Victorian Times*, London: The Batchworth Press.

Gaido, Daniel, 2003, 'Karl Kautsky on Capitalism in the Ancient World', *The Journal of Peasant Studies*, Vol. 30, No. 2.

Galarza, E., 1964, *Merchants of Labor: The Mexican Bracero Story*, Santa Barbara, CA: McNally & Loftin, Publishers.

Gangulee, N., 1935, *The Indian Peasant and his Environment (The Linlithgow Commission and After)*, London: Oxford University Press.

Garnsey, Peter (ed.), 1980, *Non-Slave Labour in the Greco-Roman World* (Supplementary Volume no. 6), Cambridge: The Cambridge Philological Society.

George, Henry, 1881, *Progress and Poverty: An Inquiry into the Cause of Industrial Depressions, and of Increase of Want with Increase of Wealth, The Remedy*, New York: D. Appleton and Company.

George, Henry, 1884, *Social Problems*, London: Kegan Paul, Trench & Co.

Gerschenkron, Alexander, 1943, *Bread and Democracy in Germany*, Berkeley, CA: University of California Press.

Gerschenkron, Alexander, 1955, 'The Problem of Economic Development in Russian Intellectual History of the Nineteenth Century', in Ernest J. Simmons (ed.), *Continuity and Change in Russian and Soviet Thought*, Cambridge, MA: Harvard University Press.

Gerschenkron, Alexander, 1962, *Economic Backwardness in Historical Perspective*, Cambridge, MA: Harvard University Press.

Giddens, Anthony, and Gavin Mackenzie (eds.), 1982, *Social Class and the Division of Labour*, Cambridge: Cambridge University Press.

González Tafur, Oswaldo B., 1952, *Peru: Población y Agricultura*, Lima: Libreria Internacional del Peru, S.A.

Goodman, David and Michael Redclift, 1981, *From Peasant to Proletarian*, Oxford: Basil Blackwell.

Goodman, David, Bernardo Sorj and John Wilkinson, 1984, 'Agro-industry, State Policy and Rural Social Structures: Recent Aanalyses of Proletarianisation in Brazilian Agriculture', in B. Munslow and H. Finch (eds.), *Proletarianisation in the Third World*, London: Croom Helm.

Government of India, 1927, *Royal Commission on Agriculture in India*, Calcutta: Government of India Publication Branch.

Government of India, 1931, *Royal Commission on Labour in India: Evidence, Vol. II – Part 2 (Punjab, Delhi and Ajmer-Merwara)*, London: HMSO.

Government of India, Ministry of Labour, 1979, *Report of the Committee on Child Labour*, Delhi: Government of India Press.

Gramsci, Antonio, 1971, *Selections from the Prison Notebooks*, London: Lawrence and Wishart.

Graves, Adrian, 1993, *Cane and Labour: The Political Economy of the Queensland Sugar Industry 1862–1906*, Edinburgh: Edinburgh University Press.

Green, F.E., 1920, *A History of the English Agricultural Labourer, 1870–1920*, London: P.S. King & Son, Ltd.

Gregor, Neil, 1998, *Daimler-Benz and the Third Reich*, New Haven, CT: Yale University Press.

Griffiths, P.J., 1946, *The British in India*, London: Robert Hale Ltd.

Groves, Reg, 1949, *Sharpen the Sickle! The History of the Farm Workers' Union*, London: The Porcupine Press.

Gruening, Ernest, 1928, *Mexico and Its Heritage*, London: Stanley Paul and Co., Ltd.

Grunberger, Richard, 1974, *A Social History of the Third Reich*, London: Penguin Books.

Guérin, Daniel, 1956 [1951], *Negroes on the March: A Frenchman's Report on the American Negro Struggle*, London and New York: New Park Publications Ltd.

Gusfield, Joseph R., 1975, *Community: A Critical Response*, Oxford: Basil Blackwell.

Gutman, Herbert G., 1976, *The Black Family in Slavery and Freedom, 1750–1925*, Oxford: Basil Blackwell.

Hagan, William W., 1986, 'The Junkers' Faithless Servants: Peasant Insubordination and the Breakdown of Serfdom in Brandenburg-Prussia, 1763–1811', in Richard J. Evans and W.R. Lee (eds.), *The German Peasantry*, London: Croom Helm.

Hammond, J.L. and Barbara, 1920, *The Village Labourer 1760–1832: A Study in the Government of England before the Reform Bill*, London: Longmans, Green, and Co.

Hammond, N.G.L., 1959, *A History of Greece to 322 B.C.*, Oxford: Clarendon.

Hannington, Wal, 1937, *The Problem of the Distressed Areas*, London: Left Book Club/ Victor Gollancz Ltd.
Hannington, Wal, 1940, *Industrial History in Wartime*, London: Lawrence & Wishart Ltd.
Hardt, Michael, and Antonio Negri, 2001, *Empire*, Cambridge, MA: Harvard University Press.
Hardt, Michael, and Antonio Negri, 2005, *Multitude: War and Democracy in the Age of Empire*, London: Hamish Hamilton.
Harriss-White, Barbara, 1996, *A Political Economy of Agricultural Markets in South India*, New Delhi: Sage.
Harriss-White, Barbara, and Nandini Gooptu, 2000, 'Mapping India's World of Unorganized Labour', in Leo Panitch and Colin Leys (eds.), *The Socialist Register 2001*, London: The Merlin Press.
Harriss-White, Barbara, D.K. Mishra and V. Upadhyay, 2009, 'Institutional Diversity and Capitalist Transition: The Political Economy of Agrarian Change in Arunachal Pradesh, India', *Journal of Agrarian Change*, Vol. 9, No. 4.
Harvey, David, 2003, *The New Imperialism*, Oxford: Oxford University Press.
Harvey, David, 2004, 'The "New" Imperialism: Accumulation by Dispossession', in Leo Panitch and Colin Leys (eds.), *Socialist Register 2004: The New Imperial Challenge*, London: The Merlin Press.
Harvey, David, 2010a, *A Companion to Marx's Capital*, London: Verso.
Harvey, David, 2010b, *The Enigma of Capital and the Crises of Capitalism*, London: Profile Books.
Hasbach, W., 1908, *A History of the English Agricultural Labourer*, London: P.S. King and Son.
Hayek, F.A. (ed.), 1954, *Capitalism and the Historians*, London: Routledge & Kegan Paul Limited.
Hayek, F.A., 1954, 'History and Politics', in F.A. Hayek (ed.) [1954].
Hayes, Peter, 1987, *Industry and Ideology: IG Farben in the Nazi Era*, Cambridge: Cambridge University Press.
Heath, Richard, 1989/[1893], *The Victorian Peasant* (edited by Keith Dockray), Gloucester: Alan Sutton.
Hegel, G.W.F., 1942 [1821], *Philosophy of Right* (translated with notes by T.M. Knox), Oxford: The Clarendon Press.
Hegel, G.W.F., 1978 [1807], *Phenomenology of Spirit* (translated by A.V. Millar; Foreword by J. N. Findlay), Oxford: The Clarendon Press.
Henderson, W.O., 1961, *The Industrial Revolution on the Continent: Germany, France, Russia 1800–1914*, London: Frank Cass & Co.
Herbert, Ulrich, 1990, *A History of Foreign Labour in Germany, 1880–1980: Seasonal Workers/Forced Labourers/Guest Workers*, Ann Arbor, MI: The University of Michigan Press.
Herbert, Ulrich, 1993, 'Labour and Extermination: Economic Interest and the Primacy of *Weltanshauung* in National Socialism', *Past and Present*, No. 138.
Herbert, Ulrich, 1997, *Hitler's Foreign Workers: Enforced Foreign Labour in Germany under the Third Reich*, Cambridge: Cambridge University Press.
Herbrechter, Stefan, and Michael Higgins (eds.), 2006, *Returning (to) Communities: Theory, Culture and Political Practice of the Communal*, Amsterdam and New York: Editions Rodopi B.V.
Herskovits, Melville J., and Mitchell Harwitz (eds.), 1964, *Economic Transition in Africa*, London: Routledge and Kegan Paul.
Hilferding, Rudolf, 1981 [1910], *Finance Capital: A Study of the Latest Phase of Capitalist Development*, London: Routledge & Kegan Paul.
Hilton, Rodney (ed.), 1976, *The Transition from Feudalism to Capitalism*, London: New Left Books.

History Task Force, 1979, *Labor Migration under Capitalism: The Puerto Rican Experience*, New York: Monthly Review Press.

HM Attorney-General, 1946, *The Trial of German Major War Criminals by the International Military Tribunal at Nuremburg, Germany: Speeches of the Chief Prosecutors*, London: HMSO.

Hobbes, Thomas, n.d. [1651], *Leviathan*, London: J.M. Dent & Sons, Ltd.

Hobsbawm, E.J., 1964, *Labouring Men: Studies in the History of Labour*, London: Weidenfeld and Nicolson.

Hobsbawm, E.J., 1967, 'Maurice Dobb', in C.H.Feinstein (ed.), *Socialism, Capitalism and Economic Growth*, London: Cambridge University Press.

Hobsbawm, E.J., 1969, *Bandits*, London: Weidenfeld and Nicolson.

Hobsbawm, E.J., and George Rudé, 1969, *Captain Swing*, London: Lawrence and Wishart.

Hodgson, Geoff, 1975, *Trotsky and Fatalistic Marxism*, Nottingham: Spokesman Books.

Hohman, Elmo Paul, 1928, *The American Whaleman: A Study of Life and Labor in the Whaling Industry*, New York London and Toronto: Longmans, Green and Co.

Homze, Edward L., 1967, *Foreign Labor in Nazi Germany*, Princeton, NJ: Princeton University Press.

Hopkins, Keith, 1978, *Conquerors and Slaves*, Cambridge: Cambridge University Press.

House of Commons Environment, Food and Rural Affairs Committee (EFRA), 2003, *Gangmasters (Fourteenth Report of Session 2002–03)*. London: The Stationery Office Ltd.

Howell, George, M.P., 1892, 'Liberty for Labour', in Thomas Mackay (ed.) [1892].

Howitt, William, 1838, *The Rural Life of England*, Volume I, London: Longman, Orme, Brown, Green, & Longmans.

Howitt, William, 1862, *The Rural Life of England* (Third edition), London: Longman, Green, Longman, Roberts & Green.

Howkins, Alun, 1985, *Poor Labouring Men: Rural Radicalism in Norfolk 1870–1923*, London: Routledge & Kegan Paul.

Howkins, Alun, 1990, 'Labour History and the Rural Poor, 1850–1930', *Rural History*, Vol. 1, No. 1.

Huque, M. Azizul, 1939, *The Man Behind the Plough*, Calcutta: The Book Company, Ltd.

Hussain, Athar, and Keith Tribe, 1981, *Marxism and the Agrarian Question – Volume I: German Social Democracy and the Peasantry 1890–1907*, London: Macmillan.

Hutt, Allen, 1933, *The Condition of the Working Class in Britain* (with an introduction by Harry Pollitt), London: Martin Lawrence Limited.

Hutt, W.H., 1954, 'The Factory System of the Early Nineteenth Century', in F.A. Hayek (ed.) [1954].

Hutton, J.H., 1941, 'Primitive Tribes', in L.S.S. O'Malley (ed.), *Modern India and the West: A Study of the Interaction of their Civilizations*, London: Oxford University Press.

Hyndman, H.M., 1919, *The Awakening of Asia*, London: Cassell and Company, Ltd.

India League, 1932, *Condition of India: Being the Report of the Delegation sent to India by The India League in 1932*, London: Essential News.

Ingram, J.K., 1895, *A History of Slavery and Serfdom*, London: Adam and Charles Black.

Institute of Marxism-Leninism of the CC, CPSU, 1964a, *Documents of the First International, 1864–1866*, Vol. I, Moscow: Progress Publishers.

Institute of Marxism-Leninism of the CC, CPSU, 1964b, *Documents of the First International, 1868–1870*, Vol. III, Moscow: Progress Publishers.

International Labour Office, 1953, *Indigenous Peoples: Living and Working Conditions of Aboriginal Populations in Independent Countries*, Geneva: ILO.

International Labour Organization, 2001, *Stopping Forced Labour*, Geneva: ILO.

International Labour Organization, 2005, *A Global Alliance Against Forced Labour*, Geneva: ILO.

Jack, James Charles, 1916, *The Economic Life of a Bengal District: A Study*, Oxford: Clarendon Press.

Jackson, Jean E., 2009, 'Neoliberal Multiculturalism and Indigenous Movements', *Latin American Research Review*, Vol. 44, No. 3.

James, C.L.R, 1938, *The Black Jacobins: Toussant Louverture and the San Domingo Revolution*, London: Secker and Warburg.

Jouvenel, Bertrand de, 1947, *Problems of Socialist England*, London: The Batchworth Press.

Kaldor, Nicholas, 1964, *Essays on Economic Policy - Volume Two*, London: Gerald Duckworth & Co.

Kalecki, Michal, 1976, *Essays on Developing Economies*, Hassocks: Harvester Press.

Kamenka, Eugene, 1982, 'Community and the socialist ideal', in Eugene Kamenka (ed.), *Community as a Social Ideal*, London: Edward Arnold.

Kautsky, Karl, 1910 [1891], *The Class Struggle (Erfurt Programme)*, Chicago, IL: Charles H. Kerr.

Kautsky, Karl, 1925, *Foundations of Christianity: A Study in Christian Origins*, London: George Allen & Unwin, Ltd.

Kautsky, Karl, 1936, *The Economic Doctrines of Karl Marx*, Hampstead: NCLC Publishing Society Ltd.

Kautsky, Karl, 1984 [1894/95], 'The Competitive Capacity of Small-scale Enterprise in Agriculture', in A. Hussain and K. Tribe (eds.), *Paths of Development in Capitalist Agriculture*, London: Macmillan.

Kautsky, Karl, 1988 [1899], *The Agrarian Question*, 2 Vols., London: Zwan Publications.

Kay, James Phillips, 1969 [1832], *The Moral and Physical Condition of the Working Classes employed in the Cotton Manufacture in Manchester*, Manchester: E.J. Morten (Publishers).

Kay-Shuttleworth, Sir James, 1973 [1873], *Thoughts and Suggestions on Certain Social Problems*, Manchester: E.J. Morten (Publishers).

Keatinge, G., 1912, *Rural Economy in the Bombay Deccan*, London, Bombay and Calcutta: Longmans, Green and Co.

Keen, B.A., 1946, *The Agricultural Development of the Middle East – A Report to the Director Middle East Supply Centre*, London: HMSO.

Kitchen, Fred, 1940, *Brother to the Ox: The Autobiography of a Farm Labourer*, London: J.M. Dent and Sons, Ltd.

Kitteringham, Jennie, 1975, 'Country work girls in nineteenth century England', in Raphael Samuel (ed.) [1975].

Klengel, H., 1978, 'Non-Slave Labour in the Old Babylonian Period', in Michael Flinn (ed.), *Proceedings of the Seventh International Economic History Congress*, Edinburgh: Edinburgh University Press.

Klinge, Gerardo, 1935, *Politica de Irrigación*, Lima: Sociedad Nacional Agraria.

Klinge, Gerardo, 1944, *La Agricultura de la Costa y la Situación Alimenticia*, Lima: Sociedad Nacional Agraria.

Klinge, Gerardo, 1946, *Politica Agricola-Alimenticia*, Peru:Imprenta Torres Aguirre, S.A.

Knauerhase, Ramon, 1972, *An Introduction to National Socialism, 1920 to 1939*, Columbus, OH: Charles E. Merrill Publishing Co.

Knei-Paz, Baruch, 1977, 'Trotsky, Marxism and the Revolution of Backwardness', in Shlomo Avineri (ed.), *Varieties of Marxism*, The Hague: Martinus Nijhoff.

Knight, Barry, Hope Chigudu, and Rajesh Tandon, 2002, *Reviving Democracy: Citizens at the Heart of Governance*, London: Earthscan.

Komarov, E.N., 1960, 'Russian Pre-Revolutionary and Soviet Studies on the Economic History of Modern India', in Tapan Raychaudhuri (ed.), *Contributions to Indian Economic History I*, Calcutta: Firma K.L. Mukhopadhyay.

Kornbluh, Joyce L. (ed.), 1968, *Rebel Voices: An I.W.W. Anthology*, Ann Arbor, MI: The University of Michigan Press.

Kotovsky, Grigory, 1960, *Some Aspects of the Disintegration of Village Communities in India in Late 18th – Early 19th Century*, Moscow: Oriental Literature Publishing House.

Kotovsky, Grigory, 1964, *Agrarian Reforms in India*, New Delhi: People's Publishing House.

Kreissig, H., 1978, "Free Labour in the Hellenistic Age', in Michael Flinn (ed.), *Proceedings of the Seventh International Economic History Congress*, Edinburgh: Edinburgh University Press.

Krissman, Fred, 1997, 'California's Agricultural Labor Market: Historical Variations in the Use of Unfree Labor, c. 1769–1994', in Tom Brass and Marcel van der Linden (eds.), *Free and Unfree Labour: The Debate Continues*, Bern: Peter Lang AG.

Kristof, Nicholas D., and Sheryl WuDunn, 2010, *Half the Sky: How to Change the World*, London: Virago Press.

Kuczynski, Jürgen, 1939, *The Condition of the Workers in Great Britain, Germany and the Soviet Union, 1932–1938*, London: Left Book Club/Victor Gollancz, Ltd.

Kuusinen, Otto (ed.), 1961, *Fundamentals of Marxism-Leninism*, London: Lawrence and Wishart.

Labour Research Department, 1944, 'Farm Workers', *Labour Research*, Vol. XXXIII, No. 1.

Laclau, Ernesto, 1971, 'Feudalism and Capitalism in Latin America', *New Left Review*, No. 67.

Laing, Samuel, 1850, *Observations on the Social and Political State of the European People in 1848 and 1849*, London: Longman, Brown, Green, and Longmans.

Lal, Deepak, 2004, *In Praise of Empires: Globalization and Order*, New York: Palgrave Macmillan.

Lawrence, Felicity, 2004, *Not on the Label: What Really Goes into the Food on Your Plate*, London: Penguin Books.

Lawson, William, Charles D. Hunter, et al., 1874, *Ten Years of Gentleman Farming at Blennerhasset, with Co-operative Objects*, London: Longmans, Green, & Co.

Lenin, V.I., 1960a [1894], 'What the "Friends of the People" Are, and How They Fight the Social-Democrats', *Collected Works*, Vol. 1, Moscow: Foreign Languages Publishing House.

Lenin, V.I., 1960b [1894], 'The Economic Content of Narodnism', *Collected Works*, Vol. 1, Moscow: Foreign Languages Publishing House.

Lenin, V.I., 1963a [1913], 'The Land Question and The Rural Poor', and 'The Agrarian Question and The Present Situation in Russia', *Collected Works*, Vol. 19, Moscow: Foreign Languages Publishing House.

Lenin, V.I., 1963b [1913], 'Child Labour in Peasant Farming', *Collected Works*, Vol. 19, Moscow: Foreign Languages Publishing House.

Lenin, V.I., 1963c [1914], 'Conspectus of Hegel's Book *The Science of Logic*', *Collected Works*, Vol. 38, Moscow: Foreign Languages Publishing House.

Lenin, V.I., 1964a [1899], 'The Development of Capitalism in Russia', *Collected Works*, Vol. 3, Moscow: Foreign Languages Publishing House.

Lenin, V.I., 1964c [1918], 'Karl Marx: A Brief Biographical Sketch with an Exposition of Marxism', *Collected Works*, Vol. 21, London: Lawrence and Wishart.

Lerche, Jens, 2007, 'An Alliance Against Forced Labour in India? Unfree Labour, Neo-liberal Globalisation and the International Labour Organization', http://www.qeh.ox.ac.uk/pdf.heyer07/lerche07-heyer-workshop.pdf.

Leslie, T.E. Cliffe, 1968 [1870], *Land Systems and Industrial Economy*, New York: Augustus M. Kelley.

Levy, Adrian, and Cathy Scott-Clark, 2004, '"He won, Russia lost"', *The Guardian Weekend*, 8 May.

Levy, Hermann, 1911, *Large and Small Holdings: A Study of English Agricultural Economics*, London: Cambridge University Press.
Lewis, W. Arthur, 1951, 'A Policy for Colonial Agriculture', in Lewis, W. Arthur, et al., *Attitude to Africa*, Harmondsworth: Penguin Books.
Lewis, W. Arthur, 1955, *The Theory of Economic Growth*, Homewood, IL: Richard D. Irwin, Inc.
Lichtenstein, Alex, 1996, *Twice The Work of Free Labor: The Political Economy of Convict Labor in the New South*, London: Verso.
Lichtheim, G., 1961, *Marxism: An Historical and Critical Study*, London: Routledge and Kegan Paul.
Lieten, G.K., 2003, *Power, Politics and Rural Development: Essays on India*, Delhi: Manohar.
London Society for the Abolition of Slavery, 1833, *Anti-Slavery Reporter*, Volume V (January 1832 to February 1833), London: J. Hatchard & Son, Piccadilly.
Lucas, Kintto, 2000, *We Will Not Dance on Our Grandparents' Tombs: Indigenous Uprisings in Ecuador*, London: CIIR.
Lukács, Georg, 1971, *History and Class Consciousness: Studies in Marxist Dialectics*, London: The Merlin Press.
Lukács, Georg, 1975, *The Young Hegel*, London: The Merlin Press.
Luxemburg, Rosa, 1937 [1899], *Reform or Revolution*, New York: Three Arrows Press.
Luxemburg, Rosa, 1951 [1913], *The Accumulation of Capital*, London: Faber and Faber.
Luxemburg, Rosa, 1954 [1916], *What Is Economics?* (Translated by T. Edwards), New York: Pioneer Publishers.
Macdonald, J. Ramsay, M.P., 1910, *The Awakening of India*, London: Hodder and Stoughton.
Mackay, Thomas (ed.), 1892, *A Plea for Liberty: An Argument Against Socialism and Socialistic Legislation*, London: John Murray.
Macleod, R.D., 1938, *Impressions of an Indian Civil Servant*, London: H.F. & G. Witherby, Ltd.
Malani, K.P.S., 1935, *Rural Indebtedness in India* (Congress Golden Jubilee Brochure No. 4), Allahabad: All India Congress Committee.
Malthus, T.R., n.d., but c. 1910 [1798], *An Essay on Population*, vols. I and II, London: J.M. Dent & Sons, Ltd.
Mandel, Ernest, 1968, *Marxist Economic Theory*, Volumes 1 and 2, London: The Merlin Press.
Mandel, Ernest, 1975, *Late Capitalism*, London: New Left Books.
Mangin, William (ed.), 1970, *Peasants in Cities: Readings in the Anthropology of Urbanization*, Boston, MA: Houghton Mifflin Company.
Mann, Geoff, 2001, 'The State, Race, and "Wage Slavery" in the Forest Sector of the Pacific North-West United States', *The Journal of Peasant Studies*, Vol. 29, No. 1.
Mann, Harold H., 1929, 'The Agriculture of India', *The Annals of the American Academy of Political and Social Science*, Vol. CXLV, Part II.
Mann, Harold H., 1967, *The Social Framework of Agriculture*, Bombay: Vora & Co.
Manzo, Kate, 2005, 'Modern Slavery, Global Capitalism and Deproletarianisation in West Africa', *Review of African Political Economy*, No. 106.
Mao Tse-Tung, 1954, 'The Chinese Revolution and the Chinese Communist Party', *Selected Works*, Vol. 3, London: Lawrence and Wishart.
Marcuse, Herbert, 1955, *Reason and Revolution: Hegel and the Rise of Social Theory*, London: Routledge & Kegan Paul.
Maren, Michael, 1997, *The Road to Hell: The Ravaging Effects of Foreign Aid International Charity*, New York: The Free Press.
Marshall, T.H., 1963, *Sociology at the Crossroads and Other Essays*, London: Heinemann.
Marshall, T.H., 1950, *Citizenship and Social Class, and Other Essays*, London: Cambridge University Press.

Martins, José de Souza, 1997, 'The Reappearance of Slavery and the Reproduction of Capital on the Brazilian Frontier', in Tom Brass and Marcel van der Linden (eds.) [1997].

Martins, José de Souza, 2003, 'Representing the Peasantry? Struggles for/about Land in Brazil', in Tom Brass (ed.), *Latin American Peasants*, London and Portland, OR: Frank Cass Publishers.

Marx, Karl, 1913, *A Contribution to the Critique of Political Economy*, Chicago, IL: Charles H. Kerr & Company.

Marx, Karl, 1972 [1861–63], *Theories of Surplus Value – Part III*, London: Lawrence & Wishart.

Marx, Karl, 1973, *Grundrisse*, Harmondsworth: Penguin Books.

Marx, Karl, 1975a [1843], 'Contribution to a Critique of Hegel's Philosophy of Law', in Karl Marx Frederick Engels, *Collected Works*, Vol. 3, London: Lawrence & Wishart.

Marx, Karl, 1975b [1844], 'Economic and Philosophic Manuscripts of 1844', in Karl Marx Frederick Engels *Collected Works*, Vol. 3, London: Lawrence & Wishart.

Marx, Karl, 1976a, *Capital – Volume 1*, Harmondsworth: Penguin Books.

Marx, Karl, 1976b [1847], 'The Poverty of Philosophy', Karl Marx Frederick Engels, *Collected Works*, Vol. 6, London: Lawrence & Wishart.

Marx, Karl, 1981, *Capital – Volume 3*, Harmondsworth: Penguin Books.

Marx, Karl, 1984 [1861], 'The Civil War in the United States', Karl Marx Frederick Engels, *Collected Works*, Vol. 19, London: Lawrence & Wishart.

Marx, Karl, 1985a [1866], 'Instructions for the Delegates of the Provisional General Council: The Different Questions', Karl Marx Frederick Engels, *Collected Works*, Vol. 20, London: Lawrence & Wishart.

Marx, Karl, 1985b [1865], 'Value, Price and Profit', Karl Marx Frederick Engels, *Collected Works*, Vol. 20, London: Lawrence & Wishart.

Marx, Karl, 1986 [1857–58], 'Economic Manuscripts of 1857–58', Karl Marx Frederick Engels, *Collected Works*, Vol. 28, London: Lawrence & Wishart.

Marx, Karl, 1988 [1861–63], 'Economic Manuscripts of 1861–63', Karl Marx Frederick Engels, *Collected Works*, Vol. 30, Moscow: Progress Publishers.

Marx, Karl, and Fredrick Engels, 1957, *On Religion*, Moscow: Foreign Languages Publishing House.

Marx, Karl, and Fredrick Engels, 1976 [1848], 'Manifesto of the Communist Party', in Karl Marx and Fredrick Engels, *Collected Works*, Volume 6, London: Lawrence and Wishart.

McCulloch, John R., 1845, *A Dictionary, Geographical, Statistical, and Historical, of the various Countries, Places, and Principal Natural Objects in the World* (Volume II), London: Longman, Brown, Green, and Longmans.

McCulloch, John R., 1967 [1854], *A Treatise on the Circumstances which determine the Rate of Wages and the Condition of the Labouring Classes*, New York: Augustus M. Kelley.

McEachern, Doug, 1976, 'The Mode of Production in India', *Journal of Contemporary Asia*, Vol. 6, No.4.

McWilliams, Carey, 1945, *Ill Fares the Land: Migrants and Migratory Labour in the United States*, London: Faber & Faber Ltd.

Mepham, John, and David-Hillel Ruben (eds.), 1979, *Issues in Marxist Philosophy – Volume One: Dialectics and Method*, Brighton, Sussex: The Harvester Press.

Meyer, Konrad, 1939, 'Discussion: The Social Implications of Economic Progress in Present-Day Agriculture', *Proceedings of the Fifth International Congress of Agricultural Economists (1938)*, London: Oxford University Press.

Miles, Robert, 1987, *Capitalism and Unfree Labour: Anomaly or Necessity?*, London: Tavistock Publications.

Mill, John Stuart, 1849a, *Principles of Political Economy*, Vol. 1, London: John W. Parker.

Mill, John Stuart, 1849b, *Principles of Political Economy*, Vol. 2, London: John W. Parker.

Mill, John Stuart, 1875 [1862], 'The Contest in America', in *Dissertations and Discussions: Political, Philosophical and Historical* (Volume III), London: Longmans, Green, Reader, and Dyer.

Mill, John Stuart, 1963, *The Earlier Letters of John Stuart Mill, 1812–1848* (edited by Francis E. Mineka), London and Toronto: Routledge & Kegan Paul/University of Toronto Press.

Millin, George F., 1903, *The Village Problem*, London: Swan Sonnenschein & Co.

Mills, Dennis R., 1988, 'Peasants and Conflicts in Nineteenth Century Rural England: A Comment on Two Recent Articles', *The Journal of Peasant Studies*, Vol. 15, No. 3.

Mills, Dennis R., and Brian M. Short, 1983, 'Social Change and Social Conflict in Nineteenth Century England', *The Journal of Peasant Studies*, Vol. 10, No. 4.

Mintz, Sidney W., 1977, 'The So-Called World System: Local Initiative and Local Response', *Dialectical Anthropology*, Vol. 2, No. 4.

Mintz, Sidney W., 1985, *Sweetness and Power: The Place of Sugar in Modern History*, New York: Viking.

Mitra, Ashok (ed.), 1974, *Economic Theory and Planning: Essays in Honour of A.K. Das Gupta*, Calcutta: Oxford University Press.

Mommsen, Theodor, 1864–67, *The History of Rome*, Vols. I-IVa, London: Richard Bentley, New Burlington Street.

Moreland, W.H., 1929, 'The Indian Peasant in History: An Introduction to the Linlithgow Report', *Journal of the Royal Society of Arts*, Vol. LXXVII, No. 3988.

Morgan, David Hoseason, 1982, *Harvesters and Harvesting, 1840–1900: A Study of the Rural Proletariat*, London and Canberra: Croom Helm.

Mosse, George L., 1982, 'Nationalism, Fascism and the Radical Right', in Eugene Kamenka (ed.), *Community as a Social Ideal*, London: Edward Arnold.

Mukherji, Partha Nath, and Bhupati P. Sahoo, 1992, 'Agrarian Structure, Contradiction and Mobilization: A Framework for the Analysis of Emerging Rural Power', *Social Scientist*, Nos. 9–10.

Munro, Dana G., 1918, *The Five Republics of Central America: Their Political and Economic Development and Their Relations with the United States*, New York: Oxford University Press.

Murray, Warwick E., 2003, 'From Dependency to Reform and Back Again: The Chilean Peasantry in the Twentieth Century', in Tom Brass (ed.), *Latin American Peasants*, Portland, OR: Frank Cass Publishers.

Murray, Warwick E., 2006, 'Neo-feudalism in Latin America? Globalisation, Agribusiness and Land Re-concentration in Chile', *The Journal of Peasant Studies*, Vol. 33, No. 4.

Myrdal, Gunnar, 1968, *Asian Drama: An Inquiry into the Poverty of Nations* (3 volumes), London: Allen Lane.

Negri, Antonio, 1980, 'Domination and Sabotage', *Semiotext(e) – Autonomia: Post-Political Politics*, Vol. III, No. 3.

Negri, Antonio, 2008, *Goodbye Mr Socialism: Radical Politics in the 21st Century*, London: Serpent's Tail.

New Unionism, 2009, 'Interview: Professor Guy Standing', www.newunionism.net/library/internationalism/Interview.

Newby, Howard, 1977, *The Deferential Worker: A Study of Farm Workers in East Anglia*, London: Allen Lane.

Newby, Howard, 1980, *Green and Pleasant Land? Social Change in Rural England*, Harmondworth: Penguin Books.

Newby, Howard, 1987, *Country Life: A Social History of Rural England*, London: Weidenfeld & Nicolson.

Newby, Howard, Colin Bell, David Rose and Peter Saunders, 1978, *Property, Paternalism and Power: Class and Control in Rural England*, London: Hutchinson & Co.

Nieboer, H.J., 1910, *Slavery as an Industrial System*, The Hague: Martinus Nijhoff.

Novo, Carmen Martínez, 2006, *Who Defines Indigenous? Identities, Development, Intellectuals, and the State in Northern Mexico*, New Brunswick, NJ: Rutgers University Press.

Nurkse, Ragnar, 1961, *Patterns of Trade and Development*, Oxford: Basil Blackwell.

O'Brien, Philip J., 1975, 'A Critique of Latin American Theories of Dependency', in Ivar Oxaal, Tony Barnett, and David Booth (eds.), *Beyond the Sociology of Development*, London: Routledge & Kegan Paul Ltd.

O'Connell Davidson, Julia, 2010, 'New slavery, old binaries: human trafficking and the borders of "freedom"', *Global Networks*, Vol. 10, No.2.

Olmsted, Frederick Law, 1953, *The Cotton Kingdom: A Traveller's Observations on Cotton and Slavery in the American Slave States*, New York: Alfred A. Knopf.

Orwin, C.S., 1917, 'The Place of Agriculture in Industry', in *Some Problems of Urban and Rural Industry*, Oxford: The Council of Ruskin College.

Oshinsky, David M., 1997, *"Worse Than Slavery": Parchman Farm and the Ordeal of Jim Crow Justice*, New York: Free Press.

Page Arnot, R., 1955, *A History of the Scottish Miners*, London: George Allen & Unwin.

Page, Thomas Nelson, 1919 [1892], *The Old South: Essays Social and Political*, New York: The Chautauqua Press.

Panikkar, K.M., 1959, *The Afro-Asian States and their Problems*, London: George Allen & Unwin.

Parker, William N. (ed.), 1970, *The Structure of the Cotton Economy of the Antebellum South*, Washington, DC: The Agricultural History Society.

Pashukanis, Evgeny B., 1978, *Law and Marxism: A General Theory*, London: Ink Links.

Patnaik, Utsa, 1986, 'The Agrarian Question and Development of Capitalism in India', *Economic & Political Weekly*, Vol. XXI, No.18.

Patnaik, Utsa, 1990, *Agrarian Relations and Accumulation: The 'Mode of Production' Debate in India*, Bombay: Oxford University Press.

Patnaik, Utsa, 1995, 'On Capitalism and Agrestic Unfreedom', *International Review of Social History*, Vol. 4[illegible], Part [illegible].

Patnaik, Utsa, 2007, *The Republic of Hunger and Other Essays*, Monmouth: The Merlin Press.

Pawate, I.S., 1953, *Contract and the Freedom of the Debtor in the Common Law*, Bombay: N.M. Tripathi Ltd.

Pedder, D.C., 1904, *The Secret of Rural Depopulation*, Fabian Tract No. 118, London: The Fabian Society.

Petras, James, 1970, *Politics and Social Structure in Latin America*, New York: Monthly Review Press.

Petras, James, 1997, 'Imperialism and NGOs in Latin America', *Monthly Review*, Vol. 49, No. 7.

Petras, James, 2002, 'A Rose by Any Other Name? The Fragrance of Imperialism', *The Journal of Peasant Studies*, Vol. 29, No. 2.

Petras, James, and Henry Veltmeyer, 2003, *System in Crisis: The Dynamics of Free Market Capitalism*, London: Zed Press.

Phillips, Ulrich Bonnell, 1918, *American Negro Slavery: A Survey of the Supply, Employment and Control of Negro Labor as Determined by the Plantation Regime*, New York: D. Appleton and Company.

Phillips, William D., Jr., 1985, *Slavery from Roman Times to the Early Transatlantic Trade*, Manchester: Manchester University Press.

Pieper, Josef, 1952, *Leisure: The Basis of Culture*, London: Faber and Faber Ltd.

Pinto, Aníbal, 1965, 'Political Aspects of Economic Development in Latin America', in Claudio Veliz (ed.), *Obstacles to Change in Latin America*, London: Oxford University Press.

Platteau, J.-P., et al., 1985, *Technology, Credit and Indebtedness in Marine Fishing – A Case Study of Three Fishing Villages in South Kerala*, Delhi: Hindustan Publishing.

Plekhanov, Georgi, 1976 [1893], 'Essays on the History of Materialism', *Selected Philosophical Works*, Vol. II, London: Lawrence and Wishart.

Polman, Linda, 2010, *War Games: The Story of Aid and War in Modern Times*, London: Viking.

Porteus, The Right Reverend Beilby, 1812 [1784], 'An Essay towards a Plan for the more effectual Civilization and Conversion of The Negro Slaves, on the Trust Estate in Barbadoes belonging to The Society for the Propagation of the Gospel in Foreign Parts', in *Tracts on Various Subjects*, London: Luke Hansard & Sons, near Lincoln's-Inn Fields.

Powell, Marvin A., 1978, 'Non-slave labor in Sumer', in Michael Flinn (ed.), *Proceedings of the Seventh International Economic History Congress*, Edinburgh: Edinburgh University Press.

Prasad, Pradhan H., 1974, 'Limits to Investment Planning', in Ashok Mitra (ed.) [1974].

Prasad, Pradhan H., 1989, *Lopsided Growth: The Political Economy of Indian Development*, Bombay: Oxford University Press.

Preobrazhensky, E., 1965, *The New Economics* (Translated by Brian Pearce), Oxford: Clarendon Press.

President's Commission on Migratory Labor, 1951, *Migratory Labor in American Agriculture*, Washington, DC: US Government Printing Office.

Pressnell, L.S. (ed.), 1960, *Studies in the Industrial Revolution, Presented to T.S. Ashton*, London: The Athlone Press, University of London.

Rabinovitch, G.S., 1932a, 'The Seasonal Emigration of Polish Agricultural Workers to Germany: I', *International Labour Review*, Vol. XXV, No.2.

Rabinovitch, G.S., 1932b, 'The Seasonal Emigration of Polish Agricultural Workers to Germany: II', *International Labour Review*, Vol. XXV, No.3.

Ramachandran, V.K., and Vikas Rawal, 2010, 'The Impact of Liberalization and Globalization on India's Agrarian Economy', *Global Labour Journal*, Vol. 1, No. 1.

Rastyannikov, V.G., 1981, *Agrarian Evolution in a Multiform Structure Society*, London: Routledge & Kegan Paul.

Rasul, M.A., 1974, *A History of the All India Kisan Sabha*, Calcutta: National Book Agency Private, Ltd.

Rathbone, Dominic, 1991, *Economic Rationalism and Rural Society in Third-Century A.D. Egypt*, Cambridge: Cambridge University Press.

Rawal, Vikas, 2004, 'Agricultural Labour and Unfreedom: Siri Workers in a Village in Western Haryana', accessed at http://www.cpim.org/marxist/200402_agri_labour_haryana.doc.

Red Notes, 1979, *Working Class Autonomy and the Crisis: Italian Marxist Texts of Theory and Practice of a Class Movement, 1964–79*, London: CSE Books.

Reed, Mick, 1986, 'Nineteenth Century Rural England: A Case for "Peasant Studies"?', *The Journal of Peasant Studies*, Vol. 14, No. 1.

Renner, Karl, 1949, *The Institutions of Private Law and Their Social Functions*, London: Routledge & Kegan Paul Ltd.

Renton, David, 2001, 'The Agrarian Roots of Fascism: German Exceptionalism Revisited', *The Journal of Peasant Studies*, Vol. 28, No. 4.

Rew, R.H., 1913 [1892], 'The Migration of Agricultural Labourers,' in *An Agricultural Faggot: A Collection of Papers on Agricultural Subjects*, Westminster: P.S. King & Son.

Rivera-Cusicanqui, Silvia, 1994, 'Rituals of Citizenship', in Rob van den Berg and Ulbe Bosma (eds.), *Historical Dimension of Development, Change and Conflict in the South*, The Hague: Dutch Ministry of Foreign Affairs/Development Cooperation Information Department.

Rocker, Rudolf, 1937, *Nationalism and Culture*, London: Freedom Press.

Roe, Merwin (ed.), 1929, *Speeches and Letters of Abraham Lincoln, 1832–1865*, London: J.M. Dent.

Ross, Andrew (ed.), 1997, *No Sweat: Fashion, Free Trade, and the Rights of Garment Workers*, London: Verso.

Rostovtzeff, M., 1926, *The Social and Economic History of the Roman Empire*, Oxford: The Clarendon Press.

Rostow, W.W., 1955, *An American Policy in Asia*, Cambridge, MA: The Massachusetts Institute of Technology.

Roth, K.H., 1997, 'Unfree Labour in the Area under German Hegemony, 1930–45', in T. Brass and M. van der Linden (eds.) [1997].

Roy, M.N., 1990 [1927–28], 'Draft Resolution on The Indian Question', *Selected Works – Volume III: 1927–32* (edited by Sibnarayan Ray), Delhi: Oxford University Press.

Royal Commission on Labour in India, 1931, *Evidence – Volume II, Part 2: Punjab, Delhi and Ajmer-Merwara*, London: HMSO.

Rudra, Ashok, 1990, 'Indian Capitalism and Marxist Theory', in Gyansham Shah (ed.), *Capitalist Development: Critical Essays*, Bombay: Sangam Books.

Rudra, Ashok, et al., 1978, *Studies in the Development of Capitalism in India*, Lahore: Vanguard Books.

Rühland, G., 1896, *The Ruin of the World's Agriculture and Trade*, London: Sampson Low, Marston & Company.

Russel, Robert Royal, 1923, 'Economic Aspects of Southern Sectionalism, 1840–1861', *University of Illinois Studies in the Social Sciences*, Vol. XI, No. 1.

Salvadori, Massimo, 1979, *Karl Kautsky and the Socialist Revolution, 1880–1938*, London: NLB.

Salz, Beate R., 1955, *The Human Element in Industrialization: A Hypothetical Case Study of Ecuadorean Indians*, Chicago, IL: American Anthropological Association.

Samuel, Raphael (ed.), 1975, *Village Life and Labour*, London: Routledge & Kegan Paul, Ltd.

Sapre, B.G., 1926, *Economics of Agricultural Progress (With Reference to Conditions in the Deccan)*, Bombay: Tutorial Press.

Schäffle, A., 1893, *The Theory and Policy of Labour Protection*, London: Swan Sonnenschein & Co.

Schnee, Heinrich, 1926, *German Colonization: Past and Future*, London: George Allen & Unwin Ltd.

Schwartz, Stuart B., 1992, *Slaves, Peasants and Rebels: Reconsidering Brazilian Slavery*, Champaign, IL: University of Illinois Press.

Scott, Emmett J., 1920, *Negro Migration during the War*, New York: Oxford University Press.

Sen, Amartya, 1999, *Development as Freedom*, Oxford: Oxford University Press.

Shapiro, Karin A., 1998, *A New South Rebellion: The Battle against Convict Labor in the Tennessee Coalfields, 1871–1896*, Chapel Hill, NC, and London: The University of North Carolina Press.

Siegel, Bernard J., 1947, 'Slavery during the Third Dynasty of Ur', *American Anthropologist*, Vol. 49, No 1, Part 2.

Singh, Chowdhry Mukhtar, 1933, *Rural India: Peasants' Poverty, Its Causes and Cure*, Allahabad: Leader Press.

Singh, Manjit, and K. Gopal Iyer 1984, 'Migrant Labourers in Rural Punjab', in Arvind N. Das, V. Nilkant and P.S. Dubey (eds.), *The Worker and the Working Class*, New Delhi: PECCE.

Singleton-Gates, Peter, and Maurice Girodias, 1959, *The Black Diaries: An Account of Roger Casement's Life and Times with a Collection of his Diaries and Public Writings*, London: Sidgwick and Jackson Ltd.

Smith, Adam, 1812 [1776], *An Inquiry into the Nature and Causes of the Wealth of Nations*, Vols. I-III, London: Cadell and Davies.

Smith, Kenneth, 1978, *The Malthusian Controversy*, New York: Octagon Books.

Sombart, Werner, 1909 *Socialism and the Social Movement*, London: J.M. Dent & Co.

Sombart, Werner, 1967, *Luxury and Capitalism*, Ann Arbor, MI: The University of Michigan Press.

Spellman, W.M., 2002, *The Global Community: Migration and the Making of the Modern World*, Stroud, Glos.: Sutton Publishing.

Stalin, Joseph, 1928, *Leninism*, London: George Allen & Unwin Ltd.

Stampp, Kenneth M., 1964, *The Peculiar Institution: Negro Slavery in the American South*, London: Eyre & Spottiswoode.

Standing, Guy, 2008, 'The ILO: An Agency for Globalization?', *Development and Change*, Vol. 39, No. 3.

Starr, Chester G., 1977, *The Economic and Social Growth of Early Greece, 800–500 B.C.*, New York: Oxford University Press.

Starr, Chester G., 1979a/[1958], 'An Overdose of Slavery', in Starr [1979c].

Starr, Chester G., 1979b/[1960], 'The History of the Roman Empire 1911–1960', in Starr [1979c].

Starr, Chester G., 1979c, *Essays on Ancient History: A Selection of Articles and Reviews* (edited by Arther Ferrill and Thomas Kelly), Leiden: E.J. Brill.

Steed, Wickham, 1944, *India and the Four Freedoms* (BBC Pamphlets No. 1), London: Oxford University Press.

Steinfeld, Robert J. 2001, *Coercion, Contract, and Free Labor in the Nineteenth Century*, Cambridge: Cambridge University Press.

Steinfeld, Robert J., and Stanley M. Engermann, 1997, 'Labor – Free or Coerced? A Historical Reassessment of Differences and Similarities', in Tom Brass and Marcel van der Linden (eds.), *Free and Unfree Labour: The Debate Continues*, Berne: Peter Lang AG.

Stowe, Harriet Beecher, 1853, *A Key to Uncle Tom's Cabin: Presenting the Original Facts and Documents upon which the Story is Founded*, London: Thomas Bosworth.

Stuckey, Sterling, 1987, *Slave Culture*, New York: Oxford University Press.

Sutch, Richard, 1975, 'The Treatment Received by American Slaves: A Critical Review of the Evidence Presented in *Time on the Cross*', *Explorations in Economic History*, Vol. 12, No. 4.

Sweezy, Paul M., 1946, *The Theory of Capitalist Development: Principles of Marxian Political Economy*, London: Dennis Dobson Limited.

Tannenbaum, Frank, 1992 [1946], *Slave and Citizen*, Boston, MA: Beacon Press.

Taylor, A.J., 1960, 'The Sub-contract System in the British Coal Industry', in L.S. Pressnell (ed.), [1960].

Temin, Peter (ed.), 1973, *New Economic History*, Harmondsworth: Penguin Books.

The Special Commissioner of the 'Daily News', 1891, *Life in Our Villages – Being A Series of Letters written to that Paper in the Autumn of 1891*, London: Cassell and Company, Limited.

Thompson, E.P., 1963, *The Making of the English Working Class*, London: Victor Gollancz, Ltd.

Thompson, F.H., 2003, *The Archaelogy of Greek and Roman Slavery*, London: Duckworth.

Thomson, George, 1941, *Aeschylus and Athens: A Study in the Social Origins of Drama*, London: Lawrence & Wishart Ltd.

Thorner, Alice, 1982, 'Semi-Feudalism or Capitalism? Contemporary Debate on Classes and Modes of Production in India', *Economic and Political Weekly*, Vol. XVII, Nos.49–51.

Thorner, Daniel and Alice, 1962, *Land and Labour in India*, Bombay: Asia Publishing House.

Tirrell, Sarah Rebecca, 1951, *German Agrarian Politics after Bismark's Fall: The Formation of the Farmers' League*, New York: Columbia University Press.

Tiwary, S.P., 1985, 'Bondage in Santal Parganas', in U. Patnaik and M. Dingwaney (eds.), *Chains of Servitude: Bondage and Slavery in India*, Madras: Sangam Books.

Tolstoy, Leo, 1900, *The Slavery of Our Times* (Translated from the Russian by Aylmer Maude), Maldon, Essex: The Free Age Press.

Trevaskis, Hugh Kennedy, 1928, *The Land of the Five Rivers: An Economic History of the Punjab from the Earliest Times to the Year of Grace 1890*, London: Oxford University Press.

Trevaskis, Hugh Kennedy, 1931–32, *The Punjab of Today: An Economic Survey of the Punjab in Recent Years (1890–1925)*, Volumes I and II, Lahore: The Civil and Military Gazette Press.

Tribe, Keith, 1981, *Genealogies of Capitalism*, London: Macmillan.

Trotsky, Leon, 1934, *The History of the Russian Revolution* (translated by Max Eastman), London: Victor Gollancz, Ltd.

Trotsky, Leon, 1936, *The Third International After Lenin*, New York: Pioneer Publishers.

Trotsky, Leon, 1946, *The Living Thoughts of Karl Marx: Based on Capital – A Critique of Political Economy*, London: Cassell and Co., Ltd.

Trotsky, Leon, 1972, *The New Course 1923*, London: New Park Publications.

Trotsky, Leon, 1973, *The Spanish Revolution, 1931–39*, New York: New Park Publications.

Trotsky, Leon, 1976, *Towards Socialism or Capitalism?* London: New Park Publications.

Tuden, Arthur, and Leonard Plotnicov (eds.), 1970, *Social Stratification in Africa*, New York: The Free Press.

Ulyanovsky, R., 1974, *Socialism and the Newly Independent Nations*, Moscow: Progress Publishers.

United Nations and International Labour Office, 1953, *Report of the* Ad Hoc *Committee on Forced Labour*, Geneva: UN and ILO.

United Nations, 1953, *Report of the United Nations Commission on the Racial Situation in the Union of South Africa*, New York: UN General Assembly.

United States House of Representatives Special Subcommittee on Labor, 1969, *Employment of 'Green Card' Aliens during Labor Disputes*, Washington, DC: US Government Printing Office.

United States Senate Commission, 1913, *Agricultural Cooperation and Rural Credit in Europe*, Washington, DC: Government Printing Office.

United States Strike Commission, 1895, *Report on the Chicago Strike of June-July, 1894*, Washington, DC: Government Printing Office.

van Pelt, Robert Jan, and Deborah Dwork, 1996, *Auschwitz: 1270 to the Present*, London and New Haven, CT: Yale University Press.

Venkateshwarlu, Davaluri, and Lucia da Corta, 2001, 'Transformations in the Age and Gender of Unfree Workers on Hybrid Cotton Seed Farms in Andhra Pradesh', *The Journal of Peasant Studies*, Vol. 28, No. 3.

Voelcker, John Augustus, 1897, *Report on the Improvement of Indian Agriculture*, Calcutta: Office of the Superintendent of Government Printing, India.

Vogt, Joseph, 1974, *Ancient Slavery and the Ideal of Man*, Oxford: Basil Blackwell.

Volkov, Vadim, 2002, *Violent Entrepreneurs: The Use of Force in the Making of Russian Capitalism*, Ithaca, NY: Cornell University Press.

von Mises, Ludwig, 1949, *Human Action: A Treatise on Economics*, London: W. Hodge.

Wakefield, Edward Gibbon, 1849, *A View of the Art of Colonization, with Present Reference to the British Empire*, London: John W. Parker, West Strand.

Walinsky, Louis J. (ed.), 1977, *The Selected Papers of Wolf Ladejinsky: Agrarian Reform as Unfinished Business*, New York: Oxford University Press.

Walker, Francis A., 1888, *Political Economy*, London: Macmillan and Co.

Walker, Kathy Le Mons, 2006, '"Gangster Capitalism" and Peasant Protests in China: The Last Twenty Years', *The Journal of Peasant Studies*, Vol. 33, No. 1.

Wallerstein, Immanuel, 1974, *The Modern World-System: Capitalist Agriculture and the Origins of the European World-Economy in the Sixteenth Century*, New York: Academic Press, Inc.

Wallerstein, Immanuel, 1979, *The Capitalist World Economy*, Cambridge: Cambridge University Press.
Ward, Barbara, 1961, *India and the West: Pattern for a Common Policy*, New York: W.W.Norton.
Washbrook, Sarah (ed.), 2007, *Rural Chiapas Ten Years after the Zapatista Uprising*, London: Routledge.
Webb, Sidney and Beatrice, 1923, *The Decay of Capitalist Civilization*, London: George Allen and Unwin.
Weber, Max, 1927, *General Economic History* (translated by Frank H. Knight), London: George Allen & Unwin.
Weber, Max, 1947, *Theory of Social and Economic Organization*, London: William Hodge & Co., Ltd.
Weber, Max, 1976, *The Agrarian Sociology of Ancient Civilizations*, London: New Left Books.
Weber, Max, 1979 [1894], 'Developmental tendencies in the situation of East Elbian rural labourers', *Economy & Society*, Vol. 8, No. 2.
Weiner, Merle, 1978, 'Cheap Food, Cheap Labor: California Agriculture in the 1930s', *The Insurgent Sociologist*, Vol. 8, Nos. 2 & 3.
Wells, Roger A.E., 1979, 'The Development of the English Rural Proletariat and Social Protest, 1700–1850', *The Journal of Peasant Studies*, Vol. 6, No. 2.
Wells, Roger A.E., 1981, 'Social Conflict and Protest in the English Countryside in the Early Nineteenth Century: A Rejoinder', *The Journal of Peasant Studies*, Vol. 8, No. 4.
Westermann, William Linn, 1929, *Upon Slavery in Ptolemaic Egypt*, New York: Columbia University Press.
Westermann, William Linn, 1955, *The Slave Systems of Greek and Roman Antiquity*, Philadelphia, PA: The American Philosophical Society.
Westermann, William Linn, 1960/[1943], 'Slavery and the Elements of Freedom in Ancient Greece', in M.I. Finley (ed.), *Slavery in Classical Antiquity: Views and Controversies*, Cambridge: W. Heffer & Sons Ltd.
Whiteside, A.G., 1962, *Austrian National Socialism before 1918*, The Hague: Martinus Nijhoff.
Wilson, A.J., 1909, *An Empire in Pawn: Being Lectures and Essays on Indian, Colonial, and Domestic Finance, "Preference," Free Trade, etc.*, London and Leipsic: T. Fisher Unwin.
Wolf, Eric R., 1982, *Europe and the People Without History*, Berkeley and Los Angeles, CA: University of California Press.
Wolpe, Harold 1980, 'Introduction' to *The Articulation of Modes of Production*, edited by Harold Wolpe, London: Routledge & Kegan Paul.
Wood, Ellen Meiksins, 1988, *Peasant-Citizen and Slave: The Foundations of Athenian Democracy*, London: Verso.
Woofter, T.J., 1936, *Landlord and Tenant on the Cotton Plantation* (Research Monograph 5), Washington, DC: Works Progress Administration, Division of Social Research.
World Bank, 1975, *Land Reform: Sector Policy Paper*, Washington, DC: World Bank.
Wunderlich, Frida, 1961, *Farm Labor in Germany 1810–1945: Its Historical Development within the Framework of Agricultural and Social Policy*, Princeton, NJ: Princeton University Press.

AUTHOR INDEX

SUBJECT INDEX